War Plays by Women

This anthology consists of ten plays from countries involved in the First World War, including plays from Germany and France never before available in translation.

The playwrights reconstruct imagined communities, challenge concepts of national identity, and rewrite history. Representing a range of dramatic forms, from radio play to street-epic, from comic sketch to musical, this anthology includes plays by:

- Muriel Box
- Alice Dunbar-Nelson
- Dorothy Hewett
- Berta Lask
- Marie Lenéru
- Wendy Lill
- Christina Reid
- Gertrude Stein
- Marion Craig Wentworth

Highly successful in their day, these plays demonstrate how women have attempted to use theatre to achieve social change. The collection explores their varied deployment of theatrical conventions and genres, and the historical context of social and gender issues raised.

Claire M. Tylee is Lecturer in English at Brunel University and is author of *The Great War and Women's Consciousness* (University of Iowa Press). **Elaine Turner** is Lecturer in Drama at the University of Warwick and Brunel University. **Agnès Cardinal** is Lecturer in European Culture at the University of Kent.

War Plays by Women

An international anthology

Edited by Claire M. Tylee with Elaine Turner and Agnès Cardinal

London and New York

First published 1999
by Routledge
11 New Fetter Lane, London EC4P 4EE

Simultaneously published in the USA and Canada
by Routledge
29 West 35th Street, New York, NY 10001

Routledge is an imprint of the Taylor & Francis Group

Typeset in Veljovic by Keystroke, Jacaranda Lodge, Wolverhampton
Printed and bound in Great Britain by TJ International Ltd, Padstow, Cornwall

British Library Cataloguing in Publication Data
A catalogue record for this book is available from the British Library

Library of Congress Cataloging in Publication Data
War plays by women: an international anthology / [compiled by] Claire
   M. Tylee with Elaine Turner and Agnes Cardinal.
      p.   cm.
   Includes bibliographical references and index.
   1. Drama-Women authors. 2 World War, 1914–1918–Drama.
   I. Tylee, Claire M., 1946– . II. Turner, Elaine, 1937– .
   III. Cardinal, Agnès.
   PN6119.8.W37   1999
   808.82 9358–dc21   99–18343
                        CIP

ISBN 0–415–17377–9 (hbk)
ISBN 0–415–22297–4 (pbk)

To our Grandmothers

Contents

Illustrations

Acknowledgements

Above all we wish to thank Gunhild Muschenheim of the Goethe Institute, London, and Odile Krakovitch in Paris for locating plays and information about the German and French playwrights for us. Without their help this project would not have left the ground. It was a footnote to *War Brides* by Margaret Kamester and Jo Vellacott in their edition of *Militarism and Feminism* (Virago, 1987: 165) that first sparked Claire Tylee's curiosity about Great War drama, so thanks to them and to Women's History Network. We are indebted to the three anonymous readers of the original proposal for their constructive comments. Many friends deserve our gratitude for their encouragement and suggestions: Meretta Elliott, Margaret Higonnet, Mary Joannou, Jane Marcus, Sybil Oldfield, Angela Woollacott, Mandy Zwarts, and all the delegates to the "Women, Drama and the First World War" conference at Brunel in 1997 who took a chance on the idea. Various archivists helped with the research: Janet Birkett at the Theatre Museum, Elizabeth Bright at the Provincial Archives of Manitoba, Ian Carter at the Imperial War Museum, Kevin Curran at Brunel University Library and Ian O'Sullivan of the British Film Institute. We are grateful to them for their care and attention to detail. Sam Walters' imaginative choice of plays and seminars at The Orange Tree Theatre was a practical inspiration; thank you, Sam, for staging Susan Glaspell and Christina Reid.

Claire Tylee wants to take this opportunity to record her appreciation of her two collaborators: we excitedly talked and argued and e-mailed to the point of exhaustion and, as readers will see, we still did not always agree. Fortunately, because of the constraints of time, space and cost, in the end we had to compromise on the choice of plays and what could be said about them. The book that has resulted is all the better for that debate between our disciplines and we hope it will inspire other inter-disciplinary work beyond the area of women's studies.

Lastly, and of course by no means least, we want to thank our editor at Routledge, Talia Rodgers, for her vision in commissioning this book, the confidence she has shown in the project throughout, and the patience with which she has awaited this polished object of desire.

Copyright Acknowledgements

General Introduction _____

In any new dispensation, the idea of a nation must be seen as an expendable construct. After all, it has never admitted of women. Its flags and songs and battle-cries, even its poetry . . . make use of feminine imagery. But that is all. The true voice and vision of women are entirely excluded.

Then why did I not walk away? Simply because I was not free to.

(Eavan Boland, *Object Lessons*)

The First World War was crucial to the formation of twentieth-century national identities and cultures. However, with the notorious exception of individuals such as Mata Hari and Edith Cavell, women are kept to the periphery of First World War history in the popular imagination. Even the writings of women like Rosa Luxemburg and Gertrude Stein have been marginalised, and the efforts of later women to write them back into history of the "Great War" have been kept in the wings. This anthology puts the "true voice and vision of women" at centre-stage, not only of national history but of world theatre.[1] Because they are so challenging to hegemonic accounts of the history and literature of the 1914–18 war, and to dominant discourses of war in general, this general introduction suggests various ways in which these war plays by women might be related to one another and positioned within cultural networks. It then makes explicit the political implications of the dramatic conventions employed by these women playwrights. Each play then has an individual introduction followed by a range of recommended reading, to identify the author and to situate the play historically, indicating cultural connections.

History

The first six plays are documentary evidence of the war's political issues as perceived by women who lived through it, and of the ways in which they tried to affect the outcomes of the war by the use of drama. The second group of four plays shows how women dramatists attempted to (re)construct historical accounts of the war later, foregrounding events and/or issues which had been obscured by dominant histories/male historians.

Hegemonic histories tend to concentrate on battles, politico-military strategy, and changes in maps and boundaries. Above all, like dominant war drama, the focus is on male experience at the battlefront.[2] By contrast, women's history/plays are more likely to focus on women's experience behind the lines, especially on the home front, and on groups opposing war. Several of these plays remind us of wider political issues raised by the war but often "lost" in national histories, such as Irish volunteers to the British Army (Reid), the conscription of African-Americans (Dunbar-Nelson), and German working-class resistance (Lask). Others recall events and experiences that are crucial to our understanding of women's history, particularly the effects of the war on the women's suffrage movement, for instance Lill's play about Canada, and the importance of the pre-war suffrage movement to women's involvement with war activities: Lenéru's heroine, a wartime nurse, had been a suffragette, and women's auxiliary groups like Box's ambulance driver were sponsored by suffrage societies. Lask's play recalls the part women played in the revolutionary situation in Germany and Russia towards the end of the war. Craig Wentworth's *War Brides* arose from the international women's peace movement, inspired by Bertha von Suttner, which was active before the war, led to the League of Nations and finally resulted in the United Nations.[3]

Women's politics particularly involved sexual politics at the time of the First World War, when women were expected to become mothers.[4] The specific relation of mothers to war is an issue in a number of the plays, especially Box's and Lenéru's. The problem of war babies, sensitive in Alsace-Lorraine where French girls had babies fathered by German soldiers in the occupying army, is hinted at in one of Stein's plays and made prominent in Craig Wentworth's.

Dominant histories also tend to be nationalistic. These plays have been selected to cross national boundaries and to foreground alternative points of view, especially those of ethnic minorities. The plays by Dunbar-Nelson, Stein, Hewett, Lill and Reid all raise questions of race, ethnicity and national identity which become acute in wartime; wars, after all, aim to define nations. The status of racial minorities such as African-Americans and Aboriginal Australians, obscured by official remembrance celebrations, is highlighted by Dunbar-Nelson and Hewett. The post-Second World War plays show the legacy for later generations of wartime recruitment/conscription into national armies. Who has the obligation or the right to defend a country? Whom does this personal sacrifice benefit? The relevance of these issues to the contemporary world is made only too apparent by Reid's play, which alludes both to the troubles in Northern Ireland and to the Greenham Common campaign.

Men alone were conscripted in the First World War, but women also were deeply affected by the war and many volunteered as uniformed auxiliaries. Celebrities such as Vesta Tilley, Lena Ashwell and Cicely Hamilton supported their government by morale-raising entertainment.[5] Plays by Lenéru, Box, Lill and Lask remind us how significant women's war activities were, not only to promoting belligerence but to opposing it. Rosa Luxemburg should be at least as well known as Mata Hari![6] The specific effects on women, as refugees, as mothers, sisters and lovers and as war workers, are interpreted by Craig Wentworth, Lenéru, Lask and Lill. Their plays are

evidence of specifically feminist responses to debates about the role of women in wartime, especially to the state's expectation that women will care for the wounded and quietly provide more cannon-fodder.

Women's studies and gender studies

All the plays challenge us to reconsider matters of gender normally taken for granted, but which were being contested at the time of the Great War, especially the idea that veterans are heroes, but that refusing to fight is cowardly and unmanly. While Lenéru's play debates how these issues affected occupied France, Hewett's play tackles them in relation to Australia and it is stimulating to set her play alongside such films as *Gallipoli*. The plays by Lask and Dunbar-Nelson recall the international socialist opposition to the war and give voice to working-class responses, but from feminist standpoints. Where the plays written before the Second World War participate in the feminist movements founded in America and Europe before the First World War, the three plays written since the end of the Second World War attempt to renew feminist consciousness by recalling that female independence. Although all the plays can be seen to contribute to the general historiography of the First World War, they also make a specific contribution to the history of women, especially to our understanding of the connections between war, the women's suffrage campaign, and the emancipation of women.[7] Above all, Lill and Reid enable us to see how patriotism may conflict with feminist solidarity.

In Western society war is pre-eminently a gendering activity where men and women are divided from each other, and primitive notions of masculinity and femininity are reasserted. The ritual commemoration of the Great War and succeeding wars in annual, so-called remembrance ceremonies, perpetuates this gender division.[8] The study of war literature can make gendering plain, and can be used to examine debates about gender roles and stereotypical expectations at particular historical moments. Most of these plays raise questions about the expectation that women will become mothers, and the centrality of nurturing and pacifity to ideas of femininity, by contrast with the

Figure 1 Vesta Tilley in a propaganda sketch at the Bradford Alhambra, 3 May 1918. [Author's own collection.]

Lenéru, Gertrude Stein and Guillaume Appollinaire take extraordinarily divergent approaches to patriotism.[10]

Literature

In Britain, the First World War is usually approached through poetry, and secondarily through novels and autobiographical fiction. This is so much the case that the names of Owen and Sassoon (followed by Graves, Blunden, Aldington and Jones) are almost synonymous with Great War literature. Associated with them are Hemingway, Lawrence, Barbusse, Remarque and Jünger.[11] Two plays about the war are also widely studied: *Journey's End* and *Oh What a Lovely War*. These are frequently performed and film versions have been televised.[12] Although over the past 25 years the dominance of male poets and novelists with their concentration on men's point of view has been challenged, up until now women's drama has not been placed alongside such plays as *Journey's End*.[13]

This collection brings together different dramatic forms, from the one-act to the four-act play, from radio drama to musical theatre, from the classical French to the modernist German and American. Even this does not exhaust women's dramatic versatility, and we have reluctantly excluded performance pieces by Ruth Draper, comic sketches written by Gertrude Jennings for Lena Ashwell's groups to entertain the troops, a wartime drawing-room comedy by Fryn Tennyson Jesse that was a West End success, a nativity play set on the Western Front by Cicely Hamilton, and a post-war expressionist drama by Velona Pilcher with music by Edmond Rubbra. Not to mention Vernon Lee's philosophic tour-de-force, *Satan, the Waster*,[14] nor any of the unpublished pageants by women lodged in the Birmingham Public Reference Library. More recent works such as Rowbotham's community drama, *Friends of Alice Wheeldon*, and the extraordinarily inventive ghost-play, *Salonika*, by Louise Page, are already widely available. What links the chosen plays is that they are all text-based dramas that are responsive to reading.

requirement that men be prepared to achieve heroism through armed combat.[9]

In the face of the traditional emphasis in men's war plays on the brotherhood of warriors, these plays suggest that war is also women's business. Some look at comradeship amongst women, and they all foreground the possibility that women could be active, autonomous agents instead of submissive victims. It is provocative to study these plays in parallel with contemporary plays by men, for instance comparing the two plays about Ulstermen, Christina Reid's *My Name, Shall I Tell You My Name* and Frank McGuinness's *Observe the Sons of Ulster*; or two plays about "Diggers", Dorothy Hewett's *The Man from Mukinupin* and Alan Seymour's *The One Day of the Year*; or Muriel Box's *Angels of War* with R. C. Sherriff's *Journey's End*, both set on the Western Front. Berta Lask's *Liberation* displays a different attitude to women's socialism from Sheila Rowbotham's *Friends of Alice Wheeldon*, Bill Bryden's *Willie Rough* or Chris Hannan's *Elizabeth Gordon Quinn*, and the plays written in wartime France by Marie

Whilst it enables us to interrogate theses propounded by Paul Fussell, Samuel Hynes, Sandra Gilbert and Susan Gubar about how war is imagined, this anthology also helps us

3

to see why women may have had difficulty using traditional dramatic forms based on theories of conflict and resolution, if they wished to counter conflict[15] and the use of force to resolve dilemmas. Most strikingly, it provokes us to consider whether if, as Fussell argues, men's war plays tend to demonstrate irony and to have a dynamic of hope abridged (Fussell 1975: 33–5), women's war plays by contrast reveal tentative optimism. Despite their confrontation with the facts of random violence, cruelty and genocide, do they suggest the possibility of change?

Some of these plays have been significant in the development of drama by national groups, or in the development of new dramatic forms. Thus, Alice Dunbar-Nelson was important to the Harlem Renaissance and the founding of an African-American theatre; Gertrude Stein was an important catalyst to the development of modernisms in various genres, including opera; and Berta Lask's experiments with epic street-theatre supported the Brechtian revolution in theatre practice. That these and other women dramatists such as Muriel Box worked with and wrote for amateur groups reminds us of the role of drama in education and the community. This role is usually lost sight of in dominant histories that concentrate on commercial theatre and national organisations, although we should not forget that Marie Lenéru's plays were premiered by the Comédie Française and at the Odéon in Paris, nor that Dorothy Hewett's *The Man from Mukinupin* was commissioned to mark the official sesquicentennial celebrations of Western Australia.

Drama

One must beware of reading plays of the past with the eyes of the present. These plays, with their focus on war, are particularly vulnerable to a projection of late twentieth-century perception and cynicism. A consideration of their structure and use of dramatic devices, especially their use of the stage space with its implicit social/political implications, can serve to mitigate against taking their apparent content for granted and provide insight into the limits and possibilities offered by dramatic form and particular performance styles.

The dominant dramatic stylistic form in the first half of the twentieth century was the realist/naturalist construct. (I use both terms because there is *still* no clearly accepted distinction and I wish to be understood!) This form assumes a one-to-one relationship between the actual world and the dramatic world and seeks its confirmation through details borrowed from the actual world. The stage-world tends to be enclosed within the static representation of an interior setting, implicitly separating characters from interaction with the larger context and forcing them into positions of re-action rather than action.

The "placing" of women in space and the larger social context is central to the feminist critique. Even today, the assumption remains that the outside world, the world of "action", is the dominion of men whereas the "inside" domestic world is the "natural" domain of women. In plays focusing on war, this assumption is inevitably at issue.[16]

Performance is the aim and temporary completion of a playtext. The text sets the possibilities and limits of its possible performance through its structure, setting and language. One element often ignored in reading plays is the visual information which makes up a considerable part of a live audience's experience. **War Brides**, for example, ostensibly takes place inside the home. It presents the women as victims of the war and of men's actions, awaiting the deaths of their loved ones in the manner of Synge's *Riders to the Sea*, and celebrates women's bravery, their stoicism and their sense of loss. The setting in a foreign country implies unity between women in contrast to the men engaged in fighting. The use of setting also offers another active opposition to male wartime activities. The outside door is open. Women are constantly seen outside, harvesting. The internal room is thus transformed from a defining environment to a threshold, a proposal for an alternative to the restrictions of the domestic environment and its demand for passivity. In other words, the use of the setting proposes an implicit active dynamic beyond the issues overtly discussed. Inside and outside interact. The internal domestic world spills out to suggest alternatives which the women are, as yet, unable to bring to fruition.

By contrast, the content of **Angels of War** is severely limited and reduced into its

Figure 2 "Goodby! Goodby!" from *War Brides* by Marion Craig Wentworth, showing Alla Nazimova as "Hedwig" in the original production at the Palace Theatre, New York, January 1915 (with Mary Alden as "Amelia" and Gertrude Berkeley as "Mother") at the threshold between the peasant home and the working-countryside.

setting. The more enclosed and permanent the setting, the more action is drawn to the personal. While the women are confined and domesticised, the war is reduced to a credible context for justifying the elaboration of personal angst. The characters are defined by personal details, few of which are related to the war or their participation as ambulance drivers. The intense personalisation finds expression in the arguably misplaced issue of "the individual vs. authority". The audience is encouraged to take sides with the "girls" against the Commandant who, instead of being allowed her rightful role as their leader and protector in a dangerous wartime situation, is presented as representative of restrictive authority. The hierarchy of responsibility and its function in wartime becomes merely a

restriction to generalised individual "freedom", and the war is virtually divested of its power and significance.

The language, disarmingly literal and middle class, also neutralises the wartime situation and dampens the emotional content. There is little build-up or suspense leading to Cocky's death, so the audience is not particularly affected by her loss. Her death, like the war, is merely an opportunity to express personal grievances rather than grief. It is these personal grievances the audience is invited to share. Although, with imagination, we can project on to the play the situation of the women ambulance drivers, with its bravery and dangers, its extraordinariness is never brought to the fore or developed.

Mine Eyes Have Seen offers a fascinating and surprisingly sophisticated use of the dramatic medium. The difficulties of the issues at stake are developed and complicated by on-stage dynamics between two specific, powerful styles, both prevalent in the period. A ruthless Realism expressed through the poverty of the setting and the incapacities of Dan and Lucy is dynamically opposed by the Expressionism of Dan's nationalistic fervour. The confrontation of these two diametrically opposed styles of expression exposes the strengths and weaknesses of each and opens a highly sophisticated discussion about "style" itself. Highlighted through their opposition, each style is elaborated as a mode of expression fitting to a particular, viable context. This overt elaboration proposes the argument that the *way* one expresses oneself determines *what* one can express; that the limits and possibilities of content are determined by the style and form of expression.

Dunbar-Nelson skilfully anchors each style with the perspective, needs and situation of each character. The closed domestic setting pins the characters to the details and difficulties of day-to-day survival. Their situation is extreme; their concerns unquestionable. The poverty of their existence and their struggle in the material world are rigorously elaborated through the realist/naturalist form which serves to engage the audience with their struggle. The only escape available is transcendence into the inspiration of spiritual goals.

Realism is unable to find expression or justification for motivating passions of the spirit (at best, it reduces them to psychological explanations). Expressionism, however, devised to express the ineffable, the spirit of ideals and passions, must override personal and mitigating details of the everyday material world and inspire with the fire of that spirit. The inspirational inclusiveness of spirit over matter is expressed not only in Chris's conversion but by the fervour of Jake, the Jewish youth.

Each style is shown to have its own focus and emotional content. Each style is at its peak of expression. Its strengths are celebrated and, simultaneously, because it is confronted by its opposite, its inherent limitations are exposed. Hence, the play offers a discussion of "style", posing, ahead of its time, questions regarding the inter-dependency between form and content.

Accents in Alsace takes us as near as we are likely to come to an "anti-play". To read it as "drama" necessitates confrontation with issues of "performance". No setting, characters or expressed narrative are indicated. There are act and scene numbers but they are erratic: some are numbered with Roman numerals and some with Arabic, and St Valentine's Day is indicated by Roman numerals. The idiosyncratic numbering calls into question assumptions about chronological narrative and the conventional means of dividing it into sections. To call attention to these issues in performance, one would need to expose them to the audience, perhaps on placards. Moreover, although called "scenes", they are more accurately "units", clusters of expression isolating a possible action or image. The play takes only minutes to read; it would take much longer to perform.

The opening indicates a general structure. A predominantly prose commentary, clearly in contrast to the verse, offers a condensed history of the Schemils, suggesting that although "Germanic" they are not "German". In comparison, the Schemmels' opening verse defines their French origins. Overriding both, the towering figure of Alsace herself promises to divide and set them against each other. The action following is presented in a series of associative crystallisations which develop a dynamic between personal responses and wider, general associations.

Performance would require fundamental considerations: Who says what? How shall they be said? Both the verse and the frequently sloganistic form of the language open possibilities: different people might speak the same lines; sentences might effectively be repeated, interchanged, spoken in unison and in different contexts. Although speeches are written as a typographical whole, they might easily be comprised of contributions from different characters, offering different perspectives. How the lines are allocated will affect both meaning and effect.

For example, consider three different approaches to the section beginning "Alphonse what is your name":

1 A teacher who is teaching the children French speaks the entire sequence as a lesson, emphasising changes in the culture as a result of the war;
2 A teacher asks and the names are given by individual children in response, presenting a situation where children are brought together for the first time;
3 Each line is said by a different person as speakers warmly introduce themselves and ask each other's names in a round, creating an image of hope in a new inclusive society.

There is enough material in structure and language to focus performance choices, but an unusual freedom to explore the range of meaning-making possibilities. When reading Stein "playlets", it is valuable to take the time to consider their possibilities as performance and how specific choices would affect audience perception and response. One could envisage an evening in which *Alsace* was performed in, say, three different ways.

The structure of Lenéru's **La Paix** [*Peace*] suggests an uneasy marriage between the realistic drawing-room play of the period and remnants of French neo-classicism. The drawing-room suffices as an area where a collection of people might credibly meet and exchange views. The central neo-classical dilemma – Love vs. Duty – is still recognisable, but diluted by the fact that the characters are in no position to turn their opinions into effective, viable action. They are limited to conversation and their characters do not evolve beyond the delivery of their opinions.

The implicit restrictions of the domestic setting, especially on women, are particularly evident. Despite her passion, Mabel is confined and rendered inactive by the domestic space. She is entirely reliant on men entering her space to bring her information from the outside, act as sounding-boards for her ideas and take action on her behalf. Her influence is limited to her effect on her personal circle. It's no surprise that, lacking an active arena, she is defeated by events taking place outside her range of influence. In the last Act, she is literally cornered in her bedroom. The image is contradictory: on the one hand, she is holding court; on the other, she is domestically isolated and disempowered.

All three women are reactive; their influence and effect minimised, if not stymied, through domestic marginalisation. One might even see Simone's idiotic bloodlust and incessant sloganising ("I am convinced that peace is a utopian dream") as a consequence of the frustrations of enforced ineffectuality ("It seems to me war and peace don't depend on me"). The question is asked "Are words enough?" Clearly not! But the women, imprisoned in their domestic setting, have nothing else to work with. Perhaps Mabel's sacrifice of private life for ideal is an expression of the limits of the merely personal?

Berta Lask's **Liberation** is an extraordinary experiment in political drama. Unashamedly agit-prop, its roots are in the "Living Newspaper", where performers exposed the political implications of current news events in street performances in order to "politicise" the audience and inspire it with the desire for change. Its enormous cast and forthright style suggest *Liberation* was envisaged as a huge street pageant, although, given enough willing performers, there is no reason why it could not be performed on stage.

The focus and strong line of development are clearly stated in the Prologue and developed through an enacted comparison between the experiences of women in Germany and Russia focusing on both class *and* gender. Lask addresses both audience and characters as "fellow women workers". Within the Tableaux, national power structures are exposed through their effects on the everyday lives of women. Simultaneously, there is an attempt to draw audience sympathy to the effects of the power structure on personal lives, especially through the development of Anna as an individual character and, most important and

necessary for a "political" play, to expose the necessity of and possibility for change.

On the whole, the "tableaux" structure enables Lask to achieve these ambitious ends. The open use of the stage calls on the audience's imagination to fill the the specific context, while the easy movement between Russia and Germany accentuates the possibilities of movement and change. The juxtaposition between Germany and Russia stimulates an automatic comparison while simultaneously implying an even larger context spreading internationally, culminating in overt manifestation in the final scene at the World Congress.

"Character" is defined through the relation of the individual to the political situation, firmly anchoring even personal sympathies to political choices. Thus, a strong focus is activated which forms and directs the expanse of action and assists the audience in responding to the significances of the information.

The weaknesses in the play lie not in its structure but in how the structure is used. The text does tend to be over-dependent on verbal information. Though the information is usually elaborated and supported through character response, there tends to be rather too much of it for an audience to take in. The presentation might arguably have been more effective if full use had been made of its formal possibilities. "Tableau" usually refers to a static image. The use of visual image to "sum up" each Tableau would have centred its emotional power while simultaneously creating an emotional and memorable through-line. A rare example is Tableau 11: both the action and its consequences are crystallised in a simple, emotive visual image when her comrades sing a hymn over Nasdja's dead body.

Liberation is a vast project in using drama to inspire political consciousness, especially as it foregrounds both a socialist and a feminist perspective. The "tableaux" format allows this expanse. The use of multiple settings and the comparisons between Germany and Russia encourage the audience to form connections and continuity between separate scenes: whilst being drawn into the characters' personal lives they are also made aware of the political implications. The final scene of the Women's Congress ostensibly includes the audience. As the women express their changing consciousness and commitment to socialist ideas, these ideals reveal themselves to have emotional content, and each member of the audience is invited to assess her own life and perspective in their light.

Radio is necessarily audience-centred. The listener must be engaged in the creation of context. All there is to go on is voice and, occasionally, sound effects. *My Name, Shall I Tell You My Name* is totally dramatic in that it makes its world as it goes along without the aid of commentary. Character is created not only by *what* is said but by syntax, vocabulary and emphasis. Cleverly, Reid makes use of the formal requirements of radio to centre issues of self-definition and extend their relevance using the fluidity of the medium to move swiftly through time and space, leading the listener not only to construct the fuller picture but to compare and assess.

An instigating opposition is set up between past and present, leading us to project the final separation of the protagonists, complete with its nostalgia and sense of loss and waste. At the same time, the context poses a central question which is not answered until near the end of the piece. We don't know exactly where Andrea is! Even if we assume from the slam of the metal door that she is in prison, we still don't know why. This question, as well as the significance of her remembering to the present situation, underlies our response to the action.

A process from unity to separation, then, is implicit in the opening, allowing Reid to elaborate the terms of its necessity and extend them from the personal to a social/political perspective. Andrea's personal memories of her grandfather, her self-definition as "Granda's pet", and his definition as her Granda, soon take root, first in family situation and then in a national and international context. His memories contrasted with hers establish his need for self-glorification while encouraging the audience to assess what is being said throughout rather than accept it wholesale.

Radio is dependent on imagery. The play's images focus on a distinction between men and women and their terms of evaluation. Men not only find self-definition and justification in war but also pass down the generations a conception of opposition and violence as admirable proof of manhood. Eddy and his father are denigrated, yet the

Battle of the Somme fought by Ulstermen as a replay of the Battle of the Boyne suggests the failures of war as a solution. Andy takes pride in his grandson's participation in the Falklands while Andrea's husband is destroyed by the unofficial use of violence as a means of gaining manful pride. The images of women centre on their caring, struggling against and surviving the consequences of male insistence on violence as a solution. Even at the end, while Andy prides himself on his rigid separation from his beloved granddaughter, Andrea longs for a "no man's land" where they can meet; a dream of resolution.

The child's innocent voice contrasts vividly with Andy's rigid, self-censored memories and the adult Andrea's growing politicisation. The child unwittingly uncovers the oppressive political hierarchy underlying her grandfather's pride. As an adult, Andrea personally experiences the results of such pride in the destruction of her husband, her separation from her grandfather, and her arrest at Greenham where giving her "name" results in misdefinition and incarceration. The image of the old woman with her cake of lighted candles, its associations with hope and loss, calls into question the images of war and puts the final tarnish on its glory.

"In the theatre everything is possible" says Clarry who, with her sister Clemmy, serves as virtual Ringmaster to the action of *The Man from Mukinupin*, creating the overall impression of Australian national identity as a "stage-managed" project. An open stage and overt theatricality give rise to a circus/music-hall structure and style presenting, instead of a linear narrative, a series of interactions forming a broad panorama through which Mukinupin becomes a microcosm of Australia. At the start of this meta-narrative, Mukinupin appears to conform to typical small-town, ordered life, its rigid class-system and materialism unacknowledged, its darker secrets – illegitimacy, mass murder, racism – hidden. After the war, its façade begins to crumble and requires acknowledgement and integration.

The opening is ambiguous and threatening, drawing the attention of the viewer by withholding sight. Suggesting dark, underlying intonations, it contrasts sharply with the comic Morris dance that follows. Because both characters and situations are drawn in broad stereotype, deviations from the norm create issues and alternative perspectives: in Brechtian terms, they serve as "distancing devices", exposing the underlying assumptions that formed the original stereotypes and encouraging comparison and assessment by the audience. The four sets of twins/alter egos accentuate the process of comparison, highlighting issues of social mores and values.

The songs not only break up the action and pump up the energy but, more significantly, they crystallise the singer's attitude and situation, setting the particular into a wider context by identifying it as a general condition. A dynamic is created between the personally particular and its archetypal representation, reinforced by the use of theatre, poetry and performance as metaphors for Life. Edie's poems, *Othello*, even Mrs Tuesday's self-presentation as "Melodrama Widow", are some examples of the multiple use of performance which call attention to the play as construction and emphasise the incidents as expressions of the archetypal process of life ("all the world's a stage"). This overt theatricality also supports the use of visual imagery as an emotive signifying device. The central image of Harry drinking beneath a cardboard war memorial, for example, crystallises a cluster of associative resonances.

The Man from Munikupin celebrates not only Australia (warts and all) but also the process of living and theatre itself. None the less, women in the audience may well be disappointed that their female counterparts are left requiring "an eligible bachelor and an eye for the main chance"!

The Fighting Days is an engaging example of a genuinely "political" play neatly linking feminist issues with international politics and confronting the audience with the necessity to assess the implications of both.

The movement of the action through time and space empowers the characters, and the characters are developed through their responses to current issues. Owing to their occupations, feminist and political issues are an integral part of their lives, centralising the political implications of everyday life and personal choices. Thus, both characters and ideas are exposed and tested through interaction and comparison. The personal is melded to the ideological and principle is

extended through practice as the characters are required to take action. This process comes to fruition in the closing scene where McNair is "forced" to sack Fanny and she rejects his proposal in order to remain a "free thinker".

The open stage encourages audience engagement with the application and effect of various ideologies in a variety of situations. Depth is given to this dynamic as the characters change and adjust their points of view. Particularly moving is Lily's confusion over the war as, affected by patriotic propaganda, she considers how emotional commitments dull ideological clarity. A further dynamic is added by the unseen Vernon, whose ideas interact with those on-stage and who suffers the consequences of his unpopular ideas. It is one of the strengths of the play that off-stage action has active effect on-stage. The voices of the Prairie women create a powerful experience of the wide-ranging influence and effect of ideas, setting a context in which perspectives on the war take on viable significance. Ironically, it is the responses of these women which force the final confrontation.

Lill's process of foregrounding and dramatising political concepts through the interaction of committed characters offers the audience credible, opposing perspectives and their implicit consequences which the audience is encouraged to consider and assess. Because Francis is constantly present, she invites a bias towards her view. However, her arguably romanticised terms of self-justification expose even Francis's final decision and its justification for audience assessment.

Theatre is inherently social. The setting and structure of any play limits and/or empowers its characters. An examination of a play's structure, and its use of the stage and formal conventions, will contribute to our understanding of the social/political possibilities inherent in the play's world and of their implications for women's role in the social order. The performance/reading of these plays enables their authors to engage with political debate and to influence public ideas. We hope that this anthology will not only enlarge the reader's appreciation of the creative vision and voice of women writers, but enable her/him to see the scope for new social roles for women and for men and new

ways of dealing with aggression in the
twenty-first century.

Notes

1 Quotation from Eavan Boland (1995)
*Object Lessons: The Life of the Woman
Poet in Our Time*, Manchester: Carcanet,
p. 145. For changes in the gender
division of national memories, see John
R. Gillis (1994) "Introduction" to
*Commemorations: The Politics of National
Identity*, Princeton, NJ: Princeton
University Press.

2 One example of hegemonic history will
suffice: the widely republished Marc
Ferro (1969) *The Great War 1914–1918*,
Paris: Gallimard (translated 1973,
London: Routledge). Newer exceptions
that explicitly take account of gender
include: Stephen Constantine, Maurice W.
Kirby and Mary B. Rose (eds) (1995) *The
First World War in British History*, London:
Arnold, which has a theoretical discussion
by Gail Braybon, "Women and the War",
pp. 141-67 that is particularly relevant to
this volume. The seminal essay which
asks whether there is a politics of gender
in the politics of war, and what they
reveal about each other, is by Joan W.
Scott "Rewriting History" in Margaret
Randolph Higonnet, Jane Jenson, Sonya
Michel and Margaret C. Weitz (eds) (1987)
*Behind the Lines: Gender and the Two
World Wars*, New Haven: Yale University
Press, pp. 19–30. Scott argues that
women's experience provides insight into
the discrepancy between private history
and official, national history, and also
(more importantly) a means of analysing
how and by whom national memory is
constructed (p. 28).

3 Beatrice Kempf (1972) *Woman for Peace:
the Life of Bertha von Suttner*, London:
Wolff. Other relevant studies, by Wilsher,
by Liddington, and by Hinton, will be
found in the lists following individual
introductions to the plays.

4 Susan Kingsley Kent (1987) *Sex and
Suffrage in Britain, 1860–1914*, Princeton,
NJ: Princeton University Press.

5 Sara Maitland (1986) *Vesta Tilley*, London:
Virago, pp. 48–9, 118–21. Lena Ashwell
(1936) *Myself a Player*, London: Michael
Joseph, chapter 8; Lena Ashwell (1922)
Modern Troubadours, London: Gyldendal.

Cicely Hamilton (1935) *Life Errant*,
London: Dent, chapters VIII–XIV.

6 Elzbieta Ettinger (1986) *Rosa Luxemburg:
a Life*, London: Harper.

7 Specific references are given after the
plays mentioned. A more general survey
is provided by Arthur Marwick (1977)
Women at War, 1914–18, London:
Fontana. Arguments about the impact of
the Great War on the Women's Suffrage
Movement in Britain are debated in
Martin Pugh (1992) *Women and the
Women's Movement in Britain, 1914–1959*,
London: Macmillan, chapter 2, and Jo
Alberti (1989) *Beyond Suffrage: Feminists
in War and Peace, 1914–28*, London:
Macmillan.

8 See Margaret Randolph Higonnet *et al.*
(1987) *Behind the Lines: Gender and the
Two World Wars*, New Haven: Yale
University Press, p. 4; and Miriam Cooke
and Angela Woollacott (eds) (1993)
Gendering War Talk, Princeton, NJ:
Princeton University Press; Bob
Bushaway (1992) "Name Upon Name: The
Great War and Remembrance" in Roy
Porter (ed.) *Myths of the English*, London:
Polity, pp. 136–67; Raphael Samuel (ed.)
(1989) *Patriotism: The Making and
Unmaking of British National Identity:
volume 1*, London: Routledge, pp. 57–89;
John R. Gillis (1994) "Introduction" to
*Commemorations: The Politics of National
Identity*, Princeton, NJ: Princeton
University Press.

9 See Cynthia Enloe (1983) *Does Khaki
Become You? The Militarisation of Women's
Lives*, London: Pluto, pp. 12–15; Marilyn
Lake and Jay Damousis (1995)
"Introduction" to their *Gender and War:
Australians at War in the Twentieth
Century*, Cambridge: Cambridge
University Press, pp. 1–20; and Malcolm
Smith (1995) "The War and British
Culture" in Stephen Constantine, Maurice
W. Kirby and Mary B. Rose (eds) (1995)
The First World War in British History,
London: Edward Arnold, pp.168–83.

10 Bill Bryden (1972) *Willie Rough: A Play*,
Edinburgh: Southside. Chris Hannan
(1985) *Elizabeth Gordon Quinne: A Serious
Melodrama* in Alasdair Cameron (ed.)
(1990) *Scot-Free: New Scottish Plays*,
London: Nick Hern. Sheila Rowbotham
(1986) *Friends of Alice Wheeldon*, London:
Pluto (reprinted 1987 ed. Blanche W.

Cook and Sandi E. Cooper, New York: Monthly Review Press). Also see: Peter Whelan (1982) *The Accrington Pals: A Play*, London: Methuen. Louise Page (1990) *Salonika*, in her *Plays: 1*, London: Methuen. Publication details for other titles are given in the reading lists following the plays in question.

11 Examples of the dominance of these male writers in studies of the First World War include: Dominic Hibberd (1990) *The First World War*, London: Macmillan; and Holger Klein (ed.) (1976) *The First World War in Fiction: a Collection of Critical Essays*, London: Macmillan.

12 These two plays are central to the thesis propounded by Paul Fussell (1975) *The Great War and Modern Memory*, Oxford: Oxford University Press, pp. 33–5, 195. Their impact has been augmented by the mass media. R. C. Sherriff's *Journey's End*, Harmondsworth: Penguin, 1983, first performed in 1928, was filmed in 1930 (directed by James Whale, GB/US), and a television version broadcast by BBC2 1995 is available on video. Theatre Workshop's *Oh What a Lovely War* (London: Methuen, 1965) was first performed in 1963 and was also adapted to film (dir.: Richard Attenborough, GB 1968). A lesser-known play by John Wilson, *Hamp* (London: Evans, 1966) first performed in 1964, was made into the successful film *King and Country* (dir.: Joseph Losey, GB 1964). In the USA, the comedy by Maxwell Anderson and Lawrence Stallings, *What Price Glory?*, first performed in New York, 1924, was similarly successful both on stage and in the cinema (dir.: Raoul Walsh US 1926; John Ford US 1952). No play by a woman has had such an impact, although Elaine Morgan's BBC television adaptation of Vera Brittain's autobiography, *Testament of Youth* (1933/1979), was broadcast worldwide.

13 Challenges to this dominance were developed in such works as: Catherine Reilly (ed.) (1981) *Scars upon My Heart: Women's Poetry and Verse of the First World War*, London: Virago; Sandra M. Gilbert and Susan Gubar (1987–92) *No Man's Land: The Place of the Woman Writer in the Modern World*, 3 volumes, London: Yale University Press; Claire M. Tylee (1990) *The Great War and Women's*

Consciousness, London: Macmillan and Iowa: University of Iowa Press; and Dorothy Goldman (ed.) (1993) *Women and World War I: The Written Response*, London: Macmillan. Despite their titles, the lack of attention to women's drama is true even of such recent studies as Samuel Hynes (1990) *A War Imagined: The First World War and English Culture*, London: The Bodley Head; and John Onions (1990) *English Fiction and Drama of the Great War*, London: Macmillan. An exception to the general disregard for women's war drama is Gillian Beer "The Dissidence of Vernon Lee: *Satan the Waster* and the Will to Believe" in S. Raitt and T. Tate (eds) (1997) *Women's Fiction and the Great War*, Oxford: Oxford University Press, pp. 107–31. A collection of essays edited by Claire M. Tylee and Rose J. Atfield, *Women, Drama and the Great War* is forthcoming from Mellen Press, Lampeter. This will form a companion to this anthology, dealing with several of the dramatists included here.

14 Fuller details of these other war plays by women, 1915–39, are given in the Appendix. The editors were particularly disappointed not to be able to include a translation of Annie Vivanti's 1918 play, *Le Bocche inutili*, or Louise Page's *Salonika*, available in her *Plays: 1*, or her unpublished radio play, *Armistice*; Sheila Rowbotham's *Friends of Alice Wheeldon* had to be omitted because of its length, although its depiction of the harassment of Anglo-Scottish draft-resistance makes it historically invaluable. These are all strongly recommended. For reasons of space we have ended the Appendix at 1939, and have restricted suggestions for further reading to books rather than scholarly articles that may be less widely available but are more easily identified through databases. This volume provides a starting-place.

15 See note 13 above. The introduction to the Methuen student edition of Caryl Churchill's play, *Top Girls*, (ed.) B Naismith (London: Methuen, 1991, p. xxii), contains pertinent remarks by Churchill about traditional dramatic structure and her need, as a woman, to find a new form.

16 Useful aids to beginning an analysis of

drama by women are: Elaine Aston (1995) *An Introduction to Feminism and Theatre,* London: Routledge; Gayle Austin (1990) *Feminist Theories for Dramatic Criticism,* Ann Arbor: University of Michigan Press; Geraldine Cousin (1996) *Women in* *Dramatic Place and Time,* London: Routledge; Lynda Hart (1989) "Performing Feminism" in her *Making a Spectacle: Feminist Essays in Contemporary Womeen's Theatre,* Ann Arbor: University of Michigan Press, pp. 1–21.

1 Marion Craig Wentworth 1872–?

War Brides
USA

Introduction

Marion Craig was born in Minnesota, in 1872. After graduating from the University of Minnesota in 1894, she studied at the Curry School of Expression in Boston and then stayed on in Boston to become a teacher of expression. She married in 1900, had one son, and divorced in 1912. A socialist, she wrote several plays on social issues, including a suffrage play, *The Flower Shop* (1912). During the pre-war American Women's Suffrage Campaign, she travelled to help raise support by giving public readings, often of the rallying speeches from Act II of the British suffrage play by Elizabeth Robins, *Votes for Women!*, which depicted an open-air suffragette meeting in London.

Thus Craig Wentworth had experience of political agitation through drama when she wrote her feminist anti-war play, *War Brides*, in September 1914. Although this was printed in the international journal, *Century Magazine*, in February 1915, and published in book form in New York the same year, the play was never licensed for performance in Britain. However, the first production opened in New York on 25 January 1915, starring Alla Nazimova, and then went on tour from coast to coast. So great was the demand to see the play that a second company was sent to tour the South, with Gilda Varesi in the leading role. In 1916 a longer, 48-minute film version of the one-act play was made, also starring Nazimova but with a larger cast. This has been widely acclaimed: "the most distinguished and sincere film of the war-period was Herbert Brenon's *War Brides*" (Butler 1974: 11), "by far the most eloquent of the anti-war films were Herbert Brenon's *War Brides* and Thomas Ince's *Civilization*" (Jeavons 1974: 27). The distributor, Selznick, made a huge profit of $300,000 from the film before America entered the war in April,

1917. Several cities and states banned the film because of its alleged pacifism, and Selznick had it re-edited to give it an anti-German bias. However, in 1917 it was suppressed for the duration of the war on the official grounds that: "The philosophy of this picture is so easily misunderstood by unthinking people" (Jeavons 1974: 27). The film was never shown in other Allied countries.

Despite disagreement about Nazimova's acting style, there is no question that the play's success was largely due to her fame and talent. Karl Schmidt praised her theatre performance, claiming that the play's more powerful effect on the stage than when read was due to Nazimova's "sincere and sympathetic acting" (*Harper's Weekly*, 13 March 1915, p. 251). The film critics were not so happy. The reviewer of *Variety* criticised Nazimova for "posing in doorways and windows, leaning against walls and supporting herself on various pieces of furniture" and suggested she might learn from another actress on the cast, Gertrude Berkeley, who played the Mother (*Variety*, 17 Nov. 1916, p. 25). The reviewer in *Motion Picture World* (*MPW*) thought that, whilst the drama achieved "tragic height never before attained by a moving picture", the Russian actress had one flaw: "in giving too freely of her inward fire" (*MPW*, 2 Dec. 1916, p. 1343). The existing stills of her stage and film performances may give an exaggerated idea of her acting as "absurdly over-dramatic" (Butler 1974: 11) because of the necessity to hold a pose for the camera at that time. Yet Nazimova is of great importance in the history of American theatre and cinema because she helped introduce current Russian practice which gave rise to "the Method" school of acting.

Alla Nazimova was born in the Crimea in 1879. She trained at Stanislawski's dramatic school in Moscow and made her debut in St Petersburg in 1904. Joining Pavel Orlenev's company she toured London, Berlin and New York, but when they broke up and she found herself abandoned in New York, she quickly learned to perform *Hedda Gabler* in English in 1906. Her success led to the Schubert brothers building her the Nazimova Theatre on 39th Street, where she played a series of Ibsen heroines. "Then came the fall" as Djuna Barnes put it (Barnes 1930: 360): Nazimova descended to vamp-roles in mediocre dramas, ending up on B. F. Keith's vaudeville circuit. *War Brides* enabled her to break into cinema, acting in 22 films including *A Doll's House* and *Ghosts* up to 1944. She made enough money to make her own version of Wilde's *Salome* in 1923, and returned to the stage in 1930 with Russian and Scandinavian classics. That a one-act play in vaudeville could make such an impact that a reviewer of the film of *War Brides* would call the story "too well-known to need repeating" was certainly due to the power of her acting.

Yet, of course, *War Brides* did not keep the USA out of the 1914–18 war. In fact, despite the internationally feminist, anti-war argument of the play and its setting in an unnamed country, the stage version – and even more so, the film version – can be seen to have strengthened the racism and nationalism that stoked America's entry into the war. Although the original place was not identified, the peasant way of life, the costumes, and the Germanic names of the characters all suggested somewhere in Eastern Europe, especially since the action is said to take place in "a war-ridden country". Perhaps because of Nazimova's accent, early reviewers supposed the location to be in Russia. Some of the names in the printed version were changed for the stage and film adaptation: "Hoffman" became "Bragg" and, more significantly, "Hedwig" (Nazimova's role) became "Joan"; yet the overbearing military officer bullying simple country-folk reinforced stereotypes of aristocratic Prussians forcing militarism on Bavarian peasants (Isenberg 1981: 157). But whatever the location, Joan's dream of invading rapists, an episode in the Brenon/Wentworth screenplay not found in the stage version, clearly shows them to be of "Teutonic appearance", wearing *pickelhaubs* – the distinctive spiked helmets of the German army uniform (see film-still, Isenberg 1981:

192). Thus, even if Craig Wentworth's original aim had been to encourage (American) women to sympathise with women from other (non-specified) countries in a struggle against militarism, visually the film accorded with British atrocity propaganda and fell in with the "preparedness", pro-war agitation that depicted Germans as bestial huns, "a lot of ruthless savages", against whom women needed defending.

On the other hand, the irony of Craig Wentworth's original script is that Joan's final gesture is completely ineffectual, since her message is destroyed and never reaches the emperor. (That ending, the off-stage suicide of a pregnant woman, announced by a gun-shot, owes much to Ibsen's *Hedda Gabler*.) Such tragic irony is removed in the film version which is politically far more effective. It shows Joan confronting the king (*sic*) in person, and ends in a climax, called "probably the most powerful ever seen on screen" (*MPW*, 2 Dec. 1916, p. 1344), with Joan's dead body being raised up by her women followers as they vow to follow her example.

The emphasis on women's right to take decisions regarding motherhood and the unborn or newborn baby was a strong theme in women's drama at the turn of the century, from the infanticide in the Robins/Bell play, *Alan's Wife*, through the abortion in *Votes for Women!*, to the vow of chastity in Angelina Weld Grimké's *Rachel*. (A similar vow is made in Marie Lenéru's *Peace*.) By contrast, it is interesting to compare *War Brides*, with its refusal of compulsory marriage and the reproduction of cannon-fodder, to another wartime play, by the British writer, Marie Stopes. Like Margaret Sanger, Stopes is well known for establishing birth-control clinics and publishing contraceptive advice. Yet her wartime play, *The Race*, argued for women to take the future of the race into their own hands in wartime by selecting their own mate to breed with and not delaying for marriage. Stopes was not gifted as a dramatist, and despite advice from Shaw, her somewhat creaking melodrama was, although published, never performed (Rose 1992: 96–7). However, her eugenicist fears were shared by British policy-makers during the war.

It is interesting to compare Craig Wentworth's *War Brides* with two contemporary films. One is the two-reeler *Women's Work in Wartime*, produced by the New York Women's Suffrage Party in 1917, to show a woman being converted to the suffrage movement by the inspiring sight of women volunteers working on farms, in munitions factories, and on transit lines, to help the war effort. The other is the film version of Bertha von Suttner's *Lay Down Your Arms* [*Ned Med Vaabnene*] made by a Danish film company for the 21st International Peace Congress in Vienna in September 1914. Suttner's Austrian anti-war novel, for which she gained the Nobel Peace Prize, was first published in 1889. It had been translated into 16 languages and ran to over 40 editions by 1914. With the outbreak of war two stage versions were banned in Germany and the Congress was cancelled, although 63 prints of the film were exported to 22 countries. It was released in the USA in September 1914 and was shown at the New York Peace Society in November 1914. Otherwise it apparently had little exhibition (Kelly 1997: 5–11).

The use of women's patriotism to support politicians and governments who had been anti-suffrage, whilst international pacifist works by women were silenced, illustrates how the war divided the women's movement both nationally and internationally.

Further reading

Primary

Grimké, Angelina Weld (1920) *Rachel*, Boston: Cornhill; reprinted in Kathy A. Perkins and Judith L. Stephens (eds) (1998) *Strange Fruit: Plays on Lynching by American Women*, Bloomington: Indiana University Press.

Stopes, Marie Carmichael (1918) *The Race*, in *Two New Plays of Life*, London: Fifield.

Synge, J. M. [1903] (1998) *Riders to the Sea* in Declan Hibberd (ed.) *Shadows*, London: Oberon.

Von Suttner, Baroness Bertha (1913) *Lay Down Your Arms: the Autobiography of Martha von Tilling*, London: Longmans. (Originally published in 1889 as *Die Waffen Nieder! Eine Lebensgeschichte*.)

Wentworth, Marion Craig (1912) *The Flower Shop: A Play in 3 Acts*, Boston: Badger.

—— (1915) *War Brides: A Play in 1 Act*, New York: Century.

—— (1917) *The Bonfire of the Old Empires*, Boston: Badger.

Secondary

Barnes, Djuna [1930] (1985) "Alla Nazimova, One of the Greatest Living Actresses Talks of Her Art" in Alyce Barry (ed.) *I Could Never Be Lonely Without a Husband*, London: Virago, pp. 352–68.

Buitenhuis, Peter (1989) *The Great War of Words: Literature as Propaganda 1914–18 and After*, London: Batsford.

Butler, Ian (1974) *The War Film*, New York: Barnes & Noble.

Isenberg, Michael T. (1981) *War on Film: the American Cinema and World War I, 1914–41*, London: Associated Universities Presses.

Jeavons, Clyde (1974) *A Pictorial History of War Films*, London: Hamlyn.

Kelly, Andrew (1997) *Cinema and the Great War*, London: Routledge.

Koonz, Claudia (1987) *Mothers in the Fatherland: Women, the Family and Nazi Ideology, 1919–45*, London: St Martin's Press.

Liddington, Jill (1989) *The Long Road to Greenham: Feminism and Anti-Militarism in Britain since 1820*, London: Virago.

Rose, June (1992) *Marie Stopes and the Sexual Revolution*, London: Faber.

Rover, Constance (1970) *Love, Morals and the Feminists*, London: Routledge.

Sanger, Margaret [1920] (1969) *Women and the New Race*, New York: Elmsford.

War Brides

[A Play in One Act]
First performed at the Palace Theatre, New York, 25 January 1915
Published New York, 1915

Marion Craig Wentworth

Characters

HEDWIG (JOAN)

AMELIA (AMY)

MOTHER

HOFFMAN (JOSEPH KERMAN)

MINNA

ARNO

HERTZ (CAPTAIN BRAGG)

PEASANTS, WOMEN and SOLDIERS

Time

Present.

Place

A war-ridden country

The war brides were cheered with enthusiasm and the churches were crowded when the large wedding parties spoke the ceremony in concert. (Press Clipping)

Scene

A room in a peasant's cottage in a war-ridden country. A large fireplace at the right. Near it a high-backed settle. On the left a heavy oak table and benches. Woven mats on the floor. A door at left leads into a bedroom. In the corner a cupboard. At the back a wide window with scarlet geraniums and an open door. A few firearms are stacked near the fireplace. There is an air of homely color and neatness about the room.

Through the open door may be seen women stacking grain. Others go by carrying huge baskets of grapes or loads of wood, and gradually it penetrates the mind that all these workers are women, aristocrats and peasants side by side. Now and then a bugle blows or a drum beats in the distance. A squad of soldiers marches quickly by. There is everywhere the tense atmosphere of unusual circumstance, the anxiety and excitement of war.

AMELIA, a slight, flaxen-haired girl of nineteen, comes in. She brushes off the hay with which she is covered, and goes to packing a bag with a secret, but determined, air. The MOTHER passes the window and appears in the doorway. She is old and work-worn, but sturdy and stoical. Now she carries a heavy load of wood, and is weary. She casts a sharp eye at AMELIA.

MOTHER   What are you doing, girl? (AMELIA *starts and puts the bag in the cupboard.*) Who's going away? They haven't sent for Arno?

AMELIA   No.

MOTHER   (*sighs, and drops her load on the hearth*) Is the hay all in?

AMELIA   Yes. I put in the last load. All the big work on our place is done, and so – (*Looks at her mother and hesitates. Her mother begins to chop the wood into kindling.*) I'll do that, Mother.

MOTHER   Let be, girl. It keeps me from worrying. Get a bite to eat. What were you doing with that bag? Who were you packing it for?

AMELIA   (*with downcast eyes*) Myself.

MOTHER   (*anxious*) What for?

AMELIA   Sit down, Mother, and be still while I tell you – (*pushes her mother into a chair*)

MOTHER   (*starts*) Is there any news? Quick! Tell me!

AMELIA   Not since yesterday. Only they say Franz is at the front. We don't know where Emil and Otto are, and there's been a battle; but –

MOTHER   (*murmurs, with closed eyes*) My boys! My boys!

AMELIA   Don't, Mother! They may come back. (*A cheer is heard.*)

MOTHER   (*starting*) What's that?

AMELIA   (*running to the door and looking out*) They are cheering the war brides, that's all.

MOTHER   Aye. There's been another wedding ceremony.

AMELIA   Yes.

MOTHER   How many war brides to-day?

AMELIA   Ten, they said.

MOTHER   (*nodding*) Aye, that is good. Has any one asked you, Amelia? (AMELIA *looks embarrassed.*) Some one should ask you. You are a good-looking girl.

AMELIA   (*in a low voice*) Hans Hoffman asked me last night.

MOTHER   The young and handsome lieutenant? You are lucky. You said yes?

AMELIA   (*shakes her head*) No.

MOTHER   Ah, well.

AMELIA   I hardly know him. I've only spoken to him once before. O Mother – that isn't what I want to do.

MOTHER   What did you tell him?

AMELIA   (*timidly*) That I was going away to join the Red Cross.

MOTHER   Amelia!

AMELIA   He didn't believe me. He kissed me – and I ran away.

MOTHER   The Red Cross!

AMELIA   (*eagerly*) Yes; that is what I was going to tell you just now. That is why I was packing the bag. (*Gets it*) I – I want to go. I want to go to-night. I can't stand this waiting.

MOTHER   You leave me, too?

AMELIA   I want to go to the front with Franz and Otto and Emil, to nurse them, to take care of them if they are wounded – and all the others. Let me, Mother! I, too, must do something for my country. The grapes are plucked, and the hay is stacked. Hedwig is gathering the wheat. You can spare me. I have been dreaming of it night and day.

MOTHER   (*setting her lips decisively*) No, Amelia!

AMELIA   O Mother, why?

MOTHER   You must help me with Hedwig. I can't manage her alone.

AMELIA   Hedwig!

MOTHER   She is strange; she broods. Hadn't you noticed?

AMELIA   Why, yes; but I thought she was worrying about Franz. She adores him, and any day she may hear that he is killed. It's the waiting that's so awful.

MOTHER   But it's more than the waiting with Hedwig. Aye, you will help Franz more by staying home to take care of his wife, Amelia, especially now.

AMELIA   (*puzzled*) Now?

MOTHER   (*goes to her work-basket*) Hedwig has told you nothing?

AMELIA   No.

MOTHER   Ah, she is a strange girl! She asked me to keep it a secret – I don't know why – but now I think you should know. See! (*Very proudly she holds up the tiny baby garments she is knitting.*)

AMELIA   (*pleased and astonished*) So Franz and Hedwig –

MOTHER   (*nods*) For their child. In six months now. My first grandchild, Amelia. Franz's boy, perhaps. I shall hear a little one's voice in this house again.

AMELIA   (*uncertainly, as she looks at the little things*) Still – I want to go.

MOTHER   (*firmly*) We must take care of Hedwig, Amelia. She is to be a mother. That is our first duty. It is our only hope of an heir if you won't marry soon – and if – if the boys don't come back.

AMELIA   Arno is left.

MOTHER   Ah, but they'll be calling him next. It is his birthday to-day, too, poor lad. He's on the jump to be off. I see him gone, too. God knows I may never see one of them again. I sit here in the long evenings and think how death may take my boys – even this minute they may be breathing their last – and then I knit this baby sock and think of the precious little life that's coming. It's my one comfort, Amelia. Nothing must happen now.

AMELIA   (*with a touch of impatience*) What's the matter with Hedwig?

MOTHER   I don't know what it is. She acts as if she didn't want to bring her child into the world. She talks wild. I tell you I must have that child, Amelia! I cannot live else. Hedwig frightens me. The other night I found her sitting on the edge of her bed staring – when she should have been asleep – as if she saw visions, and whispering, "I will send a message to the emperor." What message? I had to shake her out of it. She refuses to make a thing for her baby. Says, "Wait till I see what they do to Franz." It's unnatural.

AMELIA   I can't understand her. I never could. I always thought it was because she was a factory-town girl.

MOTHER If anything should happen to Franz in the state she's in now, Hedwig might go out of her mind entirely. So you had best stay by, Amelia. We must keep a close eye on her. (*There is a knock at the door.*) Who's that?

AMELIA (*looks out of the window, and then whispers*) It's Hans Hoffman. (*The knock is repeated.*)

MOTHER Open girl! Don't stand there!

(*Enter* HOFFMAN, *gay, familiar, inclined to stoutness, but good-looking. Accustomed to having the women bow down to him.*)

HOFFMAN (*to* AMELIA) Ah, ha! You gave me the slip yesterday!

AMELIA My mother.

HOFFMAN (*nodding*) Good day, Mother. (*She curtsies*) (*coming closer to* AMELIA) Where did you run to? Here she as good as promised me she would wed me to-day, Mother, and then –

AMELIA Oh, no!

HOFFMAN Yes, you did. You let me kiss you.

AMELIA (*taken aback*) Oh, sir!

HOFFMAN And when I got to the church square today, no bride for Hans Hoffman. Well, I must say, they had the laugh on me; for I had told them I had found the girl for me – the prettiest bride of the lot. But to-morrow –

AMELIA I can't.

HOFFMAN (*taking hold of her*) Oh, yes, you can. I won't bother you long. I'm off to the front any day now. Come, promise me! What do you say, Mother?

MOTHER (*slowly*) I should like to see her wed.

HOFFMAN There!

AMELIA (*shrinking from both him and the idea*) But I don't know you well enough yet.

HOFFMAN Well, look me over. Don't you think I am good enough for her, Mother? Besides, we can't stop to think of such things now, Amelia. It is wartime. This is an emergency measure. And, then, I'm a soldier – like to die for my country. That ought to count for something – a good deal, I should say – if you love your country, and you do, don't you, Amelia?

AMELIA Oh, yes!

HOFFMAN Well, then, we can get married and get acquainted afterward.

AMELIA (*faintly*) I wanted to be a nurse.

HOFFMAN Nonsense! Pretty girls like you should marry. The priests and the generals have commanded it. It's for the fatherland. Ought she not to wed me, Mother?

MOTHER (*nodding impersonally*) Aye, it is for the fatherland they ask it.

HOFFMAN Of course. It is your patriotic duty, Amelia. You're funny. All the young women are tickled at the chance. But you are the one I have picked out, and I am going to have you. Now, there's a good girl – promise!

(*A hubbub of voices and a cheer are heard outside. Enter* MINNA, *flushed, pretty, light headed.*)

AMELIA Minna!

MINNA (*holding out her hand*) Amelia, see! My wedding-ring!

AMELIA Iron!

MINNA (*triumphantly*) Yes; a war bride!

AMELIA You?

MINNA That's what I am. (*whirling gaily about*)

HOFFMAN (*shaking her hand*) Good for you! Congratulations!

MINNA Didn't you hear them cheer? That was for me!

HOFFMAN There's patriotism for you, Amelia!

AMELIA When were you married, Minna?

MINNA Just now. There were ten of us. We all answered in chorus. It was fun – just like a theater. Then the priest made a speech, and the burgomaster and the captain. The people cheered, and then our husbands had to go to drill for an hour. Oh, I never was so thrilled! It was grand! They told us we were the true patriots.

HOFFMAN Hurrah! And so you are.

MINNA Our names will go down in history, honored by a whole people, they said. (*They are all carried away by* MINNA's *enthusiasm; even* AMELIA *warms up*)

AMELIA But whom did you marry, Minna?

MINNA Heinrich Berg.

AMELIA (*dubious*) That loafer!

MINNA He's all right. He's a soldier now. Why, he may be a hero, fighting for the fatherland; and that makes a lot of difference, Amelia.

HOFFMAN What did I tell you?

MINNA I probably wouldn't have picked him out in peace-times, but it is different now. He only asked me last night. Of course he may get killed. They said we'd have a widow's pension fund – us and our children – forever and ever, if the boys didn't come back. So, you see, I won't be out anything. Anyway, it's for the country. We'll be famous, as war brides. Even the name sounds glorious, doesn't it? War bride! Isn't that fine?

HOFFMAN   Here's a little lady who will hear herself called that to-morrow. (*Takes* AMELIA's *hand*)

MINNA   (*clapping her hands*) Amelia a war bride, too! Good!

HOFFMAN   You'll be proud to hear her called that, won't you, Mother? Give us your blessing.

MINNA   I'd rather be a wife or a widow any day than be an old maid; and to be a war bride – oh! (AMELIA *is blushing and tremulous*)

MOTHER   (*with a far-away look*) It is for the fatherland, Amelia. Aye, aye, the masters have said so. It is the will and judgment of those higher than us. They are wise. Our country will need children. Aye. Say yes, my daughter. You will not say no when your country bids you! It is your emperor, your country, who asks, more than Hans Hoffman.

AMELIA   (*Impressed, and questions herself to see if her patriotism is strong enough to stand the test, while* HOFFMAN, *charmed by* AMELIA's *gentleness, is moved by more personal feeling.*)

HOFFMAN   (*kissing* AMELIA *on both cheeks*) There, it's all settled. (*A faint cheer is heard without.*) To-morrow they will cheer you like that; and when I go, I shall have a bride to wave me good-by instead of –

(*Enter* HEDWIG. *She stands in the doorway looking out on the distant crowds. She is tall, well built, and carries herself proudly. Strong, intelligent features, but pale. Her eyes are large with anxiety. She has soft, wavy black hair. An inward flame seems to be consuming her. The sounds continue in the distance, cheering, disputing mingled with far bugle-calls and marching feet.*)

HEDWIG   (*contemptuously*) Ha! (*The sound startles the others. They turn.*)

ALL   Hedwig!

HEDWIG   (*still in the doorway, looking out*) War brides!

MINNA   (*pertly*) You're a war bride yourself, Hedwig.

HEDWIG   (*turns quickly, locates* MINNA, *almost springs at her*) Don't you dare to call

me a war bride! My ring is gold. See. (*Seizes* MINNA's *hand, and then throws it from her.*) Not iron, like yours.

MINNA   (*boldly taunting*) They even call you the first war bride.

HEDWIG   (*furious, towering over her, her hand on her shoulder*) Say why, why?

MINNA   (*weakening*) Because you were the first one to be married when the war broke out.

HEDWIG   (*both hands on her shoulders*) Because the Government commanded? Because they bribed me with the promise of a widow's pension? Tell the truth.

MINNA   (*faintly*) No. Let me go.

HEDWIG   So! And how long had Franz and I been engaged? Now say.

MINNA   (*beginning to be frightened*) Two years.

HEDWIG   (*flinging her off*) Of course. Everybody knows it. Every village this side the river knew we were to be married this summer. We've dreamed and worked for nothing else all these months. It had nothing to do with the war – our love, our marriage. So, you see, I am no war bride. (*Walks scornfully away.*) Not like you, anyway. (*They all stare at her.*)

HOFFMAN   (*stepping forward indignantly*) I don't know why you should have this contempt for our war brides, and speak like that.

HEDWIG   (*Sits down, half turned away. She shrugs her shoulders, and her lips curl in a little smile.*)

HOFFMAN   They are coming to the rescue of their country. Saving it; else it will perish.

HEDWIG   (*bitterly*) Ha!

HOFFMAN   (*waxing warmer*) They are the saviors of the future.

HEDWIG   (*sadly*) The future!

MOTHER   (*softly, laying her hand on* HEDWIG's *shoulder*) Hedwig, be more respectful. Herr Hoffman is a lieutenant.

HOFFMAN   When we are gone – the best of us – what will the country do if it has no children?

HEDWIG   Why didn't you think of that before – before you started this wicked war?

HOFFMAN   I tell you it is a glory to be a war bride. There!

HEDWIG   (*with a shrug*) A breeding-machine! (*They all draw back*) Why not call it what it is? Speak the naked truth for once.

HOFFMAN   You'll take that back to-morrow,

when your sister stands up in the church with me.

HEDWIG (*starting up*) Amelia? Marry you? No! Amelia, is this true?

AMELIA (*hesitating, troubled, and uncertain*) They tell me I must – for the fatherland.

HEDWIG Marry this man, whom you scarcely know, whom surely you cannot love! Why, you make a mock of marriage! It isn't that they have tempted you with the widow's pension? It is so tiny; it's next to nothing. Surely you wouldn't yield to that?

AMELIA (*frightened*) I did want to go as a nurse, but the priests and the generals – they say we must marry – to – for the fatherland, Hedwig.

HOFFMAN (*to* HEDWIG) I command you to be silent!

HEDWIG Not when my sister's happiness is at stake. If you come back, she will have to live with you the rest of her life.

HOFFMAN That isn't the question now. We are going away – the best of us – to be shot, most likely. Don't you suppose we want to send some part of ourselves into the future, since we can't live ourselves? There, that's straight; and right, too.

HEDWIG (*nodding slowly*) What I said – to breed a soldier for the empire; to restock the land. (*Fiercely*) And for what? For food for the next generation's cannon. Oh, it is an insult to our womanhood! You violate all that makes marriage sacred! (*Agitated, she walks about the room*) Are we women never to get up out of the dust? You never asked us if we wanted this war, yet you ask us to gather in the crops, cut the wood, keep the world going, drudge and slave, and wait, and agonize, lose our all, and go on bearing more men – and more – to be shot down! If we breed the men for you, why don't you let us say what is to become of them? Do we want them shot – the very breath of our life?

HOFFMAN It is for the fatherland.

HEDWIG You use us, and use us – dolls,

Figure 3 Alla Nazimova as "Joan" (Hedwig) in Herbert Brenon's 1916 film of *War Brides*.

beasts of burden, and you expect us to bear it forever dumbly; but I won't! I shall cry out till I die. And now you say it almost out loud, "Go and breed for the empire." War brides! Pah!

(MINNA *gasps, beginning to be terrified.* HOFFMAN *rages.* MOTHER *gazes with anxious concern.* AMELIA *turns pale.*)

HOFFMAN   I never would dream of speaking of Amelia like that. She is the sweetest girl I have seen for many a day.

HEDWIG   What will happen to Amelia? Have you thought of that? No; I warrant you haven't. Well, look. A few kisses and sweet words, the excitement of the ceremony, the cheers of the crowd, some days of living together – I won't call it marriage, for Franz and I are the ones who know what real marriage is, and how sacred it is – then what? Before you know it, an order to march. Amelia left to wait for her child. No husband to wait with her, to watch over her. Think of her anxiety, if she learns to love you! What kind of child will it be? Look at me. What kind of child would *I* have, do you think? I can hardly breathe for thinking of my Franz, waiting, never knowing from minute to minute. From the way I feel, I should think my child would be born mad, I'm that wild with worrying. And then for Amelia to go through the agony alone! No husband to help her through the terrible hour. What solace can the state give then? And after that, if you don't come back, who is going to earn the bread for her child? Struggle and struggle to feed herself and her child; and the fine-sounding name you trick us with – war bride! Humph! that will all be forgotten then. Only one thing can make it worthwhile, and do you know what that is? Love. We'll struggle through fire and water for that; but without it – (*gesture*)

HOFFMAN   (*drawing* AMELIA *to him*) Don't listen to her, Amelia.

AMELIA   (*pushing* HOFFMAN *violently from her, runs from the room*) No, no, I can't marry you! I won't! I won't! (*she shuts the door in his face*)

HEDWIG   (*triumphantly*) She will never be your war bride, Hans Hoffman!

HOFFMAN   (*suddenly, angrily*) By thunder! I've made a discovery. You're the woman! You're the woman!

HEDWIG   What woman?

HOFFMAN   Yesterday there were twenty war brides. The day before there were nearly thirty. To-day there were only ten. There are rumors – (*excitedly*) I'll report you. They'll find you guilty. I myself can prove it.

HEDWIG   Well?

HOFFMAN   I heard them say at the barracks that someone was talking the women out of marrying. They didn't know who; but they said if they caught her – caught any one talking as you have just now, daring to question the wisdom of the emperor and his generals, the church, too – she'd be guilty of treason. You are working against the emperor, against the fatherland. Here you have done it right before my very eyes; you have taken Amelia right out of my arms. You're the woman who's been upsetting the others, and don't you deny it.

HEDWIG   Deny it? I am proud of it.

HOFFMAN   Then the place for you is in jail. Do you know what will be the end of you?

HEDWIG   (*suddenly far away*) Yes, I know, if Franz does not come back. I know; but first (*clenching her hands*) I must get my message to the emperor.

HOFFMAN   (*very angry*) You will be shot for treason.

HEDWIG   (*coming back, laughing silently*) Shot? Oh, no, Herr Hans, you'd never shoot me!

HOFFMAN   Why not?

HEDWIG   Do I have to tell you, stupid? I am a woman: I can get in the crops; I can keep the country going while you are away fighting, and, most important, I might give you a soldier for your next army – for the kingdom. Don't you see my value? (*Laughs strangely*) Oh, no, you'd never shoot me!

MOTHER   There, there, don't excite her, sir.

HEDWIG   (*her head in her hands, on the table*) God! I wish you would shoot me! If you don't give me back my Franz! I've no mind to bring a son into the world for this bloody thing you call war.

HOFFMAN   I am going straight to headquarters to report you.

(*Starts to go. Enter* ARNO *excitedly. He is boyish and fair, in his early twenties, and looks even younger than he really is.*)

ARNO   (*to* HOFFMAN) There's an order to march at once – your regiment.

HOFFMAN   Now?

21

ARNO   At once. You are wanted. They told me to tell you.

(HOFFMAN *moves with military precision to the door; then turns to* HEDWIG.)

HOFFMAN   I shall take the time to report you. (*Goes*)

MINNA   (*to* ARNO) Does Heinrich's regiment go, too?

ARNO   Heinrich who?

MINNA   Heinrich Berg.

ARNO   No. To-morrow.

(MINNA, *now thoroughly scared, is slinking to the door when* HEDWIG *stops her.*)

HEDWIG   Ha! Little Minna, why do you run so fast? Heinrich does not go until to-morrow. (*Looks at her thoughtfully*) Are you going to be able to fight it through, little Minna, when the hard days come? If you do give the empire a soldier, will it be any comfort to know you are helping the falling birth-rate?

MINNA   (*shivering*) Oh, I am afraid of you!

HEDWIG   Afraid of the truth, you mean. You see it at last in all its brutal bareness. Poor little Minna! (*She puts her arm around Minna with sudden tenderness.*) But you need not be afraid of me, little Minna. Oh, no. The trouble with me is I want no more war. Franz is at the war. I'm half mad with dreaming they have killed him. Any moment I may hear. If you loved your man as I do mine, little Minna, you'd understand. Well, go now, and to-morrow say good-by to your husband – of a day.

(MINNA, *with a frightened backward glance, runs out the door.* ARNO, *who has been talking in low tones to his mother, now rises.*)

ARNO   Well, Mother, I haven't much time. (*She clings to his hand.*)

HEDWIG   (*starting*) Arno!

ARNO   I am going, too. Get those little things for me, Mother, will you?

MOTHER   (*goes to door and calls*) Amelia! Come. Arno has been called.

(AMELIA *comes in. Each in turn embraces him, sadly, but bravely. Then the mother and sister gather together handkerchiefs, linen, writing-pad and pencil, and small necessaries.*)

ARNO   I have only a few minutes.

HEDWIG   (*tenderly*) Arno, my little brother, oh, why – why must you go? You seem so young.

ARNO   I'm a man, like the others; don't forget that, Hedwig. Be brave – to help me to be brave. (*They sit on the settle.*)

HEDWIG   (*sighing*) Yes, it cannot be helped. Will you see my Franz, Arno? You look so like him to-day – the day I first saw him in the fields, the day of the factory picnic. It seems long ago. Tell him how happy he made me, and how I loved him. He didn't believe in this war no more than I, yet he had to go. He dreaded lest he meet his friends on the other side. You remember those two young men from across the border? They worked all one winter side by side in the factory with Franz. They went home to join their regiments when the war was let loose on us. He never could stand it, Franz couldn't, if he were ordered to drive his bayonets into them. (*Gets up, full of emotion that is past expression.*) Oh, it is too monstrous! And for what – for what?

ARNO   It is our duty. We belong to the fatherland. I would willingly give my life for my country.

HEDWIG   I would willingly give mine for peace.

ARNO   I must go. Good-by, Hedwig.

HEDWIG   (*controlling her emotion as she kisses him*) Good-by, my brave, splendid little brother.

AMELIA   I may come to the front, too. (*They embrace tenderly.*)

MOTHER   (*strong and quiet, unable to speak, holds his head against her breast for a moment*) Fight well, my son.

ARNO   Yes, Mother.

(*He tears himself away. The silent suffering of the* MOTHER *is pitiful. Her hands are crossed on her breast, her lips are seen to move in prayer. It is* HEDWIG *who takes her in her arms and comforts her.*)

HEDWIG   And this is war – to tear our hearts out like this! Make mother some tea. Amelia, can't you?

(AMELIA *prepares the cup of tea for her mother.*)

MOTHER   (*after a few moments composes herself*) There, I am right now. I must remember – and you must help me, my daughters – it is for the fatherland.

HEDWIG   (*on her knees by the fire, shakes her head slowly*) I wonder, I wonder. O Mother,

I'm not patient like you. I couldn't stand it.
To have a darling little baby and see him
grow into a man, and then lose him like
this! I'd rather never see the face of my
child.

MOTHER   We have them for a little while. I
am thankful to God for what I have had.

HEDWIG   Then I must be very wicked.

MOTHER   Are you sleeping better now,
child?

HEDWIG   No; I am thinking of Franz. He
may be lying there alone on the
battle-field, with none to help, and I here
longing to put my arms around him.
(*Buries her face on the* MOTHER*'s knees and
sobs.*)

MOTHER   Hush, Hedwig! Be brave! Take
care of yourself! We must see that Franz's
child is well born.

HEDWIG   If Franz returns yes; if not – I –
(*gets up impulsively, as if to run out of the
house*)

AMELIA   Don't you want your tea, Hedwig?

(HEDWIG *throws open the door, and
suddenly confronts a man who apparently
was about to enter the house. He is an official,
the military head of the town, known as
Captain* HERTZ. *He is well along in years,
rheumatic, but tremendously self-important.*)

HERTZ   (*stopping* HEDWIG) Wait one
moment. You are the young woman I wish
to see. You don't get away from me like
that.

HEDWIG   (*drawing herself up, moves back a
step or two*) What is it?

HERTZ   (*Turning to the old* MOTHER) Well,
Maria, another son must go – Arno. You
are an honored woman, a noble example to
the state. (*Turns to* AMELIA) You have lost
a very good husband, I understand. Well,
you are a foolish girl. As for you (*turning to*
HEDWIG, *and eyeing her critically and
severely*), I hear pretty bad things. Yes, you
have been talking to the women – telling
them not to marry, not to multiply. In so
doing you are working directly against the
Government. It is the express request and
command that our soldiers about to be
called to the front and our young women
should marry. You deliberately set yourself
in opposition to that command. Are you
aware that that is treason?

HEDWIG   Why are they asking this, Herr
Captain?

HERTZ   Our statesmen are wise. They are
thinking of the future state. The nation is
fast being depopulated. We must take
precautionary measures. We must have
men for the future. I warn you, that to do
or say anything which subserves the plan
of the empire for its own welfare,
especially at a time when our national
existence is in peril – well, it is treason.
Were it not that you are the daughter-
in-law of my old friend (*indicating the*
MOTHER), I should not take the trouble to
warn you, but pack you off to jail at once.
Not another word from you, you
understand?

HEDWIG   (*calmly, even sweetly, but with fire
in her eye*) If I say I will keep quiet, will
you promise me something in return?

HERTZ   What do you mean? Quiet? Of
course you'll keep quiet. Quiet as a
tombstone, if I have anything to say about
it.

HEDWIG   (*calm and tense*) I mean what I say.
Promise to see to it that if we bear you the
men for your nation, there shall be no
more war. See to it that they shall not go
forth to murder and be murdered. That is
fair. We will do our part – we always have –
will you do yours? Promise.

HERTZ   I – I – ridiculous! There will always
be war.

HEDWIG   Then one day we will stop giving
you men. Look at mother. Four sons torn
from her in one month, and none of you
ever asked her if she wanted war. You keep
us here helpless. We don't want
dreadnoughts and armies and fighting, we
women. You tear our husbands, our sons,
from us – you never ask us to help you find
a better way – and haven't we anything to
say?

HERTZ   No. War is man's business.

HEDWIG   Who gives you the men? We
women. We bear and rear and agonize.
Well, if we are fit for that, we are fit to
have a voice in the fate of the men we
bear. If we can bring forth the men for the
nation, we can sit with you in your
councils and shape the destiny of the
nation, and say whether it is to war or
peace we give the sons we bear.

HERTZ   (*chuckling*) Sit in the councils? That
would be a joke. I see. Mother, she's a little
– (*touches his forehead suggestively*) Sit in
the councils with the men and shape the
destiny of the nation! Ha! Ha!

HEDWIG   Laugh, Herr Captain, but the day

will come; and then there will be no more war. No, you will not always keep us here, dumb, silent drudges. We will find a way.

HERTZ   (*turning to the* MOTHER) That is what comes of letting Franz go to a factory town, Maria. That is where he met this girl. Factory towns breed these ideas. (*To* HEDWIG) Well, we'll have none of that here. (*Authoritatively*) Another word of this kind of insurrection, another word to the women of your treason, and you will be locked up and take your just punishment. You remember I had to look out for you in the beginning when you talked against this war. You're a firebrand, and you know how we handle the like of you. (*Goes to door, turns to the* MOTHER) I am sorry you have to have this trouble, Maria, on top of everything else. You don't deserve it. (*To* HEDWIG) You have been warned. Look out for yourself.

(HEDWIG *is standing rigid, with difficulty repressing the torrent of her feelings. Drums are heard coming nearer, and singing voices of men.*)

AMELIA   (*at door*) They are passing this way.

HEDWIG   Wave to Arno. Come, Mother. Ah, how quickly they go! (*The official steps out of the door. There is quick rhythm of marching feet as the departing regiment passes not very far from the house.*) There he is! Wave, Mother. Good-by! good-by! (*The woman stand in the doorway, waving their sad farewells, smiling bravely. The sounds grow less and less, until there is the usual silence.*) In another month, in another week, perhaps, all the men will be gone. We will be a village of women. Not a man left. (*She leads the old* MOTHER *into the house once more*)

HERTZ   (*in the door*) What did you say?

HEDWIG   Not a man left, I said.

HERTZ   You forget. *I* shall be here.

HEDWIG   You are old. You don't count. They think you are only a woman, Herr Captain.

HERTZ   (*insulted*) You – you –

HEDWIG   Oh, don't take it badly, sir. You are honored. Is the name of woman always to be despised? Look out in those fields. Who cleared them, and plucked the vineyards clean? You think we are left at home because we are weak. Ah, no; we are strong. That is why. Strong to keep the world going, to keep sacred the greatest things in life – love and home and work. To remind men of – peace. (*With a quick change*) If only you really were a woman, Herr Captain, that you might breed soldiers for the empire, your glory would be complete.

(*The old captain is about to make an angry reply when there is a commotion outside. The words "News from the front" are distinguished, growing more distinct. The captain rushes out. The women are paralyzed with apprehension for a moment.*)

MOTHER   Amelia, go and see. Hedwig, come here.

(HEDWIG *crouches on the floor close to the mother, her eyes wide with dread. In a few moments* AMELIA *returns, dragging her feet, woe in her face, and unable to deal the blow which must fall on the two women, who stare at her with blanched faces.*)

AMELIA   (*falling at her mother's knee*) Mother!

MOTHER   (*scarcely breathing*) Which one?

AMELIA   All of them.

MOTHER   (*dazed*) All? All my boys?

AMELIA   Emil, Otto – be thankful Arno is left.

(*The* MOTHER *drops her head back against the chair and silently prays.* HEDWIG *creeps nearer* AMELIA *and holds her face between her hands, looking into her eyes.*)

HEDWIG   (*whispering*) Franz?

AMELIA   Franz, too.

(HEDWIG *lies prostrate on the floor. Their grief is very silent: terrible because it is so dumb and stoical. The* MOTHER *is the first to rouse herself. She bends over* HEDWIG.)

MOTHER   Hedwig. (*Hedwig sobs convulsively*) Don't, child. Be careful for the little one's sake. (*Hedwig sits up*) For your child be quiet, be brave.

HEDWIG   I loved him so, Mother!

MOTHER   Yes, he was my boy – my first-born.

HEDWIG   Your first-born, and this is the end. (*She rises up in unutterable wrath and despair*) O God!

MOTHER   (*anxious for her*) Promise me you will be careful. Hedwig. For the sake of your child, *your* first-born, that is to be –

HEDWIG   *My child?* For this end? For the empire – the war that is to be? No!

MOTHER   (*half to herself*) He may look like Franz.

(HEDWIG *quickly seizes the pistol from the mantel-shelf and moves to the bedroom door.* AMELIA, *watching her, sees her do it, and cries out in alarm and rushes to take it from her.*)

AMELIA (*in horror*) Hedwig! What are you doing? Give it to me! No, you must not! You have too much to live for.

HEDWIG (*dazed*) To live for? Me?

AMELIA Why, yes, you are going to be a mother.

HEDWIG A mother? Like her? (*Looks sadly at the bereaved old mother*) Look at her! Poor Mother! And they never asked her if she wanted this thing to be! Oh, no! I shall never take it like that – never! But you are right, Amelia. I have something to do first. (*Lets* AMELIA *put the pistol away in the cupboard.*) I must send a message to the emperor. (*The others are more alarmed for her in this mood than in her grief.*) You said you were going to the front to be a nurse, Amelia. Can you take this message for me? I might take it myself, perhaps.

AMELIA (*hesitating, not knowing what to say or do*) Let me give you some tea, Hedwig.

(Voices *are heard outside, and the sounds of sorrow. Some one near the house is weeping. A wild look and a fierce resolve light* HEDWIG's *face.*)

HEDWIG (*rushing from the house*) They have taken my Franz!

MOTHER Get her back! I feared it. Grief has made her mad.

AMELIA *runs out. A clamor of voices outside.* HEDWIG *can be heard indistinctly speaking to the women. Finally her voice alone is heard, and in a moment she appears, backing into the doorway, still talking to the women.*)

HEDWIG (*a tragic light in her face, and hand uplifted*) I shall send a message to the emperor. If ten thousand women send one like it, there will be peace and no more war. Then they will hear our tears.

A VOICE What is the message? Tell us!

HEDWIG Soon you will know. (*Loudly*) But I tell you now, *don't bear any more children* until they promise you there will be no more war.

HERTZ (*suddenly appearing.* AMELIA *follows*) I heard you. I declare you under arrest. Come with me. You will be shot for treason.

MOTHER (*fearfully, drawing him aside*) Don't say that, sir. Wait. Oh, no, you can't do that!

(*She gets out her work-basket, and shows him the baby things she has been knitting, and glances significantly at* HEDWIG. *A horrid smile comes into the man's face.* HEDWIG *snatches the things and crushes them to her breast as if sacrilege had been committed.*)

HERTZ Is this true? You expect –

HEDWIG (*proudly, scornfully*) You will not shoot me if I give you a soldier for your empire and your armies and your guns, will you, Herr Captain?

HERTZ Why – eh, no. Every child counts these times. But we will put you under lock and key. You are a firebrand. I warned you. Come along.

HEDWIG You want my child, but still you will not promise me what I asked you. Well, we shall see.

HERTZ Come along.

HEDWIG Give me just a moment. I want to send a message to the emperor. Will you take it for me, Herr Captain?

MOTHER (*sighing*) Humor her.

HERTZ Well, well, hurry up!

(HEDWIG *sits at table and writes a brief note.*)

MOTHER (*whispering*) She has lost Franz. She is crazed.

HEDWIG (*rising*) There. See that it is placed in the hands of the emperor. (*Gives him the note*) Good-by, Amelia! Never be a war bride, Amelia. (*Kisses her three times*) Good-by, Mother. (*Embraces her tenderly*) Thank you for these.

(*She gathers the baby things in her hands, crosses the room, pressing a little sock to her lips. As she passes the cupboard she deftly seizes the pistol, and moves into the bedroom. On the threshold she looks over her shoulder.*)

HEDWIG (*firmly*) You may read the message out loud.

(*She disappears into the room, still pressing the little sock to her lips.*)

HERTZ (*reading the note*) "A Message to the Emperor: I refuse to bear my child until you promise there shall be no more war."

(*A shot is fired in the bedroom. They rush into the room. The* MOTHER *stands trembling by the table.*)

HERTZ (*awed, coming out of the room with the baby things, which he places on the table*) Dead! Tcha! Tcha! She was mad. I will hush it up, Maria.

(*He tears up* HEDWIG's *message to the emperor, and goes out of the house, shaking his head.* AMELIA *is kneeling in the doorway of the bedroom, bending over something, and softly crying. The* MOTHER *slowly gathers up the pieces of* HEDWIG's *message and the baby garments, now dashed with blood, and, sitting on the bench, holds them tight against her breast, staring straight in front of her, her lips moving inaudibly. She closes her eyes and rocks to and fro, still muttering and praying.*)

Curtain

2 Alice (Moore) Dunbar-Nelson 1875–1935 ___

Mine Eyes Have Seen
USA

Introduction

A Black political activist, writer and schoolteacher, Alice Dunbar-Nelson wrote *Mine Eyes Have Seen* in the last year of the First World War. In it she draws on the powerful spiritual beliefs which had sustained Black Americans through slavery, adapting the Christian imagery utilised by British war propaganda to further racial equality instead. Apart from a short piece in a magazine, this is her only known play. Its one recorded performance was her own production of it with her pupils in front of an enthusiastic audience at the Howard High School in Wilmington, Delaware, where she was Head of English for 18 years. The play was published in April 1918 in the journal *The Crisis*, which had been founded by W. E. B. Du Bois as a platform for the National Association for the Advancement of Colored People (NAACP). In 1915, the NAACP had set up a Drama Committee to encourage the writing of plays about the Black experience by Black authors, to counter the racial stereotypes ignorantly reinforced by white playwrights.

The granddaughter of slaves freed after the Civil War, Alice Dunbar-Nelson was among the first African-American women to be college educated. After teacher-training in New Orleans, Alice Dunbar taught in New York City public schools and did Black settlement work in Harlem, before moving to Delaware in 1902. Her first volume of poems, short stories and essays was published in 1895 and by 1902 she had published several short stories on New York tenement life. Briefly married to the famous poet, Paul Dunbar, 1898–1902, and secretly to Arthur Collis, 1910–12, she remarried for life in 1916; her third husband was the Black political journalist, Robert J. Nelson, with whom she had worked to publish her

Masterpieces of Negro Eloquence (1914). She continued to write and edit alongside her other political activities. Between 1913 and 1915 she was associate editor of the *African Methodist Episcopal Church Review*, having remained a member of the Protestant Episcopal Church since her student days. She had been active in the Black women's club movement since the 1890s and was recording secretary for the National Association of Colored Women. During the First World War, failing to secure an appointment overseas as a war correspondent, she served the government by mobilising Black women's support for the US Council of National Defense. Thus it is clear that Alice Dunbar-Nelson wrote knowledgeably of Black experience.

On the other hand, this should not disguise the fact that Black experience was not monolithic. Dunbar-Nelson was aspiring middle-class, urban, a college graduate and a woman. Moreover, she could pass for white. *Mine Eyes Have Seen* is set in a Harlem tenement; the character who most resembles Dunbar-Nelson is the outsider, Cornelia.

Alice Dunbar-Nelson is perhaps best known today for her First World War poem "I Sit and Sew" – which contrasts the "futile" task of a woman sewing, with dreams of "that pageant terrible", war. She used the same rhetoric in "Negro Women in War Work", her chapter for Emmett J. Scott's conservative history of the American Negro in the First World War, where she claimed that "into this maelstrom of war activity the women of the Negro race hurled themselves joyously". Dunbar-Nelson's play, however, centres on the Black male experience. It is overtly political, a problem play which debates the dilemma of whether a Black American draftee should claim exemption: why should he serve a country that has treated his people so badly? Why should he risk his life on

Figure 4 "ENLIST – On Which Side of the Window are YOU?", 1917 American First World War recruitment poster by Laura Bray, the probable basis for the final tableau in Alice Dunbar-Nelson's *Mine Eyes Have Seen*. (Amongst the hundreds of propaganda posters published, none seems to have displayed or addressed African-Americans.)

behalf of white people, when it is white people who are responsible for the lynching of his father? That the play ends to the strains of *The Battle Hymn of the Republic* and a near foregone conclusion, does not reduce it to mere propaganda, despite its ready acceptance of German atrocity tales.

Dunbar's play was part of an intense contemporary debate about Black American conscription for the European War, which was at its height in 1917–18. Once the USA entered the war on the British side in 1917, American censorship was strictly enforced. It was used to silence the controversy about how Black Americans could best exploit the wartime need for them (either in factories or the army) to gain racial justice. The Black socialist editors of *The Messenger* were jailed for reminding readers that Black soldiers were being drafted to protect Europeans from atrocities whilst Black lynchings went

unprosecuted in the USA. *The Messenger* was suppressed. With a circulation of 74,000 *The Crisis* was seen as the most influential organ of radical Black American thought. When Dunbar-Nelson's play was published, the journal was already being monitored for breaches of the Espionage Act of 1917 and the forthcoming Sedition Act. Early in 1918 the NAACP had been rebuked by the Justice Department for Du Bois' powerful attacks on the government, and only avoided prosecution by promising self-censorship. Dubois' editorials started to recommend to his readers to "close ranks" with their "white fellow citizens" while the war lasted. The publication of *Mine Eyes Have Seen* was presumably part of this new placatory policy of *The Crisis*.

Mine Eyes Have Seen contributed a dramatisation of some of the issues involved in the conscription debate. It is no accident that the characters include the political types of an Irish widow and a Russian Jewish socialist. Apart from German Americans, the Irish, members of the Socialist Party and Jews were among the groups most opposed to the ending of American neutrality in 1917. Whilst German propaganda was apparently specifically aimed at Jews and Black Americans, British propaganda tried to distract attention from Russian treatment of Jews on to the massacre of Armenians by Turkey, Germany's ally. Britain also targeted the American Irish, especially after the Easter Uprising of 1916. Jake makes the connection between Black Americans and Russian Jews explicit, relating pogroms to lynchings. Yet Jake, unlike many immigrants who avoided conscription by remaining registered as aliens, is impatiently awaiting his call-up papers. Just as many American Jews were against an American–Russian alliance, Irish Americans opposed an American–English alliance. However, Mrs O'Neill approved her husband's eventual decision to "go to do his bit". It is all the more effective then, for pro-war propaganda, that these representative characters are ventriloquised by Dunbar-Nelson as agreeing with Dan that "You've got to fight to keep yer inheritance" and that racial pride is shown by loyalty to "the country where we live", in spite of persecution.

Rationally, *Mine Eyes Have Seen* debates the argument that a right to national citizenship is established by fighting for the nation. Yet the emotional power of the play comes from its demonstration of the idea of common humanity. Dan voices this idea, echoed by a litany from the women characters, and it is emphasised by the very strangeness of his claim of kinship with the Mothers of Europe. It is pity for them which will be glorious, holy, and Christlike. That claim is made more startling through the image of One Blood.

Here Alice Dunbar-Nelson has moved beyond the Black politics of her male contemporaries, such as Du Bois or Scott; she has moved beyond the feminist aspirations to earning the suffrage by war-work, which she shared with her white female contemporaries on the Women's Committee of the Council for National Defense, such as Dr Anna Howard Shaw and Carrie Chapman Catt. She is developing the Black feminism ("womanism") she shared with her Black women friends such as Angelina Weld Grimké, Mary Burrill and Georgia Douglas Johnson.

This group of women writers recognised the political power of the stage and used it as part of the Black women's crusade against lynching, especially by calling on the white woman. Much of the American and British propaganda designed to bring America in on the British side was aimed at women, trading on current discourses of motherhood. Mothers were persuaded it was their duty to encourage their sons to risk their lives to save women and children, this being the specifically female version of patriotic self-sacrifice. Dunbar-Nelson has taken that discourse and racialised it for Black feminist purposes, by claiming kinship between Black and white mothers.

She is attempting to address a varied audience with her play. Although its obvious target is young Black American men of recruitment age, it speaks to Jewish and Irish Americans too, to older Black Americans, but above all to women both Black and white to feel sorrow and pity for each other's children. Dunbar-Nelson had insisted on breaking several taboos in her play, not only by mentioning rape and lynching, but also by alluding to the provocative issue of "racial purity" by her use of the image of blood. Materially the races were linked through miscegenation (embodied in such Americans as Dunbar-Nelson herself, Weld Grimké, and Douglas Johnson); mystically they should be

linked through the Blood of Christ into a common love of humanity. If Black Americans will demonstrate to white Americans that they are prepared to sacrifice their own lives on behalf of white children, surely white mothers would be moved. Strengthening this appeal, the evocative verses of the *Battle Hymn of the Republic* remind the audience of the American ideals on which their nation is founded, calling them to union and to war: "As he died to make men holy, let us die to make men free."

Further reading

Primary

Burrill, Mary (Powell) (1919) *Aftermath*, in *Liberator*, April 1919. Reprinted in Kathy A. Perkins and Judith L. Stephens (eds) (1998) *Strange Fruit: Plays on Lynching by American Women*, Bloomington: Indiana University Press.

Dunbar-Nelson, Alice (1918) *Mine Eyes Have Seen*, in *The Crisis* 15 (April 1918) 271–75. Reprinted in James V. Hatch and Ted Shine (eds) (1974) *Black Theatre, USA: Forty-Five Plays by Black Americans 1847–1974*, New York: Free Press, pp. 173–7.

—— (1919) "Negro Women in War Work" in Emmett J. Scott *Scott's Official History of the American Negro in the World War* (n.p.). Reprinted (1969) New York: Arno.

—— (1920) "I Sit and Sew" in Alice Dunbar-Nelson (ed.) *The Dunbar Speaker and Entertainer*, Naperville: Nichols. Reprinted in Louise Bernikow (ed.) (1974) *The World Split Open: Four Centuries of Women Poets in England and America, 1552–1950*, New York: Vintage, pp. 260–1.

—— (1988) *The Works of Alice Dunbar-Nelson, 3 volumes*, (ed.) Gloria T. Hull, Oxford: Oxford University Press.

Howe, Julia Ward [1862] (1974) "The Battle-Hymn of the Republic" in Louise Bernikow (ed.) *The World Split Open: Four Centuries of Women Poets in England and America, 1552–1950*, New York: Vintage, pp. 216–17.

Miller, May [1930] (1989) *Stragglers in the Dust* in Kathy A. Perkins (ed.) *Black Female Playwrights: an Anthology of Plays before 1950*, Bloomington: Indiana University Press.

Secondary

Barbeau, E. Arthur and Florette Henri [1974] (1996) *The Unknown Soldiers: African-American Troops in World War I*, New York: Da Capo.

Collins, Patricia Hill (1991) *Black Feminist Thought*, London: Routledge.

Cooperman, Stanley (1967) *World War I and the American Novel*, London: Johns Hopkins University Press.

Huggins, Nathan Irvin (1971) *Harlem Renaissance*, Oxford: Oxford University Press.

Hull, Gloria T. (1987) *Color, Sex and Poetry: Three Women Writers of the Harlem Renaissance*, Bloomington: Indiana University Press.

Kennedy, David M. (1980) *Over Here: The First World War and American Society*, New York: Oxford University Press.

Sanders, M. L. and Philip M. Taylor (1982) *British Propaganda during the First World War, 1914–18*, London: Macmillan.

Shockley, Ann (1989) *Afro American Women Writers 1746–1933*, New York: Macmillan.

Mine Eyes Have Seen ─────────────

[One-act Playlet]
First performed Wilmington, USA, 1918
Published 1918

Alice Dunbar-Nelson

─────────────────────────────

Characters

DAN, the cripple

CHRIS, the younger brother

LUCY, the sister

MRS O'NEILL, an Irish neighbor

JAKE, a Jewish boy

JULIA, Chris' sweetheart

BILL HARVEY, a muleteer

CORNELIA LEWIS, a settlement worker

Time

Now.

Place

A manufacturing city in the northern part of
the United States.

Scene

*Kitchen of a tenement. All details of furnishing
emphasize sordidness – laundry tubs, range,
table covered with oil cloth, pine chairs. Curtain
discloses* DAN *in a rude imitation of a steamer
chair, propped by faded pillows, his feet covered
with a patch-work quilt.*

*LUCY is bustling about the range preparing a
meal. During the conversation she moves from
range to table, setting latter and making ready
the noon-day meal.*

*DAN is about thirty years old; face thin,
pinched, bearing traces of suffering. His hair is
prematurely grey; nose finely chiselled; eyes
wide, as if seeing BEYOND. Complexion
brown.*

*LUCY is slight, frail, brown-skinned, about
twenty, with a pathetic face. She walks with a
slight limp.*

DAN Isn't it most time for him to come
home, Lucy?

LUCY It's hard to tell, Danny, dear; Chris
doesn't come home on time any more. It's
half-past twelve, and he ought to be here
by the clock, but you can't tell any more –
you can't tell.

DAN Where does he go?

LUCY I know where he doesn't go, Dan, but
where he does, I can't say. He's not going
to Julia's any more lately. I'm afraid, Dan,
I'm afraid!

DAN Of what, Little Sister?

LUCY Of everything; oh, Dan, it's too big,
too much for me – the world outside, the
street – Chris going out and coming home
nights moody-eyed; I don't understand.

DAN And so you're afraid? That's been the
trouble from the beginning of time – we're
afraid because we don't understand.

LUCY (*coming down front, with a dish cloth in
her hand*) Oh, Dan, wasn't it better in the
old days when we were back home – in the
little house with the garden, and you and
father coming home nights and mother
getting supper, and Chris and I studying
lessons in the dining-room at the table – we
didn't have to eat and live in the kitchen
then, and –

DAN (*grimly*) – And the notices posted on
the fence for us to leave town because
niggers had no business having such a
decent home.

LUCY (*unheeding the interruption*) – And
Chris and I reading the wonderful books
and laying our plans –

DAN – To see them go up in the smoke of
our burned home.

LUCY (*continuing, her back to* DAN, *her eyes
lifted, as if seeing a vision of retrospect*) – And
everyone petting me because I had hurt
my foot when I was little, and father –

DAN – Shot down like a dog for daring to
defend his home –

LUCY   – Calling me "Little Brown Princess",
and telling mother –
DAN   – Dead of pneumonia and heartbreak
in this bleak climate.
LUCY   – That when you –
DAN   – Maimed for life in a factory of hell!
Useless – useless – broken on the wheel.
(*His voice breaks in a dry sob.*)
LUCY   (*coming out of her trance, throws aside
the dish-cloth, and running to* DAN, *lays her
cheek against his and strokes his hair*) Poor
Danny, poor Danny, forgive me, I'm selfish.
DAN   Not selfish, Little Sister, merely
natural.

(*Enter roughly and unceremoniously* CHRIS.
*He glances at the two with their arms about
each other, shrugs his shoulders, hangs up his
rough cap and mackinaw on a nail, then
seats himself at the table, his shoulders
hunched up; his face dropping on his hand.*
LUCY *approaches him timidly.*)

LUCY   Tired, Chris?
CHRIS   No.
LUCY   Ready for dinner?
CHRIS   If it is ready for me.
LUCY   (*busies herself bringing dishes to the
table*) You're late to-day.
CHRIS   I have bad news. My number was
posted today.
LUCY   Number? Posted? (*Pauses with a plate
in her hand.*)
CHRIS   I'm drafted.
LUCY   (*drops plate with a crash.* DAN *leans
forward tensely, his hands gripping the arms
of his chair*) Oh, it can't be! They won't take
you from us! And shoot you down, too?
What will Dan do?
DAN   Never mind about me, Sister. And
you're drafted, boy?
CHRIS   Yes – yes – but – (*he rises and strikes
the table heavily with his hand*) I'm not
going.
DAN   Your duty –
CHRIS   – Is here with you. I owe none
elsewhere, I'll pay none.
LUCY   Chris! Treason! I'm afraid!
CHRIS   Yes, of course, you're afraid, Little
Sister, why shouldn't you be? Haven't you
had your soul shrivelled with fear since we
were driven like dogs from our home? And
for what? Because we were living like
Christians. Must I go and fight for the
nation that let my father's murder go
unpunished? That killed my mother – that
took away my chances for making a man

out of myself? Look at us – you – Dan, a
shell of a man –
DAN   Useless – useless –
LUCY   Hush, Chris!
CHRIS   – And me, with a fragment of an
education, and no chance – only half a
man. And you, poor Little Sister, there's no
chance for you; what is there in life for
you? No, if others want to fight, let them.
I'll claim exemption.
DAN   On what grounds?
CHRIS   You – and Sister. I am all you have; I
support you.
DAN   (*half rising in his chair*) Hush! Have I
come to this, that I should be the excuse,
the woman's skirts for a slacker to hide
behind?
CHRIS   (*clenching his fists*) You call me that?
You, whom I'd lay down my life for? I'm no
slacker when I hear the real call of duty.
Shall I desert the cause that needs me –
you – Sister – home? For a fancied glory?
Am I to take up the cause of a lot of kings
and politicians who play with men's souls,
as if they are cards – dealing them out, a
hand here, in the Somme – a hand there, in
Palestine – a hand there, in the Alps – a
hand there, in Russia – and because the
cards don't match well, call it a misdeal,
gather them up, throw them in the discard,
and call for a new deal of a million human,
suffering souls? And must I be the Deuce
of Spades?

(*During the speech, the door opens slowly and
JAKE lounges in. He is a slight, pale youth,
Hebraic, thin-lipped, eager-eyed. His hands
are in his pockets, his narrow shoulders
drawn forward. At the end of* CHRIS' *speech
he applauds softly.*)

JAKE   Bravo! You've learned the patter well.
Talk like the fellows at the Socialist
meetings.
DAN and LUCY   Socialist meetings!
CHRIS   (*defiantly*) Well?
DAN   Oh, nothing; it explains. All right, go
on – any more?
JAKE   Guess he's said all he's got breath for.
I'll go; it's too muggy in here. What's the
row?
CHRIS   I'm drafted.
JAKE   Get exempt. Easy – if you don't want
to go. As for me –

(*Door opens, and* MRS O'NEILL *bustles in.
She is in deep mourning, plump, Irish,
shrewd-looking, bright-eyed.*)

MRS O'NEILL   Lucy, they do be sayin' as how down by the chain stores they be a raid on the potatoes, an' ef ye're wantin' some, ye'd better be after gittin' into yer things an' comin' wid me. I kin kape the crowd off yer game foot – an' what's the matter wid youse all?

LUCY   Oh, Mrs O'Neill, Chris has got to go to war.

MRS O'NEILL   An' ef he has, what of it? Ye'll starve, that's all.

DAN   Starve? Never! He'll go, we'll live.

(LUCY *wrings her hands impotently.* MRS O'NEILL *drops a protecting arm about the girl's shoulder.*)

MRS O'NEILL   An' it's hard it seems to yer? But they took me man from me year before last, an' he wint afore I came over here, an' it's a widder I am wid me five kiddies, an' I've niver a word to say but –

CHRIS   He went to fight for his own. What do they do for my people? They don't want us, except in extremity. They treat us like – like – like –

JAKE   Like Jews in Russia, eh? (*He slouches forward, then his frame straightens itself electrically*) Like Jews in Russia, eh? Denied the right of honor in men, eh? Or the right of virtue in women, eh? There isn't a wrong you can name that your race has endured that mine has not suffered, too. But there's a future, Chris – a big one. We younger ones must be in that future – ready for it, ready for it – (*His voice trails off, and he sinks despondently into a chair.*)

CHRIS   Future? Where? Not in this country? Where?

(*The door opens and* JULIA *rushes in impulsively. She is small, slightly built, eager-eyed, light-brown skin, wealth of black hair; full of sudden shyness.*)

JULIA   Oh, Chris, someone has just told me – I was passing by – one of the girls said your number was called. Oh, Chris, will you have to go? (*She puts her arms up to* CHRIS' *neck; he removes them gently, and makes a slight gesture toward* DAN's *chair.*)

JULIA   Oh, I forgot. Dan, excuse me. Lucy, it's terrible, isn't it?

CHRIS   I'm not going, Julia.

MRS O'NEILL   Not going!

DAN   Our men have always gone, Chris. They went in 1776.

CHRIS   Yes, as slaves. Promised a freedom they never got.

DAN   No, gladly, and saved the day, too, many a time. Ours was the first blood shed on the altar of National liberty. We went in 1812, on land and sea. Our men were through the struggles of 1861 –

CHRIS   When the Nation was afraid not to call them. Didn't want 'em at first.

DAN   Never mind; they helped work out their own salvation. And they were there in 1898 –

CHRIS   Only to have their valor disputed.

DAN   – And they were at Carrizal, my boy, and now –

MRS O'NEILL   An' sure, wid a record like that – ah, 'tis me ould man who said at first 'twasn't his quarrel. His Oireland bled an' the work of thim divils to try to make him a traitor nearly broke his heart – but he said he'd go to do his bit – an' here I am.

(*There is a sound of noice and bustle without, and with a loud laugh,* BILL HARVEY *enters. He is big, muscular, rough, his voice thunderous. He emits cries of joy at seeing the group, shakes hands and claps* CHRIS *and* DAN *on their backs.*)

DAN   And so you weren't torpedoed?

HARVEY   No, I'm here for a while – to get more mules and carry them to the front to kick their bit.

MRS O'NEILL   You've been – over there?

HARVEY   Yes, over the top, too. Mules, rough-necks, wires, mud, dead bodies, stench, terror!

JULIA   (*horror-stricken*) Ah – Chris!

CHRIS   Never, mind, not for mine.

HARVEY   It's a great life – not. But I'm off again, first chance.

MRS O'NEILL   They're brutes, eh?

HARVEY   Don't remind me.

MRS O'NEILL   (*whispering*) They maimed my man, before he died.

JULIA   (*clinging to* CHRIS) Not you, oh, not you!

HARVEY   They crucified children.

DAN   Little children? They crucified little children.

CHRIS   Well, what's that to us? They're little white children. But here our fellow-countrymen throw our little black babies in the flames – as did the worshippers of Moloch, only they haven't the excuse of a religious rite.

JAKE   (*slouches out of his chair, in which he*

has been sitting brooding) Say, don't you get tired sitting around grieving because you're colored? I'd be ashamed to be –

DAN   Stop! Who's ashamed of his race? Ours the glorious inheritance; ours the price of achievement. Ashamed! I'm *proud*. And you, too, Chris, smouldering in youthful wrath, you, too, are proud to be numbered with the darker ones, soon to come into their inheritance.

MRS O'NEILL   Aye, but you've got to fight to keep yer inheritance. Ye can't lay down when someone else has done the work, and expect it to go on. Ye've got to fight.

JAKE   If you're proud, show it. All of your people – well, look at us! Is there a greater race than ours? Have any people had more horrible persecutions – and yet – we're loyal always to the country where we live and serve.

MRS O'NEILL   And us! Look at us!

DAN   (*half tears himself from the chair, the upper part of his body writhing, while the lower part is inert, dead*) Oh, God! If I were but whole and strong! If I could only prove to a doubting world of what stuff my people are made!

JULIA   But why, Dan, it isn't our quarrel? What have we to do with their affairs? These white people, they hate us. Only today I was sneered at when I went to help with some of their relief work. Why should you, my Chris, go to help those who hate you?

(CHRIS *clasps her in his arms, and they stand, defying the others.*)

HARVEY   If you could have seen the babies and girls – and old women – if you could have – (*covers his eyes with his hand.*)

CHRIS   Well, it's good for things to be evened up somewhere.

DAN   Hush, Chris! It is not for us to visit retribution. Nor to wish hatred on others. Let us rather remember the good that has come to us. Love of humanity is above the small considerations of time or place or race or sect. Can't you be big enough to feel pity for the little crucified French children – for the ravished Polish girls, even as their mothers must have felt sorrow, if they had known, for *our* burned and maimed little ones? Oh, Mothers of Europe, we be of one blood, you and I!

(*There is a tense silence.* JULIA *turns from* CHRIS, *and drops her hand. He moves slowly to the window and looks out. The door opens quietly, and* CORNELIA LEWIS *comes in. She stands still a moment, as if sensing a difficult situation.*)

CORNELIA   I've heard about it, Chris, your country calls you. (CHRIS *turns from the window and waves hopeless hands at* DAN *and* LUCY.) Yes, I understand; they do need you, *don't* they?

DAN   (*fiercely*) No!

LUCY   Yes, we do, Chris, we do need you, but your country needs you more. And, above that, your race is calling you to carry on its good name, and with that, the voice of humanity is calling to us all – we can manage without you, Chris.

CHRIS   You? Poor little cripped Sister. Poor Dan –

DAN   Don't pity me, pity your poor, weak self.

CHRIS   (*clenching his fist*) Brother, you've called me two names today that no man ought to have to take – a slacker and a weakling!

DAN   True. Aren't you both? (*Leans back and looks at* CHRIS *speculatively.*)

CHRIS   (*makes an angry lunge towards the chair, then flings his hands above his head in an impatient gesture*) Oh, God! (*Turns back to window.*)

JULIA   Chris, it's wicked for them to taunt you so – but Chris – it *is* our country – our race –

(*Outside the strains of music from a passing band are heard. The music comes faintly, gradually growing louder and louder until it reaches a crescendo. The tune is "The Battle Hymn of the Republic", played in stirring march time.*)

DAN   (*singing softly*) "Mine eyes have seen the glory of the coming of the Lord!"

CHRIS   (*turns from the window and straightens his shoulders*) And mine!

CORNELIA   "As He died to make men holy, let us die to make them free!"

MRS O'NEILL   An' ye'll make the sacrifice, me boy, an' ye'll be the happier.

JAKE   Sacrifice! No sacrifice for him, it's those who stay behind. Ah, if they would only call me, and call me soon!

LUCY   We'll get on, never fear. I'm proud! Proud! *(Her voice breaks a little, but her head is thrown back.)*

(As the music draws nearer, the group breaks up, and the whole roomful rushes to the window and looks out. CHRIS *remains in the center of the floor, rigidly at attention, a rapt look on his face.* DAN *strains at his chair, as if he would rise, then sinks back, his hand feebly beating time to the music, which swells to a martial crash.)*

Curtain

3 Gertrude Stein 1874–1946

Please Do Not Suffer: A Play
USA

Accents in Alsace: A Reasonable Tragedy
USA

Introduction

Gertrude Stein is the best known and most influential of the authors included in this anthology. Born in Pennsylvania in 1874, to parents of German-Jewish descent, she spent her early childhood in Vienna and Paris, only returning to the USA when she was 5; consequently German was her first spoken language, followed by French and then English, although she read first in English. At the age of 19 she attended Radcliffe College, studying philosophy and psychology with William James, and English composition. However, she failed her Latin exams and so could not graduate. Instead, setting up house with her brother Leo, she entered Johns Hopkins School of Medicine in Baltimore and continued to study medicine until 1902. Then, partly as a result of an unhappy love affair with another woman, she spent time in Europe, finally moving to live in Paris with Leo in 1903. Supported by dividends from the family estate, the two bought paintings by contemporary artists such as Picasso, Matisse and Cézanne, and held a weekly salon at their home in Rue de Fleurus. Gertrude commenced writing for publication. She meditated and composed sentences whilst posing for the famous portrait by Picasso, and amongst her first published efforts were essays on Picasso and Matisse. In 1907 Gertrude met Alice B. Toklas, who moved into the Paris home in 1910 and became her lifelong companion. (Leo left in 1913; Gertrude never spoke to him again.)

When the First World War broke out, Gertrude and Alice were in England. They only returned to Paris, by way of Spain, after the Battle of Verdun in 1916. In 1917, when America entered the war, Gertrude obtained her first car, a Ford van, which she drove around Perpignan and Nîmes with Alice to ferry hospital supplies for the American Fund for French Wounded. In 1919 they delivered civilian relief in Alsace, which had been occupied by the Germans.

We can place Stein's wartime writing within the context of the war propaganda of the time, both government-sponsored propaganda and its unofficial diffusion through popular cultural forms such as films. Stein contested on the one hand the language used, and on the other the stories which that language promoted. So we can see her war writing partly as a reaction to the emotive uses of language that triggered stock "patriotic" responses in publications of all kinds, from guidebooks to the war verse that sprouted in newspapers. After the war, she influenced the young Ernest Hemingway, and his well-known passage in *A Farewell to Arms* may stand as a sign-post towards Stein's seemingly idiosyncratic use of language:

> I was always embarrassed by the words sacred, glorious, and sacrifice and the expression in vain . . . I had seen nothing sacred, and the things that were glorious had no glory and the sacrifices were like the stockyards at Chicago if nothing was done with the meat except bury it . . . Abstract words such as glory, honour, courage, or hallow were obscene beside the concrete names of villages, the numbers of roads, the names of rivers, the numbers of regiments and the dates.
>
> (Hemingway, 1929: 143–4)

On the other hand she was also clearly opposing the narratives by which such overblown language contributed to the dramatic illusions of the period. Her opinion of the story-line of Hollywood war films can be gauged from her spoof, *A Movie* (1920). Still recognisable are the sense of breathless speed and change, especially car chases across scenic landscapes, which function as distractions from the implausible coincidences and stereotypical characters, all absurdity of disguise and mistake justified by the exciting improbability of espionage. Such plots rely on suspense and enigma; suspense keeps the audience on edge trying to guess "what's going to happen next", and enigma puzzles them with clues in what has already happened to explain events as a sequence of cause and effect. Stein's works have neither the suspense nor dénouement traditional to Western plots. As she explains in her essay "Plays" (1935), Stein wanted her audience to be aware of the immediacy of experience, not abstracting into the past or the future but concentrating on the concrete present.

Just as turn-of-the-century painting by artists such as Picasso moved away from the historical realism of Victorian culture, and the surrealists challenged bourgeois conceptions of society, in her plays Stein turned away from the creation of an illusion on the stage typical of Victorian "drawing-room" theatre. The artists Stein knew in Paris wanted to draw attention to the very quality of the paints and materials they used, to the constructedness of the art-object. They required active work from the viewer. Instead of the paint becoming, as it were, transparent, so that the painting acted as a kind of window on to a pre-existing scene or tableau, impressing the passive beholder with a simulacrum of reality, the post-impressionists demanded that their audiences should participate in their effort to recreate the sense of mass, space and light of the world we live in, and should find pleasure in the materials explicitly used to prompt that exploration. Whereas those materials were paint and a collage of the surfaces to which paint could be applied, Stein's materials were the components of language: words and the spaces between words, words spoken by various voices. Minimising the ability of language to refer to the real world by conjuring up pictures of facts, Stein's experimental collages of words and phrases approached the language of music. As Katherine Mansfield recognised, even a less experimental early work such as *Melanctha* echoed the rhythms of African-American music and speech patterns. Indeed, the American composer Virgil Thomson set Stein's *Suzie Asado* to music in 1926, which led to her first opera libretto for him in 1927: *Four Saints in Three Acts* (premiered in 1934). Together with *Susan B. Anthony, the Mother of*

Us All (1946), this is the most frequently staged of her dramatic works, capable of producing dazzlingly kaleidoscopic effects in performance.

Stein's writing career lasted 40 years. Deliberately, playfully subversive, Stein's work is, as Barlow says, difficult to categorise by genre (Barlow 1994: 266), but for over 30 years, besides "novels", "poetry" and "lectures", she was originating "plays" – 77 in all. She commenced playwriting in the year before the First World War, 1913, and finished her last opera in 1946. Naturally, her aesthetic theory developed, and the plays are diverse in form, ranging from a collection of fragments to a four-act opera. The two early plays reprinted here give an idea of that diversity. (There is no record that either has been performed.) Both relate to the Great War. *Please Do Not Suffer* was written in 1916. Apparently set in Paris, it has references to the invasion and fighting, to Verdun and to the Dardanelles. Most of the speech is attributed to particular characters: a heterogeneous group of civilians linked by gossip. Their self-descriptions and the inconsequentiality of their words comically embody their self-centredness and the triviality of their concerns, amongst which the statements that "I ask you to believe that the french [*sic*] are winning. I believe that the french are winning" are given no greater prominence than "He does like dogs" or "I prefer veal to chicken". Implicitly, their unthinking self-absorption and pettiness contrast with the heroically patriotic propaganda of the period, yet Stein's satire is not merely rhetorical. The dialogue has danced colloquially along, with the leitmotifs of food and knitting to lightly remind us of rationing, when Stein leaves the audience suddenly reeling from the depth of hollowness revealed by Mrs Marchand: "I hate to see so much black. I do not mean by that that I am sullen. I am not that. I am delighted with the surroundings."

As Toklas recalls in *What Is Remembered* (Toklas 1963: 109–12), *Accents in Alsace* (1919) dates from the time Stein and Toklas undertook post-war relief work in Alsace, part of France invaded in 1914 and occupied by the Germans throughout the war. Although French citizens since the 1870 war between Germany and France, Alsatians speak their own, Germanic language, distinct from either French or Prussian. Much of this so-called "Reasonable Tragedy" consists of a play on language, thus referring indirectly to the armed conflict, occupation and armistice, through the struggle for authority over words. *Accents in Alsace* bears even less resemblance to conventional drama than *Please Do Not Suffer*, there being no named speakers and, although the text begins with "Act I. The Schemils", its following divisions are arbitrarily marked, for instance "Another Act", "Act 54", "Act 425", and the heading "Act II" appears several times. The opening lines are rhymed. A dialogue between the son of the Schemil family and his sister and mother is quoted before the words pass to an unidentified voice which narrates their story in doggerel and comments on it: "That is what you did with the Boche" – "you" bribed Germans. Thus the play appears to identify with a French viewpoint, but the name of the Schemils is not constant – graduating across Schemmel, Schemmil to Schimmel "which is an Alsatian name". Fragments of speech display uncertainty about language, "and then what do I say to thee", "what do you mean", and a wavering between French and German – is there a neutral language or plain fact? – "Louisa. They call me Lisela" and "When you see a Hussar. / A Zouave. / A soldier." The narrative is interrupted. There follows a patchwork that poses the nonsense rhymes by which children enjoy practising sounds – "Sing so la douse so la dim" – between contrasting snatches of conversation and the pompous rhetoric of political speech: "In the exercise of greatness there is charm." It may be, as one voice states, that "Any one can hate a Prussian", but after frequent allusions to singing and song, the play ends with one of the most lyrical passages in all Stein. Headed "The Watch on the Rhine" (a German anti-French war-song), this instead resembles a love-song, in which the Rhine, the boundary separating France from Germany, "hardly showed". Here the forest is not seen as "Black" but blue "With for get [*sic*] me nots" and "In the midst of our happiness we were very pleased". As "the best flower" is celebrated, "The flower of truth", force and bitterness give way to pleasure and delight.

Further reading

Primary

Aldrich, Mildred (1915) *A Hilltop on the Marne*, London: Constable/Boston: Houghton Mifflin.

Apollinaire, Guillaume [1917] (1997) *The Mammaries of Tiresias* in Maya Slater (ed.) *Three Pre-Surrealist Plays*, Oxford: Oxford University Press, pp. 151–207.

Hemingway, Ernest (1929) *A Farewell to Arms*, London: Cape.

Stein, Gertrude (1922) *Please Do Not Suffer: A Play* and *Accents in Alsace: A Reasonable Tragedy* and *Tourty or Tourtebattre: a Story of the Great War* in *Geography and Plays*, Boston: Four Seas; rep. (1993) in Cyrena N. Pondrom (ed.) *Geography and Plays* Wisconsin: University of Wisconsin Press.

—— (1932) *Am I to Go or I'll Say So* [1923] and *A Movie* [1920] in *Operas and Plays*, Paris: Plain Edition.

—— (1933) *The Autobiography of Alice B. Toklas*, New York: Vintage/London: The Bodley Head.

—— (1935) "Plays" in *Lectures in America*, New York: Random House; rep. (1988) London: Virago.

—— (1945) *Wars I Have Seen*, New York: Random House.

—— (1949) *Last Operas and Plays*, New York: Rinehart; rep. (1975) New York: Vintage.

—— (1972) *Selected Writings of Gertrude Stein*, ed. Carl von Vechten/New York: Random House.

—— (1975) "Relief Work in France" and "The Great American Army" and "A Deserter" in *Reflection on the Atom Bomb*, ed. Robert Bartlett Haas, Los Angeles: Black Sparrow Press.

Toklas, Alice B. (1963) *What Is Remembered: an Autobiography*, London: Michael Joseph/New York: Viking Penguin, esp. chapters 5, 6.

Wharton, Edith (1915) *Fighting France: From Dunkerque to Belfort*, London: Macmillan/New York: Scribner's.

Secondary

Barlow, Judith E. (ed.) (1994) *Plays by American Women 1930–60*, New York: Applause.

PLEASE DO NOT SUFFER/ACCENTS IN ALSACE

Bowers, Jane Pallatini (1991) *"They Watch Me as They Watch This": Gertrude Stein's Metadrama*, Pennsylvania: University of Pennsylvania Press.

Malpede, Karen (ed.) (1985) *Women in Theatre: Compassion and Hope*, New York: Limelight.

Ryan, Betsy Alayne (1984) *Gertrude Stein's Theatre of the Absolute*, Michigan: UMI.

Schlueter, June (ed.) (1990) *Modern American Drama: The Female Canon*, Rutherford: F. Dickinson University Press.

Souhami, Diane (1991) *Gertrude and Alice*, London: Pandora, esp. chapter 9.

Please Do Not Suffer: A Play

1916

Gertrude Stein

Genevieve, Mrs. Marchand and Count Daisy Wrangel.

(Mrs. Marchand.)   Where was she born and with whom did she go to school. Did she know the Marquise of Bowers then or did she not. Did she come to know her Italy. Did she learn English in Morocco. She has never been to England nor did she go to school in Florence. She lived in the house with the friends of the count Berny and as such she knew them and she knew him. She went to eat an Arab dinner.

How did she come to know the people she has known. I do not understand it.

With whom did she go to school. We are not sure. When did she first know about Morocco. Where did she hear English.

She heard English spoken to children.

(Count Daisy Wrangel.)   He speaks English very well. He has an impediment in his speech. He likes cauliflower and green peas. He does not find an old woman satisfactory as a cook. He wishes for his Italian. It is too expensive to bring her down. He does like dogs. He once had eight. They were black poodles. They were living in a garden on a duchess' estate. He trained them to be very willing and he has pictures of them all. He has often written a book. He writes about art sometimes. He also paints a little. He has a friend who paints a picture every morning and paints a picture every afternoon. He is not disagreeable. He did not come with him. He asked to see the dog he thought he had grown.

(Genevieve.)   She believes in Fraconville. What is a thunder storm. This is my history. I worked at a cafe in Rennes. Before that I was instructed by a woman who knew knitting and everything. My mother and father worked at gardening. I was ruined by a butcher. I am not

particularly fond of children. My child is a girl and is still a little one. She is living in an invaded district but is now in Avignon. I had a coat made for her but it did not fit her very well and now I am sending the money so that it will be made at Verdun. I am not necessarily a very happy woman. Every one is willing. I like knitting and I like to buy provision. Yes I enjoy the capital. There is plenty of meat here. I do not care for the variety. I prefer veal to chicken. I prefer mutton. I understand that it is difficult to have anything.

(Mrs. Marchand.)   I do not write often. I say I will mention it if a man pays attention to a woman and so I can and I can say that I have not written. I will do as I like. I find that my baby is very healthy. I hope he will not talk the language spoken here but I can not say this to him. He is too young. He is not walking. If the Dardenelles [*sic*] are not taken perhaps they will open. I hear myself speaking. I have an orange tree that is open. The sun comes in. For ten days during ten days it rains and then until December we will have good weather. There is no fire in the house. I do not like to look at that map. Will you excuse me while I give my baby his luncheon.

(Count Daisy Wrangel.)   It is the same name as an island. We were from Courland and some are Russians and some are Prussians and some are Swedes. None are Lithuanians. Mr Berenson is a Lithuanian. I have a Danish friend who has been married four times. His last wife is a singer. She is a married woman. His first wife has been married to four different men. She has been a good friend to each one of them. They do say this. I have no pleasure in my stay on the Island because I do not eat anything. I would like to have something.

(Genevieve.)   The count was here. He

wanted to see the dog and he said he would like to see him. He was not very well. He had been suffering. He did not say that his friend would come with him. He said he thought not. I am often told that the french are everything. I ask do you believe that the french are winning. I believe that the french are winning. Do you need butter for cooking.

(Mrs. Marchand.) Let me give you a peach that is softer. Do you like this one. We will come again for an evening. This is the shortest way. Yes I like walking. We say very little when we are worrying. Let us go away. We cannot because my husband cannot go away.

Nellie Mildred and Carrie

(Nellie.) Handwriting is not curving. It is not a disappointment or a service it is frequently prepossessing.

(Mildred.) It is copied. Six handkerchiefs. Two of one kind four of another.

(Carrie.) She backhands that means she takes good care of herself.

(Mrs. Marchand.) She does not know any of them. She knows Mr Rothschild.

(Genevieve.) What is the use of being tranquil when this house is built for the winter. The winter here is warm.

(Count Daisy Wrangel.) He will not stay longer than November.

William and Mary

(William.) He is fond of reading and drinking. He drinks wine. He also drinks siphon. This is water with sterilised water in it. He drinks it with and also without lemon. He is very fond of walking. He does not prefer resting. He is a painter by profession.

(Mary.) Mary is winning. She has a brother who is fighting. He has made a ring for her. She has a mother and another brother. We were asked does she like swimming. She has not a knowledge of swimming.

(Mrs. Marchand.) She is a large woman and rather walking. She walks along. We met her and Mr Marchand who were walking. We said it was too cold for walking.

(The English Consul.) All right. The dog is too closely muzzled. He can't breathe properly.

(Count Daisy Wrangel.) Why do you all speak to me. Let me tell about it. In coming into the first office I first saw one

young lady. I told her she was looking very well. I then went out and came back and went up to the other lady. I said how do you do I was sorry not to see you the other day. You were out when I called. My friend is a bear. I thought he would have come with me to call. I will come soon again.

(Mrs. Marchand.) I don't know him very well that is to say my husband has pointed him out to me and I knew he was here. It will not be a disappointment to us.

(Genevieve.) I prefer a basket to a mesh. It is the one souvenir that I will have. I do not wish to say that I am not pleased. I do not like to spend 35 dollars over again all over again. It is exact enough.

(Count Daisy Wrangel.) There is a great deal to write in a newspaper.

(Michael.) Michael was the son of Daniel. He moved into a house. He had been living at a hotel a whole winter. He has steam heat and light. We have not seen photographs of the place.

(Jane.) I have five children the youngest is three years old. Many of them died.

(Felix.) What kind of wool do you prefer black or in color, heavy or thin and for what use do you desire it. Do you also wish knitting needles and what thickness.

(Alice.) What did we have to eat today. We had very young pork. It is very delicious. I have never eaten it better.

(Genevieve.) I like to choose my meat.

(Mrs. Marchand.) I understand everything better. I like to have to think and look at maps. I hate to see so much black. I do not mean by that that I am sullen. I am not that. I am delighted with surroundings.

(Genevieve.) I wish to spend a little money on some things. I am waiting for the boat. I have nothing to do except sleep. Really not.

(Mrs. Marchand.) I understand Spanish.

(Count Daisy Wrangel.) To please him and to please me I do not dine at home.

(Harry Francis.) It hangs out in the rain and it is not dry what shall I put on underneath.
    Anything you like.

(Roger Henry.) Why do you prefer a picture of a boat.
    Because it is useful.

(Mrs. Marchand.) I am so disappointed in the morning.
    We are all of us disappointed.

(Mrs. Marchand.)   I did not meet you to-day.
  Yes you did.
  Every man swallowing. What.
(Mrs. Marchand.)   I told you that you had
  every reason to expect warm weather and
  now it's cold.
  It won't be cold long I hope. These are
  equinoxial storms. They last from seven to
  ten days.

(The English Consul.)   He has had some
  trying experiences but he has a pleasant
  home. He has a view of the sea and also of
  the woods. It is natural that he has chosen
  that house.
(Mrs. Marchand.)   I have met her. She is
  very pleasant. I did not think she was his
  wife. I thought she was his daughter.
  So did we all.

Accents in Alsace: A Reasonable Tragedy ⏤

1919

Gertrude Stein

Act I. The Schemils.

Brother brother go away and stay.
Sister mother believe me I say.
They will never get me as I run away.
He runs away and stays away and strange
to say he passes the lines and goes all the
way and they do not find him but hear that
he is there in the foreign legion in distant
Algier.

And what happens to the family.

The family manages to get along and then
some one of his comrades in writing a letter
which is gotten hold of by the Boche find he
is a soldier whom they cannot touch, so what
do they do they decide to embrew his mother
and sister and father too. And how did they
escape by paying sombody [sic] money.

That is what you did with the Boche. You
always paid some money to some one it
might be a colonel or it might be a sergeant
but anyway you did it and it was neccesary
[sic] so then what happened.

The Schemmels.

Sing so la douse so la dim.
Un deux trois
Can you tell me wha
Is it indeed.
What you call a Petide.
And then what do I say to thee
Let me kiss thee willingly.
Not a mountain not a goat not a door.
Not a whisper not a curl not a gore
In me meeney miney mo.
You are my love and I tell you so.
  In the daylight
  And the night
Baby winks and holds me tight.
In the morning and the day and the
  evening and alway.
I hold my baby as I say.
Completely.

And what is an accent of my wife.
And accent and the present life.
Oh sweet oh my oh sweet oh my
I love you love you and I try
I try not to be nasty and hasty and good
I am my little baby's daily food.

Alsatia.

In the exercise of greatness there is charm.
Believe me I mean to do you harm.
And except you have a stomach to alarm.
I mean to scatter so you are to arm.
Let me go.
And the Alsatians say.
What has another prince a birthday.

  Now we come back to the Schemmils.
Schimmel Schimmel Gott in Himmel
Gott in Himmel There comes Shimmel.
  Schimmel is an Alsatian name.

Act II.

It is a little thing to nobody to sell what you
give them.
It is a little thing to be a minister.
It is a little thing to manufacture articles.
All this is modest.

The Brother.

Brother brother here is mother.
We are all very well.

Scene.

Listen to thee sweet cheerie
Is the pleasure of me.
In the way of being hungry and tired
That is what a depot makes you
A depot is not for trains
Its for us.

What are baby carriages
Household goods
And not the dears.
But dears.

Another Act.

Clouds do not fatten with teaching.
They do not fatten at all.
We wonder if it is influence
By the way I guess.
She said. I like it better than Eggland.
What do you mean.
We never asked how many children over
  eleven.
You cannot imagine what I think about the
  country.
Any civilians killed.

Act II.

See the swimmer. He don't swim.
See the swimmer.
My wife is angry when she sees a
  swimmer.

Opening II.

We like Hirsing.

III.

We like the mayor of Guebwiller.

IV.

We like the road between Cernay and the
  railroad.
We go everywhere by automobile.

Act II.

This is a particular old winter.
Everybody goes back.
Back.
I can clean.
I can clean.
I cannot clean without a change in birds.
I am so pleased that they cheat.

Act 54.

In silver stars and red crosses.
In paper money and water.
We know a french wine.
Alsatian wine is dearer.

They are not particularly old.
Old men are old.
There are plenty to hear of Schemmel
  having appendicitis.

Scene II.

Can you mix with another
Can you be a Christian and a Swiss.
Mr. Zumsteg. Do I hear a saint.
Louisa. They call me Lisela.
Mrs. Zumsteg. Are you going to hear me.
Young Mr. Zumsteg. I was looking at the
  snow.
All of them. Like flowers. They like
  flowers.

Scene III.

It is an occasion.
When you see a Hussar.
  A Zouave.
  A soldier
  An antiquary.
Perhaps it is another.
We were surprised with the history of
Marguerite's father and step-father and
the American Civil War.
Joseph. Three three six, six, fifty, six fifty,
fifty, seven.
Reading french.
Reading french.
Reading french singing.
Any one can look at pictures.
They explain pictures.
The little children have old birds.
They wish they were women.
Any one can hate a Prussian.
Alphonse what is your name.
Henri what is your name.
Madeleine what is your name.
Louise what is your name.
Rene what is your name.
Berthe what is your name
Charles what is your name
Marguerite what is your name
Jeanne what is your name.

Act 425.

We see a river and we are glad to say that
that is in a way in the way today.
We see all the windows and we see a
souvenir and we see the best flower. The
flower of the truth.

An Interlude.

Thirty days in April gave a chance to sing
  at a wedding.
Three days in February gave reality to life.
Fifty days every year do not make
substraction.
The Alsations sing anyway.
Forty days in September.
Forty days in September we know what it
  is to spring.

Act in America.

Alsatians living in America.

February XIV.

On this day the troops who had been at
  Mulhouse came again.
They came in the spring.
The spring is late in Alsace.
Water was good and hot anyway.
What are you doing.
Making music and burning the surface of
  marble.
When the surface of marble is burned it is
  not much discolored.
No but there is a discussion.
And then the Swiss.
What is amiss.
The Swiss are the origin of Mulhouse.

Alsace or Alsatians.

We have been deeply interested in the
  words of the song.
The Alsatians do not sing as well as their
  storks.
Their storks are their statuettes.
The rule is that angels and food and eggs
  are all sold by the dozen.

We were astonished.
And potatoes
Potatoes are eaten dry.
This reminds me of another thing I said. A
  woman likes to use money.
And if not.
She feels it really is her birthday.
Is it her birthday.
God bless her it is her birthday.
Please carry me to Dannemarie.
And what does Herbstadt say.
The names of cities are the names of all.
And pronouncing villages is more of a test
  than unbrella [*sic*].
This was the first thing we heard in Alsatia.
Canary, roses, violets and curtains and bags
  and churches and rubber tires and an
  examination.
All the leaves are green and babyish.
How many children make a family.

The Watch on the Rhine.

Sweeter than water or cream or ice.
Sweeter than bells of roses. Sweeter than
winter or summer or spring. Sweeter than
pretty posies. Sweeter than anything is my
queen and loving is her nature.

Loving and good and delighted and best
is her little King and Sire whose devotion is
entire who has but one desire to express
the love which is hers to inspire.

In the photograph the Rhine hardly
showed.

In what way do chimes remind you of
singing. In what way do birds sing. In what
way are forests black or white.

We saw them blue.

With for get me nots.

In the midst of our happiness we were
very pleased.

4 Marie Lenéru 1875–1918

[La Paix] Peace
France

Introduction

There are two major facts about Marie Lenéru that are significant for our appreciation of the dilemmas in her play *La Paix*. The first is that she was born into a military family. Her maternal grandfather was Admiral Dauriac, and her father was a decorated naval lieutenant, killed on active service before she was 2 years old; her mother brought Marie up in the remote naval port of Brest, in Brittany, on the northwest tip of France. The second and more important fact is that at the age of 11 Marie was left stone-deaf by scarlet fever, and with her sight so impaired that she could read only with a magnifying glass and for conversation depended on having everything written down. Although on the surface she remained as bright, energetic and light-hearted as she had been before the illness, her private journal reveals the intense anguish caused by her isolation and sense of loss. The courage with which she faced her affliction gave a seriousness and depth to her studies and subsequent writing.

In 1902 Marie and her mother moved to Paris where Marie gained access to literary circles. In 1905 one of her essays appeared in *Mercure de France* and three years later her story "La Vivante" [The Awakening] gained a prize. Following an unsuccessful attempt to publish a novel, in 1908 she sent a copy of her first play, *Les Affranchis* [Free Souls], to the famous poet and playwright, Catulle Mendès. He was enthusiastic and his wife submitted it for the literary prize, *La Vie Heureuse*, that carried publication by Hachette. The play won. However, Mendès died shortly after. It was the founding editor of *La Mercure de France*, Rachilde (Marguerite Eymery 1860–1953), herself a successful dramatist as well as influential journalist, who took the play to the leading theatre

director, Antoine. Having persuaded Lenéru to reduce the four-act structure to three, he produced *Les Affranchis* at the Odéon theatre in 1910. As remembered by Lenéru's friend, the writer Mary Duclaux, the play was "a triumphant success . . . the huge theatre rocked with applause" (Lenéru 1924). The production was widely reviewed by such important critics as Léon Blum and the play was awarded another prize, the *Émile Angier*. Her second play, *Le Redoutable*, was produced at the Odéon two years later but to such negative response that Antoine advised Lenéru to withdraw it after only four performances. Undaunted, and with the aid of Léon Blum, she submitted her third play, *La Triomphatrice* [Woman Triumphant] to the national theatre company, Comédie Française, in 1914. It was accepted provided that she reduce its four-act structure to three, but the production was delayed by the war. So it was not until January 1918 that Marie Lenéru became the third woman dramatist in a hundred years – after George Sand and Delphine de Girardin – to have her name on the playbills of the Comédie Française.

In the meantime, as her journal and letters reveal, the war had changed her fundamentally. In his introduction to the posthumous edition of her journal, the playwright François de Curel, who had been influential on her writing, recognised that the war was a personal catastrophe for Lenéru, signalling a total transformation. Her only thought became to manifest the unspeakable horror which had seized her. Curel judged that in 1914, when the journal became forgetful of Lenéru's own misfortune and consisted of reflections on the atrocities of war, it loses interest. To the contrary I would say, for Marie Lenéru had lost her religious faith but encountered a subject worthy of her spirit. Unable to nurse or perform other useful work, in December 1914 she decided that her war-work would be to write a play, *La Paix*. She regarded this effort as like a religious vocation and dedicated it to those who had died for her country. *La Paix*, which bears the marks of her reading and thinking of the war years, is concerned with the need to ensure lasting peace by establishing a Permanent Committee of Heads of State, in place of ambassadors and secret treaties. Finished by 1917, yet set after the war, the play was performed at the Odéon in 1921. But Lenéru did not live to see either her play or the peace conference it predicted. She died in September 1918 from the virulent flu epidemic.

Lenéru received world-wide attention after her death on the publication and translation of her journal in 1923/4. This led to the appearance in print of her letters, three of her unperformed plays and the re-publication of the others, as well as a retrospective of her work at Natalie Barney's salon and a new production of *Les Affranchis* by the Comédie Française in 1927. Despite such phenomenal success, Lenéru was ignored by later theatre historians, probably partly because her work was realist in form. They have been more interested in the radical experiments of such plays as Jarry's *Ubu Roi*, the theories of Artaud, and finding the roots of post-Second World War absurdist drama. Yet Lenéru shares with later playwrights such as Beckett and Sartre a close adherence to the unities of time, place and plot – a restraint which places them all in the classical tradition of French drama, even if Lenéru's plays aspire to an idealism markedly absent from Beckett's. Lenéru's plays also inherit earlier French tradition in giving strong central roles to female characters, which may indicate why it is only with the development of feminist literary history that her work has resurfaced.

Some of the reasoning inherent in *La Paix* is to be found in an essay called "Le Temoin" [The Witness] which Lenéru published in *The Book of France* (1915), one of the many anthologies published to raise money for war-relief. The esteem with which Lenéru was held at the time can be measured by the other contributors alongside whom she is ranked: Henry James, H. G. Wells, André Gide and Thomas Hardy. Although she does not refer to the *Ligue International des Femmes pour la Paix Durable*, established in Paris by Dorothy Buxton and Gabrielle

Dûchene, her arguments resemble their pamphlet "An Urgent Duty for Every Woman". Speaking on behalf of women, Lenéru claimed that it would eventually be their duty not to be silent and resigned, but to judge and revolt. Women must reject men's puerile arguments about the inevitability of war and refuse to regard it as splendid. Heroism must be achieved in other ways. If, during the war, women submitted to it, it was with the proviso that their agonised witnessing of the sorrows and pain gave them a motive to go on living in order to demand that men never let this happen again. Going against the conservatism and militarism of her upbringing, yet recognising the need to defend France, the value of sacrifice, and the glamour of the man of action, Lenéru was converted to socialism and pacifism by the war. She publicly affirmed her pacifism at Natalie Barney's Temple in 1917. What might be entailed by pacifism, meaning not merely a wish for peace but an urgent commitment to change the political conditions that lead to war, is explored in her play. It is clear why the Comédie Française found *La Paix* too controversial to stage during the war.

Some of the sources for her theoretical ideas in the play are cited in the essay, including Bernard Shaw and Norman Angell, as well as Bertha Von Suttner. Germs for the plot of *La Paix* may also be found in *The Book of France*. That anthology included a piece entitled "Diary of a Hospital Nurse" written by the Duchess of Rohan Douairière, and translated into English by Millicent, Duchess of Sutherland. The "Diary" briefly recounts the Duchess's basic training for Red Cross work at an Auxiliary Military Hospital in Rennes, Brittany. This was a base hospital, not a dangerous, front-line ambulance of the kind that Millicent Sutherland had organised in Belgium in the same period. The Duchess, evidently a widow, had two sons in the army. Her diary ends with her departure from the hospital, tired and ill from an infected needle. The Duchess of Rohan was well known to Marie Lenéru, having arranged for the first public reading of her play *Les Affranchis*, and seems to have been the model for Marguerite de Gestel in *La Paix*. Marguerite has lost an arm due to infection while war-nursing and no longer rides nor makes music. Her false arm and hand symbolise the mutilation of her life, the appearances by which she disguises her

Figure 5 Millicent Gower, Duchess of Sutherland (1867–1955), with wounded soldiers at her hospital in France, 1916. The author of *Six Weeks at the War* (1914) and decorated with the French Croix de Guerre and Belgian Red Cross for her war work, she is a likely original for Lenéru's heroine, Lady Mabel Stanley. [IWM photo Q2606]

crippled state. Such woundedness is a recurrent trope of modernist literature, yet usually it is male protagonists rather than females who are war-cripples.

There is no one obvious model for the character of Lady Mabel Stanley, whom Marguerite met whilst nursing. Rather, she is typical of upper-class British feminists such as Millicent Sutherland, Mrs St Clair Stobart or the Hon. Evelina Haverfield, who were renowned for their courage in front-line nursing and could then speak out against the war with the authority of experience. The epigraph to Lenéru's essay, "O sacrifices effroyables . . . " [Oh hideous sacrifices . . .] is by Maurice Barrès, the nationalist novelist, essayist and politician to whom she had dedicated her essay on Saint Juste. During the war Barrès wrote daily patriotic articles in *Echo de Paris*, a newspaper Lenéru quoted from critically in her essay. It seems likely that his example gave her the idea for

DeLisle in *La Paix*. The figure of Graham Moore stems from the example of several British politicians of the war period, including Ramsay MacDonald. It perhaps seemed less treasonable to attribute the pacifist arguments to British characters, especially since the movement for negotiated peace was stronger in Britain than in France – understandably, since France had been invaded. The patriotic sentiments of General Peltier and the idealism of Simone and her uncle were typical of both countries as evidenced by wartime propaganda such as the writing of Mrs Humphry Ward, or a book like *A General's Letters to His Son* (Anon. 1917). Simone's attitudes are similar to Lenéru's own as expressed in her diary when younger.

I have stressed the historical veracity of Lenéru's play because whilst commentators have wonderingly likened her to the Brontës for their supposed ability to write without experience, she has also been criticised for her unworldliness. As the daughter of a war-widow, in an invaded country, Lenéru had much at stake in this play. The cogency with which she presents the confrontations between the characters, with their emotional commitment to their viewpoints, displays to us at a later era the difficulties that lay in establishing the institution that we now take for granted, the United Nations Assembly.

Further reading

Primary

Anonymous (1917) *A General's Letters to His Son on Obtaining His Commission*, London: Cassell.

Lenéru, Marie (1915) "Le Temoin" translated as "The Witness" by Lady Frazer, in Winifred Stephens (ed.) *The Book of France*, London: Macmillan/Paris: Champion, pp. 241–6, 247–52.

—— (1921) *La Paix*, in *Annales Politiques et Littéraires*, Paris: Grosset. 1973–96.

—— (1923) *Lettres à un combattant* (1915–18), intro. by Albert Puech, Paris: Editions de la Revue Indo-chinoise.

—— (1924) *Journal of Marie Lenéru*, translated by William A. Bradley with an introduction by François de Curel and a reminiscence by Mary Duclaux, London: Macmillan.

—— (1996) *Woman Triumphant* [*La Triomphatrice*] translated with an introduction by Melanie C. Hawthorne, in Katherine E. Kelly (ed.) *Modern Drama by Women, 1880s–1930s*, London: Routledge, pp. 147–82.

Shaw, George Bernard (1914) "Common Sense about the War" in *The New Statesman*, supplement, 14 November 1914. Reprinted in *New York Times*, 15 November 1914.

—— (1914) *Heartbreak House*, London: Constable.

Wells, H. G. (1914) *The World Set Free: a Story of Mankind*, London: Nelson.

Secondary

Barney, Natalie (1992) "Retrospective of Marie Lenéru by Magdeleine Marx Paz" in *Adventures of the Mind*, translated with an introduction and notes by John Spalding Gatton, New York: New York University Press, pp. 191–8.

Hinton, James (1989) *Protests and Visions: Peace Politics in 20th Century Britain*, London: Hutchinson.

Holmes, Diana (1996) *French Women's Writing 1848–1994*, London: Athlone. (Holmes does not mention Lenéru.)

Keith-Smith, Brian (1997) "Bertha von Suttner" in *A Library of German Women Writers 1900–1933*, volume 6, Lampeter: Mellen.

Schulz, Gerhard (1967/1972) *Revolutions and Peace Treaties, 1917–20*, translated by Marion Jackson, London: Methuen.

Thébaud, Françoise (1986) *La Femme au temps de la guerre de 14*, Paris: Stock.

Wiltsher, Anne (1985) *Most Dangerous Women: Feminist Peace Campaigners of the Great War*, London: Pandora.

Peace [La Paix]

[A Play in Four Acts]
First performed at the Théâtre de l'Odéon, Paris, 12 February 1921
Published in French, 1921
Translation by Claire Tylee

Marie Lenéru

Characters

	Aged
LADY MABEL STANLEY	33
GENERAL PELTIER	47
JEAN GESTEL	22
PAUL DELISLE	55
GRAHAM MOORE	42
MARGUERITE GESTEL	45
SIMONE DELISLE	18
PERRINE BOTTOREL	20
A CHAMBER MAID	

Act I

In 1918, during the Paris Conference

The salon of a chateau in the autumn. In the plant pots, the vases and the fireplace, everywhere there are red sages. A young woman in black, dressed for the town with a Brest head-dress, black gloves and an umbrella, is standing expectantly.

Scene 1

PERRINE and JEAN

Enter JEAN in mourning. He crosses the room, letters in his hand. He takes his hat off and throws it on a chair.

JEAN Perrine! Are we really seeing each other again!

(He clasps her hands for a long time as one does after a bereavement.)

PERRINE Well, it was up to you to come back to Lehane.
JEAN As soon as I could; Lord, nothing has changed here. I'd almost prefer it if it had.
PERRINE Yes, you'd hardly think there'd been a war . . . It's only been over for six months . . . the village, the chateau . . .
JEAN Shirkers?
PERRINE Yes, but not the servants.
JEAN At your home, how many are left?
PERRINE *(lowering her voice)* All gone . . . my three brothers and my brother-in-law . . . Except for Yvon of course, but both his legs . . . Well, that's what saved his skin.
JEAN Why didn't Yvon come with you?
PERRINE He didn't like to. He said that it would hurt Madame, because he was alive while Gerald and Louis and Sir . . .
JEAN I'm very much alive, and I've got both my legs.
PERRINE That's not your fault. You volunteered.
JEAN Mother was always against it . . . but when the others were gone, she had nothing more to say. I don't think anything mattered to her any more.
PERRINE You were part of Sir's staff at headquarters?
JEAN No, in his brigade. I was in the trenches.
PERRINE They say he died in front of your eyes.
JEAN No, no . . . it wasn't quite like that. I went up with the relief. We were lined up in a communication trench when a stretcher was brought by. A gloved hand passed. Mechanically I lifted the tarpaulin. *(Reliving the experience, his voice becomes harsh.)* They hadn't closed his eyes yet; his face was untouched, although his head . . . The stretcher-bearers didn't know me. It was only an hour later, I think, that the rumours began to circulate . . . I told the captain that it was him we had passed . . . But at that time, you see, when I left others to carry my father while I went on up to where he was coming from . . . at that moment I felt why we follow each other on earth, I felt the energy of France.

PERRINE *(very moved)* And Louis?

JEAN Louis died in Germany, picked up by their medics at Charleroi, very gravely wounded. He was treated properly. But all the same to end up there . . . My mother who had looked after so many, seen so many die in the ambulance, did not watch any of her own family recover.

PERRINE I feel very odd at the idea of seeing Madame again.

JEAN She's just the same, not even any grey hair, except that she sleeps badly.

PERRINE *(shyly)* Her arm . . .

JEAN Only the forearm. You don't notice it much. She always wears a glove.

PERRINE How did it happen?

JEAN The pus from one of the wounded . . . Her rubber gloves were split . . . She knew but she didn't have any others and wounds won't wait.

PERRINE What bad luck all the same . . .

JEAN Especially for music, that's awful for her.

PERRINE It must be . . . When Madame played the piano, and we were in the linen room, we left the doors open . . . sometimes it went on all day . . . It was like a great storm which filled the house – you could hear it from the village.

JEAN I don't know if she'll have the courage to start again. She used to make music so much with her sons . . . It's like her other great pleasure. I haven't dared to get her to go out on horseback yet, less because of her arm than because of our rides together in the past.

PERRINE When you think of all that! Has there been any news of Gerald yet? Do you know how . . . ?

JEAN Nothing. He went missing on 25 August. No one has seen him. I keep getting the impression that someone knows something but doesn't want to tell us . . . *(harsh)* that they can't . . .

PERRINE *(agitated)* Gerald was Madame's favourite.

JEAN Oh – and yours too. *(His voice drops)* He was the most decent of the three of us, physically – perhaps morally too. *(Violently)* And to think they can't even admit to us that he may have had a rotten death.

PERRINE *(softly)* He died for France.

JEAN For France . . . what an idea that is to have got hold of us! When you've done so much for your country, what can you

expect will become of you? The only thing left is to carry on.

PERRINE Will you go on being a soldier even now the war's over? You'd be the only one not in the army.

JEAN Me? I went to the Quai d'Orsay before coming home. I'm even an officer now, it's been gazetted; I'm a lieutenant.

PERRINE What does Madame say to that? She'll be very alone.

JEAN Oh, my mother – we haven't talked about the future yet – nor about the past either . . . she doesn't stray from the here and now . . . She plays with the dogs – but at night her door is always open and the light left on . . . don't speak to her about anything at all except yourself . . . your family – I can hear her coming. See you soon, Perrine, I'm off to find Yvon.

Scene 2

MARGUERITE and PERRINE

MARGUERITE, *a tall, strong woman, still young. Well-dressed, in full mourning. She has that life and assurance of women who are used to a masculine atmosphere. The mother of three sons, she has kept in her bearing, her movement, her voice, something of the mateyness, the decisiveness and the alacrity of a young man.*

MARGUERITE Perrine, how kind of you to have come to see me first. *(She hugs her with the evident intention of not making a drama.)*

PERRINE As soon as I knew Madame had come back – I couldn't wait to get to Lehane.

MARGUERITE Always so beautiful! The flowers – you see how they have arranged them . . . outside it's as if none had been picked.

PERRINE Madame is going to stay long?

MARGUERITE Yes, of course, just at first, after, after . . . *(She speaks with the wish above all to avoid whatever is not to be said.)*

PERRINE You are looking very well, Madame.

MARGUERITE I have a constitution of iron.

PERRINE The only thing that bothers me is that Madame does not do her hair in the same way.

MARGUERITE I don't do my own hair myself, any more.

(For a moment PERRINE dares to look at MME

DE GESTEL'S *right hand in its black glove, which resembles those hands with a slightly affected gesture that one sees in the showcases of glove shops.)*

PERRINE   Yvon hasn't come today . . .

MARGUERITE   *(energetically)* It isn't for Yvon to put himself out to come and see me . . . but I have a favour to ask him. I want him to wear Gerald's watch . . .

(PERRINE is a bit taken aback at the ease with which MME DE GESTEL says the name of her missing son.)

PERRINE   Oh Madame, such a thing, a keepsake . . . keep it for yourself.

MARGUERITE   *(quickly)* I want it to be Yvon's. *(Then, gaily)* You remember the tree where my husband carved your initials . . . I walked by it yesterday, it's wonderful, and the letters are as big as a hand.

PERRINE   *(surprised, embarrassed)* Jean has grown a lot . . .

MARGUERITE   Yes, since the war I have been the shortest, yet . . . *(She laughs, then bursts into sobs.)*

PERRINE   Madame . . . oh Madame . . .

MARGUERITE   *(she sobs wildly, with all her strength. With stifled cries, she apologises)* Oh God, they used to play with you!

PERRINE   Madame . . . if I had known . . . that it would hurt you at all . . .

MARGUERITE   No my dear, let me, go on . . . and cry or not cry *(beginning again, more violently)* for what has changed!

PERRINE   It's too much for you . . . all three . . .

MARGUERITE   *(stopping a little)* Oh, you know, in cases like yours and mine . . . I've seen too many die. My sons, of all those whose eyes I have closed . . . *(She calms down, but she is more natural than she was at first with her false gaiety.)* My little Perrine, at your home too there is a gap . . . Poor dear Yvon . . .

PERRINE   At Dixmude . . .

MARGUERITE   Dixmude! *(The sobs threaten again; she masters them)* This is really idiotic . . . Don't think that I spend my whole day crying. They would be proud of me, my dear children, my soldiers . . .

PERRINE   You have done a lot for them. You have helped many to recover.

MARGUERITE   Yes, those . . . but you know, it's the others that one doesn't forget.

PERRINE   *(after a while when both have collected themselves)* They were so happy to go . . . I remember at the station, it was so beautiful . . .

MARGUERITE   *(bursting out in fury)* Beautiful enough never to get over it, beautiful to make you mad for life . . . People from the village waited at the door when Gerald and Louis and my husband were leaving . . . They didn't sing; no, it was worse: under their breath, as if to themselves, they murmured the *Marseillaise* . . .

PERRINE   Yet they knew that they wouldn't be coming back.

MARGUERITE   That night, like all the men in France, all three of them had made their wills . . . But what is death to such hours? Myself, I was stirred like them . . . *(She gets excited)* There is then one death, one at least, that you can face with enthusiasm? Oh, life, the future meant so little on that day, a rapid goodbye to all that wasn't our country . . . That came so quickly . . . Yesterday we lived, we wanted to live . . . Yesterday is no longer, the heart swells . . .

PERRINE   Yet . . .

MARGUERITE   Yet what, Perrine?

PERRINE   I don't know . . . *(The two are quiet as if, on the contrary, they did know.)*

MARGUERITE   I am expecting one of my former patients . . . a great leader, an army general. I know him well . . . I looked after him for 6 months in my hospital. He'll be here with another of his nurses, Lady Mabel Stanley. She's English. She's giving me three months of her time because I didn't have enough company. And then . . . I'm also expecting my brother with his daughter, Simone . . . do you remember Simone?

PERRINE   That's the Mr Paul Delisle who writes for the papers?

MARGUERITE   That's the one! He's a member of the Academy, a poet . . . have you read any of his poetry?

PERRINE   We used to sing it at school.

MARGUERITE   He's quite a celebrity . . . especially since the war . . . He's known all over the world. He really cares about the soldiers. *(She speaks to cheer her visitor up.)* And now, my little Perrine, we must pull ourselves together, get on with living again. How old are you?

PERRINE   Twenty.

MARGUERITE   Twenty and you didn't lose a

fiancé at the front . . . there is always that, my dear . . .

PERRINE They might as well have killed him as far as I'm concerned . . . because I've changed my mind.

MARGUERITE Don't despise heroes. Let's see, Perrine, amongst all those who have come back . . .

PERRINE *(very quickly)* Oh never! If it hadn't been for Yvon, I would have become a nun, but because Yvon . . .

MARGUERITE But it would be happier for Yvon to see children around him.

PERRINE Children – I don't want any. *(To the astonishment of* MARGUERITE*)* I know what they make of children later. No, once is enough.

MARGUERITE That is not like a good Frenchwoman, my dear.

PERRINE I'll tell you everything. I've sacrificed my happiness in this world. So that God should not allow them to kill anyone else's, I've made a vow not to have any children of my own as long as I live. *(Confronted by* MARGUERITE*'s silence)* Don't you think that's right, Madame?

MARGUERITE My poor child, if it were enough to sacrifice oneself . . . which of us would not give her life?

PERRINE Then, what's to be done?

MARGUERITE *(firmly)* Nothing.

Scene 3

LADY MABEL *enters.*

MARGUERITE *(to* LADY MABEL*)* What happened to you after lunch? I didn't like to go upstairs to you. Here, Perrine, this is Lady Mabel whom I was just telling you about. *(To* LADY MABEL*)* My little friend, Perrine Bottorel. *(*LADY MABEL*, also in full mourning, looks at the young woman's black dress.)*

MABEL I see we're dressed alike.

MARGUERITE *(rapidly)* Her three brothers . . . Perrine is a childhood friend of my sons and now she's almost made up her mind to enter a convent . . .

MABEL That's very serious . . .

MARGUERITE It's her way to fight war.

PERRINE *(embarrassed)* Oh I know quite well that I shan't do anything about that.

MABEL *(ardently)* It's already enough to have had the idea of doing something.

PERRINE *(more and more awkward)* Goodbye

Madame . . . . Madame won't be needing me this week?

MARGUERITE I'll let you know . . . or I'll come and find you. There's so much to put straight in the house. *(They kiss.)*

MABEL Goodbye, Miss Perrine, I've enjoyed meeting you.

Scene 4

MABEL *(when the young woman has left the room)* What kept me upstairs longer than I intended was my post. I found a long letter from Graham Moore had arrived which worried me.

MARGUERITE You take this conference too much to heart . . .

MABEL *(heatedly)* My only reason for living is hope about what it will achieve.

MARGUERITE Be careful not to ask too much of them.

MABEL I only ask them to do their job. Tell me, please, why they have got together if it's not to give us peace?

MARGUERITE Don't play with words, Mabel; you know quite well that they and you don't mean the same thing by peace. They will make us a treaty which will be respected so long as we are the stronger – say for 15 years, the time it will take for Germany to recover her economy, and her army, and her navy. My brother says that with good frontiers and bridgeheads, it's possible for hostilities to be put off longer.

MABEL You could tell me it would be 100 years . . . a day will still arrive when people will be on the eve of what we have seen. Never, never again!

MARGUERITE *(coming out of her prophetic dream)* It will arrive however . . . the time will come once again . . .

MABEL Can it be you saying that? Who admits that? Yet if all the women on earth knew what to be content with . . . If I had the right to count on someone else as I count on myself . . . *(She is very excited.)*

MARGUERITE You are young and full of fight; I don't expect anything any more.

MABEL *(lively)* And that's what I don't forgive you for. You've done with it, all right. You're not searching the earth any more for the right occasion to die, and because you've settled yourself into a state of despair you make the best of what it will cost the world . . .

MARGUERITE *(harshly)* I don't have enough of the world left to wish it well.

MABEL *(annoyed)* You are a lost cause!

MARGUERITE But my poor child what would you have me do?

MABEL Everything . . . give everything . . . use up all your energy . . . live only for that . . . have no body, have no soul except for that . . . so that one more time at least if the horror must fall upon the world it should be in spite of us, in the face of all our effort, in the ruin of all our hopes; a second time at least we should not be found indifferent, slumbering where we were living – under the protection of bullies.

MARGUERITE Mabel . . .

MABEL Yes . . . that's the worst. Before . . . which of us was thinking of war? Which of us even knew that it existed, that it always threatened? Did our hearts flutter, did we feel a shiver? War . . . it was politics, "foreign affairs" . . . Nonsense! . . . What was arousing our emotions? our novels, our plays, always life, happiness more or less menaced by one person . . . *(Ironically)* We would write tragedy with only one man, and the great tragedy which operates through thousands and millions we would never think of. We would weep about the fate of one woman yet war existed. We would weep about just one shattered life . . . when everything there was could be left in utter ruin.

MARGUERITE *(also ironically)* Yes, I can think of heated discussions about women's fate.

MABEL *(sarcastically)* The fate of women. Really, but like the fate of empires, it's decided on the battlefield. *(A pause. Both are crushed by their memories.)* They won't catch me twice. I've sworn to remember and every hour of my life will be a fight against forgetting. Even if I must live a hundred years, I want to keep on until the end, bracing myself with the sense of horror, the convulsive protest that I rose up with on the day after that unspeakable vigil.

MARGUERITE I wonder if our General Staff was not right to ban women from the battlefield.

MABEL You're one of those who turn away when the condemned pass? *(Harshly)* If men must suffer, we owe them the courage to bear witness to it.

MARGUERITE For four years I did not turn away.

MABEL You were in a hospital . . . with those who could be brought in . . . they were not the worst . . . yet God knows how much you saw . . . I was with those who couldn't be lifted, who couldn't be touched.

MARGUERITE *(with a stifled cry)* And your brother was one of those. *(vehemently returning to herself)* At least you saw him again, you helped him . . . whereas I!

MABEL Don't envy me . . . I didn't leave him, it's true. But I wasn't with him.

MARGUERITE *(softly)* Was he conscious?

MABEL I would have preferred him not to be . . . I saw him suffer so . . . I saw him go pale and quiet while we dressed his wounds, and smile and thank us afterwards . . . That is suffering, cruel indeed, and worse than we imagine . . . but still bearable, still human . . . whereas later on! You see . . . there is a stage where the heart itself means nothing any more. I couldn't even meet his eyes . . . there was nothing left but his suffering . . . the indescribable despair, the absolute misery of his face . . . *(Both are drawn together in deadly recollection.)*

MARGUERITE *(whispering)* How do you have the courage to speak about it?

MABEL *(her voice louder)* I only want to live in order to speak about it. I made a vow that night. I only want to live in order to remember. To carry the memory wherever it has never been. To carry this arrow with you across the centuries, countries of Europe. You can never be reminded enough about what your sons suffered, so that you won't have let them suffer in vain. Their achievement must live, it must endure. Not just for 10 years, 20 years, 100 years, but for evermore. Because if this abominable thing ever begins again it will be the destruction of all they did, the uselessness of their sacrifice, the end of that precious scrap of paper which they paid for so dearly.

MARGUERITE The life of the world is only the history of these costly pieces of paper.

MABEL I haven't paid the cost for the others that I paid for this one. I am determined that the treaty will last, that it be permanent . . . that another war should never come to put it in doubt . . . My brother didn't die for less than that . . .

he said what he wanted: it must be the last war.

MARGUERITE   At any rate, no one will challenge the generosity of your utopian dream.

MABEL   Utopian dream! Don't use such stupid words, Marguerite. Utopia, that's an opinion we don't share, it's the opposite of the market place. Everything is utopian from the point of view of the adversary: the projects of revolutionaries, the rebuilding of the past. Nevertheless it all happens: today the utopian dream of a few, tomorrow the utopian reality of others. Everything today, everything which we take for granted, was once someone's utopian dream, someone else's incredulity. The first General Conference they said that about the Red Cross: it's a very noble ideal, but unrealisable.

MARGUERITE   *(incredulously)* Do you really think, Marguerite, that you and your fellow Englishmen are going to establish permanent peace in Europe?

MABEL   Sorry! . . . I didn't tell you we were going to establish peace. I only told you we were going to do everything towards it.

MARGUERITE   And you are hopeful?

MABEL   I don't know. I only know that before hoping for anything at all on earth we have to have done with war.

MARGUERITE   But what are you going to do, then? What are you banking on?

MABEL   First of all I am banking on the Congress, or rather, on the pressure that a formidable league can exert on it, a league composed of men of all parties, who have finally been able to organise themselves into concern, who are agreed on a programme, a sort of "copybook" of peace, which they will impose on their representatives, on Parliament to begin with and through that as an intermediary to the world leaders at the Congress.

MARGUERITE   And this programme, if the Congress adopts it, it will be the advent of permanent peace in Europe?

MABEL   It will be a considerable step out of the system of permanent war which we live in today.

MARGUERITE   Then they won't adopt it.

MABEL   *(resolutely)* That's quite possible: war is atrocious, war is absurd, personally it horrifies everyone . . . But there is something which we are even more frightened of than war, and that is to admit

before everyone that there could be an end to the whole human race.

MARGUERITE   But if you convert me, my poor child . . . I don't have your talent. I don't know how to write for the papers and magazines. I don't have your political friends whom you inspire with your fervour and your eloquence. I'm not able to prompt the most distinguished men of my country to action, yet all the same that's what we need . . .

MABEL   I'm only asking for ten in all, not even ten from each of the capitals of Europe! Ten men of courage and authority. But I am also asking for women, I'm keeping a mission for them, the mission which belongs to them and is mine too, which is to remember. *(She speaks softly at first, but then more and more fervently.)* I have reached this conviction, that only one thing is necessary, one thing alone will be enough, but humanity is incapable of it: Not to forget . . . if only each person had seen; if just one of the horrors which have passed by in thousands in front of our cowardly imagination belonged truly to the real life of each of us; if we truly felt ourselves to be the just avengers . . . Your brothers are being murdered in your house and you listen behind your locked door . . . You won't open it, you won't throw yourself forward, attack and die . . . And don't I too forget? What has happened to the time when every night I heard those terrible screams again? I would wake up and call back: I'm here, I'm coming! They gave me drugs to get rid of the hallucinations. Hallucination! As if that was not the material and pressing reality, as if forgetting it was not the hallucination!

Scene 5

A lovely September light rests in the sky and over the park. In the frame of a glowing window JEAN appears and stands for a moment. He is wearing his blue uniform and fawn-coloured boots; with two fingers in a salute at his kepi. There are particles of sunlight on the pale uniform. It is a radiant apparition. He goes to his mother, kneels, takes his hat off, takes her gloved hand and kisses it.

JEAN   Mother dear . . . *(His head rests on MARGUERITE's shoulder.)*

MARGUERITE   *(ironically)* You've got

something to ask of me, then, since you are deploying all your graces?

(In front of the charming group of mother and son, MABEL's *face contracts.* MARGUERITE *sees, understands and, pushing the young man, she gets up brusquely. Quickly her son does the same and they stand face to face, nervously.)*

JEAN Won't you let me hug you?

MARGUERITE I don't know, you took me by surprise. A great devil like you.

JEAN It's this uniform, isn't it? You haven't seen it again here, since . . . I wanted to put it on again precisely to ask you . . . Depending on what you say it could either be for the last time . . . or else I won't get rid of it ever again. (MARGUERITE *is silent.)* You're not saying anything, Mother? You don't want your last remaining son to be a soldier like the others?

MARGUERITE *(without revealing her feelings)* You will do what you want.

JEAN *(quietly but obstinately)* No, it's not like that. I want your consent. I want my mother, who was almost my brother-in-arms, to be willing and to decide with me. I want to be a soldier by your choice as well as my own.

MARGUERITE *(still keeping her true feelings hidden)* Why do you doubt it? Why this play-acting? Were you frightened that I might not be opposed to it? *(The young man looks towards* LADY MABEL.)

MABEL You're frightened of me, Jean?

JEAN You have a great influence over my mother. She loves you and she admires you. You support the men of your country who want to put an end to war. Your friend, Graham Moore, whom I admire as a champion of the struggle, is today at the heart of the cabinet, the accredited representative of final peace.

MABEL *(moved)* And so?

JEAN *(with growing severity)* Daughter of a First Lord of the Admiralty, sister of a soldier killed in Flanders, yet you don't believe in our profession. (MABEL *tries to speak; he stops her with authority.)* Lady Mabel, I know you are nobility itself, that everything which is noble in us could not be unknowingly rejected by the woman who ran our dangers on the battlefield, but if my mother said: "You decide. Must I let my son be what he wants?", what would you answer?

MABEL *(very moved)* I'm going to ask you a question. Since you know by your own experience that you can defend your country without being a career soldier, why, Monsieur de Gestel, do you want war to be your only care, why do you want your country to find no other use for your devotion, except at times of grief and catastrophe?

JEAN Because I have acquired the conviction that we must always be thinking of those times, that in times of peace we must prepare for war each day, that there will never be sufficient numbers of us in arms, we need to be countless, that we shall never have enough time in our lives to ponder over weapons, to make them ever more powerful, more diverse, more cunning and more decisive.

MABEL *(with a cry)* You see, Marguerite, look at the alternative, see the choice we have.

MARGUERITE *(indifferent, unmoved)* He will do what he wants.

JEAN *(urging)* Mother, I don't need your resignation, your passive acceptance. What about other vocations. You wanted those, accepted them with enthusiasm. *(More emotional, beseeching)* Darling, remember everyone you have loved has worn this uniform . . . The progress of the conference isn't so reassuring. Its work will create discontent. France needs far-sighted sons . . . It could all begin again . . . (MABEL *has fallen to her knees next to a table.)* Mother, victory is always precarious . . . It is not enough to be stronger today, we've got to be stronger forever. It's not enough to offer one's life to save France in the hour of tragedy . . . we need effort, thought, daily obsession. What is a peace that must come to an end? Life is only an armed watch . . . Allow me to be one of those who work and invent and never sleep. The war which I shall perhaps not see, the war of tomorrow, so colossal and so wild, beside which this one will seem mild, let me play my part in its effort and sorrow . . . Yesterday's victory means nothing without victory tomorrow. Without that, my father and my brothers will have died in vain . . .

MARGUERITE *(with a laugh and a sob)* Died in vain! Mabel also said that to me.

JEAN Look at her. She feels the truth of my words, my prayer . . . Lady Mabel, what have you to say to me?

MABEL *(jumping to her feet, wildly)* You are right.

Curtain

Act II

The same set, 9pm

Scene 1

PELTIER *in civilian clothes, with* MABEL. *They are standing. She holds the* GENERAL's *hand and is making his arm bend at the elbow.*

MABEL It's wonderful . . . and can you also lift it?

PELTIER *(raising his arm slowly)* Long live England!

MABEL *(very attentively)* Now hold it out.

PELTIER Oh, whatever you want. *(He holds it out.)* That's the most difficult – you remember?

MABEL It's a miracle!

PELTIER *(smiling)* A miracle you had something to do with.

MABEL *(briskly)* And Dr Carrell too . . . Do you realise that when you arrived, God knows in what state, we seriously dreaded amputation?

PELTIER *(still smiling)* Me too . . . when I saw you sit up with me night and day, I really thought the case wasn't worth the effort.

MABEL *(coldly)* The case or the fellow?

PELTIER *(still lit up by the same strange smile)* Really . . . you include people? I thought the nurse's zeal was purely professional.

MABEL All the same . . . all equal, a Boche is a Boche and a Frenchman . . .

PELTIER Be careful, you're frightened of giving me too much pleasure, you're taking back what you said. *(Disappointed)* It's true. I wasn't a Boche.

MABEL I'm not taking anything back.

PELTIER Carrel told me that my dressings at first were the most difficult he'd ever seen, and that you alone touched them . . . that your notes, your observations, were remarkable, that you prevented any accident, especially where I was concerned . . .

MABEL I'm very fond of my profession.

PELTIER *(smiling less)* That's a cold shower.

MABEL What?

PELTIER It was so fine earlier and now it's icy.

MABEL I don't understand you, General.

PELTIE I believe that in your country women don't flirt?

MABEL *(firmly)* No, never.

PELTIER Only at Lyon you were so gentle, so considerate, so caressing even, that the memory of that time is dangerous.

MABEL Well, I was treating you . . .

PELTIER Like all the others, I don't doubt it. Only I didn't treat all the others like you. It seemed to me that once I was near to declaring myself; I was cured . . . we chatted a lot at that time. It wasn't my wound that interested you . . . you replied to me: "Later" . . . I remembered your brother, and then the war went on . . . It wasn't yet the right moment to think of ourselves. I waited. You wrote to me less and less. I wanted to be heart-free. I questioned Madame de Gestel. She replied to me: "Come." *(A pause. Agitatedly)* And you, Madame, how do you reply to me?

*(*MABEL *is at first taken aback and visibly searches for an answer. Then, in a toneless voice:)*

MABEL I don't have anything to reply, because I don't understand your question.

PELTIER *(reproachfully)*. Is that possible? It isn't the first time . .

MABEL *(pulling herself together, in a lower voice)* I don't understand why you are making advances to me.

PELTIER Why not? Haven't the times changed? We have won, our countries are no longer at war, we have both served them well . . . we can think of ourselves . . . Now is the time for happiness.

MABEL *(with an effort)* You will be happy. You deserve it. But I . . .

PELTIER *(gently)* What's the matter? Where's the difficulty? You don't love me enough for this? *(*MABEL *is silent, but by no means disconcerted.)* It rather matters to me that you don't protest. I had the impression that you did love me enough . . . otherwise I wouldn't be here . . . not with the kind of love that arises in the drawing-room. We were still so near the battlefield. So what's the matter? Why do you hesitate?

MABEL I'm not hesitating. I am quite firmly decided . . . whatever it costs me . . . to say no to you.

PELTIER *(completely stunned)* To say no to me. *(*MABEL *is silent. Rejecting an idea which seems absurd to him.)* It's not, it's impossible that it could be, it's not the fact I'm a soldier that repels you, is it?

MABEL *(rapidly)* I wouldn't love you any better if you were not a soldier.

PELTIER Then? I can't accept your refusal . . . Never, on any point, have I known you clash with me . . . not even over the war, about which you are so vehement and so sensitive. I have always been in favour of the women's revolt. I completely agree with you about the war, its absurdity, its pointlessness . . . Just as you grant to me, as far as possible, that there is nothing for a man to do than to be either a pacifist or a soldier, and perhaps the two together, with the same passion, the same fury, the same entire devotion of his being, in life and in death. Isn't that what you said to me, during our walks in the hospital garden?

MABEL *(her throat tight)* Well, what would you think of a woman who, at the moment when the clouds piled up in the ministries, came to you asking for your resignation?

PELTIER *(calm)* I'm not with you. You would require . . .

MABEL If I required it, what would you say?

PELTIER *(sharply)* That you were not the same woman.

MABEL I only want to hear your reply.

PELTIER Well, to the woman who would ask me to act against my honour as a soldier . . .

MABEL *(stopping him)* That's exactly what I wanted to make you say. *(Sadly)* Now it's not me who requires your resignation, it's you who are calling for mine . . . And I too have my honour as a soldier.

PELTIER *(sharply)* But you are absolutely wrong. I would never ask you to abdicate your ideas, which – I say it again – I am in favour of in a woman . . . and even in a man. *(Brightly)* Look, I really think it would be impossible for me to love anyone but a pacifist. If you knew how much warlike women, or simply the submissive woman, resigned to the war . . .

MABEL *(disgusted)* They haven't seen what we have! They don't know . . .

PELTIER Well, I assure you that the woman who is not disgusted by war because it has always been there and always will be, such a woman horrifies me. And if, as I suspect, her deference to public opinion about "utopian ideas" and the obstinacy of her enthusiasm for war stem from the ulterior motive of capturing men's attention,

(sternly) I declare that such a calculation is quite wrong, and not the way to please us.

MABEL Thank you. You are right. Because I confess I've worried about what people might think. I have been so frightened you wouldn't find me very heroic.

PELTIER You – you! Mentioned in despatches . . . it isn't you saying that?

MABEL Heavens – next to all those who are too frightened that others do not sacrifice enough . . .

PELTIER People should only claim heroism in their own name, and I tell you again, I would never hamper your freedom of action. You work for peace, that's woman's mission in life, and I for war, which is man's. Haven't you told me a hundred times that the two efforts could run side by side?

MABEL *(desperate)* Yes, very well, between us two . . . if there were only us. But you are a leader, a great leader, how could you . . . how could you make people understand? . . . Certainly not . . . It's more impossible than you imagine. And then . . . if, leader as you are, you had superiors . . . they would never accept it. It is inadmissible that your wife should sign her name. Such an instrument would scare no one coming from Lady Stanley, but it would be your name your wife would sign.

PELTIER *(a bit shaken)* In your turn, wouldn't you make some concessions for me? Wouldn't you give up flagrant demonstrations?

MABEL Flagrant? You know me . . . You know I would never hurt anyone's honourable feelings . . . but there are misunderstandings. You could not be led to fight three times a year to defend the patriotism of your wife . . . And then, if it were enough to give up writing . . . however useful it were, because all the same there are those who understand . . . I have two secretaries to reply to letters I receive . . . Oh, if only all hearts knew what they could dare . . . Poor human heart, intimidated by utopias, if it only knew that there is no utopia except for the one engendered by timidity . . . But there isn't only the pen, there are still my friends . . . My friends, the wild athletes for peace, always into the breach in all the allied parliaments . . . *(Lower)* And then at last there are the others, those to whom I have sworn . . . I made a vow on the field of agony, to live only for them, to be forever haunted . . .

PELTIER   Oh Mabel, forget! The nightmare is over.

MABEL   *(fervently)* Not for me, no . . . the nightmare is not over as long as it hovers over the world . . .

PELTIER   *(begging)* One isn't a heroine all one's life.

MABEL   *(simply)* A heroine, oh no . . . a woman in mourning, a sister at prayer, a sort of auxiliary to souls on the battlefield. *(Coldly)* Women have entered convents for less than that.

PELTIER   Those who are in glory don't need you.

MABEL   They do need something: they need us to respect what they did, which can never be altered. And I too have a need: not to doubt, not to give in . . . I want to become more powerful in the sense of their death, to give full scope to their sacrifice . . . My brother thought he died for peace, not for a truce, but for peace . . . *(Very agitated)* Like the early Christians, I must go on to complete what is missing from the sacrifice.

PELTIER   *(sadly)* It costs you a lot then?

MABEL   *(in a rapid admission)* Almost as much as him.

PELTIER   Then? Because you won't accept useless sacrifices . . . Don't play with our pain. How would you be perjured? Can't you be loyal to the dead with a little love for the living?

MABEL   It's impossible . . . you can see that.

PELTIER   *(persistent, begging)* Happiness, doesn't that seem magnificent to you after all the effort that has been made to chase it from the world? Listen, it's still one of the wounded who is calling to you . . . Happiness, human happiness, so massacred, so left for dead . . . It wants to live, it stretches out its arms to you . . . Save it, have pity on the joy that could still be had on earth.

MABEL   I could not . . . I wouldn't know how to any more.

PELTIER   Be careful, you are bound by a false sense of honour . . .

MABEL   Alas . . . we are no longer living in a time of gratuitous tragedies. You have already forgotten what we just said . . .

PELTIER   *(struggling with himself)* What if I persist? Look . . . isn't there any hope?

MABEL   *(slowly, hesitantly)* Well . . . I have

sometimes thought . . . at first, when I hoped for so much from the Conference . . . when I saw war truly withdrawing in front of us before the cheering efforts of my friends . . . I thought perhaps a day would come when they wouldn't need me any more . . .

PELTIER   *(clutching at straws)* That's it, oh that's it! *(Persuasively)* Your friends are our leaders and our masters . . .

MABEL   *(sighing)* They are not alone at the Conference . . .

PELTIER   Hope, you must have hope! Oh, if you want to make me a pacifist! What's needed, what has to be gained for you to declare yourself confident of peace?

MABEL   Only one thing . . . a thing which would make all hopes possible . . . which would open such horizons to Europe.

PELTIER   *(joyfully)* Tell me, tell me quickly, and I will spread the propaganda in the army. I promise you all the troops and all the officers, the whole power of the armed forces.

MABEL   *(smiling)* I don't ask that much.

PELTIER   Then tell me, what is this thing that the Conference can do? Limit the number of weapons?

MABEL   Not even that, not yet.

PELTIER   What then?

MABEL   What that great Englishman, H. G. Wells, has called for . . . Decide not to break up.

PELTIER   The Conference?

MABEL   Vote to be permanent, to stay in session forever, a world council, a universal parliament, and to replace forever all our medieval ambassadors, that disastrous system which brought about the failure of 1914.

PELTIER   If that's all you need.

MABEL   When Graham Moore gets here he will explain it better. It would truly lay the first stone . . . Perhaps that would be enough for one generation.

PELTIER   Then you would believe in the right to be happy and to make others happy?

MABEL   *(sadly)* Don't count on it too much.

PELTIER   It's so simple.

MABEL   *(discouraged)* Is that any reason?

Scene 2

A car is heard to draw up although it remains unseen, off-stage, and PAUL DELISLE, MARGUERITE, *and* SIMONE *get out.* MARGUERITE *is wearing a black crepe veil which fits closely to her head. Her niece is wearing less severe mourning.*

MARGUERITE *(entering, speaking to her brother and niece)* They're in the drawing-room. Come in for a little and I'll introduce you. *(To* MABEL *and the* GENERAL*)* My brother, Paul Delisle, and my niece, Simone.

    *(*DELISLE *bows to* MABEL *and shakes the* GENERAL*'s hand warmly, while the women get together.)*

DELISLE I'm so pleased to meet you again at my sister's. Our last meeting was at army headquarters . . . you hadn't yet got your glorious command.

PELTIER *(smiling)* On the other hand, you were already the great cheerleader, the loudest voice in France.

DELISLE I only wrote for you. What is a poet's voice on the battlefield? But in the rear they were happy that I spoke about you . . . that I expressed in words the great feats you were performing on the battlefield . . .

SIMONE *(interrupting effusively)* General, isn't war noble!

*(*JEAN *enters on this cue, and pauses expectantly.* PELTIER, *rather taken aback, hesitates to reply.)*

DELISLE *(laughing)* Don't be *too* surprised, General, that my daughter is so enthusiastic.

SIMONE Oh, I don't mean . . . don't think . . . War is terrible, abominable, but what would men be worth without sacrifice? Pacifism is so squalid.

DELISLE *(faced with a general silence, flies to his daughter's rescue)* It is certain that in the abject materialism of modern societies, only war transfigures people, reviving dormant virtues, resurrecting idealism and beauty again on the earth . . .

MARGUERITE *(brusquely)* Idealism and beauty . . . we can do very well without them!

SIMONE *(scandalised)* Oh Aunt!

MARGUERITE You'll agree with Jean's wish to stay in the army. He'd have done better to have asked you for a blessing rather than me. *(Forestalling her guests' surprise)* Simone and Jean have been engaged to each other since they were ten years old.

JEAN *(laughing)* It was Simone herself who made me ask you.

SIMONE You didn't have to be coaxed. As for your decision, I counted on it quite rightly after talking with you. We had the same idea. I'm quite happy.

JEAN Really?

DELISLE And as for me, I am absolutely in favour. There is still a future for that career.

PELTIER But I hope you are not aiming to start again tomorrow?

DELISLE *(short and sharp)* We shall have war again within ten years. *(During all this, but without addressing her directly,* DELISLE *is as if haunted by* MABEL. *His glances and his expectant looks, even his silences, are made in her direction. She listens intensely attentively, but she holds herself aloof and keeps quiet.)* Ah! I am not exactly a pacifist!

SIMONE Goodness! If we could only have peace! But we know very well that that is only a utopian dream.

DELISLE *(sadly and knowingly)* War happens periodically. It recurs every 50 years.

SIMONE *(taking it up)* There have always been wars and there always will be. As long as there are men you can't stop them from being human, and from throwing themselves at each other.

DELISLE *(in the same way)* Human passions defy all calculation and all prudence . . . aggression will always express itself between nations. You have to recognise instincts: human beings are greedy, they are belligerent, they are cruel too, and even when they're only envious . . .

SIMONE Humankind is a sad thing.

MARGUERITE Come along, you must eat. It's half past nine. I'm afraid we didn't wait dinner for you. You can go on talking about war and peace tomorrow, because Lady Mabel claims that, unless you are so holy that you live with God, you shouldn't have any other preoccupation in the world.

(They exit, leaving MABEL, JEAN *and* PELTIER *in the room.)*

Scene 3

JEAN *(to PELTIER)* Well, now you've heard . . . is he convincing, the poet? And even Mother begins to talk about war!

PELTIER It's the young woman who struck me. Good Heavens! That's someone who really makes the most of slaughter.

JEAN Lord! She's got her father's ideas. Don't expect too much of her . . . But Lady Mabel, why . . . why didn't you protest? Why didn't you say anything?

MABEL *(agitated)* Oh, *me!* You see, the idea that one could discuss it . . as if no other opinion mattered . . . as if one could be for or against . . . and when they are a thousand times right, when they must have "always wars because there always are wars", does that exempt them from going mad . . . from breaking their heads against the eternal cannons, before at least having their heart broken?

PELTIER Certainly these old men and young women are resigned rather prematurely.

MABEL *(getting excited)* There is only one thing in the world still more revolting than war; it's the eternal sticking to the idea that it costs us so little to accept it . . .

PELTIER *(quietly, sadly)* As long as there are men . . .

MABEL *(devouring him with her eyes)* Oh you too, you say that too! You believe in war, human passion, in war, national aggression, in war because people are belligerent, greedy, envious and cruel!

PELTIER *(compliantly)* And isn't it like that?

MABEL *(excitedly)* You have seen men die . . . you, a soldier, don't insult your fallen enemy. "As long as there are men!" Really, to parrot that phrase is an unpardonable blasphemy! But people are only admirable in wartime . . . there is no heroism or self-denial, there are no disciples or voluntary martyrs! *(Ironic, acerbic, excited)* "The aggression between nations!" Do you really think that a general mobilisation is called in order to serve the passions of men snatched from their firesides?

PELTIER No, Lady Mabel, no, I don't think that, and certainly there are many fine-sounding phrases that come ready-made . . . but I do believe in collective madness.

MABEL *(looking at him)* For using ready-made phrases I congratulate you.

PELTIER *(smiling)* You don't believe in collective madness?

MABEL *(shrugging)* Facile words . . . pedantic words. War would not be so tragic if it were a matter of madmen. The truth is that none of these madmen stopped repeating, "What madness!" Yes, human beings are belligerent, greedy, envious and cruel; they are ignoble, as much as you like, but war is their sanctity, it is not their crime. War is their most cruel self-possession, it is not their madness.

(PELTIER takes MABEL's hand and kisses it. JEAN looks at her in great surprise.)

JEAN I haven't seen you like this, Lady Mabel . . .

MABEL *(without hearing him)* So, when the Guards, and when our armed fighting divisions marched against each other, singing their hymns, you drew this lesson, that "man is a wolf to other men" and whatever one did, one couldn't stop the heroes from devouring each other? *(She is gasping for breath.)* If war is unforgivable in those who let it loose, it's because it is *not* human fate. There is no instinct in an animal that makes it walk towards cannon.

PELTIER You'll forgive Delisle when he has written beautiful verses about our soldiers.

MABEL *(as if coming out of a dream)* It's true. They'll sing the praises of our heroes and in reading them we'll sob with enthusiasm. But will that be all – trumpets echoing their fame? Won't you find other voices? Never a yell of revolt, a shout of more than enough horror . . . or simply a cry of sorrow . . . Always the conventional swaggering about "glory", the sterile: "How I envy the Dead" and never a loyal outburst, a zeal that might achieve something. "Oh! Action for the sake of action. They were our defenders, let's change roles . . . it's our turn to carry arms, to die for them . . Perhaps you will still go on the battlefield, soldiers of Europe, but it will be over our dead bodies . . . "

JEAN *(after a moment that shivers with future wars)* Don't count on that too much, Lady Mabel. Peace is not everyone's business like it is yours. Each one to his own calling, his usual habits. They'll go back on it like before . . . There isn't a fancy that won't carry them away from the strain of everyday life.

PELTIER You'll run up against universal indifference.

MABEL *(almost shouting)* Indifference to that?

JEAN It's because I am persuaded that you see me a soldier. If men wanted peace, but, there, what is called *wanting*, that's to say, not vaguely wishing . . . what stops them from organising as you suggest?

MABEL *(lively)* Oh, I have asked them. Soldiers usually tell me that it is economic laws, and economists that it is the warlike spirit of soldiers and civilians.

PELTIER *(laughing)* So you see, you must despair.

JEAN In the end, no one gives a damn . . . and without that, how can one live?

PELTIER Meanwhile, I'm anxious to see how you are going to manage to live under the same roof as Paul Delisle.

MABEL Oh, that's very simple. I only ever talk about war with pacifists or soldiers. And then I am counting on Jean for a favour.

PELTIER *(surprised)* Oh?

MABEL *(to JEAN)* You will demonstrate that he is not indifferent, and that it is necessary for men to put themselves on active service for peace.

JEAN *(highly astonished)* You are counting on me?

MABEL You are very intelligent, well educated, very argumentative . . .

PELTIER *(laughing)* And I'm none of those things?

MABEL *(also laughing)* I need soldiers in both camps. I'm conscripting you. You are my international sanctions force.

JEAN *(seriously)* Be assured that I believe myself to be of more use to my country on this side rather than on the other.

MABEL *(taking his hands)* Do you mean that . . . do you really say it sincerely?

JEAN *(moved to compassion by MABEL's enthusiasm)* Who would not mean it?

MABEL *(briskly)* What time is it?

PELTIER *(smiling)* No, it's not time yet . . . Graham Moore will never get here before eleven o'clock, half past eleven.

MABEL *(to JEAN)* I'm longing for you to talk with him, promise me.

JEAN But he's a charming man, and we've talked a lot already. We agree about heavy artillery and aerial torpedoes and particularly about naval guns . . .

MABEL He's a great man of action and I only hope that the writers and thinkers will march when their public marches. Moore has an enormous influence on the Labour Party. He raised new recruits. He gave us 35,000 men a week. He'll do as well as that for peace.

JEAN *(guardedly)* I'm not a socialist.

MABEL *(briskly)* He'll be enchanted by that. He doesn't allow peace to be a party-political matter.

Scene 4

MARGUERITE *returns.*

MARGUERITE They've gone to bed. They were exhausted. She's pretty, my niece, isn't she?

MABEL *(looking out of the window)* She's hideous!

MARGUERITE *(laughing)* Really! You can't insist on her being a pacifist. But she's a good girl, I assure you, and she knitted for the troops.

MABEL *(walking up and down, absorbed by what is going on outside in the night, in the distance)* And what did women think about while they were knitting? *(She comes and goes, crossing in front of the windows.)*

PELTIER *(to MABEL)* You'll hear the car before you see it. Sit down, Lady Mabel. Moore may have taken a sleeper. It's not likely he could have caught the train this morning.

MABEL *(on edge)* That's why . . . *(She suddenly goes out on to the terrace.)*

MARGUERITE It's waiting for Moore that's making her fidgety. She's begun her coming-and-going an hour before he's due here. She's going to catch her death of cold . . . it's freezing tonight.

PELTIER *(calling out)* Lady Mabel, come back inside. *(He goes out on to the terrace. MABEL can be seen in the dark with a shawl. She moves away and calls.)*

MABEL I'm not cold.

PELTIER *(coming back inside, worried)* We'll just have to leave her to it. *(Resentfully)* She only lives for this Conference.

JEAN I'm afraid she's not well prepared for disappointment.

PELTIER *(harshly)* She's prepared for everything. Who exactly is this Graham Moore?

MARGUERITE He's a former Secretary of State. Today he's a representative at the Conference.

PELTIER How old is he?

JEAN   He's wild enough to go through fire. He's all the more wild because he's suffering from consumption. Kitchener opposed him and fairly militarised the government on the spot.

PELTIER   *(who has not received the answer he is looking for)* And what is he to Lady Mabel?

MARGUERITE   He's a colleague, they're working together.

PELTIER   *(impatiently)* I mean, a relative, a friend?

MARGUERITE   Not related at all. Moore is from a working-class family. Mabel, after her brother's death, is – by royal decree – a peeress in her own right, heir to a peerage which she will transmit to her children, if she should marry a commoner.

PELTIER   *(annoyed)* I didn't know she was such a great lady.

MARGUERITE   Since the war she has renounced everything. Even though she is the greatest landowner in England, she doesn't live in a stately home any more; just a hotel room in one European city or another. And she won't stop wearing black, any more than a nun would. She has seen too many men die. She told me that before the war she hadn't known what it cost to live on earth, but now she's had the experience and accepts what it means: that her life certainly wasn't worth that.

PELTIER   How old is she?

MARGUERITE   Thirty-two. She adored her brother. He was wonderfully cultivated and intelligent, and handsome in the way they are over there . . . handsome like an animal. They travelled together, and it was him who brought her up. Even before her conversion, I would say, she was the most aware and well-informed of aristocrats. *(Harshly, hoarsely)* She watched this brother die for 14 hours, in a manner she has never talked about. *(She stops suddenly, she has gone rigid. She is so pale, her throat tight, her chin raised, that her son goes to her.)*

JEAN   Mother . . . why talk about things like that? What are you thinking about? You don't know anything, you have no right to suppose . . . there are others dead on the battlefield . . .

(MARGUERITE as if exasperated, pulls away from her son, and, her hands to her head, with the speed of a young woman she suddenly runs from the room.)

PELTIER   *(sadly)* Well – you've never heard anything about your brother, Gerald?

JEAN   *(worriedly)* No – but there are days when I wonder if my mother has.

Scene 5

MABEL *enters with* GRAHAM MOORE

MABEL   *(introducing)* General, Mr Graham Moore is pleased to meet you. You are one of the rare people he admires.

PELTIER   And I have certain things to thank him for personally. I remember the welcome arrival of some heavy artillery that did not come from French saucepan factories.

(They shake hands coolly, in the manner of the English.)

MOORE   Yes, we worked hard for you. *(Shakes hands with* JEAN.*)*

JEAN   Well, Lady Mabel, are you satisfied with the news?

MOORE   I expected a better welcome. *(To* MABEL.*)* I find you very cool.

PELTIER   You've brought some hope with you?

MOORE   Lots . . . I've talked at length with all the heads of mission, with their technical advisers, the secretaries, the rulers themselves . . . I've sounded out the whole Conference. All my consultations were satisfactory . . . I've laid the foundations and I can say that for everyone I have established a safety-hatch, a way of getting out of the conventions, common diplomatic grounds . . . No one can see any insurmountable obstacle to two or three prime reforms which are cardinal points for us. I have everybody's agreement. *(He looks towards* MABEL *who seems turned to stone.)* Well let's see. Would it be best to start from there?

MABEL   *(shrugging her shoulders)* Oh, individual agreements! I know those. I've dealt with those before.

MOORE   But the agreements of the war-lords?

MABEL   *(shrugs again)* Do you know the fable by Baroness von Suttner?

PELTIER   *(smiling)* *The Fury of Peace?*

MABEL   It's a very good title and she's proud of it. I only ask to lift up her arms and her name.

JEAN   I don't know Baroness Suttner's fable.

MABEL   "A crowd of a thousand and one men look enviously at a marvellous garden which has its gate locked. The job of the gate-keeper is to let people in if the majority want it. He calls the first person: 'Sincerely, do you want to come in?' 'Myself, of course, but not the others.' The gate-keeper notes this reply down. He calls the second, who says the same. He notes this in his register: one yes, a thousand no. And so on until the last. He adds up the sum of a thousand yes's, and a million no's. The gate stays shut because the majority of no's was overwhelming. Each man felt obliged to vote not only for himself but also for the others."

(PELTIER *lets out a burst of sarcastic, careless laughter.* JEAN *looks profoundly at* MABEL.)

MOORE   We'll keep a good look-out, Lady Mabel, we'll scrutinise the vote. Now, don't you want to look over my report? I have to leave tomorrow about five o'clock to be at the station by eight.

PELTIER   You will hardly have slept.

MOORE   (*looking at* MABEL) I would not have been able to see our friend for the whole Conference if I slept . . . and since she has promised Madame de Gestel to extend her stay . . . How much longer are you going to make me carry on with this profession, Lady Mabel?

(PELTIER *follows the conversation very attentively.*)

MABEL   Am I so indispensable to you?

JEAN   Mr Moore, I hope you're not manoeuvring to carry Lady Mabel away from us?

MOORE   That is my intention . . . she's indispensable to us. This young woman, trained in all the sports and particularly those of the battlefield, has a doctorate in peace. She has read everything, she knows everything by heart. From Henry IV to Sully she knows everything that has been tried, everything that has been thought on the subject of peace. Before the war she only read novels; now she plunges into economists, military writers, diplomats and statesmen. Blue books, or yellow, green, orange, grey, white or red books, none holds any secrets from her. She can cite you chapter and verse. There is only one such woman who has given herself so wholeheartedly to a cause. (*He ends with a tremor in his voice.*)

JEAN   I admire Lady Mabel with all my heart.

MABEL   (*looking at* MOORE) It's him you should admire. He cried tears of blood at not being able to fight. Then he waged the munitions campaign, and you know with what drive. We'll get the same drive behind our peace campaign. He'll be the man of future sanctions, the terrorist for peace.

JEAN   (*very struck*) Mr Moore, do you really believe that the question of permanent peace can be pledged in advance of defeat?

MOORE   It's not a matter of what is "pledged in advance of defeat". There are only men who are more or less resolute, more or less persistent, more or less invincible, pledged to the service of these questions.

PELTIER   And now we'll let you work. (*Looking over the big table and the lights*) Have you got everything you need? (*Going to the fireplace*) Above all, don't let the fire go out . . . the servants have gone to bed . . . You must stay at least until tomorrow evening, Moore.

MOORE   Impossible. A king is expecting me during the day.

PELTIER   (*gives* MABEL *a neat, athletic bow. Curtly*) Goodnight, Madame.

(*He takes his leave of* MOORE *as* JEAN *kisses* MABEL*'s hand. The two men leave the room, picking up their books and papers as they go.*)

Scene 6

MOORE   The rest of my report is being copied out. (*Opening his briefcase and turning over a pile of papers*) There is nothing else to tell you before next week . . . I knew beforehand that you would not count on the recent news. But I've come all the same.

MABEL   (*embarrassed*) You must be worn out.

MOORE   Given a choice between tiredness and anxiety, I wouldn't hesitate.

MABEL   (*softly*) Anxiety?

MOORE   (*with authority*) You ought to be in Paris. Your absence at the present time is equivalent to desertion. A month's stay with your friend while she is in mourning is more than enough.

MABEL   (*with an effort*) I'll be in Paris in a couple of days.

MOORE   You'll be sick at heart to leave this place.

MABEL   You know quite well that my sadness or happiness could not depend more on you.

MOORE   *(moved)* Mabel . . .

MABEL   *(coldly)* On the work that you've done.

MOORE   We have only one thought, we are devoted to the same cause, devoted life and death. We are each other's witness, each day we have valued each other more. There is not an effort in the world that excites me more passionately than this, and I have given all my energy to it, both as a man and as a fighter. Yet when it comes to loving, to loving me as a woman, it is not me that you come to. The man of peace, the peace you would give your life for, you will not give him your heart. The magic glamour of war means more to you and has stolen your love from me. You prefer a soldier to me.

MABEL   *(tired)* No, Moore, no. If I could . . . do you think a soldier could love me?

MOORE   You deny it very badly. You're suffering from a bad conscience. If you haven't yet decided to give in, Mabel, you must leave with me at once. Yes, I know, I know only too well. I know the terrible power of war, of death over the heart, and it takes great resolution to resist that glamour when it's so near. We shall be loved less, Mabel, and we shall deserve it less. That ruthless side of war is perhaps what we have not recovered from. A dreadful life at heart, but what a life!

MABEL   *(shocked)* No, no . . . we mustn't think of that. Our love is not at that price.

MOORE   Yet . . . what will we be in comparison with others? Others who have sovereign rights over you, whose life adorned for you the precious, stirring frailty of the battlefield. Mabel, if we only listened to, only thought of ourselves. To fall, wounded in my turn, to tear from your woman's heart the only true cry of love, the cry of torn entrails.

MABEL   *(standing up)* But I don't want to. I don't want to love like that! My love is not an executioner.

MOORE   *(profoundly)* Yet, Mabel, it's death you love. Because a lifeless body has weighed down your arms, because the paleness of a dying face has turned your heart over, you can never any more love a man who is not consecrated by sacrifice.

MABEL   *(fighting with herself)* That's too terrible, it's not true.

MOORE   *(very simply)* What haven't men done to be loved?

MABEL   *(beside herself)* It's not that . . .

MOORE   *(gently and sadly)* Yes, it is that. Don't ask too much, Mabel. People will always have grief . . . grief and death to drive their love to despair. Don't dread the idyllic . . . don't be afraid of certain happiness. In war and in heroism, what troubles you so deeply is death. It won't fail us. That arrow thrills the human heart right till the last day. Don't be jealous of war-loves. *(Refusing to reflect on his own conduct, mastering his feelings)* Cruelty for the sake of cruelty . . . be satisfied with the human lot. Don't only give your soul, Mabel, your courage and your devotion. Now that victory is achieved, it's your woman's heart you must snatch away from war, from death, and which you must give passionately to life and peace.

MABEL   But I don't want all that . . .

MOORE   *(discouraged)* Nevertheless, it's Peltier that you love.

Curtain

Act III

The same set

Scene 1

SIMONE, JEAN, DELISLE *and then* LADY MABEL

SIMONE   I don't understand my aunt . . . the General and Lady Mabel here at the same time.

JEAN   She was his nurse for three months. My mother particularly wanted them to meet again.

DELISLE   You don't suppose he's going to make the blunder of marrying her!

JEAN   I don't suppose he doesn't want to.

DELISLE   Stop there! I won't let my heroes be damaged. This concerns me. Peltier is one of our great prides. I shall have to step in.

SIMONE   It would be scandalous.

JEAN   I think Peltier has cooled off a little since he realised Lady Mabel's social rank.

DELISLE   That's the thing. She's a royal princess.

SIMONE   He's the one who'd be marrying beneath him.

JEAN   You really don't like Lady Mabel.

SIMONE   I have more than enough reason not to.

DELISLE   (following his own train of thought) Besides, I'm wrong to make a tragedy out of the matter; she will insist on his resignation and Peltier will have second thoughts about it all.

JEAN   He would never resign . . . but I don't think she would ever ask him to.

SIMONE   (very excitedly) Really, it would be absolutely ridiculous.

DELISLE   I can't see Peltier, that magnificent leader, proceeding with his aides-de-camp into his wife's pacifist salon.

JEAN   They haven't got to that point yet.

DELISLE   In the meantime, it seems to me sheer stupidity to be in love with someone not of one's own rank.

JEAN   Peltier is nearly 50 but he does not look 40 yet.

DELISLE   (who has no liking for Mabel) Women should choose: either be a flirt or be political. For them to be both is too much for a man!

JEAN   You cannot call Lady Mabel's quasi-religious vocation political. Nor can you call a woman a flirt who has given herself up to the mission of experiencing the shock of war in the way that Carmelite nuns identify with the passion of Christ.

DELISLE   (excitedly) Then you think like she does?

JEAN   (pressured by his uncle's aggression, measuring his words) If I thought it possible to obtain any practical result whatever in that way . . . victory having been won today, France having reacted to the war as she ought . . . well, I would give all this over, I would live like Moore and Lady Mabel, I would think like them, like them I would see in every activity which was not aimed at finishing with war, which benevolently, stupidly gave its tomorrows to destruction, I would see any other activity as a symptom of madness, sheer adolescence, the behaviour of apemen.

SIMONE   How dare you speak like that while wearing uniform!

DELISLE   Calm down, he won't be wearing it for long. And we are quite right to be worried about something else. It's not a question of Peltier's resignation, but of his own.

JEAN   (whispering) You're mad!

SIMONE   I knew it would come to that. I knew that woman was dangerous.

DELISLE   Do you seriously mean what you're saying?

JEAN   (regretfully, slightly testily) What do you want, Uncle? I'm no intellectual. I've got no philosophy about the respective merits of war and peace, and I chose the incomparable blessings that war brings the world.

DELISLE   Let me draw your attention to the fact that you had the choice between a peaceful career and the one you have opted for.

JEAN   I'm a fireman, but it's not because I admire fires; it's to put them out.

DELISLE   You do at least recognise that fires make heroes.

JEAN   (gravely) Do you think it gives me any pleasure to tell me that? I can assure you that we would have little zest in fighting for beauty. People don't go to the battlefront to put up their own statue. I wish my country had less need of heroes.

SIMONE   (moved) Not all soldiers think like you!

JEAN   What do you know about it? What do you take us for? Are we made for war or is war made for us? Are we merely mice on a wheel and do we have to keep war going because war is what keeps our feet moving? We get enthusiastic about a useful job which is necessary to our country, but if we could avoid this nauseating work, I can tell you, ask any soldier, not the people who read your books . . . and if you are bent on keeping the system for sake of the system, war for war's sake, death for death's sake, art for art's sake, I've had enough. I'm no artist.

SIMONE   (very moved) You could only argue like that if you were no longer ready to do your duty.

JEAN   Choose your words carefully . . . I am still a soldier!

SIMONE   (passionately) You no longer have the right.

JEAN   (looking at his uncle) It's you who's responsible for this madness. Is that a woman's role? I ask you! Is it a fiancée's place to preach the Kaiser's mentality?

SIMONE   Just look how excited you're getting because I'm not a pacifist.

JEAN   I'm sorry for you.

SIMONE   Be sorry for yourself if you still love me a little, because the Jean who was just talking, the Jean who sees something else in the world more beautiful than his career as a soldier . . .

JEAN *(heavily)* Get on with it!

SIMONE The man who lets himself be seduced by false and dangerous doctines, the man who is capable of throwing up his uniform and his military service . . .

DELISLE Be careful, Simone! You're getting worked up. Don't exaggerate.

JEAN *(his voice upset)* I want to hear her to the end.

SIMONE Jean knows very well that I will only ever marry a soldier . . . a soldier I can rely on.

JEAN That's enough.

SIMONE Will you give me your word that you will never, ever resign?

JEAN *(very distinctly)* I have never yet been asked to.

DELISLE Simone is right to ask you that question because from now on you are going to have to ask it yourself.

JEAN I haven't reached that point yet. And I don't ever want to either. *(To SIMONE)* Does that satisfy you?

SIMONE If you ever did, if you ever resigned, for me that would be letting your brothers down, you would make yourself unworthy of them, and you would be letting yourself down too.

JEAN *(worried)* That would be a sacrifice I can hardly bear to think about . . . I couldn't bring myself to do it without very serious reasons . . . That might be something that would raise me in your eyes.

SIMONE That's possible. But I'm sure it would mean the end of our plans together for always.

JEAN *(badly affected)* You decide.

SIMONE *(bitterly)* I didn't expect to have to fight her. How strong is this woman then?

JEAN You can only see a woman in this?

SIMONE *(passionately)* I'm convinced that peace is a utopian dream.

JEAN *(sombrely)* There are days when I would like to be so sure.

SIMONE Papa, tell him that you can never get the better of war, that war is bound to happen, it's human fate, that he could never . . . *(DELISLE is not listening and doesn't reply.)* What are you thinking about, Papa?

DELISLE I was thinking of a man in the past, a diplomat who was well known for being strong-minded and quick-witted. To such a man the survival of war in modern society would be so incomprehensible that he would see it as a miracle, a whim on the part of Providence, a scheme to impose on the world the bloody libations of redemption, and, too profound to judge war a human calamity, he would only be able to see it as a divine calamity.

JEAN You're speaking of Jean de Maistre?

DELISLE *(mocking)* So, young man, you got there right away. Unfrock yourself, throw away your uniform. War, modern warfare, which bears no comparison to wars of the past, this war is not human. Only imbeciles would think so. Shameful idiots who, without realising it, insult heroism. In every country mobilisation is a holy thing. War is not human. War is divine, and that's why I value it.

JEAN *(bewildered at first, then serious)* Do you believe in God, Uncle?

DELISLE Me? No. But I believe in the divine.

JEAN That's too subtle.

[Scene 2]

MABEL *(who has been watching and listening from the terrace, after standing there for a while, advances like a ghost)* At least you admit it. You admit it to yourself. That's what I'm sick and tired of telling people. You "want" war. They don't have your vision, nor your cynicism. They are persuaded that they can't help peace.

DELISLE *(untroubled)* And you, Lady Mabel, highly bred as you are, remember this: you can't repudiate your race. You would be the first to lose interest in a world without heroism and without splendour, without sacrifice and with none of the nobility which only military valour still inspires.

MABEL *(slowly)* I don't want heroism, I don't want nobility at that price!

DELISLE *(peremptorily)* A nation that doesn't know how to fight any more, a nation of sensualists, is good only to be struck from the face of the earth.

MABEL *(in a holy rage)* "A nation of sensualists" – historian's words. The world is not organised in such a way that there could be on the earth, "nations of sensualists".

DELISLE *(obstinately)* I repeat my question and ask women: What do you love, what can you find to love, in a world where all the military virtues of war have disappeared? Before attempting utopia . . .

MABEL *(fiercely)* No woman will answer you. No woman would acknowledge such a question. The nurse who watches over a wounded man doesn't wonder whether his recovery is a utopian dream; she doesn't wonder whether it is more beautiful for a man to die for his country. She knows she must save him and gives her life up to that.

DELISLE Lady Mabel, if you were only a nurse, I would not argue with you. But you are my opponent. You are championing a cause I do not accept. Let's see. I sincerely ask the sister of Lord Stanley, do you want to see this boy *(he looks at his nephew)* . . . do you want to see Lieutenant Gestel, who has proved himself on the battlefield, do you want to see him lay down his arms and his men, and follow you to become a civilian champion of peace?

MABEL *(looking at the young man hopefully)* Oh! Are you frightened of him doing that?

DELISLE You are very eloquent, Lady Mabel, very dangerous because you are so convinced. You won't be a party to this wrong?

MABEL *(calmly to the young man)* Would you think of doing that?

JEAN If it is wrong, set your mind at rest. You would have nothing to reproach yourself for. Something else gave me far more food for thought than your rebellion and your despair.

DELISLE It would be the last blow to your mother.

JEAN That's what you haven't understood . . . You fail to see that everything is ruined. You haven't the sense to despair. My mother is dead to everything. You can't play with human heart-strings with impunity. Be careful not to preach to us about death too much; there is something in us which responds only too quickly. *(He leaves the room, followed by SIMONE.)*

DELISLE The harm is more advanced than I thought. Lady Mabel, I abandon him to you. In any case, he's not 25 yet. He was commissioned too soon, for expediency. But there is something else better not mentioned: he must die in uniform or be a disgrace to his country.

MABEL *(who had gone pale)* I don't want desertions. I don't bear any soldier ill-will, I only bear ill-will to war. And nothing, nothing in the world *(impassioned, but with a shade of defiance)* it was a different, most secret voice in my heart, nothing will wrench my strength away from my first duty, my sworn duty . . .

DELISLE Even the most solemn oath gives way to the lure of happpiness.

MABEL *(as if she must repeat herself and burn the bridges behind her)* The lure of happiness? For those who have understood, there is no more happiness. There is nothing any more. There is only one reason for living. There is only one excuse to keep for oneself what so many others were deprived of, there is only one pardon for escaping the shame of survival, and that is to live only to prolong their achievement, to maintain forever what they have won for us: peace. To live only to be against war, to be no more than a scream, a yell of horror and rebellion, a desperate shout, a call to vengeance, a cry to rally all our efforts, all our strength . . .

DELISLE *(cold and hard)* Then I am quite easy in my mind. Peltier will never marry you. *(He goes towards the door.)*

MABEL *(in agreement, but sadly)* He will never marry me!

Scene 3

PELTIER *and* MABEL. DELISLE *leaves the stage after a few cues.*

PELTIER *(entering, crumpled-up newspapers in his hands)* It's all in favour of your friend. That man is decidedly a force to be reckoned with . . . he's roused everyone up, and without using the slightest trick; his report consisted only of facts, of precise details. What fine realists you have in your country! It's such a pleasure to see a well-developed mind at work. I'm bowled over by him!

MABEL *(sceptical)* His programme is on the agenda?

PELTIER The debate is going to take all this week. Aren't you pleased? I'm as happy as victory-day. You can see the ravages peace works in me!

MABEL *(nervously)* You're not hoping for too much?

PELTIER *(on the alert)* What do you mean?

MABEL *(rapidly)* You, me . . personally, we have nothing to expect from peace.

PELTIER Sorry. I was left with a quite different impression. What has happened?

MABEL   I got my self-possession back, especially when other people took it on themselves to remind me about you. We were indulging in illusions!

PELTIER   *(inquisitorially)* What has Delisle been saying about me?

MABEL   Oh, you have nothing to fear. He's only trying to help you. He wishes you nothing but good. He only wanted to keep you away from what you should not get too close to.

PELTIER   Happiness, for instance.

MABEL   *(brusquely)* Scandal, and in the end I understood. We have been fooling ourselves. Our dream can't come true.

PELTIER   *(getting angry)* He's managed to convince you of that?

MABEL   I was already prepared . . .

PELTIER   And you're worried about scandal?

MABEL   *(nervously, but with authority)* I believe in scandal, in misunderstanding, in continual harassment. I believe in constraint, even between us two. I believe in a false situation . . . I can already see the look in the eyes of young officers . . . I believe in insults you could not avoid! I believe in worse, in provocation, in spilt blood perhaps, or worse still, in resignation, in a retreat you never dreamed of.

PELTIER   *(dully)* You have to love me more than your ideas.

MABEL   *(desperately)* That's what you want? Now it's my turn, it's up to me to leave, to tear myself away. The hour of sacrifice, the moment to win you if I can . . .

PELTIER   Stop . . . I've never asked that of a woman, it's a monstrous sacrifice. The time of action is over for you, everything proves it. You can leave your friends at the moment of victory. The first step is taken, you're not deserting anyone.

MABEL   *(bitterly)* Victory! Wait! We've only had words so far, they've got to be put into practice.

PELTIER   *(authoritatively)* I won't give you up. Certainly I've looked for other things in the world than love. I wanted action, I wanted to exert myself . . . perhaps I wanted glory, too. I wanted to use myself up, to lavish myself on something . . . to give myself over to something other than caresses. I loved great causes which a man could serve entirely . . . I aspired to rank with those who really counted, amongst those who were excellent and mattered!

But if I wanted all that, can't I admit it to a woman? If I wanted to be a lion among men, it was with the secret hope of increasing my rights, so that in love too I might win something to be proud of. Mabel, I am so proud. I don't have one of those facile hearts which finds two happinesses, two loves . . . *(Heatedly)* Don't make me lose hope.

MABEL   *(passionately)* Yes, you are stronger than the rest, you could put up with . . . You have something much more . . . your life could be so beautiful, so complete! To have been what you are is to have paid the price for happiness.

PELTIER   But I don't want that! You're mad. How could I find the happiness I want without falling? I have been arrogant. Mabel, if you only knew . . . I had a horror of myself with the happinesses on offer. It's a sign, you see, a sign that something else is in the offing. We both rank high. I am everything that you could wish for. Don't give all that up. You used to love my life, Mabel; you were enthusiastic about my profession.

MABEL   You still have your profession. Isn't that finer than my love?

PELTIER   But I need both of them! Remember. There was a time when you dreamed of Chad and Central Africa. That journey where you would have travelled with me, how it fascinated you, because, without saying so, we both knew quite well we could only do it as a married couple.

MABEL   *(sadly)* But I wasn't then . . .

PELTIER   Yes, I know . . . But . . . challenge the idea of excess. Peace doesn't need it!

MABEL   *(still sad)* It needs it even more. This isn't the fanaticism of just one woman, but of all women.

PELTIER   *(begging)* Stay faithful to peace, but love me. I have suffered more than I can say. I've known real distress. At Crayonne, when I was at the point of death, when I thought it was all over . . . other men had pictures, something to cherish. But I was dying like an animal, without even having a name to murmur.

MABEL   *(in an outburst, as if to wrap him in her arms)* Hush, there, it's over now.

PELTIER   And do you want it to start again? Because I was less alone in No Man's Land than I shall be in my hut in Africa.

MABEL   Do something for me: go and talk to Paul Delisle; I don't know where I am any longer. I shall do something silly. In Africa, yes, clearly . . . but wouldn't it be desertion for you? And I would do nothing except be happy . . . No, even there I couldn't escape from remorse. There isn't a safe corner left in the whole universe, there isn't a desert left where one could forget. There is no horizon that war hasn't driven to despair.

PELTIER   But no one could go on living if they were always thinking of that!

MABEL   (with authority) No one could go on living if they truly understood what has happened. No one could go on living if they had enough emotion to feel the sacrifice of others and enough pride of spirit not to accept it without revulsion.

PELTIER   Then it's over; you have sacrificed both of us. You'll leave tonight with Graham Moore, you'll only be able to live by fighting, shaking at the door of Parliament. In spite of all you've said, you're no longer a woman. There will be nothing intimate about you. You will have given your heart to crowds, to crowds of sad people, to crowds of heroes from the battlefield. But you won't have known a soldier's love.

MABEL   (very shaken) But that's cruel! You know how to strike home! Why are you so wounding? Let someone else take my place . . . I don't want any more of it . . . I don't know anything any more, I can't decide anything. I believe whatever anyone says. I will be your wife if you think I ought to.

PELTIER   You might come to care for me then?

MABEL   (upset) That's nothing to be proud about.

PELTIER   You're going to say it and promise it . . . we can announce our engagement tonight?

MABEL   (nervously) You're in such a hurry to see what they'll say?

PELTIER   (joyfully) If you only knew how little I care about that. But I want to trap you so there's no way for you to get out of it.

MABEL   (still nervous) That's it, make it irreversible as quickly as possible!

PELTIER   Now, Mabel, you must kiss me.

MABEL   (seriously) No. That's very serious.

PELTIER   (reproachfully) See, I'm right to be diffident. (Fervently) Until I hold you in my arms I shan't believe anything!

MABEL   (very affected) Leave me, let me alone for a little while. (Gives a slight sob.)

PELTIER   (hearing a door open and voices in the next room, makes an irritated gesture) This house is completely impossible. When, where shall I see you again?

MABEL   It's Miss Delisle. I think you'd better go.

PELTIER   Miss Delisle can find us having a tête-à-tête.

MABEL   Not with the way you look. You're quite capable of not even being polite. (Softly) Trust me, Peltier, and take yourself off. Leave me to deal with her.

PELTIER   I feel a foreboding. I shan't find you again as you've just been. I already see the scene: there are only goodbyes!

MABEL   Go on, please. I won't be able to control myself if you're here, but it would be much better if it's me she finds.

(The door opens. PELTIER obeys.)

Scene 4

MABEL and SIMONE

SIMONE   I don't know where my aunt is . . .

MABEL   No one ever knows . . . I think she's gone out.

SIMONE   I hope it's not like the other day . . . when the victoria came back empty and she got in it without a hat on, without a cloak . . . and exhausted the horses by careering across the countryside all day long. She covered 60 kilometres. Everyone saw her go by hatless and in only a light dress. They're going to say she's gone mad.

MABEL   (sharply) She's in her right mind.

SIMONE   She's at such a loose end . . . I think it's her arm. She can't ride a horse any more, nor make music, nor hold a needle.

MABEL   It's not her arm that stops her from reading.

SIMON   If only she still saw a few people . . . we don't count, she's never with us. But her neighbours. Why doesn't she go and see poor Madame de Tragannat who also lost her son? Mme de Tragannat lives for her memories, waiting to see her son in heaven. She is so courageous.

MABEL   (deeply) He remains her great hope.

SIMONE   (continuing) She's wonderful.

MABEL   (in the same voice) Oh dear, is it wonderful to be consoled?

SIMONE   She would do my aunt good.

MABEL   But you see that Marguerite avoids her. (Sadly) It's natural, she doesn't have faith in such a meeting.

SIMONE *(dogmatically)* I don't understand how my aunt can go on living if she doesn't believe in the beyond.

MABEL To die . . . if it were enough just not to be able to live.

SIMONE Anyway, she still has Jean. She doesn't look as if she knows he is anything more to her than you or me . . . I even wonder if she would suffer much if Jean happened to do anything completely vile . . . to hand in his resignation, for instance. *(She watches the effect this has produced on MABEL.)* Am I shocking you, Lady Mabel?

MABEL Because among all the men on earth you prefer those who have chosen to be specialists in courage and devotion?

SIMONE If you think that too, why do you fight them?

MABEL I don't fight them. I'm serving them. I don't want them to get killed.

SIMONE *(peremptorily).* You're not logical.

MABEL *(smiling)* You, on the other hand, Mademoiselle Simone, you are logic itself. You do not want war to stop killing them, because you want to love a soldier.

SIMONE If it depended on me to prevent war . . .

MABEL *(calm and grave)* It depends uniquely on you.

SIMONE You're making fun of me. But if I disarmed him . . .

MABEL Who asked you to do that? Let the soldiers busy themselves with their arms and you, like other women, confine yourself to women's business, be a specialist in peace.

SIMONE *(bursting out)* I'm convinced that peace is a utopian dream.

MABEL *(mocking)* Then I have to start by convincing you of quite the opposite . . . because conviction is enough to bring about everything one wants, black or white, for or against, peace or war. There is no reality in the world except in our convictions.

SIMONE That's too hard for me to grasp.

MABEL I'll make it easy for you . . . it is enough to say that a thing is fatal to make it probably fatal in fact. The woman who declares, "I am bound to give in" is not exactly arming for the fight. It might take a long time alongside competent men before you learned how little war is inevitable. But, believe me, learn to say, without even believing it, since you don't, "Peace is not a utopian dream."

SIMONE And then?

MABEL *(smiling)* They say that women's power lies in their ability to go on saying the same thing for 20 years . . . as well as repeating the opposite.

SIMONE If words were enough . . .

MABEL First set words against words and you will be amazed to see how actions fall into step with them.

SIMONE I wish I could believe you.

MABEL *(who has had enough of the young girl, goes towards the door)* No, my dear, you don't wish anything of the sort.

(MABEL stays in the room, seeing DELISLE entering by the terrace.)

Scene 5

MABEL, SIMONE, DELISLE, JEAN *and* PELTIER

DELISLE *(to his daughter)* Do you know where your aunt is?

SIMONE She's not in her room.

DELISLE But I must let her know we're leaving. I shall have to find her.

SIMONE By all means, but if you think that'll be easy . . . She may be with the woodcutters, and they are at the far end today, at the top of the trees. *(Noticing JEAN and PELTIER ready to go out together, calls through the window)* Jean, do you know where my aunt is?

JEAN *(who doesn't know either)* Probably with the woodcutters.

SIMONE *(without enthusiasm)* You're not sure?

MABEL I'll go and look for her for you. I need a walk. I'll bring her back with me.

DELISLE *(to his daughter)* You ought to show Lady Mabel the path. Come on, shake yourself, you're always scared of walking.

JEAN She refused to come with us.

DELISLE *(to the two men)* Are you going far?

(LADY MABEL and SIMONE disappear together.)

JEAN As far as the signal-station. I've a telegram to send.

DELISLE Does the General have anything to do at the signal-station?

PELTIER Nothing at all . . . I'm yours to command if you want anything.

DELISLE Thanks, Peltier, I really wanted to talk to you. I'm leaving and shall scarcely have seen you.

JEAN   I'm off, it's going to rain. The ladies were wrong to set out for the woodcutters. *(He leaves.)*

Scene 6

PELTIER *and* DELISLE

DELISLE   I'm called back to Paris. I swear, General, that you're all I regret leaving behind at Lehane. My sister's thoughts are far away. My nephew . . . I'll talk to you about that later. Lady Mabel is interesting, so charming, but I find her suspicious – or at least I don't have her sympathy . . . But there's you, Peltier, we have had a few, brief moments. *(He has taken his time to arrive at what he wants to say.)* Are you planning to stay on here a little longer?

PELTIER   No – at least I don't think so! *(Correcting himself)* We haven't yet spoken to Madame de Gestel.

DELISLE   *(stealing a glance at him)* Forgive me! You have no friend, no more enthusiastic fan than myself . . . May I . . You are not aiming to leave with me . . . you're not aiming to leave at all!

PELTIER   *(very coolly)* I would be grateful to you, Delisle, for not venturing further in that direction.

DELISLE   *(as if he had recieved an open avowal)* Ah! *(Abandoning the subject)* They are deluding themselves with hopes in Paris. That Graham Moore is intelligent. He has Wilson's authority on his side. For you who have chosen, and been married to war for 20 years, doesn't it all affect you?

PELTIER   *(gravely)* My vocation is not a warlike wedding. In so far as men have the duty to risk themselves for their country, one can wish to be among them, that's all.

DELISLE   And you would have no regrets to see this duty disappear?

PELTIER   No regrets, certainly, none at all. I have a loaded memory. I know too many of the realities this duty represents. Without nostalgia, perhaps not, but that is entirely personal. And when there would still be a share in sacrifice . . .

DELISLE   *(losing his self-control)* Reason like that and you'll finish by resigning . . . especially when other longings . . .

PELTIER   *(his voice altered)* You absolutely insist on talking about it?

DELISLE   *(with pent-up violence)* A man such as you dies in uniform.

PELTIER   I would never give up my uniform, you've nothing to fear on that score!

DELISLE   *(as if he had received a second avowal)* Permanent peace. Perhaps they'll make it one day, that's their affair. But it's a long way away, very far away from us! France could suffer the suprise of an unprovoked attack.

PELTIER   *(who has not moved, whispering)* I will be there!

DELISLE   If you were only a soldier. We're not fanatics. But you're in the first rank of the national defence. The man who is charged with taking advance measures, with commanding future sacrifice, future slaughter if you like, cannot live in the incredulous atmosphere of pacifism. He cannot draw from the eyes of a woman in mourning, in the arms of a rebellious woman, the assurance, the calm, the certainty of accomplishing the necessary work, the indispensable work, the supreme mission of salvation!

PELTIER   *(very wearily)* Obviously not; you're right.

DELISLE   *(in another tone of voice, determined to have done with it)* Then this is sacrifice, Peltier? These are goodbyes? I'm ten years older than you, let me . . . I am a leader too, in my way, close to the same rank as yourself. Both of us are answerable to France, not in the face of peace, but in the face of enemy forces. Perhaps our role is restraint. Voices which can speak loudly may one day silence ours, it's possible, I don't deny it. It's possible that this woman is right and I am wrong. It's possible she serves my country better than I do. It's possible that she's admirable and more worthy of your passion than anyone else. But what I do know is this: that you have no right at all to love her.

(PELTIER is very gloomy and keeps silent. DELISLE recovers all his charm as a "master", as a seducer of men.)

DELISLE   She has never appeared to me more affecting, I have never been so near to kissing the hem of her robe, than today when I behave like her mortal enemy, when I withdraw your love from her . . . because you do understand, Peltier, that there can be no subterfuge, even a liaison is impossible!

PELTIER   *(making an abrupt gesture)* She

wouldn't allow it and I . . . free as she is . . . it would be an insult.

DELISLE It would be enough for people to talk . . . you would be suspected . . . Just yesterday I spent the day in town summoned by a telegram from Captain Milhaud to meet him there.

PELTIER *(startled)* Milhaud? Without my orders? Without my knowledge?

DELISLE Your aide-de-camp had superior orders . . . he was coming simply to make enquiries.

PELTIER *(exasperated by the proceedings)* Stop. Such proceedings are within an inch of a resignation.

DELISLE If you had heard Milhaud! If the General does not take care . . . he has enemies. He will be obliged to leave the army. He must remain with us. Besides, what other activity do you see him in? At his age, you don't retire.

PELTIER I shall never leave the army. No one will ever make me leave it. They're not going to shove me out by the shoulders!

DELISLE General, those are pointless words. You know quite well that without seizing you by the shoulders . . .

PELTIER *(impatiently)* You have been determined to meddle in what does not concern you. You have muddled matters up for pleasure. Your imagination has worked out all the eventualities. Can't you see that in the situation I find myself in, no one from the outside can make me take a decision? What I shall do . . . we shall see. I am old enough to give it mature consideration.

DESLISLE I spoke to you in the name of our country . . . a little on behalf of Captain Milhaud.

PELTIER No thank you . . . I don't want your advice.

(At the moment when the two of them are about to leave the room, JEAN appears.)

Scene 7

DELISLE Has your mother come home yet?

JEAN *(preoccupied)* No one has seen her since lunch. If she's not here in the next quarter of an hour, I'm setting off to search for her.

PELTIER Rely on her usual way of behaving . . .

JEAN Yes, she keeps disappearing more than is polite and I don't know how to excuse her to you . . .

PELTIER Good heavens!

JEAN But today, really she's gone beyond the limit . . . I've been all round and no one has seen her anywhere.

PELTIER If Madame de Gestel is not here in a quarter of an hour, we'll all set out to meet her.

(PELTIER leaves with DELISLE. JEAN installs himself in an armchair from where he can look out of the window. He glances at his watch. A CHAMBERMAID in a headdress brings in two lamps.)

JEAN Marivonne, ask someone to light a lantern and bring it to me here. Madame is not home yet and it's about to get dark.

MARIVONNE Madame is back. The dogs have just arrived and for sure they were with her. I heard her whistle to them before going out.

(The peasant-woman exits. JEAN gets up and looks out over the borders of the terrace, then he opens the French windows. Two big sheep-dogs rush in with a strong gust of wind.)

Scene 8

JEAN *and* MARGUERITE

JEAN *(distressed)* Mother, where have you been? We've been looking for you at the woodcutters. I was about to set off again.

MARGUERITE *(with a great peasant's mantle but bare-headed; she has her gloves on)* I was on the beach.

JEAN On the beach at this time, at high tide when there isn't any beach?

MARGUERITE I had my back up against the cliff.

JEAN *(looking at her)* Your hair is drenched. You haven't got your feet wet?

MARGUERITE It was the spray. The sea was so close, the waves were breaking with such force, I could feel it all through my body . . . they took the place of my heart.

JEAN You could have been cut off.

MARGUERITE It wouldn't have been the first time that I was caught on the rocks!

JEAN *(beside himself)* With your arm . . . Mother! Even for me that would have been dangerous.

MARGUERITE *(almost merrily)* Do you

remember the day when we got caught with Gerald, coming back from the signal-station? I had on a white dress and white stockings and shoes . . . when we had to wade through the water they took turns to carry me. In the end night fell, Gerald had used up all his matches. You were little and you made a fuss, you grizzled. We were in the middle of the rocks when you suddenly categorically refused to go on . . .

JEAN *(surprised and happy to hear her speak about the past)* You know we narrowly missed being stranded there.

MARGUERITE *(who is getting more and more animated)* Hang it, I know quite well. They grabbed you by the scruff of the neck . . .

JEAN *(correcting her)* By my tennis belt.

MARGUERITE They passed you from hand to hand. They shouted: "Come on, Jean, come on, Mother, keep your chin up, we're only 20 yards from the steps up the cliff."

JEAN *(also caught up by the memories)* We'd gone a long way but we were always 20 yards from the steps.

MARGUERITE *(suddenly passing a hand over her face)* Where is everyone?

JEAN A fine time to ask me that. They're looking for you. They're a bit politer than you are, Mother.

MARGUERITE *(who is scarcely listening, walks up and down the room)* Oh!

JEAN They were anxious enough to go as far as the top woods. The woodcutters are a long way away today. We thought you were with them . . . They'll be back by dinner. *(To* MARGUERITE, *who is moving away)* Where are you going, Mother? Can't you stay still for a bit?

MARGUERITE What do you want me to do here?

JEAN Talk to me a little.

MARGUERITE You've got something to tell me?

JEAN *(laughing)* Can't I talk to you even when I've got nothing to tell you? Give me your cape and sit down. *(*MARGUERITE *gives him her mantle but stays on her feet to wander about the room.* JEAN *carries her mantle to the vestibule.)* Mother, I'm getting old and I shall go raving mad. I have a horror of you walking round me.

MARGUERITE You're annoying me.

JEAN When people are really active, Mother, and they can't stay in one place, they get busy. *(Unable to stand it any longer)* You do nothing. You don't even attend to your guests and it's me that orders the meals.

MARGUERITE It was to tell me that?

JEAN No, for something else, but that escaped into the bargain. Mother, why don't you read anything, not even a newspaper?

MARGUERITE *(defends herself, soothingly)* But I do read the papers.

JEAN *(looking for a test)* What do you think of the report about Graham Moore?

MARGUERITE I haven't read that yet.

JEAN I think the headlines stare you in the face.

MARGUERITE As soon as I get a book in my hands, I think of something else.

JEAN *(reproaching her sadly)* Mother!

MARGUERITE *(sharply)* No, no, it's not what you think. But it's true that I find it hard to concentrate on anything.

JEAN You must react . . . you absolutely must interest yourself in something . . . even if it's only in me.

MARGUERITE Darling Jean, I love you, but if you knew how everything . . .

JEAN Come on, say it!

MARGUERITE Everything which concerns me . . . it all seems to be to do with someone else, some stranger . . . Me, I was the woman in a white dress in the middle of you all . . . This person I don't know any more, I don't want to be her.

JEAN Mother, you are too young to let yourself go; at 45 you have years in front of you; you've got to fill them!

MARGUERITE Don't talk nonsense!

JEAN You must stir yourself, occupy yourself, not live here as if it were someone else's home: give orders, know what is happening . . . listen, read, talk, not run wild, whistling to the dogs or sitting in a chair gazing at empty space.

MARGUERITE If that amuses me . . .

JEAN But it's not doing you any good.

MARGUERITE I don't need what does me good. I don't need anything, I don't want anything.

JEAN You can't spend your life in despair.

MARGUERITE But I am very calm. You can see, I don't cry. I don't hide myself away to cry, I promise you.

JEAN But you are broken-hearted.

MARGUERITE *(brusquely)* At the very least.

JEAN And you want me to help in that. But I love you, Mother. Can't I bring any sweetness into your life?

MARGUERITE   There was a great sweetness and it's gone. You were in it, you too, my little Jean. I love you because you are one of them. But the Jean of after, like the me of after, that doesn't exist any more. It's like with the books, I can't fix my attention . . . don't ask that of me.

(JEAN *has managed to get her to sit down, and he is on his knees on the floor, with his arms around her.)*

MARGUERITE   *(not too sadly)* They were so nice about being your big brothers! They would say, "Mother's boy" as if you were closer to me. I had no worries when they were around. Nothing could happen to you. The moment you fell in the water or got too near the fire, always a great stride, a rapid grasp . . . they were so quick.

JEAN   I remember too . . . life may have cruelty in store for me but I shall never be gloomy, Mother, because of the rays of morning sunshine that shone on me in your home.

MARGUERITE   I can only see them again in happiness . . . even at the moment of leaving . . . after that I can't do any more. I would, but I can't follow them into the horror. *(Her nightmare is going to take hold of her again.)*

JEAN   *(rocking her in his arms)* There's no horror, Mother. They died for France! *(*MARGUERITE *wrestles with a powerful emotion.)* Think of them again on the day of the cliff . . . They were in white like you . . . They kept calling to us: "Come on, Jean, come on, Mother, keep your chin up!"

MARGUERITE   They kept theirs up right to the end.

JEAN   *(reproachfully)* Mother! We don't know anything . . . perhaps they died very gently.

(With a start MARGUERITE *releases herself from his arms, springs up to escape and runs into her brother, who is just entering the room.)*

DELISLE   *(shocked)* Marguerite . . . what is it?
JEAN   *(clenching his fists)* Let her go.

*(*MARGUERITE *disappears.)*

Scene 9

JEAN *and* DELISLE

DELISLE   But what's the matter with your mother? What were you talking about?

JEAN   *(curtly)* Gerald.
DELISLE   *(alarmed)* Oh. *(After a pause)* What did she tell you?
JEAN   I think, I am convinced that she knows how Gerald died.
DELISLE   *(tapping his foot)* She doesn't.
JEAN   *(bluntly)* Do *you* know then?
DELISLE   No, but . . .
JEAN   *(fiercely)* You both know. I have the right too. If they finished him off . . . I can spend my whole life, all my strength, in getting revenge for the crime. There may be greater tasks in the world, but there won't be for me.
DELISLE   *(very pale)* There was no crime. Calm down. The Major wrote to me.
JEAN   *(breathing heavily)* Ah! the Major . . .

(But DELISLE *is trembling, unable to go on.)*

DELISLE   I agree with you, you do have the right to know, the duty perhaps . . . *(With a gasp)* His skull was torn away by machine-gun fire . . . the brain was left exposed for 29 hours.
JEAN   *(his hands clenched against his breast)* But perhaps he felt nothing . . . a coma?
DELISLE   He was howling. *(*JEAN *goes limp, clasping his hands to his chest, he doesn't move.* DELISLE, *facing him, his head down, has lost control. He pants.)* Never let your mother know that you know.

Curtain

Act IV

MABEL's *room, at night. The window is wide open and from top to bottom only stars are visible through it. The Great Bear can be clearly made out. In full view on the mantelpiece is a large photograph of an officer in khaki. Around the room are the same red sages that blazed in the salon.* MABEL *is still dressed, but her hair is down on her shoulders in two plaits. She is writing at a small table. The bed is turned back for the night. There is a knock at the door.* MABEL *lifts her head in surprise. The knock comes again.*

Scene 1

MABEL *and* JEAN

MABEL   Come in! *(*JEAN *comes in silently. Without taking off his cape he removes his hat and goes to lean his back against the foot of*

75

the bed, facing MABEL, *who asks anxiously)* Where have you been? It's midnight.

JEAN It's done.

MABEL What's done?

JEAN I've been to the post; my resignation has gone off.

MABEL Be careful not to act too quickly.

JEAN There was nothing to hesitate for . . . My mind was made up a long time ago . . . All that was needed was something in my heart, I don't know what, to give me the will to do it . . . whatever takes you by the shoulders, outside of yourself . . . I have been waiting. *(Very moved)* The incident has just been of use to me, it's helped me with interest! . . . *(He stops speaking.* MABEL *waits, hands joined together fervently, stretched out, but without triumph.)* There's something personal I must say . . . perhaps we need that . . . *(Very simply and rapidly)* I know how Gerald died . . . (MABEL, *not changing her attitude, turns her head towards the portrait of her brother and keeps her eyes there.*) I thought at first that my brother died on the battlefield . . . To live to avenge him? That idea came to me. But it wasn't that . . . it was worse . . . (MABEL *keeps her eyes on the portrait on the mantelpiece.)* The crime was worse . . . but the killer escaped me! . . . So anonymous, so formidable, so untouchable . . . I will avenge my brother's agony! I, too, shall say: I want no more of it, I resist . . . (MABEL *has closed her eyes; she remains withdrawn, in an attitude of suffering.)* Lady Mabel, do you think that there is anything to be done in this country?

MABEL *(opening her eyes brightly)* Lots. More than anywhere else.

JEAN *(still leaning on the end of the bed)* Without having wealth like yours at my disposal, I too have inherited something from the war . . . The inheritance of my brothers has made me rich. *(Roughly)* Such a fortune can't just be spent like any other . . . I don't want to keep any of it.

MABEL I understand you. Be calm. You will have work to do. You can lay the foundations in France.

JEAN *(after a while, his voice low and distinct, harsh with emotion)* The sacrifice is immense, harder than you can imagine . . . The ambition to continue . . . to follow in my brothers' footsteps . . . I can only see myself as a soldier. I loved that profession as a monk loves the rules of his order. I loved it to the point of scandal, to the mark in our flesh . . . to silence and passion.

MABEL There will still be a need for soldiers, Jean. They'll be necessary for a long time yet!

JEAN I know there won't be a lack of them, whereas others . . . Lady Mabel, you're right: the heart will do nothing, look at women, they push the wheel. Intelligence will do nothing, look at my uncle, he's asking for a second helping! But man, energy, virile action? Let's leave the ulcer to grow in the flank of our country because that fight pleases us less, because it is newer and more unprofitable, badly maintained by women and the mob . . . Because, alas, let's admit it, because we are loved better as soldiers of war than as soldiers of peace? Yes, what I like in myself and what I adore in my profession, is that call to the heart, the enthusiasm, the highest image of myself that I was taught to dream of . . .

MABEL *(whispering)* You are not ripe for resignation. *(Warmly)* You will be a soldier no less than your brothers. You will serve your country magnificently . . . and perhaps one day you will have to give your life for it . . .

JEAN *(thankfully)* You do find the right things to say!

MABEL *(gets up, goes over to him and takes his hands)* I'm very fond of you, Jean.

JEAN *(getting back to a gruffer emotion)* Perhaps I hadn't suffered enough . . . I didn't understand until today the truth of what you've been saying . . . Since the war, with that experience, we can't live any more as we used to in the past. Our one-time careers, our passions, our activities . . . childishness, thoughtlessness, miserable distractions . . . the condemned who gamble, who smoke and drink with the guards right up to the dawn! I want to prepare an escape. Like the Christians called up the idea of death, I want to call up the idea of war, and startle people with it, make them work for this other salvation, closer and more human, but which men are no more lukewarm about, more feeble or more indifferent . .

MABEL *(ardently)* Fine battles call to you . . . don't regret all the others.

JEAN *(dully)* If it had only been up to me, I would have asked for nothing more than suicide on the next battlefield. *(With growing strength)* Because really what can we be expected to do? What is left in the world? Family, love, patriotism, art, science, kindness . . . what good are they if my effort has to stop when it had scarcely begun to serve them? What good is all that if I must not lift a finger towards the only effective defence? What good is all that if I accept in advance the threat of their destruction?

MABEL If only others possessed your sense of responsibility . . . But here, like everywhere, responsibilities are shrugged off. No one feels responsible for peace. The most clear-sighted, the best forewarned, it's almost insane to say it: *They lack zeal!* The idea that they could take over the reins themselves doesn't even enter their minds. Oh, when you cry, when you suffer sackcloth and ashes, when you outlive your own heart, surviving those who are dead for our cowardice, you have what you deserve. You weep at the slaughter of your sons, hypocrite nations, then just raise a finger so that their agony should be spared tomorrow! If only all nations, all states were not gasping before a future threatened by their peace, by their "victory", if only an order could descend from on high: "Enough! Once and for all, enough!" *(There comes a knock, this time at the other door, the door to her dressing-room.)* Is that you, Marguerite? Come in!

Scene 2

MARGUERITE *enters.*

MARGUERITE Graham Moore has just arrived. He's with my brother and asking if he can come up.

MABEL *(full of life)* Moore? At such a late hour? Then he has bad news?

MARGUERITE *(turns and sees* JEAN, *greatly astonished)* What on earth are you doing here?

JEAN Don't be surprised, Mother. I was giving Lady Mabel a piece of news more important to her than to you.

MARGUERITE At this time of night! That's very indiscreet.

JEAN I saw from the window that her light was still on.

SIMONE *(at the dressing-room door, a lamp in her hand, a dressing-gown on over her nightdress, and a becoming cap covering her*

curlers) The gentlemen are asking if they may see you . . .

MABEL Well of course, ask them up.

(She pulls up the bedclothes and rearranges the bedspread. JEAN *leaves the room with* SIMONE *before the visitors arrive.)*

MARGUERITE Fortunately no one had gone to bed yet. Mr Moore never comes this late . . . Have you noticed the stars tonight? They are splendid.

MABEL They make me afraid . . . They fill me with horror!

MARGUERITE *(surprised)* Oh Mabel, the stars?

MABEL *(violently)* They are so alien! Haven't they kept looking at us like that ever since they could do nothing for us!

Scene 3

SIMONE lights the way in for MOORE, DELISLE and JEAN, *followed by* PELTIER.

MOORE *(going to* MABEL *and seizing her by the arms)* Take heart, Mabel! The Congress is breaking up. Not one of our measures has been carried. I didn't want you to find out tomorrow from the papers.

MABEL *(weakly)* Not even . . .

MOORE Nothing at all. To each of my motions, one voice – mine. *(*MABEL *gives a nervous giggle.)* Don't let go, my dear!

DELISLE *(decently)* What do you expect them to do? It was certain that public opinion wasn't ready, it wouldn't have followed them.

MOORE *(sarcastically)* That's what everyone told me. Each one repeated to me, "If it was only up to me, or up to my government . . . but we have to look to the country! Opinion would be against us." I am their leader, so I must follow them. "Get the public on your side first, and then you can count on us." These polite nothings never cease: "After you, please. No, after *you*," until the day when someone has the nerve to resolutely go first . . . and not even to be very surprised to see each one follow after him, in an orderly succession.

JEAN Meanwhile, it's a lost cause.

MOORE *(always unconstrained and determined)* We'll have to start again. Perhaps we'll have to go on until the atomic bombs predicted by H. G. Wells; it's true of course that their declining conflagration *(ironically)* could last months and transform the capitals of Europe into so many volcanic furnaces, unapproachably hot . . . perhaps we'll see the earth rased of towns, that is: rased of the past, of human beings.

DELISLE   *(to* MOORE*)* What are you going to do now?

MOORE   Try the parliamentary way. That will drag on . . . trying to alert public opinion.

DELISLE   I rather think that we are entering a resolutely militarist period . . . War, a treaty, even a congress, only generates conflicts, wrangling, indefinite struggles.

MOORE   *(definitely)* I absolutely agree with you. It's the impossibility of arriving at any solution whatever . . . I'm hardly encouraging, am I! *(Squeezing* MABEL*'s hands)* You have to forgive me . . . it's not my fault . . . Are you going to be able to sleep?

MABEL   I can hardly stand it. But if you have brought me harsh news, I can go one better. *(Pointing to* JEAN*)* Here is a collaborator!

MOORE   *(astonished)* An army officer?

JEAN   Not any more!

MOORE   *(awkwardly)* Has he resigned?

DELISLE   You haven't done that!

JEAN   Don't reproach me, uncle, considering it's you who made up my mind.

DELISLE   Oh yes, you said that before, just after our conversation.

JEAN   *(gently)* No, no, it wasn't our conversation . . . just a few words later, before dinner – do you remember? *(His face contracted,* DELISLE *looks at his nephew, very upset.)*

MARGUERITE   What did your uncle say?

DELISLE   *(very troubled)* It wasn't what your brothers would have asked of you?

JEAN   *(gently)* How do you know? What right have you got to speak on their behalf? I was closer to them in the trenches. I have seen what they saw . . . I have thought what they thought.

*(*MARGUERITE *looks intently from one to the other, but asks no questions.)*

SIMONE   There is another side to the question. I think it can't be very important to you, Jean, because you haven't spoken to me about your decision . . . But it's a matter of course that it would mean the end of our joint projects.

JEAN   You did tell me that. But I swear I never thought that . . . the idea that a woman could put that price on her love . . . the everlasting acceptance of war.

SIMONE   I have sworn only to marry a soldier!

MABEL   *(moved)* The day when each woman in the world will be so resolute about what concerns her as to dedicate her life to peace, that she will be so convinced that, next to death on the battlefield, there is nothing finer than a life of action and struggle for peace, that she will resolve to bring up her sons . . .

SIMONE   I want my sons to be soldiers!

MABEL   In future we shall need soldiers to take up all kinds of arms, we shall need soldiers for peace. They won't be less brave, less adventurous, nor less warlike.

SIMONE   Then even I would make pacifists of them, but it's not that . . .

MABEL   Yes, it's precisely that . . . The part each one can play towards the common good. There's no greater force in the world.

SIMONE   I don't want to harm my country.

MABEL   *(drawing herself up)* My dear child, you have nothing to teach me about the way to serve one's country!

MOORE   Come on, it'll take time to get the women on your side. *(Looking at* MABEL*)* For each one who is a fanatic like her, there are also others! *(He gestures towards* MARGUERITE, *who is sitting aside: lost in her own thoughts, she hasn't even heard.)*

SIMONE   *(lifting her chin, her voice ringing out)* Because I am convinced, Mr Moore, that peace is a utopian dream.

DELISLE   *(annoyed)* Keep your voice down.

SIMONE   There have always been wars, and there always will be. Humankind is a sad thing. While men exist, you won't be able to stop them from throwing themselves at each other's throats.

JEAN   *(making a violent gesture which stops three inches from* SIMONE*'s mouth)* You are in Gerald and Louis's home. Shut up! *(Completely silenced,* SIMONE *is near to tears.)*

MARGUERITE   Jean, you're behaving outrageously. I thought you were going to hit Simone.

JEAN   *(looking at his uncle)* That's not *my* job. Why don't you get this little wretch to hold her tongue?

DELISLE *(with a certain acerbity)* Because that would be as useless as your gesture, Jean. After all, Simone has only expressed her natural acceptance . . .

MABEL *(cries out)* Natural!

JEAN Such acceptance is revolting enough, but it's absolutely scandalous coming from a woman. *(He is pale and severe, but calm enough.)*

SIMONE *(snivelling)* But I didn't mean . . . I know quite well that soldiers are heroes.

JEAN Every man is a soldier in wartime.

SIMONE *(in the same way)* I only meant that you couldn't prevent it.

JEAN *(looking at her unkindly)* Heroes devour each other.

(SIMONE bursts into tears.)

MARGUERITE Leave Simone alone. Can't you see what you've done to her?

JEAN She is very easily touched. She has plenty of tears when it comes to herself. But I've seen enough. We've got to get rid of the woman who, in the face of women in mourning for their sons, in the face of men of action and thinkers who devote body and soul to work for peace, dares to recite her old tale of inertia.

SIMONE *(turning her face to her aunt)* Goodnight, Aunt Marguerite. *(From the door she turns to address JEAN)* I don't understand what you are blaming me for. It doesn't seem to me that war and peace depend on me . . . but that I am innocent . . .

JEAN *(wanting justice)* It is innocents like you who let antiquated ideas drag on, the state of mind which lets war go on being possible . . .

(SIMONE goes out.)

MARGUERITE *(to her son)* You have been unspeakably abusive.

MOORE *(to JEAN)* You are one of us . . . you carry the flaming torch of peace.

JEAN It's time to raise the horse-whip, to frighten their complacency and vanity . . . let the sceptics go somewhere else and see if they are fit in any other respect. Peace too is a matter of public welfare. They hawk bad news around. Here is a state of martial law; elsewhere, mouths and arms and hearts are of no use.

MOORE *(unrestrained)* Enough! every reform in the world is made of an attack on fantasy and utopia . . . In 50 years such people will be reproaching us for breaking down an open door.

MARGUERITE *(sighing)* In 50 years! . . . in a hundred years perhaps, from now till then . . .

MOORE *(without constraint)* From now to then the world is uninhabitable. Shame on those who would forget it! *(To MARGUERITE)* Goodbye, Madame, count on us. We're not afraid of the stigma, whatever they say, we're only up against a few of them. Everything in this world is a struggle of a few with a few. The masses are only an illusion.

MARGUERITE It's all the same to me. I've given everything already.

JEAN *(softly)* Not quite, Mother!

(MOORE makes his goodbyes and leaves with the other men. Jean lights the way.)

Scene 4

MARGUERITE Perhaps there are others who will be able to live again . . .

MABEL Who will be able to sleep, love, think . . . Your brother will look for rhymes and your niece for embroidery patterns . . . Each one will pick up their own hobby again and think about other things . . . They will forget, they'll forget everything! *(She gives a bleak laugh, like a mad woman.)*

MARGUERITE My brother isn't so indifferent, really. He's looking for ways to ensure peace . . . a space of time, to limit conflicts.

MABEL What an illusion! That really is a utopian dream! It takes no account of war! It's less impossible to finish with the existing system once and for all than to hope for something else from this system than provisional peace, short-term truces. If only each one of us knew, imagined, represented to ourselves in earnest what our diplomats, our statesmen know today, the desperate world would run mad.

MARGUERITE *(kissing her before leaving)* My poor child! And all the same you are going to set yourself that task!

MABEL I couldn't go on living otherwise.

MARGUERITE Well, after all, you've found a reason to live. It's as good as any other! Good night.

MABEL *(excitably)* Can you tell me any better reason?

MARGUERITE *(leaving abruptly)* There are other reasons one can do without!

Scene 5

PELTIER *enters slowly through the door left open on the lit corridor, without closing the door throughout the scene.*

PELTIER   I leave at six in the morning. So I shan't see you again . . . it hurts me to see you in such distress. *(MABEL is suffering silently, screwed up in pain.)* Mabel, give it up – it's hopeless. Be content with the precarious happiness a soldier can offer you.

MABEL   *(without looking up)* You are right . . . Leave . . Go and work for France, she needs you . . . Go and prepare for the atrocious war that is coming tomorrow. *(She recalls JEAN's words)* "So savage and so monstrous that this one will seem merciful beside it". Go on!

PELTIER   *(gently)* The world will become peaceful little by little, do believe it . . . but it will take time. You can't rush the work of time.

MABEL   *(with increasing passion)* Time! But what is time if it's not human beings? What is time if it's not their actions? From century to century, you wait for time to bring a man of energy, a man of action. Really, is your generation so poor? Hasn't war taught you how to restore your strength and anticipate the work of time, that is to say, of other shoulders . . haven't you already got all you need to act?

PELTIER   *(looking for a way to calm her down)* It will all end . . . as everything comes to an end . . . war will fall into disuse . . .

MABEL   *(sadly)* And we shall have done nothing to bring that moment closer. It will end . . . after one, after 10, after 20 other wars. Everything has to start all over again. Waxen masks on death-beds again . . . that agony again, that exhaustion of the poor human face . . . that absolute misery, Christ's despair on the cross . . . All that for us, the survivors, because we haven't wanted, haven't known, haven't dared . . . perhaps because we haven't even wished. *(She is filled with distress, but continues, heart-rendingly)* Oh my best-beloved! When

you fought to grips with your agony, didn't you expect that at least a little of the force of that agony would pass into our hearts, to command an end to war? *(She breaks into sobs which shake her whole frame, but without making a sound and with a kind of restraint.)*

PELTIER   *(who is saying anything)* Mabel! my dear, don't give up, there's no need to cry!

MABEL   *(stopping a little, with a cold irony)* Oh really! There's no need to cry?

PELTIER   Don't poison the little space of time we have left to forget, to live . . .

MABEL   Oh, that space of time! Is it worth what it cost?

PELTIER   You must want happiness.

MABEL   *(getting up and looking at him, calmly and certainly)* You can't tempt me with happiness.

PELTIER   Oh Mabel!

MABEL   Everything is too horrible . . . Really, who wants happiness today? You have taught me how it is despised and everything that is preferred to it . . . I shall give up my life, my heart, my joy . . . I shall give up everything as they did. I don't want to keep anything.

PELTIER   *(imploringly)* Mabel, you don't have to go mad.

MABEL   I have the right to formulate not just a prayer, not a vow, but a command to all those who are responsible, a command I see as the only reason to go on living: War must never happen again.

PELTIER   *(very sadly)* Mabel, it will happen again . . . and you and I, we shall agree to it once again, for our country . . .

MABEL   "For our country"? Is there nothing else we can do for our countries than go on agreeing to this agony?

PELTIER   *(in the same way)* You put the question; others will resolve it.

MABEL   *(shouting)* Others? But where are those who really care about it? *(With a desperate gesture she pushes PELTIER away forever.)* Where are those who only want to live to make peace?

Curtain

5 Berta Lask 1878–1967

[Die Befreiung] Liberation
Germany

Introduction

When Berta Lask saw *Liberation* staged in 1925, she was 48 years old and well established in Berlin's theatrical world. Earlier that year she had scored a major triumph with *Thomas Münzer*, a play about the sixteenth-century German peasant uprising. Like *Liberation*, *Thomas Münzer* is a study of the processes of political revolution. Four hours long, it was performed in grand spectacular style during a communist rally in an open-air stadium at Eisleben, a small industrial town in Eastern Germany. Some three thousand workers flocked to see it and their enthusiasm was such that the police, though under orders to disperse the crowd, dared not move in. But henceforth Lask was marked down by the authorities as a dangerous left-wing agitator. In 1927, her documentary drama *Leuna 1921*, written at the request of the Leuna factory-workers and probably her best dramatic effort, was closed down during rehearsals. After this, none of her plays was ever again performed in public. When Hitler came to power in 1933, Lask chose exile in the Soviet Union, only returning to East Berlin 20 years later.

Born in 1878 in the Galician town of Wadowice, the daughter of a wealthy Jewish manufacturer, Lask had moved to Berlin in 1901 after her marriage to a welfare doctor. Her husband's work brought her into daily contact with the stark misery of urban working-class life, and this stimulated her interest in Marxist-Leninism and the revolutionary events then unfolding in Russia. Two of her early plays explore questions about the nature of civic power and social justice; neither was ever published. She was more successful with the poems she wrote from 1910 to 1920, which came out in two collections after the war and established her reputation as an Expressionist poet of considerable force. These poems are particularly interesting in that they bear witness to her development, over the crucial second decade of this century, from lyrical introspection to civic awareness and political commitment.

Indeed, in her fictional autobiography, *Stille und Sturm* (1955), Lask would come to identify the First World War as the single most important factor in her conversion from a bourgeois housewife to a socialist

Figure 6 Theatre placard for the first performance of Berta Lask's play, celebrating the tenth anniversary of Soviet endurance: *Gas Warfare against Soviet Russia!*, 8 July 1927.

revolutionary and writer of political literature. Her outrage at "the Great Massacre" forced her to abandon an individualist stance. From now on, three major aims alone were to determine her writing: to unmask the corrupt system of capitalism as manifested in the class structure, in nationalism and in militarism; to portray the explosive moment of revolution; and to invoke the prospect of a socialist utopia. She believed the role of women to be crucial to these three aims. From 1919, Lask began to produce a steady stream of dramatic poems, choral dramas, essays and politically explicit plays, in an effort to convert German workers to the socialist cause. She joined the Communist Party in 1923 and in the same year had her first major success with *Die Toten rufen* [The Dead are Calling], a dramatic poem about the death of Karl Liebknecht and Rosa Luxemburg. Performed in true agit-prop fashion by proletarian-speaking choirs, it became so popular that it had to be repeated more than 30 times all over Berlin, although it was never published.

Thus, for a brief time, Lask became one of the best-known and most discussed writers of political theatre in Berlin; so much so that, in August 1925, Erwin Piscator's high-profile Workers' Theatre Group staged her play *Liberation* at the Zentral-Theater. That Piscator should be interested in *Liberation* is hardly surprising, for just a few weeks earlier, he had made the headlines with a spectacular production of *Trotz alledem!* [In Spite of Everything], a cycle of 23 scenes showing political moments in Germany's history from 1914 to 1919 with a script drawn exclusively from authentic political documents. Lask's *Liberation*, with its loose succession of tableaux portraying recent political events as they affected ordinary people, offered him a ready opportunity to pursue his current interests. Furthermore, in calling for the extensive use of slide-projections and placards, Lask's play was picking up on the novel stage devices which Piscator had introduced a year earlier in his production of Alfons Paquet's *Fahnen* [Flags].

But *Liberation* has further traits which were at the cutting edge of dramatic innovation at the time. When, in the very first moments of the play, before the curtain even rises, a woman pops up from amongst the crowd to berate her fellow workers for wasting their time and money on the theatre's "bourgeois

lies", the way is prepared for an ongoing dialogue between the spectator and the stage. Twice more, the play *per se* is interrupted by similar altercations between the audience and the theatre director. These "Interludes" effectively create a frame which not only unifies the 16 disparate episodes but also establishes a mode of reception whereby the enactment of war and revolution in Germany and Russia becomes directly relevant to the onlooker in the theatre. These intrusions are of crucial importance to the impact of a play whose prime function was to engage the audience in a critical appraisal of the current political situation.

As a product of its age, *Liberation* also reflects many aspects of the Expressionist mode which had dominated the German stage since the turn of the century, including depersonalisation of the hero, stylisation of action, and sparse intensity of verbal expression. Lask's characters – her peasants, soldiers, woman fighters and neighbours – are clearly no more than types, and they function solely in terms of their public personae. This is true even of the two heroines Darja and Nasdja, who, despite enjoying proper names, could hardly claim real individuality. Introspection and psychological depth are of no concern to Lask. Moreover, her dialogue is clipped and laconic, and revolves in a most basic way around key issues such as survival, social justice, politics and revolution. Her 16 tableaux are brief, minimal, and, as the term suggests, static. They are like a series of snapshots with emphatic captions: the Russian peasants worrying about the outbreak of war, a German mother and her hungry children, a wartime food queue, a police raid, a battlefield, a conference of socialist women. These cameos are conceived as a political argument, so that the play abandons any individual story in order to foreground the logic and urgency of the socialist revolution, both for Germany and the world at large.

Is *Liberation*, then, strictly a war play? The main locus of the play is not the battlefield, nor the chambers of military strategists, as one might expect of a typical war drama. Instead we are presented with altercations on the home front, in the peasant cottage, in a woman's kitchen. In this regard, Lask is of course following an age-old tradition of "alternative" war plays: Aristophanes'

Lysistrata, Shakespeare's *Troilus and Cressida*, Brecht's *Mother Courage*. These are all plays that focus on the domestic impact of war rather than on the clash between embattled forces. Such plays implicitly subvert the dominant narratives of war. Unsurprisingly, such an approach is particularly attractive to women playwrights. Like most civilians, women are apt to experience war through its repercussions within the community. Hence a woman playwright might well seize upon a war as the pretext to explore the tensions that surface in a community *in extremis*.

This can be demonstrated by two other First World War plays by German women: Friede Kraze's *Erfüllungen* [Fulfilments] of 1915 and Ilse Langner's *Frau Emma kämpft im Hinterland* [Frau Emma Fights behind the Lines] of 1928. Kraze's play is symptomatic of the heady atmosphere and idealistic patriotism of the first year of the war. Ilse Langner wrote her war play more than a decade later, at a point when, having experienced defeat and revolution, along with social and economic turmoil, the German population had had time to reflect on the costs of the war. Both plays take place inside a German family home although, unlike Kraze, Langner depicts the war's practical impact on civilian lives. Though moving to a rather conciliatory resolution, *Frau Emma* is a celebration of the resourcefulness of women as well as an attack on traditional patriarchal values. As such, its message stands in marked contrast to the patriotic idealism of *Erfüllungen*. Nevertheless, in their form, both plays retain the conventional three acts and, in the tradition of the German *Gedankendrama* [Theatre of Thought], concentrate upon the development, in purely psychological and intellectual terms, of a few central figures.

The distinctiveness of Berta Lask's play could not be more pronounced. *Liberation* stands out for privileging the interest of the group over that of the individual, highlighting the political dimension rather than the psychological moment. In terms of form, it also heralds new departures. The use of slides and placards, the interaction between the public and the stage and, above all, the hurried tempo of the many short scenes combine to forge a dramatic idiom which lends impact to the play's revolutionary message.

Even so, it has to be acknowledged that *Liberation*, like *Erfüllungen* and *Frau Emma*, is a play rooted in its time. The unequivocal urgency with which it seeks to summon support for the revolution is clearly symptomatic of the extreme contemporary situation, when political polarisation into left and right factions was threatening to rip Weimar Germany apart. Lask's was of course by no means an isolated voice. International Socialism, in alignment with the revolution in Russia, was viewed by many German intellectuals as the only appropriate response to the lurch to the political right at grass-roots level at home. Playwrights such as Kaiser, Toller, Brecht and especially Piscator all wrote and produced political plays in the 1920s which, if not overtly socialist, put forward the case of the dispossessed and the exploited. But Lask went further than most of her contemporaries in her revolutionary zeal and uncompromising dedication to the communist ideal. This is why, as the decade drew to a close, she found herself in clear opposition to colleagues with whom she had worked only a few years earlier. By 1930 she was writing a blistering attack on Piscator, arguing that his political theatre was faltering for lack of ideological direction, and was in danger of selling out to defunct bourgeois values. By contrast, Lask maintained, the true proletarian revolutionary theatre, in spite of all its difficulties, was forging steadily ahead.

Today we can only view that faith ironically. Even so, *Liberation* must be admired for its optimism. Where other postwar playwrights portrayed hapless heroes floundering in a world corrupt beyond redemption, Lask offered hope and a way forward to audiences who had borne the brunt of a terrible war and its aftermath.

Yet it may be that what will most interest today's readership is Lask's view of the role of women. Particularly striking in her play is the spontaneity and naturalness with which women are shown to assume roles of power. At no point in the text is there any discussion about gender roles or whether women are actually suited to undertake "men's work": from the outset, women simply dominate the action. Indeed, Lask's portrayal of the role of women still has much to offer the women's cause of today. In her 1916 poem "Selbstgericht" [Self-Indictment], she insists that women are as much to blame for the catastrophe of war as men. With their traditional reluctance to get involved in politics, their acquiescence in the face of power, not to say their cowardice and laziness, women have made themselves just as culpable as men. The vigour of Lask's approach to the woman question is particularly striking if we turn to Kraze's *Erfüllungen*, where women are shown to be no more than passive, anguished bystanders in the war debate. Even in Langner's *Frau Emma*, the notion still persists that war, and by extension the public domain, are strictly man's purview. Perhaps the most important message of *Liberation*, still valid today, is its robust rallying-cry to women to "wake up", to declare themselves of age, and to assume responsibility in the shaping of the body politic.

Further reading

Primary

Eisenmenger, Anne (1932) *Blockade: The Diary of an Austrian Middle-class Woman 1914–24*, London: Constable.

Kollwitz, Hans (ed.) (1955) *The Diary and Letters of Käthe Kollwitz* (translated A. and C. Winston), Evanston: North Western University Press.

Kraze, Friede (1915) *Erfüllungen: ein Stück von heut für morgen* [Fulfilments: a Play of Today for Tomorrow], Stuttgart: Bonz.

Langner, Ilse [1928] (1979) *Frau Emma kämpft im Hinterland: Chronik in drei Akten* [Frau Emma Fights behind the Lines], Darmstadt: Neudruck.

Lask, Berta [1916] (1988) "Selbstgericht" [Self-Indictment] in *Deutsche Dichterinnen vom 16. Jahrhundert bis zur Gegenwart* [German Women Poets – from the 16th Century to the Present], Gisela Brinker (ed.), Frankfurt: Fischer, p. 302.

—— (1924) *Die Befreiung: 16 Bilder aus dem Leben der deutschen und russischen Frauen 1914–1920* [Liberation: 16 Tableaux from the Lives of German and Russian Women 1914–20], Berlin: Remmele.

—— [1929] (1980) "Frauen im Kampf: eine Erzählung aus dem Weltkrieg" [Women in Battle: a story from the World War] in Gisela Brinker (ed.) *Frauen gegen den Krieg* [Women against War], Frankfurt: Fischer.

—— [1955] (1974) *Stille und Sturm* [Calm and Storm], Mira Lask (ed.), Halle: Mitteldeutscher Verlag.

Lazars, Maria ("Esther Grenen") (1933) *Der Nebel von Dybern* [The Fog from Dybern], Berlin: Stettin.

Piscator, Erwin (1980) *The Political Theatre* (translated H. Rorrison), London: Methuen. (Originally published as *Das politische Theater* in 1929.)

Toller, Ernst (1935) *Transfiguration* in *Seven Plays* (translated E. Crankshaw *et al.*), London: John Lane. (Originally published as *Die Wandlung* in 1919.)

Secondary

Cardinal, Agnès (1993) "Women on the Other Side" in D. Goldman (ed.) *Women and World War I: the Written Response*, Basingstoke: Macmillan, pp. 31–50.

—— (1997) "Three First World War Plays by Women" in Wolfgang Görtschacher and Holger Klein (eds) *Modern War on Stage and Screen* [Der moderne Krieg auf der Bühne], Lampeter: Mellen, pp. 305–15.

Hoffmann, Ludwig and Daniel Hoffmann-Ostwald (1973) *Deutsches Arbeitertheater* [German Workers' Theatre] *1918–1933*, Munich: Rogner & Bernhard.

Loewenberg, Peter and Alyson Jackson (1996) "Germany on the Home Front (1) and (2)" in Hugh Cecil and Peter H. Liddle (eds) *Facing Armageddon: The First World War Experienced*, London: Lee Cooper, pp. 554–72.

Smith, Brian Keith (ed.) (1997) *A Library of German Women Writers 1900–33: Exemplary Readings with Biographies and Bibliographies*, Lampeter: Mellen.

Stürzer, Anne (1991) *Dramatikerinnen und Zeitstücke* [Women Dramatists and Plays of the Time], Stuttgart: Metzler.

Liberation [Die Befreiung] ————————————

[Sixteen Tableaux from the Lives of German and Russian Women 1914–1920]
First performed at Zentral-Theater, Berlin, August 1925
by Erwin Piscator's Workers' Theatre Group
Published in German 1924
Translated by Agnès Cardinal

Berta Lask

————————————————————————————

Characters

DARJA, a young Russian peasant

WASSIL, her husband

TWO CHILDREN

MITJA, brother of Wassil

MATRENA, his wife

NASDJA, a young Russian teacher

ANNA, a worker in Berlin

PAUL, her husband

ROBERT ⎫
          ⎬ their children
ERNST ⎭

LITTLE GIRL

NEIGHBOUR (female)

RUSSIAN NEIGHBOUR

WOMAN FIGHTER

1ST COMRADE FROM HAMBURG (female)

2ND COMRADE FROM HAMBURG (female)

3RD COMRADE FROM HAMBURG (female)

CLARA, a young worker

PERSIAN WOMAN

INDIAN WOMAN

WOMAN PEASANT FROM SIBERIA

1ST WOMAN

2ND WOMAN

3RD WOMAN

4TH WOMAN

OLD RUSSIAN PEASANT

OLD RUSSIAN WOMAN PEASANT

VILLAGE ELDERS

1ST RUSSIAN PEASANT

2ND RUSSIAN PEASANT

3RD RUSSIAN PEASANT

1ST MEMBER OF PARLIAMENT

2ND MEMBER OF PARLIAMENT

THE CONSCIENTIOUS OBJECTOR

FRANZ, deserter, then sailor

LANDOWNER

GENTLEMAN

POLICE SERGEANT

1ST POLICEMAN

2ND POLICEMAN

A MEMBER OF THE SECRET POLICE

THE SPY

HANS, the comrade from Hamburg

RUSSIAN FACTORY OWNER

SOAPBOX ORATOR for the Social-Democrats

1ST REDGUARD

2ND REDGUARD

3RD REDGUARD

4TH REDGUARD

5TH REDGUARD

1ST OFFICER OF THE CAVALRY
  SHARP-SHOOTERS

2ND OFFICER OF THE CAVALRY
  SHARP-SHOOTERS

3RD OFFICER OF THE CAVALRY
  SHARP-SHOOTERS

4TH OFFICER OF THE CAVALRY
  SHARP-SHOOTERS

5TH OFFICER OF THE CAVALRY
  SHARP-SHOOTERS

WORKERS

PEASANTS

SOLDIERS

1ST CITIZEN

2ND CITIZEN

3RD CITIZEN

4TH CITIZEN

WOMEN, CHILDREN, THE PEOPLE,

WOMAN

THEATRE DIRECTOR (female)

OLD WOMAN

Table of Contents

(These content summaries should appear as transparencies before each tableau.)

Prologue

A woman pushes her way through the auditorium towards the stage.

WOMAN   This is just too much! A bloody disgrace, that's what it is: seeing my fellow women workers like this. It simply stinks!

CALLS   What's up? What are you talking about?

WOMAN   You! You sitting here in this theatre gawping at the pictures the bourgeoisie conjures up for your benefit.

CALLS   What! What d'you mean! We don't!

WOMAN   Well, why do I see you sitting here then? You should be ashamed of yourselves! Every day, each one of you works your fingers to the bone for a pittance. Our children perish in filth and disease. Protection of women workers has been abolished. Those who open their mouths end up in prison. Our KPD[3] comrades who fight for better wages are given the sack. Our best people are in jail. And you, you women workers, spend your last lousy penny on this crap.

THEATRE DIRECTOR   Do you mind! This isn't crap!

WOMAN   Don't make me laugh. I know what's what. Bourgeois lies and nothing else! Theatre or boozer, either will do to dull our senses. Nothing like a bit of a tickle to make us forget our misery and stop us from fighting back.

THEATRE DIRECTOR   Dear comrade, you really are mistaken. We are putting on a piece for the woman workers here, a piece of reality taken from life.

WOMAN   Well, that I'd like to see! If that's what you are about, the play would need to be called "The women prols and the Dawes Report"[4] or such like.

THEATRE DIRECTOR That's exactly what we're doing and you, comrade, are part of it. Go on, get yourself on the stage and show us what it's really like out there. How about next week?

WOMAN You're on! If this is what it takes to open my fellow women workers' eyes. But for now I'll leave you to your fleapit.

WOMAN REGISSEUR Today we are showing what happened to the woman worker during the war and revolution. How she hungered, struggled, and slowly waking, developed a class solidarity with other women.

WOMAN Hhh! as to "awakening" – haven't noticed much of that so far. But I will have a look at your thing here. As far as I am concerned the show can begin.

1st Tableau

A Russian village. Some disparate huts. A peasant hovel. A WOMAN FIGHTER *with a headscarf, a knapsack and a walking stick comes striding along. She stops in front of the peasant hovel.*

WOMAN FIGHTER Hey, sisters, are you still asleep? Do you intend to go on sleeping through the millennia? From mother to daughter in a never ending chain? Together with your menfolk the slaves of the rich and powerful – you're the slaves of your men to boot! Bearing a double yoke, dumb and ignorant. How much longer, my sisters? How much longer are you going to carry such a heavy burden, walk with chained feet and unseeing eyes? Wake up!

(The young peasant woman DARJA *comes along carrying two large wooden buckets full of water.)*

WOMAN FIGHTER Do you live here?
DARJA Yes.
WOMAN FIGHTER Does the place belong to you?
DARJA It belongs to my father-in-law. He lives here with his wife and with my husband's brother and his wife, and my husband and myself and all our children. We all live here.
WOMAN FIGHTER Is there that much room in this hut?

DARJA We sleep on the stove, on mattresses, on straw. Why are you asking, little mother? Where should we live? In the stable we keep our cattle. And when it's cold we even take the piglets indoors, and the chickens, and the baby goat.

(The OLD PEASANT *comes out of the hut limping along with his stick.)*

OLD PEASANT What do you think you are doing, you lazy goose, gossiping and letting your work pile up. Indeed, my son has taken a bad wife: quick with her tongue and slow with her hands! And for me, nothing but trouble in my old age. Go on, take those buckets indoors!

DARJA Why are you scolding me again, father-in-law? Look, the sun is high in the sky and I have been at it since dawn: I fed and milked the cows, nursed the child, gathered firewood and kindling and dug the field.

OLD PEASANT Shut up and learn to hold your tongue! Lazy sluts, all these women! They fill one's house with brats and noise and are no good for anything. *(He hits* DARJA *on the neck.)*

DARJA You shouldn't beat me, father-in-law. I work for you and your son like an ox. I'll tell Wassil.

OLD PEASANT He'll learn you to talk back to an old peasant, you stubborn wife.

WOMAN FIGHTER Is this woman your slave? Is she your mule? Why do you beat her? Is she not a free person just like you?

OLD PEASANT You keep out of this, old woman. Who's asking you?

(The young peasant WASSIL *comes along)*

OLD PEASANT Your wife isn't working, she's stubborn and a chatterer. You must beat her.

WASSIL Why don't you do as you are told, woman?

(He raises his hand so as to hit her.)

DARJA Do not hit me, Wassil! I am not your serf!
WASSIL What aren't you?

(The OLD PEASANT *woman comes out of the house.)*

OLD PEASANT WOMAN Just look at her, this young woman, my daughter-in-law! Afraid for your tender flesh, for your soft bones, are you? I too was beaten but I gritted my teeth and said nothing. But you, of course, you want to rebel? Want to be better than the likes of us. Carry on, Wassil, beat her by all means! After all, I was beaten too.

DARJA I am not your serf! I am not your mule!

WOMAN FIGHTER *(putting herself between* WASSIL *and* DARJA) Peasant, do not beat your wife.

WASSIL She is my wife. Why shouldn't I beat her?

WOMAN FIGHTER She is your comrade. You should love and honour her.

WASSIL I don't understand you, old woman. You are probably from a different place. When the tax collector comes, he will want his taxes. How am I to pay him if the wife is lazy?

WOMAN FIGHTER Peasant, you are not seeing sense. Just because your masters and those in power exploit you and rip you off, do you really want to do the same to your wife?

WASSIL I too want to be master somewhere. Who else can I beat up and exploit but my own wife? I get enough abuse and blows myself.

(Excited cries. Men and women peasants arrive together with a VILLAGE ELDER. *Out of the hut come* WASSIL's *brother* MITJA *and his wife* MATRENA.)

WASSIL What's up? What's all the shouting about?

1ST PEASANT Is it true what Dimitri said yesterday? Our Czar is going to war. In all the villages they are signing up.

EVERYBODY Signing up?!

1ST PEASANT WOMAN They've carted away my husband. What's to become of me? Dear Mother of God, help me! Those heathens will kill him. And my children will starve.

VILLAGE ELDER *(turning to the* OLD PEASANT) Vladimir Ivanovitch, I am really sorry. Both your sons will have to go to war. They must leave tomorrow.

OLD PEASANT Both of them? Both sons? Take one! That's enough!

DARJA Why should they be sent away? I am not having my Wassil sent anywhere!

VILLAGE ELDER He has to go and fight against the foreigners, against the enemy.

DARJA What enemy? I don't know of any enemy. What does he want?

VILLAGE ELDER They say that he is after our land.

DARJA Our masters have plenty of land. They can give it to him.

VILLAGE ELDER And our little peasant plots? If he takes those?

DARJA We'll invite him into our huts. He will see that we are poor and return back home. We will give him a piece of bread for his journey.

VILLAGE ELDER But the Czar gives the orders. It is for the Czar that Wassil must go to war.

DARJA And where is this Czar? I don't know him.

WASSIL I don't know him either. You are quite right, my wife.

VILLAGE ELDER He lives in the great town of Petersburg where the houses and the church towers reach into the heavens. All the towns and all the land belong to him. He is the master. He gives the orders.

DARJA Well, he can chase the enemy away on his own! What business has he calling Wassil from his village? Here is the field Wassil has still to plough and here is Wassil's hut. His children and his wife are here too.

MITJA Yes, for whom must we go to war? For the Czar who lives in his castle? For all these masters who take away our last bit of grain in taxes. Let them rot!

WOMAN FIGHTER Well done, peasants! Take no notice of these calls. This is not your war, it is your masters' war.

SOME PEASANTS Listen to what they say!

OTHER PEASANTS No point talking. We'll have to go to war.

VILLAGE ELDER Stop the idle chatter, my brothers. Those who are conscripted have to go. There is no choice. Whoever disobeys is shot.

DARJA Cowards! Don't you care that village and land will be ruined?

WOMAN FIGHTER The woman is right. You have to unite against the great masters who want to lead you into war. Your blood will flow and they will gain more land.

1ST PEASANT But it's good to go to war. You march. You pillage. You get drunk. Life is good in war. Vodka and women.

SEVERAL To march, to vanquish. Drinking, shooting, looting. It will be fun!

(A peasant arrives out of breath.)

PEASANT Ten miles from here, in the

village of Lubinka, a few fellows have mutinied, they didn't want to sign up. So the Czar's Cossacks arrived on their fast horses, surrounded the village and whipped the lot, women and men. The mutineers they took away in chains.

WOMAN FIGHTER   Rebel against the Czar and his Cossacks! Rebel against the war!

PEASANTS   Off with you, woman! Do you want to ruin us?

(They force the woman to leave.)

WASSIL   *(to DARJA)* I have often beaten you, wife. When I return it will not happen again. But now I have to leave. Plant the field with Matrena and look after our parents, the children and the cattle.

DARJA   Why do you want to go and kill strangers? Make your children fatherless? Desert your wife? Haven't you sworn your oath to me in church?

WASSIL   Stop arguing, Darja, my wife. The man who has been made a soldier must go to war.

DARJA   The Czar is a long way away and this land is vast. Hide in the forest. They won't find you there!

WASSIL   We have to go.

MITJA   We have to go.

(NASDJA, the young teacher, arrives.)

NASDJA   Goodbye, Wassil, Mitja!

MITJA   You who can write so well, teacher Nasdja, do write to us about how things are going at home.

NASDJA   I promise I will.

2nd Tableau

1914

A big town. Soldiers are marching out. Enthusiastic crowds. Women and girls are bringing flowers. A small group of people are standing gloomily aside.

SOLDIERS   *(singing)* "Heil dir im Siegerkranz"[5] etc. *(first stanza)*

1ST CITIZEN   Long live our strong army!

EVERYONE   Hip hip hurray!

1ST CITIZEN   Long live our Kaiser Wilhelm the Second!

EVERYONE   Hurray! Hurray!

2ND CITIZEN   Our brave young field-grey[6] boys, our volunteers, hip hip hurray!

EVERYONE   Hurray! Hurray!

2ND CITIZEN   Our fleet which rules the seas, the Imperial Marine, our wonderful Blue-Jackets,[7] hip hip hurray!

EVERYONE   Hurray! Hurray!

1ST CITIZEN   "I am leading you into wonderful times" says the Emperor.

2ND CITIZEN   A united people of brothers. A people free and armed.

1ST CITIZEN   The same pulse pounding in officer and soldier alike!

2ND CITIZEN   Factory owner and worker marching side by side in brotherly union intent on saving the fatherland!

1ST CITIZEN   One people, one will. And out there awaits the enemy. Destroy the French pigs! Chase off the Russian wolves! Down with the English traitors, the miserable shopkeepers and traders. Just keep on going!

2ND CITIZEN   Just keep on going!

1ST WOMAN   I am sending three sons to the front and am proud of it.

1ST CITIZEN   A hero's mother!

2ND WOMAN   I am sending my husband and two sons to the front.

2ND CITIZEN   German heroism! German women's strength!

ANNA   Will they ever return?

OLD WOMAN   The poor women! They don't know what they are doing.

CALLS   Cowards! Those who think like that are scum!

(POLICEMEN emerge from a sidestreet bringing with them a prisoner.)

1ST CITIZEN   What have you got here?

1ST POLICEMAN   A conscientious objector.

1ST CITIZEN   What kind of animal is that?

2ND CITIZEN   Such a thing does not exist in Germany!

1ST POLICEMAN   He doesn't want to go to war.

CONSCIENTIOUS OBJECTOR   Listen to me, my friends! To kill human beings is a sin! Our Christian religion forbids it!

1ST CITIZEN   Shut his filthy mouth for him!

2ND CITIZEN   Beat him up.

CONSCIENTIOUS OBJECTOR   Fellow Germans, we are told to love our neighbour!

CALLS   Down with the scoundrel! Pull out his tongue! Gouge out his eyes!

ANNA   You dogs!

(The POLICEMEN, barely managing to save

the CONSCIENTIOUS OBJECTOR *from the wrath of the people, take him away.)*

1ST POLICEMAN   Don't worry. He will be shot in an orderly fashion. *(Exit)*

(Several POLICEMEN *bring along a bound worker.)*

2ND CITIZEN   And who is that?

2ND POLICEMAN   He tried to desert, kept himself hidden, didn't want to go to war!

CALLS   The wretch! Miserable dog!

1ST CITIZEN   With God for Emperor and Fatherland!

EVERYONE   With God for Emperor and Fatherland!

DESERTER (FRANZ)   Fellow workers, you are shouting too? Is it not you who are the traitors? Are you really ready to go to war for your class enemies? For the fat cats and their bank accounts?

CALLS   Let's beat him up!

(They rush at the DESERTER *and beat him up until he collapses.* POLICEMEN *drag him away.* CLARA *arrives.)*

CLARA   Franz! Franz!

*(*CLARA *follows him. Social-Democratic* MEMBERS OF THE REICHSTAG *arrive.)*

1ST CITIZEN   Here come the Social-Democrats from the Reichstag.

1ST MEMBER OF REICHSTAG   We have voted for war credits.

2ND MEMBER OF REICHSTAG   We have all voted for war credits.

1ST CITIZEN   At last you are truly German! Honest and decent!

2ND CITIZEN   They have found their way home after going astray. Now we are truly a people of brothers!

1ST CITIZEN   Peace at home! Peace at home! Long live Germany's Social-Democratic Party!

PEOPLE   *(singing)* "Es braust ein Ruf wie Donnerhall!"[8]

(The crowd disperses together with the SOLDIERS. *The gloomy group remains. A* WORKER *ambles by.)*

WORKER   What are you doing, standing about so suspiciously? Why don't you join in?

OLD WOMAN   You must be as drunk as all the others. Don't you know what war is like? I know! My husband fought in Africa against the Hereros.[9] I feel sorry for the poor lads who are marching now.

WORKER   Women's gossip! War is natural. Our members in the government have voted for war credits.

ANNA   Are you a Social-Democrat? I, myself, am not political, never bothered much about your affairs. But I do remember you saying that workers don't go to war for the capitalists. What do you say now?

WORKER   We don't believe in attacking anyone. But this is different. It is we who have been attacked. All our enemies have fallen upon us like wild dogs.

OLD WOMAN   You are all drunk!

ANNA   My husband has to go too. He's gone all quiet. What was all that big talk about, a few months ago? – In Switzerland – Workers of all nations unite against war? And now? And now you run amok in the streets like mad dogs! I am not a political animal. But even I can see that something does not make sense here.

WORKER   Our deputies have voted for war credits. They must know what they are doing.

ANNA   Yes, it is easy for them to cast a vote while my husband has to march.

(Anna's husband, PAUL, *arrives, puts his hand on* ANNA'S *shoulder.)*

PAUL   Shhh! Anna. There is nothing you can do. This time we have had it. But when our boys are grown up it will be different. You must bring them up well, Anna, even when it's hard.

ANNA   Paul, what are you saying? And your face! As if you didn't expect to come back!

PAUL   Never mind, now! Be quiet! Come, let's gather our things.

(The WOMAN FIGHTER *arrives pursued by several people.)*

1ST CITIZEN   High treason!

2ND CITIZEN   Seize this woman! She incites the people to rebellion. She argues against the war!

3RD CITIZEN   She is a spy! Hang her!

WOMAN FIGHTER   I am not a spy. All I want is to tell the truth. But you can't hear it.

(The gloomy group takes the WOMAN FIGHTER *into its midst and fends off the pursuers.)*

3rd Tableau

The same Russian village as in the first tableau. A few men standing in a group. The VILLAGE ELDER *has a piece of paper in his hand.* DARJA *and* MATRENA *arrive.*

VILLAGE ELDER Where've you come from, Darja and Matrena?

DARJA We have been in the field, ploughing.

VILLAGE ELDER You are efficient women. No one can tell from looking at your homestead, that the men are away. The land is ploughed and the cattle are thriving.

MATRENA Well, there is not much choice, dear grandad. Who would do it if not us?

VILLAGE ELDER A lot of land lies fallow in Russia these days. There are no men. There are no horses. And the government needs grain and meat for the soldiers. The cattle are taken from peasants.

MATRENA They take the cattle?

VILLAGE ELDER Yes, what the government needs it takes from the peasant.

1ST PEASANT They're after the few poor cattle we've got? Why don't they take them from the rich farmers and those fat landowners?

2ND PEASANT Yes, why don't they take them from the landowners, who can't even count their herds? Not very good government, is it!

1ST PEASANT Ha, it would be against God's world order, I suppose.

VILLAGE ELDER Don't talk like that! What can we do? The government has a strong arm and a ready hand. When it reaches out it grabs. Peasants like us are easily crushed. Before you know what's what, the Cossacks come charging in – and you are finished. And then come the lawyers and the courts – and you are done for.

DARJA Because you're cowards, all of you! They won't take anything from me, I can tell you that!

1ST PEASANT With scythes and forks we shall welcome the people from the government. Anyway, what kind of a father is this man who calls himself our Czar?

2ND PEASANT He knows nothing about us peasants, this Czar who lives far away in his great city. As far as he is concerned we can all go and starve!

EVERYONE We'll all starve! Starve! And what about our seed corn? The seed corn?

1ST PEASANT When will it arrive, this seed corn which we have asked for? Everyone knows that we had to hand over so much of our own harvest that now we have nothing left to sow. We shall all starve next autumn if the government does not give us the seed it has promised us. Do other governments have more than ours?

VILLAGE ELDER Yes, of course, the seed corn! The seed corn! Darja, Matrena, have you got enough?

DARJA Just enough for our field.

VILLAGE ELDER Ah, you see: these clever women! Grew their corn like everyone else, gave their share to the government, and still have enough to sow.

DARJA That's because there are two of us. Many are alone and their fields are spread far and wide.

ANGRY CALLS My plough is broken! They have taken my horse! There is no seed corn! We shall all starve, starve, starve!

1ST PEASANT Oh, do shut up! What are you all moaning about? Nobody will starve as long as the grain barns on the big estates are still full. If our masters do not give us our corn we shall go and get it ourselves. They all say that there is plenty there.

(A THIRD PEASANT *comes running.)*

3RD PEASANT The Cossacks are coming! Those blood-hounds!

CALLS What? Where?

3RD PEASANT In the village of Lubinka the peasants stormed and pillaged the estate. It appears that they were after seed corn. It wasn't long before the Cossacks arrived, cut them down, shot at them and burnt their cottages.

DARJA Let's get going then, village comrades! Let's go and help the peasants of Lubinka!

1ST PEASANT Yes, let's get going, let's help them!

3RD PEASANT They are past any help! They are lying dead in their own blood and the Cossacks are long gone!

1ST PEASANT All this must change. Things must change!

SOME WOMEN *(frightened)* Don't stand together like this! Let's all go home. Otherwise the Cossacks will get us too.

(They leave.)

DARJA   Comrades! Matrena and I, we don't want to tend our own field while you have no seed to grow. We have decided to leave half our field fallow and share our seed with you.

1ST PEASANT   That is really kind of you, Darja.

2ND PEASANT   Spoken in true Christian spirit. You are a good woman, Darja!

VILLAGE ELDER   I won't have anything said against women, ever again. Wassil will be well pleased when he comes home.

DARJA   Stop nattering on! Go home!

(They disperse. DARJA *and* MATRENA *stay behind.)*

DARJA   If half the field remains fallow we won't all be able to live here. There might be just enough for you and your children. I shall move into town with the little ones and look for work. They say they that the factories need workers.

MATRENA   Yes, perhaps you should go and try your luck. There is plenty of hard work everywhere. But there is famine in the village and famine in town.

DARJA   I won't let my children starve, Matrena!

NASDJA   I'll come with you to the city, Darja, and work in a factory where I'll tell the workers about the revolution.

4th Tableau

Berlin 1916

The kitchen of a worker's family. ANNA *is sitting at a sewing-machine busy working. A small child is playing. Two bigger boys are returning from school.*

ROBERT AND ERNST   Mother, we're hungry! What's for dinner?

ANNA   *(without looking up from her work)* There are some turnips left over from yesterday. You make up the fire, I haven't got the time.

ROBERT   Just turnips? No potatoes?

ANNA   You know very well: there were no potatoes yesterday. Where am I supposed to get them from today?

ERNST   *(close to tears)* And I am so hungry!

ROBERT   Me too!

ANNA   Well, you may go to the cupboard. I did keep just eight potatoes – two for each. You can cook those.

ROBERT   *(pleased)* Ooo! Potatoes!

ERNST   Not enough, though, to get really full.

(The boys make up a fire in the stove and put turnips and potatoes on. ANNA *keeps on sewing. A* NEIGHBOUR *appears.)*

NEIGHBOUR   I see you've got some work, Schulzen?

ANNA   *(sewing)* I've got work alright, but the pay is terrible.

NEIGHBOUR   What are you making?

ANNA   Bed linen for the military hospital.

NEIGHBOUR   Paper or material?

ANNA   Real material.

NEIGHBOUR   Do you know, one can earn a pretty penny in the munitions factories. And they get bits of bacon too.

ROBERT   Yes it's true. Fritz's mother works in the munitions factory and sometimes Fritz has bacon in his sandwich. Yesterday he even had a bit of real sausage.

ALL TOGETHER   Real sausage?

ERNST   You don't mean mussel-sausage?[10]

ROBERT   No. It was a real sausage, all red and white, with bits of fat in it. He let me take a bite. I got all dizzy just from the smell, because I was so hungry.

NEIGHBOUR   Listen to the boy, Schulzen! Why don't you go and work in the munitions factory? Do you want your kids to starve?

ANNA   *(looking up from her work, angry and determined)* You know very well that I shall never again work in a munitions factory. When I assembled those grenades I felt as though I was about to shoot my own man.

NEIGHBOUR   Rubbish! Those grenades are for the enemy!

ANNA   And who is this enemy, tell me? Aren't they all workers just like us? Like our men they had to go into battle whether they wanted to or not.

NEIGHBOUR   Oh well, you always want to be cleverer than ordinary folk and you end up hungrier than any of us. My old man is doing very nicely. He's been promoted to sergeant and spends his time in a castle in Belgium. Quaffs wine every day. Sent me some silk for a blouse and a pound of butter.

(She leaves the room.)

ROBERT   Mum, Ernst has pinched a whole spoonful of turnips!

ANNA   *(gets up and holds her head with both*

hands) When will all this end? When will things change?

5th Tableau

28 June 1916

A large crowd, mostly women and children, gathers in front of a food store. There are some men. A policeman lingers nearby.

1ST WOMAN   *(just arriving)* What's up? What are all these people doing?

2ND WOMAN   Monkey grease from America and cubes of dried mock-peas!

1ST WOMAN   Right, where can I join the queue? But I won't bother with the mock-peas. I've had some: it's ground chestnuts laced with sand. But I won't say no to the monkey grease.

(THIRD WOMAN comes out of the store.)

2ND WOMAN   What's the grease like?

3RD WOMAN   If you hold your nose, it's just about edible. And its stink doesn't reach further than 3 metres. But there is only half a pound for each customer.

(A FOURTH WOMAN leaves the queue.)

4TH WOMAN   I am not going to queue for that!

ALL THE WOMEN   Well, look at her!

1ST WOMAN   I suppose you get your creamery butter sent direct from your country estate?

2ND WOMAN   And they send you special officer's parcels from behind the lines?

3RD WOMAN   I know! Her bloke is a black marketeer!

1ST WOMAN   Monkey grease is not good enough for her, just because it pongs a bit.

(A passing GENTLEMAN stops.)

GENTLEMAN   What's all the fuss about? I don't believe it! These women are getting their regular rations and still they are not satisfied. Don't they know there is a war on? This is a time for gritting one's teeth and keeping going. Think of our brave soldiers in their trenches! They are the ones who are really suffering. Often they get no hot food from morn to night. You should thank God on bended knees for your turnips and potatoes, and for the fact that the frontiers of your fatherland are safe, and that the foreign robber hordes cannot invade your land.

1ST WOMAN   Who the hell is he? Talks like a regular clergyman.

2ND WOMAN   And why, may I ask, are you not with those "brave soldiers in their trenches" yourself?

GENTLEMAN   I have been deemed indispensable to the service of of the fatherland in a different capacity.

2ND WOMAN   Let's have a closer look at this "Mister indispensable".

1ST WOMAN   Isn't it amazing how well he looks on his diet of turnips!

2ND WOMAN   Yes, while our children hobble about in shoes with wooden soles, he wears an exquisite pair of boots.

GENTLEMAN   You insolent bunch of prols!

WOMEN   Whack him one behind the ears!

(The GENTLEMAN flees. ANNA leaves the queue. A fat LANDOWNER arrives.)

ANNA   I could strangle those pontificators and cheats! Here we are struggling and slaving. Our children get thinner and thinner. Old folk die from want and the weak perish. And then there comes along some idiot, sticks out his fat belly and begins to preach.

LANDOWNER   Someone ought to get the police on to you! You unpatriotic rabble. The motto is "Grit your teeth and keep going until victory is ours!" For the Fatherland no sacrifice is too big.

1ST WOMAN   I know him. He is from Pommern, has a smoking house chockablock with hams and sausages, guzzles milk every day. While our babies die he feeds his pigs with spuds and bran.

LANDOWNER   Long live the Kaiser! Grit your teeth and keep going!

WOMEN   Listen to the bastard! Punch him in his fat gob! Down with him!

LANDOWNER   Outrageous rabble! Nothing but prols!

(He flees. The SHOPKEEPER comes out of his shop.)

SHOPKEEPER   There is no more grease.

WOMEN   No more grease? Do you mean to say that we've queued in vain?

(A woman faints.)

1ST WOMAN   Lehmann has fainted. Give her something to eat!

ANNA   Let's get into the shop and check whether there is really no grease left. He might be selling it more dearly on the quiet.

WOMEN   Let's go. Let's check!

(They turn towards the shop. There are a lot of voices talking together and the sound of footsteps. A FIFTH WOMAN *arrives in a hurry.)*

5TH WOMAN   Can you hear them? They are coming from the factories.

WOMEN   From the factories, now, in mid-morning?

5TH WOMAN   They are striking!

WOMEN   Striking?!

5TH WOMAN   They are striking for Karl Liebknecht. Today is the day of his trial.

NEIGHBOUR   They must be mad! They are madder still than Liebknecht himself.

SOME WOMEN   A strike? Now? When there is a war on? Isn't that against the law?

OTHER WOMEN   They are quite right but they should be striking against the war.

NEIGHBOUR   They are all mad. Striking is against the law.

ANNA   And is it perhaps against the law that our children starve? Is it against the law that your husbands are torn to pieces out there at the front? Is it against the law that you are blown sky-high in your munitions factories?

*(*POLICEMEN *arrive)*

1ST POLICEMAN   It is against the law to create a gathering in a street. The shop is closed. There is nothing here for you. Move along. Clear off!

(The POLICEMEN *chase the* WOMEN *away. For a little while the stage remains empty until a few of the women return,* ANNA *and* CLARA *amongst them.)*

ANNA   Aren't you the girlfriend of Franz? The one they threw into prison because he wouldn't sign up and play at being a soldier?

CLARA   Yes, I'm his bride.

ANNA   Is he still holed up?

CLARA   Still there – *(*FRANZ *arrives.)* Franz!

FRANZ   I've been looking everywhere for you!

CLARA   What happened? Did you escape from prison?

FRANZ   I have signed up. I'm with the Navy. Tomorrow I'm off.

CLARA   You have – what? – Signed up?

FRANZ   I'm after the Iron Cross, First Class!

CLARA   You're after – what?

FRANZ   *(laughs)* Don't worry! They won't have much fun with me out there. I shall agitate against the war once I am in the ranks. *(Quietly)* I shall prepare the soldiers for the revolution.

(A revolutionary WOMAN FIGHTER *arrives.)*

WOMAN FIGHTER   Have your heard? They've put our Karl Liebknecht into prison.

EVERYONE   Into prison!

FRANZ   Good job they haven't shot him. He won't stay long in prison, we shall see to that! I'll get him out myself!

ANNA   I'll go with you, Franz! Isn't Liebknecht the one who is against the war and fights for the workers?

CLARA   That's the one!

FRANZ   I come out of prison and he goes in. That's what you call shift work! Don't worry, Karl Liebknecht, relief is on its way!

WOMAN FIGHTER   Here, come closer. I want to tell you something! Ever heard of Spartacus?

WOMEN   Who's that?

WOMAN FIGHTER   He lived two thousand years ago. He freed the Roman slaves. He was a freedom fighter!

1ST WOMAN   There aren't any slaves any more.

ANNA   That's what we are now, and our men.

WOMAN FIGHTER   Karl Liebknecht and Rosa Luxemburg have founded a group and called it Spartacus. Its aim is to fight against the war and to liberate the workers.

1ST WOMAN   What about the Social-Democrats?

WOMAN FIGHTER   They have given up fighting for the liberation of the working class and are now in the service of power and capital.

ANNA   Send Rosa Luxemburg to us. She must speak to us!

WOMEN   Yes, let her speak to us!

WOMAN FIGHTER   Here are some leaflets. Letters from Spartacus. Read them and distribute them!

FRANZ   Give me some too, comrade! I'll put them between the soles of my boots and take them to the front.

WOMAN FIGHTER   There you are!

(Two POLICEMEN *arrive.)*

FRANZ   *(puts his arm around Clara's shoulder)*

Let's go to your place, Clara. Tomorrow I shall be in the Navy.

CLARA   Two years I have waited for you, Franz!

FRANZ   We are all waiting, all the time. The day will come when we won't have to wait any more.

Interlude

WOMAN   *(in the auditorium, stands up)* So many scenes and not a word about the Russian Revolution? I suppose you've forgotten about that?

THEATRE DIRECTOR   *(steps out in front of the curtain)* No, we haven't forgotten. We are coming to it now.

WOMAN   Make sure it's the real revolution of the Bolsheviks. There was another one before.

THEATRE DIRECTOR   Yes, that was the March Revolution of Kerenski and the government of the Mensheviks.[11]

WOMAN   I suppose that was a bit like our Ebert-Scheidemann government?[12]

THEATRE DIRECTOR   Yes, you are quite right! It was very similar.

WOMAN   But in Russia the people soon got wise to that swindle.

THEATRE DIRECTOR   Yes, gradually, after a few months they realised they'd been tricked.

WOMAN   They must be cleverer over there than we are here. For Christ's sake! Just look at us! While we were still all yelling "Long Live Willem",[13] they were already on to their second revolution. How did it all happen? Go on! Tell us!

THEATRE DIRECTOR   Well, briefly! We've got to get on with our play. Well, it was like this. The people were hungry. The peasants were given no land at all. And there was never any peace for the soldiers. So they came to realise that these were not the right leaders to represent the workers and the peasants. People became restless, handed in petitions and finally they took to the streets. Lenin and the Bolsheviks showed them the way.

(The THEATRE DIRECTOR steps back behind the curtain.)

WOMAN   And then – ?

(The curtain goes up.)

6th Tableau

1917

The kitchen of a worker's family in Petersburg. DARJA *with two small children. Evening. A small lamp is burning.*

CHILD   Is there anything to eat, mother?

DARJA   Not today, my darling. Go to sleep and when you wake up tomorrow morning there will be bread. The baker has promised it. *(She takes the* CHILD *on to her lap.)*

CHILD   *(close to tears)* I'm hungry, mother! Hungry! Horrible baker! He won't have any bread even tomorrow.

OLDER CHILD   Isn't father coming home soon? We used to live in a village but father wasn't with us. Then we moved to town and still father stayed away. Soldiers marched past but father was not amongst them. The Czar has left his castle and still father is at war.

DARJA   Just wait, dear boy. Father will soon return. He will plant corn and your mother will bake bread. And you children won't be hungry any longer. We shall take as much land as we need from the landowners and shall plough, sow and harvest. The field will yield plenty and there will be bread in our house.

OLDER CHILD   When will that be mother? Why don't you go and work in the factory where machines rattle all day and where there are all those foreign people? When will father take us back to the village?

(There is a knock on the door. NASDJA *enters.)*

NASDJA   Good evening Comrade Darja. I've brought some bread for your children.

CHILDREN   Look mother, bread, bread! *(The* CHILDREN *eat.)*

DARJA   But now it's bedtime children! *(The* CHILDREN *go to bed.)* Take a seat, comrade Nasdja. Look, I have received a letter from our village and I can read it. You have taught me well. My eyes used to be so stupid, unable to see the writing on the paper. But now I am able to pick out words from the page.

NASDJA   What are they writing from the village, Comrade Darja?

DARJA   My sister-in-law Matrena writes: "Dear sister Darja! The teacher from Lubinka is here on a visit. I tell him the words and he is putting them on paper for me. He writes this letter. Dear sister Darja! Did you find work in town? Do you have bread for you and your children? May God see to it that you don't starve to death. Dear sister Darja! Things are not good here in the village. Everyone is just waiting. Morning comes and then evening and still we wait. Morning comes again and evening and nothing happens. I tell you what the peasants are saying, sister Darja. 'They have chased away the Czar and toppled the old government. But what good has it done? The poor peasant did not get any land. The great lords are still sitting on their estates amongst their huge fields and their barns filled to bursting. But we have nothing at all.' – I am telling you what the peasants are saying, dear sister Darja so that you can tell everyone in town. 'What are the new masters doing?' ask the peasants. 'They send us letters and pieces of paper, but they leave the land to the great robbers. We don't want letters and pieces of paper. We want the land. We shall wait today and perhaps tomorrow, but then we shall go and get the land ourselves. We shall wait today and perhaps tomorrow, but then we shall chase away the new masters who speak and write so much but keep the land to themselves.' That's what the peasants say. And I can tell you, dear sister Darja, when the peasants set out to get the land, I shall go with them. Before I let my children starve, I shall take my scythe and join the peasants in their fight against the new masters. – And something else, dear sister Darja. I have received a letter from a foreign country which lies beyond our frontier. It says that my Mitja has been wounded. Will I ever see him again, who can tell me that? Whether you will ever see your Wassil again, who can tell you that? Why is it that our men do not return to us? I am asking you, dear sister Darja, and you must tell the people in the town: Why is it that even though we have chased the Czar away the war still goes on? They ought to make peace, these new masters of ours, who claim to be men of the people. If they do not make peace soon, we shall come and chase them away too. All we want is land and peace. Matran, the old peasant wife, says it too and so say all the poor peasants around here. – Do give Nasdja this letter so that she can read to you what is

written on its paper, as I told it to the teacher from Lubinka, and as he has written it down according to my words on 1st November 1917."

NASDJA *(laughs)* She has never as much as looked a Bolshevik in the face and has never even been to a party meeting, your Matrena. But she tells us what we ought to do.

DARJA Yes, you Bosheviks know what the peasants need, and what they want.

NASDJA They are very patient, the peasants in your village. Elsewhere they have already begun to take away the land from the landowners. You won't have to wait much longer for the signal, my dear old Matrena. Go and fetch your scythe from the barn! And don't wait until your children have died of hunger.

DARJA When? Comrade Nasdja, when are we going to start fighting openly?

NASDJA Be on the ready, Darja! I've got to go now, I am in the courier service. At this very moment our troops are surrounding the Winter Palace. *(Some gunshots ring out)* Did you hear that?

DARJA Are you off to the Smolni Institute where Lenin and the Bolsheviks are?

NASDJA Yes, I must join them, need to bring them some news.

DARJA And are we going to the factory tomorrow?

NASDJA If the streets are quiet and if the factory is open we shall go there.

DARJA How long do you think the letter took to get here? What day is it today?

NASDJA It's the 6 November. Good bye!

(NASDJA leaves. DARJA hums a song and carries on with her sewing. Then she turns off the lamp. For a while the stage remains dark and quiet. Then the marching feet of a great crowd can be heard from outside. The stage remains dark. The sound of marching feet continues. Now and then there are commands given in a soft voice.)

DARJA Time to go to bed.

DARJA *(sleepily)* What is it? Am I dreaming? What is all this marching? – Listen! Left, right, left, right, marching red, marching red. They have started! *(She goes to the window to peep out.)* Soldiers. And more soldiers. Up and down the street, as far as the eye can see, nothing but soldiers! But it is so dark! Ah, but here comes the moon from behind the clouds. Soldiers! Soldiers everywhere! Could it be the enemy? Or are they ours? Oh, to sit here and not to know! Ah, a man on horseback! With a red armband and a star. He is speaking to the officers. These must be our soldiers. Comrade Lenin is leading us to victory!

(There is a knock on the door. DARJA *switches on the lamp. The* NEIGHBOUR *comes in, very scared.)*

NEIGHBOUR   I am terrified. I wake up and hear these men marching. Then I fall asleep again, wake up once more and still they are marching. What is happening? My son came home an hour ago and says: "Everybody in town is marching: workers, peasants, soldiers. The people are on the move." *(A shot is heard.)* Dear mother of God! Now they are shooting! *(There is a second shot.)* Dear mother of God! Come to our rescue!

DARJA   *(at the window, cheering)* These are our soldiers! This is our victory!

NEIGHBOUR   What are you on about?

DARJA   You need not be afraid, dear neighbour. This is the night of the Bolsheviks! It is the red night of the people!

NEIGHBOUR   What are they after, those people out there?

DARJA   They want land for the peasants and freedom and bread for the workers. And peace for everyone.

NEIGHBOUR   Peace, yes we could all do with that – and bread. *(Worried)* But tell me, neighbour, will the Bolsheviks too keep all the bread to themselves?

DARJA   You fool! Their bread is for the workers. They are marching, left, right, left, right like our true Reds.

*(*NASDJA *rushes in and embraces* DARJA.*)*

NASDJA   It's going well, Comrade Darja! The soldiers are to a man behind the Bolsheviks. Almost all the regiments from Petrograd are with us.

DARJA   What are they doing now? Where are they going?

NASDJA   They are occupying the government buildings and stations. They are chasing out Kerenski's people, the cadets, the Mensheviks, the neutrals and the Whites. Open the window, Darja! Have a look!

(Both stand at the window. The marching of feet and the noise of many voices can still be heard.)

NASDJA   Don't you have a red cloth somewhere, Darja? Give me your headscarf! *(She takes the scarf and waves it out of the window.)* Long live the Bolsheviks!

CALLS FROM THE STREET   Long live the Bolsheviks! All power to the councils! All power to the councils! Peace! Peace!

(The CHILDREN *get out of bed, run to the window and begin to shout too.)*

CHILDREN   Long live the Bolsheviks! Peace! Peace!

DARJA   Tell me what happened at the Smolni Institute, Nasdja!

NASDJA   The old government sits in the Winter Palace surrounded by our troops. The new government sits in the Smolni Institute: the new revolutionary military committee, the Bolsheviks. The Institute has become a fortress. It's tightly guarded and secured from above by machine guns. The telephone rings night and day and on the roads couriers rush along at great speed. Messages arrive from all over the place.

(Cries of jubilation can be heard from outside.)

DARJA   Listen, what are they shouting?

CALLS FROM THE STREET   Hurray for the Semenov Regiment!

DARJA, NASDJA, CHILDREN   Hurray, hurray, hurray!

NASDJA   The Semenov Regiment, Kerenski's own Regiment has joined the Bolsheviks! *(More jubilation outside.)*

CALLS FROM THE STREET   Hurray for the pioneer squadrons!

NASDJA   *(calls out of the window)* Fetched by Kerenski? On the march towards St Petersburg? A telegram for us?

CALLS FROM THE STREET   Hurray for the anti-aircraft batteries! Hurray for the cavalry!

NASDJA   Kerenski went for reinforcements from the front, fetched his most loyal regiments, the pioneers, the cavalry and the artillery. On their way to St Petersburg they have contacted our committee: "They are all for the Bolsheviks! They support the workers' and soldiers' councils."

CHILDREN   Everyone is for the Bolsheviks! Everyone is for the workers' and soldiers' councils!

CALLS FROM THE STREET   The National Bank has been taken! The most powerful weapon of the capitalists is now in our hands!

CHILDREN   Long live the Bolsheviks!

DARJA   Look our town is alive! The streets are full of people! Workers, peasants, all free! And we women are part of it! A red day and a red night. The people have woken!

NASDJA   Soldiers, soldiers. New delegations of the regiments. Here come the first soldiers from the front, dirty and barely able to walk. Look Darja, just look!

DARJA   Wassil! It's my Wassil!

WASSIL   *(from outside)* Darja!

DARJA   Where are you going, Wassil?

WASSIL   To the Smolni Istitute, to the Bolsheviks. We want peace!

DARJA   Peace! Peace! Long live the Bolsheviks!

CHILDREN   Father! Father! Long live the Bolsheviks!

7th Tableau

January 1918, Hamburg

An undercover office. A room in an empty hotel. Tables, chairs, typewriter, a copying machine. An open door leading to another room. Telephone. WOMAN REVOLUTIONARY FIGHTER *and a female* COMRADE *sitting at the typewriter.*

WOMAN FIGHTER   I'll dictate the new leaflet. Take it down in shorthand. It has to be duplicated and distributed as soon as possible. "Workers! Men and Women! More than two months ago the Russian proletariat laid down arms and offered peace to all nations. But the capitalist states insist on continuing with the dreadful massacre. Every day tens of thousands of human beings bleed to death on the battlefields of capitalism. Our children starve and the people are about to perish. Right now the German government is playing a criminal game in Brest-Litowsk. It is trying to break up and then subjugate free Russia. It is seeking to break the power of the Russian worker state so as to be able to enslave its own workers more ruthlessly. Workers! Men and Women! Declare your solidarity with your Russian brothers! Join forces with Soviet Russia! Refuse to make ammunition which will be used against Soviet Russia. There must be no ammunition to help the exploiters and marketeers prolong the war! Leave the factories! Strike for peace, for the Soviet Union, for the setting free of political prisoners, for the freedom of the Press! Strike against the state of siege we find ourselves in, strike against hunger rations and against the dying of thousands of innocent people! Strike for a free German republic! Workers! Men and women! Everywhere in Germany and Austria your fellow comrades are joining the strike. Keep the strike going! And you who are not on strike yet, walk out now!" *(A* WOMAN COMRADE *arrives.)* Already back from Berlin?

1ST COMRADE   *(out of breath)* Comrades, five hundred thousand workers are on strike in Berlin!

BOTH   Five hundred thousand workers?

1ST COMRADE   In Leipzig, in all the big towns, all over Germany workers are going on strike. We are not alone here in Hamburg.

WOMAN FIGHTER   Write it down! Write it down! Our leaflet must be out today! *(A* SECOND COMRADE *arrives.)* Have you been in the harbour?

2ND COMRADE   The dockers! Those cowards! Had it not been for the women . . .

WOMAN FIGHTER   What happened? Has the strike collapsed?

2ND COMRADE   The strike continues. Thanks to our women. Early this morning the women marched to the harbour. And, would you believe it, at six o'clock they met one group, and then another and another, more and more, strike breakers who had been scared rigid by threats of bringing in the army. But the women joined hands and made chains, one behind another, a living wall blocking the entrance to the harbour. The men hung around unable to decide what to do. Some tried to push past but did not succeed. There was no way anyone could get into the harbour. So the men, embarrassed, began to disperse. *(A* THIRD COMRADE *arrives.)*

3RD COMRADE   The women are fighting at the entrance of the harbour. The police arrived but were not let through. The resistance of the women remains strong. They are throwing stones and bricks and anything they can lay their hands on and shout: "Give us bread! Give us peace!"

WOMAN FIGHTER   Let's all go to the harbour and help them. You stay here and finish the leaflet.

(*All but the* FIRST COMRADE *rush out of the room. The* FIRST COMRADE *begins to type. Enter* COMRADE HANS *and a* SPY.)

HANS   I have brought a comrade from Kiel.

1ST COMRADE   (*gets up and takes* HANS *to one side*) Don't you know that you shouldn't bring just anyone to this place?

HANS   He is a good old comrade, comes from Kiel and has been working for the last three weeks at my factory. He's been very helpful to me in my work. I assure you, you can trust him.

(FIRST COMRADE *gives him some leaflets.*)

1ST COMRADE   Here are some of the last of the old leaflets. There are not many left. I am going to the printers and the new lot should be ready within the hour.

HANS   An hour?

1ST COMRADE   I must go! There is going to be a meeting here tonight.

(FIRST COMRADE *leaves.*)

HANS   There are not many leaflets here but it's important that we distribute them right away. How shall we do it?

SPY   You go and distribute them and I'll stay here and wait until our comrade comes back.

HANS   All right, but don't let anyone in without the password.

SPY   Don't worry! I know about these things!

(HANS *leaves. The* SPY *goes to the window and watches him walk away. He begins to look through all the papers. He goes to the window, opens it and whistles. Soon afterwards a* SECRET POLICE AGENT *arrives.*)

SECRET POLICE AGENT   That was quick!

SPY   (*laughs*) Yes, I am getting good at this. After all, this is my fourth year of doing this sort of work. I've got a lot of experience!

SECRET POLICE AGENT   For three months now we have been chasing these bastards without success. And they are becoming more and more daring – they flood working places with their leaflets – and we could never trace them back to their lair.

And then you arrive from Kiel and within three weeks you have found them out. Is this really their underground office?

SPY   Yes.

SECRET POLICE AGENT   Well, let's get going!

(*He goes to the window and whistles. They then search through the papers and put files into their briefcases. A* POLICE SERGEANT *and several* POLICEMEN *arrive.*)

SECRET POLICE AGENT   This is their secret office. Hide yourself in the other room. Anyone who enters will be arrested.

(*The* POLICEMEN *disappear into the other room.*)

SPY   I'm off. I don't want to blow my cover.

SECRET POLICE AGENT   Right. Off you go! Remember, you don't know anything.

(*Immediately afterward the* THIRD COMRADE *comes rushing in.*)

3RD COMRADE   The leaflets! The leaflets. They are done beautifully!

SECRET POLICE AGENT   You are under arrest!

(*Two* POLICEMEN *enter.*)

POLICEMAN   Stand over here and keep completely still otherwise you will have to answer the consequences.

3RD COMRADE   But I don't understand, who has been accusing me . . . ?

POLICEMAN   Keep quiet. You are not allowed to say anything.

(*He leads the* THIRD COMRADE *into the back room.*)

SECRET POLICE AGENT   (*at the window*) Here come some more! It's going well!

(*Enter* WOMAN FIGHTER *and* SECOND COMRADE.)

WOMAN FIGHTER   Those brave women! We can be proud of them! What's this . . . ?

SECRET POLICE AGENT   You are under arrest!

WOMAN FIGHTER   I would strongly advise you, Officer, not to arrest us. You don't seem to be aware of the situation. If you arrest us there will be such an outcry that I can't guarantee a peaceful end to the matter.

POLICEMAN   Don't worry, there won't be any trouble.

WOMAN FIGHTER   Do you know what is

happening? The reign of the military is over. All over Germany and Austria the workers are on strike. In Berlin alone 500,000 workers are striking. The people are fed up with the war. There is a general wave of indignation . . .

POLICEMAN   Quiet! Someone is coming! Not a word! Not a sound!

(Policemen push the WOMAN FIGHTER *and the* SECOND COMRADE *into the backroom.* HANS *arrives.)*

VOICE OF WOMAN FIGHTER   Watch out, comrade!

HANS   What is this? Have we been betrayed? Where is my comrade who stayed behind?

SECRET POLICE AGENT   Your comrade from Kiel has been arrested. And you too are under arrest!

HANS   We have been betrayed!

SECRET POLICE AGENT   Hold your mouth, scum! You agitators are all going to jail and the workers you lured into a strike are heading for the trenches.

8th Tableau

6 November 1916

A prison cell. The WOMAN FREEDOM FIGHTER *in jail clothes.*

WOMAN FIGHTER   There is an atmosphere here today like never before. We can't bear being cooped up in here. Our agitation grows day by day. Why is my comrade still not answering? *(She knocks on the wall. From the neighbouring cell there comes a reply.)* Ah, at last! Liebknecht and Luxemburg free, amnesty! Karl and Rosa are out! Wonderful! It's dawn at last! We leave the terrible night of blood behind us. Ah, if I could get out now! Join the others! Crush the darkness with these arms and plant the red flag against all murder battalions, against poisoned gas, tanks and fighter planes! Listen! They are calling! *(One can hear a crescendo of voices.)* It's coming nearer, it's getting louder. This is the voice of the Revolution. Will they think of us in here? Will they get us out? Here they are! Storming against the gates. But these gates are heavy and well locked – Keep trying, comrades! – A shot! What a tremendous noise! Are those the cries of prisoners?

PRISONERS' VOICES   Freedom! Freedom!

WOMAN FIGHTER   They come flooding down the corridors. They are here!

1ST WORKER   Comrade, you are free!

WOMAN FIGHTER   What is going on? Tell me! Take me with you! Put me somewhere where I can be of use!

1ST WORKER   Victory to the Revolution in Kiel. The Navy put to sea but the sailors mutinied and sailed back into the harbour.

WOMAN FIGHTER   What happened then?

1ST WORKER   Street battles. Soldiers' councils. Victory for us.

WOMAN FIGHTER   And what is happening here?

1ST WORKER   General strike in Hamburg. General strike in Lübeck. The workers' and soldiers' councils are fighting to seize power.

WOMAN FIGHTER   And the Social-Democrats?

1ST WORKER   *(laughs)* The Social-Democrats tell everyone not to be too hasty. They issue decrees and plead for peace and order.

WOMAN FIGHTER   They are against the Revolution?

1ST WORKER   Against the Revolution.

CALLS   Come on! Come on! Into battle! For the workers' and soldiers' councils!

WOMAN FIGHTER   For the workers and soldiers' councils. Long live Spartacus!

9th Tableau

9 November 1918

ANNA   You're not going to school today, kids, today there is trouble afoot.

ROBERT   But can we go into the street and play?

ANNA   Let's wait and see. *(She is sewing but gets up after a while.)* I can't go on stitching, can't settle down. My fingers are trembling.

*(*NEIGHBOUR *arrives.)*

NEIGHBOUR   (suppressing a sob) I can't bear being on my own any more. I'm all . . . I feel all . . . *(Sits down on a stool and puts her head on the kitchen table.)*

ANNA   *(putting her arms around her)* It's difficult, I understand only too well. What is there to say?

NEIGHBOUR   And he had such a good time in Belgium in that castle, with wine and lots of food. And then, suddenly, six weeks ago, totally out of the blue, suddenly it was all over, gone, torn to bits by a grenade. And he was such a good man, so dependable . . .

ANNA   Yes, I know. A good man.

NEIGHBOUR   And to think how stupid I was, my dear Schulz. Yes, we only begin to understand what's going on when it's too late. Remember January, the time of the great strike? You were mad keen about it and, at the time, I thought you were quite mad. Fool that I was! It didn't dawn on me what was at stake. And now . . .

ANNA   Well, you know, when the Revolution is at stake, when it's about freedom for the workers and freedom for all humankind, the way Rosa Luxemburg puts it, well, then, perhaps it is worth sacrificing a husband; I could even see myself going out there and sacrificing myself, even if it meant leaving the children behind. But to lose a husband in a capitalist war, as you did, that is truly awful.

NEIGHBOUR   I am left completely alone: no husband, no children, nothing. (Once more she lets her head fall on the table.)

ANNA   Pull yourself together, Malwine, and don't give up. After all, you are in my kitchen now and you are not alone. If two people are together, and they are kind to each other and get a bit of love from each other, well, then they become strong again and all the shit and evil of the world can't touch them. Kindness is like a bit of sunshine which makes things grow. Ah well, I can't really say what I mean, but you understand, don't you . . .

NEIGHBOUR   Yes, I know what you mean. I do feel a little better, when you speak like this.

ANNA   If it works for us, it must work for all of us. We give each other strength. It's true, we must be tough, we must learn to fight . . . but if we can't hold on to a bit of love for each other then we might as well not bother.

ROBERT   (at the window) Mother! All these people. The street is black with them!

ANNA   That's the Revolution. Look! They are walking side by side and all together. Men and women for a better human life. Let's go and join them and go wherever this may lead us. Liebknecht and Luxemburg are at the head of the march. Our Russian brothers are showing us the way.

NEIGHBOUR   I'm coming too. I'm joining in.

We have been betrayed. From now on things will be different.

(CLARA and FRANZ arrive.)

CLARA   Look, comrade, this is my Franz from Kiel, my Franz, the sailor.

FRANZ   Are you in Spartacus too?

ANNA   Last week, I heard Rosa Luxemburg speak. Now I know what's going on and where all this will lead.

FRANZ   Right.

ANNA   And what's happening in Kiel?

FRANZ   It's going better than here. In Kiel they already have workers' and soldiers' councils; but we will get them here as well.

2ND SAILOR   (comes rushing in) What's keeping you Franz? Here: Liebknecht's leaflet.

FRANZ   (reads) "We demand: the disarming of the police and of all officers. All commandoes to hand power to the workers' and soldiers' councils. All weapons to the workers' and soldiers' councils. Traffic control administered by the workers' and soldiers' council." That's sounds about right.

2ND SAILOR   Yes, and now we must distribute these quickly! The Social-Democrats are busy spreading their poison: "Quietness and order! Fairness!" they preach.

FRANZ   Let's go to the barracks! Let's storm them!

ANNA   I'm coming too! Malwine, you stay with the children.

(Exit ANNA, CLARA, FRANZ, SAILOR.)

CALLS FROM THE STREET   General strike! All power to the workers' and soldiers' councils!

10th Tableau

1919

The Bolshevik Front facing the army of General Denikin on the bank of the Don. A large room in the log cabin. NASDJA. *Men from the* RED GUARD *are pushing into the room, amongst them* WASSIL

1ST RED GUARD   What am I doing here?

WASSIL   It's time for your lesson with Comrade Nasdja.

1ST RED GUARD   Is this woman going to teach us how to shoot?

WASSIL   No, but she'll teach you how to read

and write and other things, which we fools never learnt.

1ST RED GUARD What the devil! How much more is one supposed to learn?

WASSIL She'll tell us what the Whites want, and what the Reds want, and the reasons why we are fighting.

1ST RED GUARD Oh well, let her get on with it!

WASSIL There are lots of us here already, you can start, Comrade Nasdja.

NASDJA Red Guards, comrades, let's not waste time. Any moment now you might be called back to the battlefield. This is our third meeting. And why, do you think, are we meeting like this?

WASSIL Because the soldier of the Red Guard must not be a stupid ox.

NASDJA That's right, comrade.

3RD RED GUARD Because the Red Soldier wants to know what he is fighting for.

NASDJA Does the Red Soldier behave just like a White Soldier?

4TH RED GUARD No, he does not.

WASSIL The White gangs devastate the land,trample the corn and burn cottages. They beat and murder the peasants, and cruelly torture and kill their prisoners.

NASDJA Indeed, they do that. But you, comrades?

3RD RED GUARD The Red Soldier loves his land. He looks after the fields, does not beat up peasants and only kills in honest battle.

NASDJA Whom does the Red Soldier protect?

WASSIL The Red Soldier protects the free workers who have ousted the exploiters and the bosses.

3RD RED GUARD The Red Soldier protects the Soviets of the workers and peasants.

NASDJA Right, comrades. And why do the Whites fight against us?

WASSIL They want to put us back under the yoke.

3RD RED GUARD They want to put the Czar and his men back in power.

4TH RED GUARD They want to impose new and heavy taxes on the peasants. And when the peasants can't pay, they will force them into starvation.

5TH RED GUARD They want to see his delicate white bones lord it over heavy black bones. But our brother Lenin has called upon the millions of black bones to rise with him against the Whites.

NASDJA And why are you no longer fighting for the Czar at the front? Why did you throw away your rifles? And why are you now picking them up again to fight of your own free will at the Red Front? Why are you doing this, comrades of the Red Guard?

1ST RED GUARD Why are you asking all these questions when everyone knows why we are doing this? Over there we were fighting for the bosses and not for the people.

NASDJA Tell me, are the Germans, the French, the Japanese our enemies?

5TH RED GUARD Holy Saint Nicholas! This woman is trying to ask our soul from our body!

WASSIL The capitalist governments are our enemies. But the oppressed classes of all nations are our brothers and comrades. We shall never again want to fight against them.

NASDJA Do we want to make conquests?

3RD RED GUARD No.

NASDJA Do we want to conquer foreign people in Europe and Asia in order to rule over them, exploit them, and get fat on their wealth?

SEVERAL No.

NASDJA Who are those who do?

WASSIL The capitalists and the governments of all states want to do this.

NASDJA Do we want to be great soldiers, excel in war, strive after decorations and make war our single preoccupation?

SEVERAL No, never.

3RD RED GUARD We want to protect our brothers, the workers and the peasants, and once the enemy is beaten we want to do peaceful work at home.

NASDJA Yes, comrades, that's how it is. The capitalists states need military murder machines in order to oppress foreign people. We however refuse to become professional murderers of human beings. We refuse to murder other mothers' children for robbery and material gain. Peace and freedom of all workers, that is our aim.

(A COURIER enters.)

COURIER The comrades are in a difficult battle over the bridge. They need reinforcement.

(All the soldiers of the RED GUARD rush outside. Only NASDJA remains. Searchingly she walks through the room and checks some bundles which are lying about.)

NASDJA   No gun here which I could use. Maybe if I go to the gun depot down at the river? I'm sure they will have some use for me there. *(She dons a soldier's coat, puts on her scarf and quickly leaves.)*

11th Tableau

The Bolshevik front. Grassland – shrubs. In the distance, a river with a bridge. Soldiers of the Red Guard run about. Gunfire can be heard.

1ST RED GUARD   The Whites have had another reinforcement. They are everywhere! *(More gunfire)* Grenades again!

2ND RED GUARD   Who is that? Grey coat and that grey headscarf waving in the wind?

1ST RED GUARD   It's a girl. Looks like a grey moth. Look, she's waving!

(NASDJA arrives.)

NASDJA   I want to join the fight, comrades. Give me a gun!

1ST RED GUARD   Got any identification?

(NASDJA shows him her papers.)

1ST RED GUARD   Good!

(Several SOLDIERS come running. They are fleeing.)

RED GUARDS   They are shooting with artillery and machine-guns. Our supplies are exhausted. We can't hold them any longer. It's impossible. Everyone is fleeing.

(Another FLEEING SOLDIER arrives.)

FLEEING SOLDIER   Everyone is retreating across the bridge. If only we had just a few machine-guns!

2ND RED GUARD   Over there in those bushes is our machine-gun – out of action.

NASDJA   Come on, let's get to it!

(NASDJA runs off into the bushes. Two soldiers of the RED GUARD follow her.)

FLEEING SOLDIER   Look how they're retreating over the bridge, running and throwing away their guns! The enemy is just too strong.

(Noise of a machine-gun very close.)

1ST RED GUARD   Our machine-gun is firing again! The Whites are advancing towards the bridge but our machine-gun is mowing them down.

2ND RED GUARD   Look, the grey moth rushes forward with the gun! They are storming the bridge!

SEVERAL   Let's follow them! Get together and follow!

(Most of the RED GUARD soldiers rush forward. There is constant noise of machine-gun fire. Three RED GUARD soldiers appear from back-stage.)

3RD RED GUARD   Our lot were fleeing but now they are gathering themselves again. A machine-gun out in front is holding the bridge.

(Constant shouts and gunfire. Soldiers of the RED GUARD are rushing forward. Others are walking past.)

CALLS FROM THE FRONT   The Whites are running away. Follow them! The bridge is free!

(After a while the soldiers of the RED GUARD return. One carries the corpse of NASDJA.)

3RD RED GUARD   Things are looking up. The enemy is in retreat. What are they carrying over there? A girl.

2ND RED GUARD   It's our grey moth. Stormed the bridge with the machine-gun. A good comrade.

(Enter WASSIL)

WASSIL   This is Nasdja, Instructor of the Red Guard.

SEVERAL VOICES   A good comrade.

WASSIL   Farewell, Comrade Nasdja! You knew how to teach and how to die.

(They lay NASDJA on the ground, take off their caps and sing a funeral hymn.)

12th Tableau

Winter 1919

A large textile factory where Darja works. Storage room with rolls of cloth lying about. Workers are gathered for a meeting.

1ST WORKER   You're taking your time joining us, comrade!

2ND WORKER   Still early enough to hear the bad news, I'm sure.

1ST WORKER   Yes, things are bad: no raw

materials, no wood, no coal. Broken machines. How are we supposed to do our job? The commissioners keep driving us on and we don't know where to turn.

3RD WORKER I wonder whether the director is really doing all he can. I'm beginning to have doubts.

1ST WORKER Oh, he's all right really, and knows the outfit inside out. After all, he used to be the owner.

3RD WORKER Well, there you are! He used to own the place and now he no longer does. I'm not accusing anyone of anything. But – perhaps that's where the trouble lies.

(DARJA arrives.)

DARJA What's this? Another general meeting? Haven't you got any work to do, comrades? Standing around like this? The soldiers of the Red Guard have no coats, the textile shortage is getting worse all over Russia. And we? We are having a party! As if we didn't have anything to do.

1ST WORKER Come off it, Comrade Darja. You, for one, haven't been seen around much in the factory, these last few days. Been running about in town. And now you have the cheek to reproach us!

DARJA If others before me had run around town as I did just now, perhaps the factory would now be running again.

SEVERAL What d'you mean? What are you saying?

DARJA Who's convened this meeting?

1ST WORKER The comrade director.

DARJA Well then, he must have found some means of carrying on production and wants to tell us about it.

SEVERAL That's not what we think.

DARJA You don't believe it? What else might he want? Surely he's not going to whinge and tell us yet again about his difficulties. We've heard it all before!

1ST WORKER It hasn't got any better.

DARJA And why not? That's what we must find out. What kind of director is this who can't keep his factory going?

SEVERAL Comrade Darja is right. That's what we must ask him.

(Enter factory DIRECTOR.)

DIRECTOR Comrades, I am herewith opening this general meeting. Comrades, you know how, these last few weeks, we have have been struggling. You know that

our difficulties are getting worse and worse. A few days of production meant that we ran out of fuel. A further few days of production brought us to the end of our raw material and there is no prospect of any further supplies. And the worst of it are the machines themselves.

SEVERAL Yes, it's true. The machines!

DIRECTOR You know, comrades, there are no spare parts for the machines. Small but important bits of machinery are now missing.

DARJA How is it possible, Comrade Director, that bits of machinery can simply vanish?

DIRECTOR That's indeed a difficult question, Comrade Darja. I don't want to point the finger at anyone, of course, but it would be perfectly understandable if, say, now and then, some worker . . . Well, times are hard. The need is great. It's obvious. One can buy a piece of bread, some butter . . .

2ND WORKER Are you suggesting that there are such bastards amongst us?

DIRECTOR I didn't say that this is what happened. I'm merely suggesting the possibility. In any case, the machines are now beyond repair. The missing parts are unobtainable. And with the current unreliability of railways, there is no way of getting any raw materials. There is nothing for it, comrades, and it is very sad indeed, but we have no option but to close the factory. *(Despondent murmur amongst the workers.)*

SEVERAL It's a sad state of affairs. But what can we do?

DIRECTOR There is nothing anyone can do, comrades. You know that we have tried everything. I shall therefore propose the motion that we close down the factory and suggest we vote accordingly.

DARJA Just a minute! Don't vote just yet! I posit the motion to set up an enquiry.

SEVERAL *(astonished)* An enquiry?

DARJA Yes, an enquiry with a committee who agrees to accompany me straight away to the director's home.

DIRECTOR What's the meaning of all this?

DARJA It means that, after we have been to your cellar, we shall be able to put the factory back to work within a few days. *(The DIRECTOR tries to move unnoticed towards the door.)* Don't let him go, comrades! Don't let him out. Follow me!

(DARJA *and several* WORKERS *leave. Two workers move to either side of the* DIRECTOR *and lead him away. The rest remain in the room.*)

1ST WORKER It's difficult to know what to think!

3RD WORKER Yes, comrades, I did have my doubts, but didn't want to say anything.

2ND WORKER Darja is no idle talker. She usually holds her tongue but seems to keep her eyes open. But when she does open her mouth she knows what she is talking about. Look, they're back!

(DARJA *and the others return without the* DIRECTOR.)

1ST WORKER Where is the director?

4TH WORKER Under guard in his house. – And here are the missing spare parts. (*Two* WORKERS *bring a wooden box full of small bits of machinery.*)

2ND WORKER Where were they?

4TH WORKER In the cellar of the director's house. You tell them, Darja.

ALL Darja, tell us!

DARJA Well, I was so miserable, comrades: the thought of our soldiers out there without coats while our cloth factory stood idle! And I just knew it in my bones that the director was planning to close us down. So I opened my eyes, ran around a bit, did some snooping. I'd much rather do an honest day's work, I can tell you, comrades. Spying is a job for scoundrels. But this was an emergency. Indeed, it turned out that the director was selling our raw material and hiding parts of the machines in his cellar. He was out to prove that the factory could not be run along our lines and that it would be better to put it back into private ownership.

WORKERS The bastard. The cheat!

DARJA Let's not lose another minute in idle talk. Let's put the machines together once more and then it can all start up again. By the way, we also managed to get some raw material.

1ST WORKER Comrades, Darja has put our factory back in business. How about making her our manager?

ALL Comrade Darja for manager! She knows what she is doing!

DARJA If you really think so, comrades, I shall try to do my best, but you must all help me! This way we shall succeed. And now, back to work!

ALL To work! Long live the Soviet Republic!

13th Tableau

Berlin, 14 January 1919, evening

Anna's flat as in the other tableaux. The children are in bed asleep. ANNA *is sitting at her sewing-machine near a small lamp. There is a knock at the door. It makes* ANNA *jump. The* NEIGHBOUR *enters.*

ANNA (*walking towards the* NEIGHBOUR) Where have you come from, Malwine? What's going on out there?

NEIGHBOUR Things are bad. Trouble everywhere. And nobody knows what's going on. I've lost all my contacts. There must be an awful lot of troops in Berlin. Our lot has been totally dispersed. Any news from your husband?

ANNA Nothing at all.

NEIGHBOUR Has no one from the advance guard been to see you?

ANNA No one – Ah well, Malwine. Go home, go to bed. There is no point in doing anything any more. Things are just too awful. It's all over. Our hopes, all these past years . . .

NEIGHBOUR It seems the tables are turned. Now it's my turn to buck you up. You mustn't give up, you know.

ANNA What's the point in carrying on, if they are determined to do us in with their cheating and their bullying? We have been betrayed and sold out, and most of the workers don't even notice it. As usual they are dozing on, dreaming their beautiful dreams. Between snores they conjure up wonderful images for themselves. Go to bed, Malwine! Nothing good will come of this day.

NEIGHBOUR Well, good night, then.

(*She leaves.* ANNA *walks up and down in her room. She is uneasy; looks out of the window, looks at the clock.* PAUL *and* FRANZ *arrive, wearing dirty and torn clothes.*)

ANNA Paul, Franz, what a relief! You're alive!

PAUL Not so loud! We must be careful. Was Karl here?

ANNA Karl Liebknecht? No.

PAUL And Rosa?

ANNE No, not her either.

FRANZ In that case I must carry on looking for Karl. He's got to leave Berlin before daybreak. They are looking for him and Rosa. Moabit[14] has been cordoned off. General Hoffmann[15] and his gang are disarming the workers.

PAUL Try to get to Wedding.[16] You are bound to find him there. You know where to look, don't you?

FRANZ Yes.

(FRANZ *leaves quickly.* PAUL *sits down, exhausted. He puts his head on the table.*)

ANNA My dear, tell me, can you stay here? Or are they after you too?

PAUL I've got to go. Just one hour's sleep. I can't go on. (ANNA *brings coffee and bread.*)

ANNA Here, drink this and have something to eat.

(PAUL *takes a sip and swallows a bite. He throws the rest of the bread on the table and jumps up.*)

PAUL This bread tastes bitter and the coffee seems poisoned. Four years I spent in the trenches, got wounded. They patched me up and I carried on; helped chase out the landlords and take over the government; and now, after just two months of revolution, we are betrayed, sold, and driven on to the knives of the white officers. With their artillery they shot at us in our revolutionary hideout. After that they tried gas. They murdered our seven Members of Parliament. Seven unarmed Members of Parliament! And who, do you think, has betrayed us to these white bastards? Our own brothers, the Social-Democratic workers and their leaders. Traitors on the one side, blind fools on the other. And why do they hate us so much? It's because we fight for their rights and their freedom. That's why they hunt us like wild animals. The few who are honest and remain loyal to the workers' cause, these are the very ones they want to kill.

ANNA But Noske,[17] our new leader, is a Social-Democrat too.

PAUL Why doesn't he follow the example of the Russians? They got rid of the Czar's officers, dispersed the old military and formed a new Red Army. Instead of which our Social-Democrats lick the old officers' boots and put weapons in their hands against the workers. I've got to go now. Keep up your spirits. I shall be back when things are sorted out.

(PAUL *leaves quickly.* ANNA *sits down on a*

chair and sobs silently. Soon after there is a loud knock at the door. The house door is pushed in violently and there is a noise of heavy boots coming upstairs. The door flies open and a LIEUTENANT *and two* SOLDIERS *enter.*)

LIEUTENANT Karl Liebknecht is in this house.

ANNA Nobody is here except me and my children.

LIEUTENANT (*puts his gun to* ANNA's *chest*) Tell me where you have hidden that Spartacist pig or else I'll shoot.

ANNA There've been no pigs in this flat – not until now.

LIEUTENANT What's this? What? (*The* SOLDIERS *search the cupboard and the bed.*)

1ST SOLDIER There is no one here, sir.

LIEUTENANT Let's go! Into the next flat! (*Turns round at the door*) When we come back we'll break every bone in your body, you Spartacist slut.

14th Tableau

15 January 1919

A street in a working-class district of Berlin. A public speaker stands on a wagon. People gather around him. On a wall nearby hangs an anti-Soviet poster. ANNA *comes along holding little* ROBERT's *hand. She carries a basket.*

ROBERT Mother, look at that picture!

ANNA It's the picture of someone being murdered with a knife. Underneath it says "That's Bolshevism".

ROBERT Mother, what's that man on the cart saying?

ANNA Let's go and listen. (*They mingle with the crowd.*)

PUBLIC SPEAKER Thanks to the wisdom and clear thinking of our Social-Democratic leader it has been possible to avert the catastrophe. Spartacus is no more!

CALLS FROM THE CROWD Thank God!

PUBLIC SPEAKER Slowly peace and order are returning to Berlin thanks to our general commander Gustav Noske.

CALLS FROM THE CROWD Peace and order!

OTHER CALLS Yes, and blood and hunger too!

PUBLIC SPEAKER General Hoffmann and his troops are on the advance everywhere. The sharp shooters of the loyal cavalry guard promise you that they won't leave Berlin until order has been restored once and for all.

A WORKER   Are the officers republicans too?

PUBLIC SPEAKER   No need to worry, the officers have sworn allegiance to the republic.

WORKER   That's all right, then.

PUBLIC SPEAKER   People, you have no idea what a dreadful danger had been hanging over you. Bolshevism with all its terror. Boshevism is synonymous with death. Bolshevism means robbery.

ANNA   You are lying.

PUBLIC SPEAKER   Bolshevism means fire storms and meaningless persecution of all against all. It means the distribution of our wealth amongst the rabble of the street. It means the theft of all property and a free for all against women.

1ST WOMAN   Just listen to him!

ANNA   He is lying.

PUBLIC SPEAKER   Those who have two shirts must hand over one. Those who have two cooking pots must give one up. Those who have a wife or a daughter have to abandon them to anyone who will have them. Women are the property of the state. Everything is the property of the state. In Russia no soldier will ever again obey an officer. Lawless hordes swarm the country. Here, on the other hand, our noble and trusty officers put themselves at the service of the state.

CALLS   Long live our army!

1ST WORKER   Let's be a little bit more cautious where these noble officers are concerned.

ANNA   Butchers of working people, that's what they are.

PUBLIC SPEAKER   Seize that woman over there!

ANNA   Judas! Traitor!

(ANNA *is pushed away. A* MAN *with a special edition of a newspaper arrives.*)

MAN   Liebknecht and Luxemburg are dead. Liebknecht arrested and killed while escaping. Rosa Luxemburg has been lynched by the mob.

ANNA   Murdered! Our leaders have been murdered!

CALLS   Get rid of that woman!

PUBLIC SPEAKER   People! It is a great pity that two people who until recently belonged to the Social-Democratic Party had to find their death in this way. Wild fanaticism drove them to their doom. The people themselves have judged them.

ANNA   Judas!

15th Tableau

15 January, evening

A room in the Hotel Eden. Several OFFICERS *from the sharp shooters division of the Cavalry Guard.*

1ST OFFICER   Long live the Sharp Shooters of the Cavalry Guard!

ALL   Hurray! Hurray!

1ST OFFICER   Actually, my friends, I didn't think a revolution would be quite so much fun. Really, it was more like a prank in fancy dress!

2ND OFFICER   Yes, and to think how worried we were only two months ago!

3RD OFFICER   It feels all the better now – as if waking up from a bad dream.

1ST OFFICER   A few tame donkeys – I shall name no names *(laughter)* – a few tame donkeys donned a lion's hide and ended up being frightened of their own appearance and their own roar.

3RD OFFICER   Yes, my dear fellows, who would have thought that the so-called revolutionary representatives of the people, saddlers, basket makers etc. etc. *(laughter)* would, with their tails between their legs, plead for our support against the workers, the very people to whom they owe their position. Who would have thought it?

2ND OFFICER   Well, there you are. It is obvious, the Germans are a nation of heroes.

1ST OFFICER   Steady on! One can go too far with one's mockery, you know. We, the élite, we are the heroes. The others are just rabble and will always remain rabble. And if the rabble begins to rebel, one shoots it down. As you saw yourselves, most of them beg for the whip and a bit of discipline themselves.

2ND OFFICER   No serious arguments, here, if you please, gentlemen. Tonight we are going to have fun. Spartacus is finished. Let's celebrate! After all, we did have some difficult moments. Let's raise our glass to the red light of Jerusalem, to the leader of the people, Rosa Luxemburg! *(Loud laughter)*

1ST OFFICER   Yes, a head with a lot of brain

inside is just as easily broken as one with none. Let's ask –

2ND OFFICER   Sh! No names!

1ST OFFICER   But we are all friends here!

2ND OFFICER   Even so.

4TH OFFICER   Friends, I am really astonished, outraged even, at your cavalier attitude. The events which have occurred in Germany these last few weeks are very serious indeed and will have fateful consequences. In fact . . .

1ST OFFICER   Enough of that, my young friend. We are not in church here. We are drinking Sekt and are celebrating our victory. Life is short and the power is ours. Long live the Sharp Shooters!

EVERYONE   Hip hip hurray! Hip hip hurray! Hurray!

2ND OFFICER   Long live the spirit of the old Prussian Officer Class!

EVERYONE   Hurray! Hurray!

3RD OFFICER   And all the saddlers and basket makers! *(Laughter)*

EVERYONE   Hip hip!

Interlude

THEATRE DIRECTOR   We can't put on stage everything that happened in those years. The heroic struggle of the proletariat in the Ruhr region after the Kapp-Putsch,[18] for example, or the worker taking up arms to save the Revolution and being brutally mowed down by Noske's guards, the generals and their white mob. Or workers who helped to save Ebert's republic languishing in prison to this day. The thousands who were killed. Battles in Bavaria, the uprising in Middle Germany, the great strike and the famine riots during the year of the great inflation. The daring and brilliant struggle of the workers of Hamburg and their women. The proletariat of Germany, weakened by hunger, restrained by imprisonment, and paralysed by terror. And the Russian workers, who, after a hard struggle have triumphed over all enemies, who are now building up a new world for the workers. One last time the curtain will rise to show you how working women the world over continue the struggle.

16th *Tableau*

World Congress of Communist Women in Moscow. A large meeting room. Women Delegates from all over the world.

DARJA   Greetings from the women workers of the textile factory in Petrograd. We have had a long struggle and have suffered much. Our machines were broken up and raw materials difficult to obtain. But despite all this we continue to work and keep our factory in good repair. We have even organised a refectory for our workers and a nursery for the children of working mothers.

MATRENA   Greetings from Materka and Lubinka, the village soviets where we come from, four village women of the new village welfare. No longer despised as we used to be, we are now part of the village council. We have acquired a steam plough for our region and the soil gets worked much better now. The time of the greatest poverty is over.

ANNA   In Germany there has been much suffering. Again and again our hopes have been dashed as we were beaten by our enemies. We lost our leaders, Liebknecht and Luxemburg, and many good comrades during the January battles. And after the attack by Knapp thousands perished in the west. Many of our best fighters are either dead or dispersed across the world. Often we came close to abandoning all hope and giving up. But now that I am here in Russia and see how you are all still struggling and working, my courage is returning. I want to go home and report to my comrades what I have seen here.

FARMER'S WIFE FROM SIBERIA   I'm from Siberia, from the steppes of Kirgiz and am only a poor and ignorant woman. In my head it was dark and my heart was used to being a slave. Now I feel as if I'm awakening to a new life. I come and go as I please in the very house of the Czar and I greet you as my sisters. We make decisions about what is good for the land and for our children and will carry them through for the benefit of all.

WOMAN WORKER FROM PERSIA   We are Islamic women from Persia. Not so long ago we didn't even know that we were human beings. We were the slaves of the rich, and the slaves of our men. But when the light of the Red Star went up over the Russian people, it shone as far as Persia.

INDIAN WOMAN   India is a long way from here but for us Bolshevik women it was not too far. We felt we must come and greet our sisters and get advice and sustenance from you. Over India too, the red dawn is rising and we, the communists, realise what the light means. We shall not relent in our struggle against our formidable enemy. Our men will not be able to do it without our help: we must fight by their side. Our strength must combine with theirs to establish the new order, which will be one unifying principle encompassing all human beings, both men and women.

WOMAN FIGHTER   Welcome to you all, comrades from all the world! Welcome, communists, of all lands! There was a time when women were isolated everywhere, powerless and lost. Unaware of the relentless historic process, they lived like plants and beasts, isolated in their huts and hovels. They were condemned to slave labour on the land and in the factory. But now the Red Star has risen in the sky of humanity and the great storm of revolution has seized these working women and drives them inexorably towards the fighting front of the awakening slave workers. The light of this star will reach into the nooks and corners of the darkest and most distant hovel. Its light touches the helpless, the lonely and the enslaved. Working women of the world, Communism calls all of you to a new life! Under Lenin's banner we unite. Our insignia will be the Hammer, the Sickle and the Red Star.

Working women: the world awaits you! Mothers of the proletariat, humankind waits you! Without you the revolution will be nothing but a half measure. It will turn to dust. Without you the struggle will count for nothing and the old powers will not be destroyed. Without you there will be no new beginning and no new society. Therefore, stand up and be counted! Communist women of the world, go to work now, and begin the fight. Become the mothers of the future! The Red Star be our light, the Sickle and the Hammer our Sign!

WOMEN   *(They sing the "Internationale")*

Curtain

Notes

1 Karl Liebknecht (1871–1919) left-wing socialist. He was the joint leader, with Rosa Luxemburg (1870–1919), of the communist Spartacus Group which staged an unsuccessful uprising in 1919. Liebknecht and Luxemburg were both assassinated by officers of the counterrevolutionary volunteers.

2 Anton Ivanovitch Denikin (1872–1947). Russian General during the First World War. After the Russian Revolution of 1917 he led the offensive against the Bolsheviks (the Reds) until his defeat in 1920.

3 Kommunistische Partei Deutschlands (German Communist Party).

4 Dawes Report: International Plan, signed in London in 1924, which outlined the extent of Germany's War Reparation after her defeat in 1918.

5 Popular German war-hymn.

6 Field-grey: colour of the German Infantry.

7 Blue-Jackets: uniform of the German Navy.

8 Popular German war-hymn.

9 Hereros: a tribe of Bantus living in north and middle South-west Africa. In 1904 they staged a heroic but unsuccessful revolt against German colonial rule which virtually destroyed them.

10 Sausage made of minced shellfish.

11 Aleksander Fedorovich Kerenski (1881–1970) Russian political leader. He tried to introduce democratic reforms after the March Revolution of 1917 by forging a coalition between Socialist Revolutionary and Menshevik members of the newly formed soviet. He was deposed on 6 November 1917 when the Bolsheviks under Lenin seized power.

12 Friedrich Ebert (1871–1925) and Philipp Scheidemann (1865–1938), both Social-Democrats, shared power in 1919 in the first government of the Weimar Republic.

13 Willem, colloquial for Kaiser Wilhelm II.

14 Moabit: district in the west of Berlin.

15 Max Hoffmann (1869–1927). He was Chief of Staff on the Eastern Front from 1916 onwards and in 1919 became an efficient strategist against the revolution at home.

16 Wedding: district in the north of Berlin.

17 Gustav Noske (1868–1946). Social-
    Democrat. Under his command
    government troops quashed the Spartacus
    movement in 1919.

18 Wolfgang Kapp (1858–1922). He led an
    unsuccessful right-wing attempt to seize
    power in Berlin during the night of 11
    March 1920.

6 Muriel Box 1905–91

Angels of War
UK

Introduction

Angels of War was published in 1935 as part of a collection of full-length plays for all-women casts. The first play written by Muriel Box, *Angels of War* is one of the few works published under her own name rather than as a result of collaboration with her husband, Sydney Box. Although she is best known today as one of the first British women film directors, she also wrote nearly 100 plays and over 15 major film scripts with Sydney, winning an Oscar for the screen-play for *The Seventh Veil* (1945) before their partnership broke up in 1958. Sydney, a journalist, had already won prizes for his one-act plays and in 1934 he had a curtain-raiser, called *Murder Trial*, produced in the West End with Alastair Sim and Peggy Ashcroft, whereas Muriel was still working as a continuity-girl while she wrote *Angels of War*. It was a play for amateurs and we have no evidence that it was performed professionally until 1981. In that year the feminist theatre group, Mrs Worthington's Daughters, took it on tour around Britain.

It is very much a beginner's piece of work with regard to dialogue and stage impact. Nevertheless, it repays consideration. Muriel Box was (re-)discovered in the 1980s as a "quasi-feminist" film-maker for certain films which she both wrote and directed in the 1950s, such as *Too Young to Love* (the film adaptation of a play about teenage prostitution, *Pick-up Girl*) and *Street Corner* (about London policewomen), where she managed to privilege women's points of view within the male-dominated commercial cinema of her time. *Angels of War* was an attempt to achieve the same for the theatre. Box's work can be fruitfully regarded as an example of the ways in which feminism survived "underground" in the apparently fallow interwar period. Despite not belonging to any explicitly feminist organisations or networks such as *Time and Tide*, Muriel Box did benefit from the informal support of other strong women like Flora Robson and Mary Field, and she did manage to inherit and transmit remnants of the powerful political movement that had existed prior to and during the First World War. Her approach can be clearly distinguished from the conservative anti-feminist works of such writers as Diana Morgan, whose virulently anti-suffragette play *The House on the Square* was a minor success on the London stage in 1940.

Furthermore, although contributing nothing original to the formal development of British theatre, *Angels of War* is significant partly because it is evidence of the genteel interest in amateur dramatics which was a feature of British culture in the interwar period, and also because it illustrates aspects of the inherited memory of the First World War and anxiety about another world war, which were features of popular consciousness in the interwar period. Thus, together with its transmission of popular feminist history, we can regard *Angels of War* as a useful cultural indicator – perhaps the more so because Box had a deprived background, little education and no influential connections. As she wrote in her autobiography *Odd Woman Out*, she was "born into the Respectable Poor" (Box 1974: 15). Hers was at the time genuinely a voice from below, not one of the dominant voices of the élite.

It is helpful to place *Angels of War* within two contexts. One is the obvious, wider context of the literature remembering the First World War which suddenly flourished in Britain from 1928/9, with the first performances in London of R. C. Sherriff's *Journey's End* and Sean O'Casey's *Silver Tassie*. O'Casey's play may be the more creative, but it was Sherriff's which seems to have stirred the English response, making a huge public outpouring suddenly possible. That outpouring was, like Sherriff's trigger, primarily male-authored and to do with male experience, and it led to male-dominated war films (such as Asquith's *Tell England*, on which Muriel Box worked as a continuity-girl). Yet it also resulted in two influential war books by women: Vera Brittain's *Testament of Youth* (1933) and Evadne Price's *Not So Quiet* (1930), which were both aimed at presenting a woman's point of view. These were direct responses to male-authored, androcentric texts – Brittain's to Robert Graves's *Goodbye To All That* (1929) and Price's to Erich Remarque's *All Quiet on the Western Front* (1929). Both became best-sellers. The romantic *Testament of Youth* is better remembered today, thanks to the 1970's TV adaptation by Elaine Morgan. It is a story which tends to reinforce traditional, conservative notions of femininity, taking as

its protagonist a young woman who sacrifices her own ambitions to take up the stereotypically auxiliary role for women, that of nursing wounded warriors. Yet at the time of the Great War, it was the subject of Price's novel which made the greater impact on the imagination of girls and women: all-women ambulance units at the battlefront. Inspirited by the pre-war feminist movement and following the extraordinary example of the Heroines of Pervyse, women ambulance drivers broke traditional moulds. They drove unchaperoned, they had to be expert mechanics, cleaning and repairing their own vehicles, and their arduous work demanded not only stamina but courage, since they frequently drove at night, during air-raids and under bombardment, and at risk of gas attacks.

It was to Price's example that Muriel Box turned when seeking material for an all-women cast. Yet, although about an all-women ambulance unit on the Western

Figure 7 British women ambulance drivers with the Belgian Army, May 1918. (Although Box specifies WAAC drivers' uniforms, only FANYs drove ambulances on the battlefront.) [IWM photo Q3257]

Front, her play is in no way a straightforward dramatisation of the taboo-breaking events of Price's novel (such as abortion and pre-marital sex) nor of its modernist style. However, many of Box's facts and ideas are drawn from that source, particularly the crucial ones of the coarsening of women through war experience, looser sexual mores, the rejection of facile patriotism, and the conflict between the ordinary drivers and their Commandant. To turn that material into a play Box very closely follows the structure of Sherriff's *Journey's End*. Although not concluding in tragedy, like his, her three-act play introduces the audience to the war-front by means of a newcomer, whose experiences contradict the wartime propaganda. *Angels of War* does not make the impact of Sherriff's play, for Box did not share Sherriff's talents for dialogue and characterisation, nor for significant incident and suspense, yet the precise differences between the two plays, and the precise reasons for Box's difficulties, are instructive. These have partly to do with the differences, arising from gender stereotyping, between men's and women's experiences at the Front, and partly to do with the point of view with which the audience is encouraged to identify. Whereas Sherriff's protagonists are officers, and the focus is on displaying the heroism and bonding of two men, Box focuses on the rank-and-file women drivers and she distributes her interest equally across all eight of them, making the group the protagonist rather than any individual. Furthermore, for all its deficiencies, her play avoids the pitfalls which beset a direct dramatisation of Price's novel by a far more experienced and accomplished playwright, Kenyon Nicholson. His *Stepdaughters of War* reached the Broadway stage in 1930, only to be savaged by critics for its diffuseness and similarity to a novel. Box's play is both more concise and more unified in place and theme than Kenyon's, and she downplays the romantic love aspect which Kenyon foregrounds.

The second context in which it is helpful to situate *Angels of War* is that of other 1930s' plays by women dramatists which also focused on communities of women confronted by a military ethos. There are two plays which, although largely forgotten now and out of print, made a significant impact in the 1930s: *The Years of the Locusts* (1935), by

the American playwright Constance Marie O'Hara, which was first performed at the Hedgerow Theatre in Philadelphia in 1933, and *Schoolgirls in Uniform* (1933), an adaptation by Barbara Burnham of the play *Gestern und Heute* [Yesterday and Today] (1930) by the German writer, Christa Winsloe. That play had been adapted to film in German in 1931 as the notorious *Mädchen in Uniform* and the English version was performed with success in London in 1932/3 and then on Broadway. *The Years of the Locusts* was based on a Great War history, *The Irish Nuns at Ypres*. All three plays interrogate ideas of motherhood and use them to resist militarism. They also point, guardedly, to emotional and sexual satisfactions for women outside marriage. These three women playwrights, in their respective countries, drew on a shared sense of women's values to depict, analyse and stand out against the militarist ethos that threatened those values in the early 1930s. Looking back at the First World War, they all manifest a premonition of another war to come. Although their plays constructed imaginary communities of women, these are precisely historically located; part of patriarchally controlled institutions, these are not fantastic amazon utopias and they do not constitute "no-men's-zones" outside the dominant order of class, religion and the army. However, they indicate a resistance from within, a subversive fifth column, isolated and weak but definitely anti-war. So the plays can be seen as providing a link from the international women's movement before the First War to the international women's movement that succeeded the Second War, particularly between those branches which worked to avoid war.

Further reading

Primary

Box, Muriel (1935) *Angels of War* in John Bourne (ed.) *Five New Full-Length Plays for All Women Casts*, London: Lovat Dickson & Thompson.
—— (1974) *Odd Woman Out*, London: Leslie Frewin.
Brittain, Vera (1933) *Testament of Youth*, London: Gollancz.
Columban, Dame M. (1915) *The Irish Nuns at Ypres*, London: Smith Elder.

Morgan, Diana (1940) *A House on the Square* in *Five Plays of 1940*, London: Hamilton.

O'Hara, Constance Marie (1935) *The Years of the Locusts*, Boston: Baker.

Price, Evadne ("Helen Zenna Smith") [1930] (1988) *"Not So Quiet . . . " Stepdaughters of War*, London: Virago.

Sherriff, R. C. [1929] (1983) *Journey's End*, London: Penguin.

Winsloe, Christa (1933) *Children in Uniform* (adapted by Barbara Burnham), Boston: Baker.

Secondary

Bidwell, Shelford (1977) *The Women's Royal Army Corps*, London: Leo Cooper.

Box, Sydney (1939) *The Amateur Stage: a Symposium by Flora Robson et al.*, London.

Gale, Maggie B. (1996) *West End Women: Women and the London Stage, 1918–62*, London: Routledge.

Jesse, Friniwyd Tennyson (1919) *The Sword of Deborah: First-hand Impressions of the British Women's Army in France*, London: Heinemann.

Kuhn, Annette and Susannah Radstone (1990) *The Women's Companion to International Film*, London: Virago.

Marshall, Norman (1947) *The Other Theatre*, London: Lehmann.

Mitton, G. E. (1916) *The Cellar-House of Pervyse*, London: Black.

Angels of War

[A Play in Three Acts]
Published London, 1935
First performed by feminist theatre group, Mrs Worthington's
Daughters on UK tour, 1981

Muriel Box

Characters

IRENE COX ("Cocky")

EDNA CLARKE ("Nobby")

SALLY LOMAX ("Salome")

HON. MILLICENT WESTBROOKE ("Moaner")

JOYCE OVERTON ("Jo")

VICTORIA NEWMAN ("Vic")

MARY SKINNER ("Skinny")

ELIZABETH TURLEY ("Creeping Lizzie")

THE COMMANDANT

MRS GORDON MYERS, OBE

Time and Place

The action takes place in a cottage behind the
British lines in France, during the year 1918.

Act I

*A farm labourer's cottage several miles behind
the British lines at —— in France. It is March
1918, and the cottage is at present occupied by
seven members of the Queen Mary's Army
Auxiliary Corps (more generally known as "the
Waacs".) Its living-room has become their mess-
room. It is furnished with a rough trestle table,
covered with American cloth, an ancient upright
piano and several chairs. Light is provided by a
hurricane lamp and heat by a "bogey" stove.*

*The room has bare whitewashed walls, with
here and there pictures torn from illustrated
magazines and crude pencil sketches to relieve
the monotony. A door down S.R. opens on to the
yard and another, back centre, leads to the
sleeping quarters. There is a window in the
left-hand wall. Close to the door S.R., is fixed a
notice-board, from which hangs a pencil. Each
member of the detachment writes her name on
this as she comes in and crosses it through when*
*she goes out on duty again. When the curtain
rises the room is empty. Then the outer door is
opened violently by* IRENE COX, *a sturdy
Lancashire lass, known to the rest of the girls as
"COCKY". She is followed by* EDNA CLARKE, *a
newcomer who becomes known, immediately
and inevitably, as "NOBBY". Both girls are
dressed in Q.M.A.A.C. uniform, but* NOBBY *is
neat and clean in comparison with* COCKY *the
oldtimer.*

NOBBY *(dropping her kit and moving over to
the stove to warm her hands)* I'm simply
frozen. I never dreamed it could be so cold.

COCKY Aye. It's a bit on chill side.

NOBBY A bit! It's like being at the North
Pole. And this stove doesn't seem to give
any heat. Is it always like this?

COCKY That's least of what you'll have to
put up with, out here. *(She starts to write on
the list pinned to the notice-board.)* Clarke's
the name, didn't you say?

NOBBY That's right. Clarke with an "e".

COCKY I shouldn't worry about the "e", lass.
Ye'll be Nobby to everyone except
Commandant.

NOBBY Nobby!

COCKY That's right.

NOBBY But why?

COCKY Search me. Because Clarkes always
are called Nobby – whether they've got an
"e" or not – so you'd best get used to it.

NOBBY *(in a forlorn voice)* It doesn't sound
very pretty.

COCKY Nothing's very pretty out here.

NOBBY What are you writing?

COCKY Come and look. *(NOBBY crosses the
room and looks over COCKY's shoulder.)*
Every time you come in you write name on
board – at bottom of list, see? When you
have to go out you cross name off, like
these are. When yours is top name *not*
crossed off, you're next for high jump
when whistle goes. Got it?

115

NOBBY   Yes. I think so.

COCKY   Good. Now you're number twelve – you'll be taking Tilly's place.

NOBBY   Why did she go?

COCKY   *(laconically)* Double pneumonia.

NOBBY   Oh! How ghastly! Was she nice?

COCKY   *(shortly)* She was a good driver, if that's what you mean. *(She turns away abruptly and opens the door to the sleeping quarters.)* We sleep in here. That's your cot in the far corner. Roof leaks when it rains. Best roll this way a bit when you get into your flea-bag.

NOBBY   *(more shocked than she would care to admit at the squalor of the place)* Oh. I'll try and remember that. Thank you.

(She pushes the door to and turns back into the mess-room. COCKY is warming her hands at the stove.)

NOBBY   What's your name?

COCKY   Cocky.

NOBBY   *(slightly bewildered)* You mean I'm to call you that?

COCKY   You'd better – if you want an answer.

NOBBY   What's your proper name, though?

COCKY   Irene Theodora Cox. Bloody awful, eh? *(NOBBY makes an instinctive gesture which reveals how much this remark has shocked her, but COCKY is looking at the stove and doesn't notice it. She goes on cheerfully.)* Did you have a bad crossing?

NOBBY   Simply vile. I'm feeling frightfully tired. I think I'll have a wash and then turn in.

COCKY   That's a good one, that is!

NOBBY   I don't see anything to laugh at.

COCKY   You would if you'd been here as long as I have. There's a few surprises in store for you lass.

NOBBY   *(rather haughtily)* For instance?

COCKY   You can't have a wash for a start.

NOBBY   Why not?

COCKY   Because we've only got enough water for drinking – unless you'd like to take a pail across yard to pump.

NOBBY   *(looking round for pail and picking it up)* Where's the pump?

COCKY   *(taking the pail from her)* Ee, don't be so soft, lass. It's sure to be frozen if you go.

NOBBY   But I feel filthy.

COCKY   That's nothing – I'm lousy. Haven't had a bath for three weeks.

NOBBY   How appalling! I shall never get used to *that*!

COCKY   You will. It's only what you might call a surface irritation. There's worse things than that to get you down – cold and wet and bad grub and the Old Cow.

NOBBY   *(opening her eyes very wide)* The . . . *(She changes the subject hurriedly.)* Well, of course, one doesn't expect active service to be a picnic. I knew there were hardships before I came and I'm quite prepared to rough it as long as I know that I am doing my bit. After all, the Tommies have far worse things to put up with.

COCKY   Aye, much worse – if you can imagine anything worse than this.

NOBBY   *(laughing a little uneasily)* You know, I believe you're ragging.

COCKY   Ragging?

NOBBY   Exaggerating, just to frighten me.

COCKY   Don't you fret, lass. You'll be frightened enough without any assistance from me.

NOBBY   It can't be as awful as all that.

COCKY   Oh, can't it. *(She turns and takes NOBBY by the shoulders.)* Look here, lass, I'm not trying to frighten you. I'm only telling you so that you can go out there with your eyes open. It's not such a shock that way. War's awful all right – bloody awful! It's hell – worse than anything you can imagine – but you've got to keep a stiff upper lip and say nowt. Otherwise the Old Cow'll have you back to Mother before you can say "Jack Robinson" and you know how you'd feel then. *(She pauses for a moment.)* Well, aren't you going to say anything?

NOBBY   There's nothing to say, is there?

(She turns away.)

COCKY   Then you'd better get unpacked.

NOBBY   All right. *(She kneels by her kit and then pauses and looks up at COCKY.)* You know I don't want you to think I'm a prude or – or anything, but do all the girls use – well – bad language like you?

COCKY   *(with a laugh)* Wait till you hear Jo . . . There, don't you worry; you'll pick it up soon enough.

NOBBY   I'm sure I could never say the sort of things you do.

COCKY   Oh, you'll find it helps. They're the only two consolations we've got – swearing and smoking. Ee, that reminds me. Got a cigarette?

NOBBY   No, I'm sorry. I'm afraid I don't smoke.

COCKY   Strewth! (She turns away.)

NOBBY   (looking up again) Do they never stop?

COCKY   (puzzled) Stop?

NOBBY   The guns.

COCKY   Oh, them. After a while you won't be able to sleep without that row going on. When I was on leave the quiet nearly sent me daft.

NOBBY   Of course we had air raids at home but they didn't go on and on like that.

COCKY   Oh, air raids are all right – unless you happen to be on the road with an ambulance full of Blighty cases. Driving without lights is a tricky business.

NOBBY   (anxiously) I say, I hope they won't give me an awful lot of driving to do just at first. I'm not really a first-class driver yet you know.

COCKY   Who cares? The Old Cow certainly won't. You'll be all right as long as you keep your nerve.

NOBBY   Well, I'll try. . . . I say, who is the old – er – you know what?

COCKY   You'll know soon enough!

(The outer door is pushed violently open and four Waacs stagger wearily into the room. They are SALLY LOMAX ("SALOME"), the HON, MILLICENT WESTBROOKE ("MOANER"), JOYCE OVERTON ("JO"), and VICTORIA NEWMAN" ("VIC").

SALOME is by far the prettiest. She has fair fluffy hair, a neat figure and slim ankles. MOANER is thin, with a pale, miserable countenance, dark shadows under her eyes and a weak mouth. JO might almost be taken for a man. Her hair is cropped short and every line of her figure betrays unusual strength. VIC, the last of the four, is good-looking without being striking and manages to be popular without asserting herself particularly. One by one they sign their names at the end of the list and make for the stove.)

MOANER   (the last to reach the stove) Move up somebody. I'm nearly stiff with cold. Jo! You might let me have a look at the fire.

JO   (making room for her) Stop whining.

MOANER   I can't help it – I'm all in. I've hardly the strength left to stand up.

SALOME   Oh shut up, Moaner! We're all tired.

MOANER   Well, my head aches.

NOBBY   Would you like some aspirin? I've got plenty.

(The new arrivals turn and look at the stranger in their midst.)

JO   Crippen! Where did you spring from?

COCKY   Just arrived. She's taking Tilly's place.

JO   Oh. Got a cigarette?

(A hungry look comes into the eyes of each of the girls as the question is asked.)

NOBBY   No, I'm afraid I –

COCKY   The lady doesn't smoke and she –

NOBBY   (to COCKY) I say, won't you introduce me to everybody?

COCKY   I suppose I must. This healthy youngster you see standing before you was christened Joyce Overton but we thought that was too ladylike for her, so we changed it to Jo.

NOBBY   How d'you do? I'm very pleased to meet you.

JO   I'm glad somebody's pleased. (She turns her back, rudely.)

SALOME   No need for you to be rude to the poor kid, Jo. She'll have enough to put up with here, goodness knows. (To NOBBY) My name's Sally Lomax, but I'm always called Salome – for short, you know.

NOBBY   How d'you do? Mine's Edna Clarke but it's already been changed to Nobby.

SALOME   That's the style.

COCKY   (catching MOANER by the shoulder and turning her round) This little ray of sunshine is the Honourable Millicent Westbrooke alias "The Moaner". She's always such a bright cheerful little soul, you'll find.

MOANER   Oh, leave me alone!

VIC   And I'm Vic. I should think that's enough to be going on with for a bit.

NOBBY   It's such fun meeting you all. I've been simply dying to get out here, of course.

JO   Why "of course"?

NOBBY   (slightly embarrassed) Well – er – you know what I mean. Mother was awfully bucked when the order came through. She said she was only sorry Ruth wasn't old enough to come with me. I was sorry in a way, myself. It would have been such fun being together.

SALOME   Who's Ruth?

NOBBY   My sister. She's nearly seventeen – frightfully keen on nursing and all that, but naturally she hasn't trained at anything yet and you can't come out here knowing absolutely nothing, can you?

117

VIC Pretty nearly. If you can't drive a car you can always clean the lavatories!

MOANER And that takes a hell of a lot of training I can tell you. The Old Cow's pushed it on me twice this week.

SALOME Fat lot you've to grouse about! What about me? Cleaned her ruddy bus out this morning as well as my own, and because I was three minutes late for inspection she gave me hell by way of a thank you.

VIC Well, I've had tea-orderly all this week, so you're not the only ones. Nobby will think we're always grumbling.

NOBBY Oh, no I shan't. I'm sure you're awfully thrilled really, to think that you're doing your bit, even if it is hard at times.

(The others stare at her, too full for words, but the tension is broken when the door opens and MARY SKINNER *clumps into the room. She is commonly known as "*SKINNY*". After signing her name on the list she joins the group round the stove. She is very plump, red-faced and slow moving and even her present weariness cannot altogether hide her good-natured grin.)*

COCKY You're late, Skinny.

SKINNY Spotted fever case twice running.

JO My God, you stink!

NOBBY It's disinfectant, isn't it? *(Sniffing the air.)*

SKINNY That's right. Been sprayed twice. Are you the new girl?

NOBBY Yes. My name's Edna. . . .

JO Her name's Nobby.

SKINNY *(eagerly)* Got a cigarette?

NOBBY I'm frightfully sorry. I'd have brought some with me but I didn't know they'd be in such demand.

JO You wouldn't!

SKINNY *(the last spark of life having departed from her)* Any tea going?

VIC Not a whiff.

SKINNY Too late, I suppose?

JO *(sweetly)* How did you guess?

(The outer door is pushed open again and ELIZABETH TURLEY *stumbles in, loaded with brown paper parcels and a bundle of letters. She is the Commandant's right hand and is generally suspected of a little espionage work as well. For this reason she is known as "*CREEPING LIZZIE*". A cadaverous Cockney, shiny-nosed and spotty-faced, she is immensely detested. When the girls see the mail, they make a concerted rush towards* LIZZIE.*)*

ALL *(shouting together)* Letters! At last! My God you've been long enough sorting. Any for me? No? That's my parcel, you swine! Five for me, hooray! Come on, Creeping Lizzie, where's mine? There must be! Here, that's addressed to me. Hand it over! Only two? Hard luck! You had four last time, greedy! etc.

LIZZIE *(hidden behind a seething mass of humanity)* Aow! Let go! You're hurting. Stop shoving, Cocky. No, there's only one for you – a parcel. I don't know . . . There – now you've torn it. Get off my foot! If Commandant hears this row, you'll get it in the neck good and proper, I tell you!

JO If she doesn't Creeping Lizzie will tell her, you bet.

LIZZIE I'll make you pay for that, Jo Overton, you see if I don't.

MOANER Oh, shut up, you two!

LIZZIE But she called me a name.

VIC Clear out, we want to read our letters in peace.

LIZZIE You say it again and I'll report you to Commandant – see if I don't.

JO Tell the Old Cow. *(As she undoes her parcel)* I don't give a damn!

*(*LIZZIE *flounces out angrily and slams the door hard.)*

SKINNY Cigarettes! I'm rolling in 'em! *(She throws several packets in the air and catches them gleefully.)*

VIC So am I! Abdullas and all!

JO Swop fifty for a Bovril? *(She holds up a bottle of Bovril.)*

SKINNY What-ho! Coming over! *(She throws the packet across to* JO *who catches it neatly and throws her the bottle in exchange.)*

JO Got a match?

(Cigarettes are passed round and matches produced. The girls light up and puff with satisfaction.)

COCKY *(holding up a woollen garment)* Ee! One fine body belt going begging! Any offers?

SKINNY Bloater paste – one tin?

COCKY Done! Chuck it across.

MOANER God! They've forgotten my soap!

VIC I'm flush. Here's a cake. *(She throws a tablet to* MOANER.*)*

MOANER *(catching the soap and smelling it)* Heavenly!

VIC Got any butter?

MOANER Pounds! Look! (*Holds up a large packet.*) Mother's been thieving again!

VIC Wicked old woman! You can keep me a bit.

COCKY (*who is halfway through a letter*) Ee! Would you believe it!

SKINNY What?

COCKY Remember the Scotties I told you were billeted on my mother?

SALOME Jock and Wullie?

COCKY Aye.

SKINNY Well?

COCKY Went off week before last and left my sister Gracie in family way.

SALOME Phew! Which one?

COCKY She doesn't know. That's the trouble.

VIC (*excitedly*) Hurrah! (*She gets up and dances around the room.*)

JO Hey? What's the matter with you? Something bitten you?

VIC He's got it! He's got it!

JO Who's got what?

VIC Raymond's wangled his leave to start on the 12th – same day as mine. We'll have a whole week together.

SKINNY And who is Raymond?

SALOME What! You don't know Raymond? (*She sings dramatically*) Oh, Raymond's the only boy in the world.

SKINNY Go on! I didn't know. Well I hope you have a nice time. Better make sure he marries you first.

(VIC *throws a ball of paper at her.*)

COCKY Damn! (*She pores carefully over her letter.*) I can't read it.

JO Why not, Cocky?

COCKY Censored, blast it!

JO All the best bits are.

SKINNY "Chu Chin Chow" is still running. Jim's been to see it for the fourth time.

VIC Father says we're winning the jolly old war. He's read so in the papers.

MOANER My brother's finished his training at Sandhurst, the little louse. Expects his marching orders any moment. Won't that be nice for the great British army!

JO Hell!

VIC What's the matter?

JO George has got shell-shock. Poor devil! That'll send my sister cuckoo, all right.

VIC Hard luck!

JO Can't grumble. Might've been a double dose of gas. Oh, and Betsy has foaled, bless her heart!

SALOME Ernie's won the D.S.O.

COCKY (*laconically*) He's welcome!

(*The door opens and* LIZZIE *slouches in.*)

LIZZIE Commandant's orders and . . .

JO Go away!

LIZZIE Commandant's orders and you're to be ready in five minutes to receive Mrs Gordon Myers. If you're not tidied up here, you'll get what for. She's on the war-path.

SALOME Would you mind saying it all again? I wasn't listening.

LIZZIE I ain't goin' to repeat it. If you didn't 'ear, you'll just be unlucky, that's all.

SALOME Who is she?

LIZZIE Dunno!

COCKY What's she coming for?

LIZZIE Inspection or somethink.

JO Hell!

SKINNY Haven't been in five minutes and we get this.

SALOME Where's she come from?

LIZZIE 'Ow should I know?

JO You're the Old Cow's right ear, aren't you? You ought to know.

LIZZIE You better be careful, Joyce Overton! Commandant'll have her knife into you if this place ain't cleared up by the time she comes, and 'ere's one as won't be sorry, so there!

(COMMANDANT's *whistle interrupts the argument.* LIZZIE *exists, banging the door as usual. The girls begin to tidy themselves and the room generally.*)

JO Little rat!

MOANER If the Commandant ever left us in peace for five minutes, I'd never recover from the shock!

SKINNY Four hours' sleep last night.

MOANER And only three the night before. God! I'd like to strangle her!

COCKY You want jam on it, that's what's wrong. After all, three hours' sleep a day ought to be enough for healthy young lassies like us with the light duties we have to get through. (*She chuckles malignantly.*)

SALOME Inspection! Stared at like a lot of performing animals – that's what!

JO Who is the bitch?

COCKY Never heard of her.

NOBBY Oh, I have. I've seen her pictures in the *Sketch* and the *Mirror*. Why, she's quite famous.

JO Really!

MOANER Yes, I remember now – the *Tatler*.

Mrs Gordon Myers, a noble mother who has turned her stately mansion into a convalescent home for the dear, brave wounded Tommies.

JO   What's the hell's that got to do with us?

VIC   Oh, she probably is related to some big bug at the War Office and wants to make sure we're doing our bit.

MOANER   Dear, sweet thing!

JO   *(scrutinising herself in small cracked mirror)* Gosh, my neck's black!

COCKY   Pull your collar up – won't show.

JO   *(obeying the instruction)* Cocky, you're a ruddy marvel!

SALOME   Look out! They're coming!

(The door is opened and the COMMANDANT *enters, followed by* MRS GORDON MYERS. *The* COMMANDANT *is a forbidding woman, hard-featured, tight-lipped and steely-eyed. She carries herself very erect and enunciates precisely in a harsh tone.* MRS GORDON MYERS *has an excessively genial smile and is dressed in expensive mufti. Her rich furs cause the girls' eyes to gleam enviously as they stand stiffly to attention.)*

COMMANDANT   This is the mess-room.

MRS MYERS   *(as she comes down towards the girls)* And these are the brave ambulance drivers we hear such glowing reports about, I'm sure . . .

COMMANDANT   These are some of them. The others are on duty at the moment. Cox, your handkerchief! *(COCKY tucks away a filthy handkerchief that is dangling from her coat pocket.* COMMANDANT *makes a painful attempt at being pleasant.)* Mrs Gordon Myers honours us highly by her visit here this afternoon and I am sure each of you appreciates her interest and generosity on our behalf as deeply as I do. We all know how much the wounded owe to her kindness, and I feel certain you will all join with me in extending our sincere thanks to Mrs Myers for coming here to-day.

(At a sign from the COMMANDANT *the W.A.A.C.s salute.)*

MRS MYERS   *(fluttering)* Oh, please. I didn't wish this to be a formal visit in any way. *(She starts to warm up to her platform tone.)* I only wanted to see with my own eyes the splendid work being carried on by Britain's brave daughters in the face of danger and sometimes even death. I'm sure every British mother would give a great deal to be in my place at the moment, actually in contact with those who are bringing honour and glory to the name of English womanhood by their gallant service in this war to end wars. I wish I were a few years younger, so that I might throw in my lot with yours and join in the noble work. I have given my sons and if it were possible, I would gladly give my daughters in such a magnificent cause, but fate has decreed otherwise. Nevertheless, I am with you in spirit, the spirit which has built our glorious Empire and inspired our men to sacrifice their lives for its protection and continuance in this time of danger and stress. Believe me, when I say that words cannot express my admiration for the way you are keeping the flag flying so gallantly, and may you always do so. I am proud to have met you.

(COMMANDANT claps vigorously and the others join in, a trifle reluctantly.)

COMMANDANT   We are proud to have met you, Mrs Myers. After all, we are only doing our duty in a very humble way. Now perhaps you would like to see the other quarters before you leave?

MRS MYERS   Delighted, Commandant. Charming of you to take so much trouble.

COMMANDANT   Not at all. This way, please. *(She crosses to the door and, opening it, waits for* MRS MYERS *to precede her.)*

MRS MYERS   *(as she drifts out)* Wonderful work! Wonderful work!

(The moment she has passed the threshold the COMMANDANT *wheels round.)*

COMMANDANT   *(in a harsh undertone)* Skinner!

SKINNY   Yes, Commandant?

COMMANDANT   Your appearance is disgraceful. Report to me at ten o'clock to-morrow for extra orderly duty.

SKINNY   Yes, Commandant!

(COMMANDANT exists and closes the door crisply behind her. The girls fall into their chairs and breathe hard with relief.)

JO   Of all the prize cows!

COCKY   Which one?

JO   Both!

SALOME   Britain's brave daughters!

MOANER   Brave! And I'm sick with fear every time I take out my bus!

VIC   I know. Terrified at every pot-hole in
case you shake up some poor devil inside
with his legs half off.
COCKY   Ploughing through blinding
snow –
SALOME   Or a bombing raid on a moonlight
night –
SKINNY   Noble work!
JO   Cleaning lavatories!
MOANER   Swilling out your ambulance –
blood and filth, till you vomit at the sight of
the muck.
VIC   Britain's brave and beautiful
daughters. . . .
SALOME   Doing their bits, bless 'em.
COCKY   Keeping the old flag flying!

(NOBBY, *who has been standing in a strained
attitude, suddenly bursts out.*)

NOBBY   Stop it! Stop it!

(*They are all suddenly silent, surprised at her
outburst.*)

NOBBY   I'm sorry, but I couldn't bear it any
longer. You don't really feel like that – you
couldn't. I suppose you think it funny to
say these things in front of me just to make
me scared, but you needn't. It won't have
any effect. I'm proud of being British – and
I'm proud to do my bit.

(JO *bellows with laughter. The others are
silent.*)

NOBBY   (*turning to* JO) You can laugh as
much as you like. I don't care! If you don't
like being here, why don't you go home?
MOANER   I'll tell you. Because we're afraid
of being pointed at and told we showed the
white feather and ran away. We don't go on
because we like it. We'd go home
to-morrow if we could – but it would only
be more misery than this. There's a nice
position for you – afraid to stay and afraid
to go home. That's war!

(COMMANDANT's *whistle sounds outside
very shrilly.*)

JO   There she is again, blast her!
MOANER   That damned whistle never lets
you alone – even in your sleep.
COCKY   I'll shove it down the Old Cow's
throat one of these days.
JO   Better hurry – I'd promised myself that
pleasure.

(VIC, *who is reading another letter, suddenly*

*exclaims sharply. The others turn to look at
her. She sits staring straight ahead with
unseeing eyes, her face very white.*)

JO   Hey, Vic! What's up?
VIC   (*dully*) Nothing.
JO   You look pretty sick! What's wrong – bad
news?
VIC   Raymond was killed last week. He must
have written that letter a few hours before
he died.
JO   Rotten luck. I'm sorry.
VIC   (*pulling herself together*) Silly of me. I was
quite bowled over for the moment. Ought
to be used to that sort of thing by now, I
s'pose. But I was quite looking forward to
that leave . . .
SKINNY   Were you engaged?
VIC   In a way. It was an understanding. (*She
pushes the letter into her pocket.*) Well, that's
that.

(*The other door opens and* COMMANDANT
*enters the room briskly. She consults the list at
the door and then turns round to the girls.*)

COMMANDANT   (*sharply*) Clarke!
NOBBY   (*stepping forward*) Yes,
Commandant?
COMMANDANT   (*looking her up and down*)
Why haven't you got ready for duty?
NOBBY   I was just starting to when Mrs
Myers arrived.
COMMANDANT   I see you are very ready
with an excuse. You have had plenty of
time to arrange your kit. Slackness is not
tolerated here, and you will be well advised
to make an early note of it.
NOBBY   I see, Commandant. I'm sorry.
COMMANDANT   That will do. Newman!
Didn't you hear the whistle?
VIC   Yes, Commandant.
COMMANDANT   Then why are you sitting
there?
VIC   (*vacantly*) I – er – I don't know. (*She rises
with an effort.*)
COMMANDANT   It would be hard to explain,
no doubt. Clarke will accompany you on
convoy duty this evening. I understand
sergeant has allotted you Number Five.
When you have finished, you will show
Clarke round the camp indicating the
various routes from the station to the
hospitals and such general information as
will give her a thorough acquaintance with
the routine here. She will then be prepared
to take over her own ambulance when the
ten o'clock convoy is due.

VIC   Yes, Commandant. (She starts to button up her coat and pull on her gloves.)

NOBBY   (nervously) Oh, but I –

COMMANDANT   If you have any difficulties, Newman will assist you with them.

NOBBY   It isn't that, Commandant, but I've only just arrived. Surely, I'm not to take over an ambulance right away?

COMMANDANT   We don't waste any time in this camp, Clarke, whatever you've been accustomed to elsewhere. You're an experienced driver, I presume?

NOBBY   Yes, though I've never driven at night. I'm afraid I should be a bit nervous on strange roads.

COMMANDANT   Then you will have an opportunity to conquer your nerves.

NOBBY   Before I came I was given to understand I should be on probation for a month with an older driver who would help me a little at first.

COMMANDANT   You will receive all the help that is necessary from Newman within the next hour. (She snorts.) A month's probation. Less charitable people might call that shirking.

NOBBY   (shrinking) Oh no, really. I was only thinking of the wounded. I'd hate to make them suffer from my incompetence.

COMMANDANT   (brutally) If you are incompetent, you should never have come, and had better go back at once. You were sent to me as an experienced driver, and will be treated as such. Do you wish to go or stay? Make up your mind.

NOBBY   Of course, I'll stay, Commandant.

COMMANDANT   Then put on your overcoat and gloves and be prepared to start at once. You've wasted nearly five minutes already.

NOBBY   (obediently) Yes, Commandant.

(COMMANDANT turns to the others.)

COMMANDANT   Cox, Westbrooke and Overton, you will stand by for duty at midnight. Lomax and Skinner will take the ten o'clock convoy.

SEVERAL   Yes, Commandant.

(COMMANDANT exists and the girls relax with the exception of Vic, who has been standing rigid all this time.)

MOANER   Sometimes the very sight of her makes me wonder how long I can keep my hands to myself.

COCKY   Don't fret, lass. Your nerves won't stand it. Now if you had my iron constitution you could hang, draw and quarter her three times daily without turning a hair.

SKINNY   She really is a bitch, but what can we do?

JO   We're too bloody ladylike, that's our trouble.

(COMMANDANT's whistle blows twice sharply. VIC is roused to action.)

VIC   (to NOBBY) Ready?

NOBBY   Yes, I think so.

VIC   Come on then, we're late.

JO   (as NOBBY passes on her way out) So you came out to do your bit, did you?

NOBBY   Yes.

JO   Let's know how you like it when you get back, will you? I'm interested.

COCKY   Don't take any notice kid. She's only ragging. Cut along or you'll get it in the neck.

VIC   (after crossing off her name on the board) Here! Cross your name off and let's start.

(NOBBY does so and they go out.)

JO   Nice guileless little worm she is.

COCKY   She'll be all right when she settles down. Give the poor kid a chance.

JO   She's not the sort I feel like giving anything to.

COCKY   Have it your own way. As for me, I'm going to snatch a little shut-eye. We've got till twelve to amuse ourselves.

JO   Not a bad idea. Anyone else following suit?

SALOME   If I turned in now, I'd never turn out at ten.

SKINNY   What are you going to do?

SALOME   Smoke and keep myself awake.

SKINNY   Same here.

COCKY   Come along, Moaner. You could do with a month's back exercise by the look of it.

MOANER   Six months, you mean! And that wouldn't make up for all the sleep I've lost since I came out here. What with the guns and the cold and the lice and that blasted whistle.

COCKY   Oh, come to bed! I'll fix you a hot water bottle and some Bovril if you'll only stop jawing.

MOANER   All right. I'm coming.

(MOANER gets up and goes with COCKY into the sleeping quarters.)

SALOME   Nightie-night, children.

(JO *also goes, leaving* SALOME *and* SKINNY *together.* SKINNY *gets up from her chair and goes to the outer door.*)

SALOME   Where you going?
SKINNY   To get some coke.

(*She goes out.* SALOME *stubs out the cigarette she has been smoking nervously, and lights another. She moves over to the window and peers out cautiously. The door slamming suddenly makes her wheel round jumpily.* SKINNY *has come in and crossed to the stove. She lifts the lid, shovels in the coke, and then closes it. Going to the piano, she sits down and begins to play softly.*)

SALOME   What's the time?
SKINNY   (*glancing at her wrist watch*): Quarter past seven.

(SALOME *crosses to the window again and glances out; then turns back decisively. She whips off her hat and, looking in the small mirror hanging on the wall, combs her pretty hair and fluffs it out.* SKINNY *watches her lazily as she goes on playing.* SALOME *takes a box of powder and dabs some on her face.*)

SKINNY   (*without stopping her playing*) Out on the loose again?
SALOME   (*airily*) And what if I am?
SKINNY   You'll do it once too often, that's all.
SALOME   And the dear Old Cow will catch me and pack me off to Blighty in disgrace, I suppose? Well, she won't unless you tell on me.
SKINNY   That's likely, isn't it. But you're a B.F. to take the risk, all the same.
SALOME   (*putting on her hat at a coquettish angle*) Well, a girl has to have a little fun sometimes.
SKINNY   Who is it this time? Patterson?
SALOME   No, ducky, Miles Newton. He's taken Field's place at the station. Said if I could sneak over to-night about 7.30, there'd be a slap-up dinner going, bottle o' fizz 'neverything. I'll just be able to make it if I go now.
SKINNY   Buzz off then. I'll cover your retreat this end.
SALOME   You're a pal, Skinny, old girl.

(*She starts to climb out of the window.*)

SKINNY   Keep your weather eye open. Creeping Lizzie's on the snoop around these nights.
SALOME   Just let me catch her peeping through keyholes!

SKINNY   You mind she doesn't catch you climbing through windows. Or drinking champagne with strange young men.
SALOME   Miles Newton's not a strange young man – he's an officer and a gentleman.
SKINNY   Well you're supposed to be a W.A.A.C. and a lady – but don't let a little thing like that stand in your way.
SALOME   (*pausing with one leg on either side of the window-sill*) Really, Miss Skinner!

(*She hides her eyes, mock-modestly, and then slips over the window-sill and disappears.* SKINNY *who has been playing softly all this time, changes to "If You Were the Only Girl in the World." She is thumping this out very loudly as the curtain falls.*)

Act II

Scene 1

The mess-room some months later, on Sunday evening, November 10, 1918. NOBBY *is seated at the table writing a letter home. A cigarette hangs from the corner of her mouth. Her appearance has deteriorated considerably, and there are deep shadows under her eyes. Her pen spurts and makes an ugly blot.*

NOBBY   (*slamming it down in disgust*) Blast the pen!

(*She screws up the paper, throws it away and starts afresh.* COCKY *comes in at this moment in a hurry, leaving the door open. She seems very restless.*)

NOBBY   (*shouting*) Shut that blinking door!
COCKY   Sorry, sweetheart! (*She shuts the door and walks back to the table, jabbing her hands into her pockets with a vicious thrust.*) Got a fag?

(NOBBY *takes a packet from her pocket and throws it down on the table without speaking. She continues with her letter.*)

COCKY   Thanks . . . Talkative young thing, aren't you?

(COCKY *extracts a cigarette from the packet and lights it.* NOBBY *says nothing but, finding that her own is nearly finished, takes one and lights it from the stub.*)

NOBBY   You can afford to be cheerful, going on leave tonight.
COCKY   To-morrow, you mean.

NOBBY *(mildly surprised)* Thought you were going with Salome.

COCKY I was. But the Old Cow's ditched that for me.

NOBBY How?

COCKY Detailed me for midnight convoy to pay me out for cheeking her last week.

NOBBY That was nice of her.

COCKY Aye, she doesn't forget things in a hurry. It cuts my leave down by a day, that's what gets my goat. Ee! But I'd like to dot her one. *(Her face suddenly lights up as an idea occurs to her.)* Nobby!

NOBBY *(still writing without looking up)* Hallo?

COCKY *(rising and leaning over the table towards* NOBBY*)* Are you game for a wangle?

NOBBY *(glancing at her cautiously)* Depends. What is it?

COCKY *(excitedly)* A swop. You go on at midnight in my place, and I go on at seven in yours. That'll just give me time to get back here and sling my hook with Salome.

NOBBY Don't be a B.F.!

COCKY She'd never twig unless somebody split. *(NOBBY goes on writing and says nothing.)* Go on, be a sport! *(NOBBY still says nothing.)* All right, if you're scared.

NOBBY For God's sake leave me alone, can't you? I'm on midnight convoy myself, so I couldn't swop if I wanted to – and if I could, I wouldn't, so put that in your pipe and smoke it.

COCKY Then why couldn't you say so in the first place?

NOBBY Oh, shut up! Go and worry someone else. Can't you see I'm trying to write a letter.

COCKY Mother's little ray of sunshine!

(MOANER comes out of the sleeping-quarters buttoning up her overcoat. She starts to go towards the door, changes her mind, and comes up to COCKY, with her hand held out.)

MOANER Nearly forgot. You'll be gone by the time I get back. Better say cheerio.

COCKY Bit premature, love. I'm not off till morning – the Old Cow's booked me for midnight, blast her eyes.

MOANER Hard luck. See you later then. *(She turns to go.)*

COCKY Aye. *(She has a sudden brain wave and catches MOANER by the arm.)* I say, Moaner. . . .

MOANER Hallo?

COCKY Would you be a sport and let me take your place this trip?

MOANER What on earth for?

COCKY If I have to go on the midnight convoy, I can't start my leave this evening. But if you'd change with me now and take over my bus at midnight, I can slip off with Salome.

MOANER It's too risky.

COCKY Go on. I'll take the blame if the Old Cow finds out.

MOANER Oh, I don't mind about that – she can't give me any more punishments than I've got – unless she adds a couple more hours to the twenty-four.

COCKY *(hopefully)* Then you'll do it?

MOANER All right! *(COCKY embraces her.)*

COCKY You're a sport – I'll bring you back a hundred Abdullas for this!

MOANER We must hurry though! You'd better slip round the back way to my bus. I'll walk through the yard so that the Old Cow can get a good eye-full if she's on the look-out. Buzz off, or I'll get it in the neck for being late.

COCKY You're champion! I'll make it two hundred.

(She leaps across the room and climbs nimbly out of the window.)

MOANER I'll keep you to that! *(She turns and pulls on her gloves.)*

NOBBY Got an envelope, Moaner?

MOANER Sorry. Used my last to-day.

NOBBY Know anyone who has?

MOANER 'Fraid not. *(COMMANDANT's whistle blows twice, shrilly.)* All right – I'm coming.

(She hurries out into the yard. She is barely out of the room when JO *comes in from the sleeping-quarters carrying a newspaper. She drops into a chair by the stove and starts to read.* NOBBY *folds up her letters.)*

NOBBY Got an envelope by any chance?

JO Yes.

NOBBY Good! I'm cleaned right out and this must go off to-night.

JO Must it?

NOBBY Yes, it's to the boy friend. *(There is a pause. She looks at JO expectantly.)* Well, aren't you going to hand it over?

JO No.

NOBBY But you said . . . Oh, I see. It was silly of me to expect you to be obliging.

JO I am occasionally – to deserving cases.

NOBBY   *(angrily)* You make me sick!

JO   I wish I could. It would do you good.

NOBBY   Oh, go to hell!

(She goes into the sleeping-quarters, slamming the door violently behind her. JO *smiles and resumes reading the paper. The door opens and* MOANER *slips back into the hut like a shadow.* JO *notices her furtive entrance and looks up in mild surprise.)*

JO   Hullo! Thought you were on a convoy.

MOANER   So I was – and still am, as far as the Old Cow's concerned. *(She starts to take off her hat and coat.)*

JO   Dodged it?

MOANER   Yes, thank God!

JO   How did you manage it?

MOANER   Cocky's gone in my place.

JO   Oh, she has, has she? What were you booked for?

MOANER   Number Five.

JO   The longest, lousiest route of the lot! You certainly have got a nerve.

MOANER   *(indignantly)* It wasn't my choice.

JO   You don't have to tell me that.

MOANER   Nobody ever has to tell you anything.

JO   Nobody has to tell me you get cold feet whenever there's two penn'orth of danger. It's written all over your face.

MOANER   *(hysterically)* Well, we can't all be bloody heroes like you. And anyway, I didn't ask Cocky – she offered to go . . .

JO   She would. She's decent.

MOANER   You . . . ! *(She raises her fist and rushes at* JO, *who stands smiling at her.* MOANER *does not hit her, but pauses suddenly and drops her hands.)* Oh, you beast, you beast! *(She turns and runs into the sleeping-quarters.)*

*(*JO *laughs as she goes. Almost at once,* VIC *comes in. She crosses to the stove, loosens her coat and throws down her gloves.)*

VIC   Hullo! What's the joke?

JO   There isn't one. It's a bloody tragedy.

VIC   *(raising her eyebrows)* Really, then I think I'll make some cocoa.

JO   You can't.

VIC   Why?

JO   There isn't any.

VIC   Are you sure?

JO   Absolutely.

VIC   But where's it all gone, then?

JO   Your little friend Nobby could probably tell you.

VIC   Has she been at it again?

JO   Only for the third time.

VIC   The rotten little thief!

JO   I'm glad somebody else has realised that at last.

VIC   She's always up to some dirty trick or other. It's time someone told her just where she gets off.

JO   Why don't you? If you want something to drink, I've got a spot of Bovril.

VIC   Didn't know you were so flush.

JO   I have exactly half a teaspoonful, which I have been carefully hoarding for two days.

VIC   Then hoard it a bit longer. We'll have it together when I get back. The Old Cow's determined to keep me on the run to-night.

JO   What's up?

VIC   I'd give a lot to know. The end of the world – or the end of the war, I shouldn't wonder. You'd be surprised at the number of rumours floating round the camp.

JO   They've been floating for days. You can't fool me. This bloody war'll never end. *(There is an appalling noise just outside, caused by someone beating a tin with a stick.)* There! What did I tell you. Just a nice friendly air raid on the way. Better douse the glim.

(She turns the light out, leaving the room lit only by the faint glow from the stove.)

VIC   I know, but still it's queer. We've never had so many stories coming through before. They keep on saying it's the finish.

JO   You tell that to the marines.

VIC   Tell 'em yourself.

JO   I'd like to! Gee! What could I do with a squad of marines.

(There are two loud explosions as bombs drop close at hand, followed by a burst of gun fire. This noise continues intermittently during the next three or four minutes and the dialogue is spoken in pauses between the explosions.)

JO   You did say the war was over, I believe?

VIC   Oh yes. This is just one of those silly practical jokes.

JO   Such a sense of humour, the Germans, don't you think?

VIC   Yes indeed!

*(*NOBBY *comes back from the sleeping quarters with an envelope in her hand. She sits at the table and strikes a match to enable her to address it.)*

JO   Where did you pinch that envelope?

NOBBY   Mind your own business.

JO   I am. It looks like one of mine.

NOBBY   Well, it isn't. Salome gave it to me.

JO   Scrounger!

NOBBY   You shut up or there'll be a bloody row!

JO   It's time there was. What about my cocoa?

NOBBY   Well, what about it?

VIC   It's all gone, that's all.

NOBBY   And I took it, I suppose.

VIC   You know damn well you did.

NOBBY   That's right, blame me.

VIC   *(who has not heard because of a bang)* What?

NOBBY   I said: "That's right, blame me."

VIC   Who else is there to blame? I wouldn't mind if you'd take your fair share – or even say so, but you hog the lot and say nothing.

NOBBY   Oh, I'll pay for the bloody cocoa.

VIC   I don't want you to pay for it. I just want you to behave decently.

NOBBY   Huh!

VIC   You may not know it but we're all just about tired of the way you're going on.

NOBBY   Huh!

JO   It's no good talking, Vic. The only way to treat people like that is to knock some sense into them.

NOBBY   You try, that's all!

JO   For two pins, I would.

NOBBY   All right, you try. You may be a great hulking bully, but I'm not afraid of you.

JO   *(moving in her direction)* Well, you asked for it, don't forget that.

NOBBY   You keep your hands off me or you'll be sorry.

VIC   *(getting between them)* Stop it, both of you! You won't do any good by fighting. Hasn't the war taught you even that?

JO   *(gruffly)* Oh, we'd have got it out of our systems. That would have been something. Anyway, she needs a good hiding.

NOBBY   It'd take more than you to give me one.

JO   Oh, you'd . . .

VIC   SHUT UP! *(They are both silent.)* Look here, Nobby, I want a talk to you.

JO   If you're going to try preaching to her, I'm going. It's all I can do to keep my hands off the young cub. *(She goes into the sleeping quarters.)*

NOBBY   *(after a pause)* Well, go on. Let's have the sermon and get it over.

VIC   There's not going to be any sermon.

NOBBY   Well, thank God for that, anyway.

VIC   You know, you've changed out of all recognition in the last couple of months.

NOBBY   Thanks.

VIC   It's a fact. You were a decent kid when you came out here. A bit of a snob, but decent.

NOBBY   And now I'm indecent and immoral, I suppose.

VIC   No, just rotten.

NOBBY   *(angrily)* If I am, who made me like it? All of you were quick enough to teach me, weren't you? You saw to it that I didn't keep any of my illusions, all right. When I came out here, I thought it was going to be pretty wonderful – that I was doing my bit for King and Country. But you soon showed me different, didn't you?

VIC   Well, it was for your own good. You would soon have learned for yourself what war was really like and it would have come as more of a shock that way. I'm not suggesting you ought to have stayed a nice innocent little girl – none of us is that after six months out here in hell. But there *is* a limit.

NOBBY   And I suppose you think I've gone beyond it.

VIC   I think you're pretty near it. Seriously, Nobby, you'll have to pull yourself together. There's no very strict code of life or morals out here, and we all let ourselves go a bit. But you've got to draw a line somewhere. Once you let yourself go too far, it's a hell of a job climbing back.

NOBBY   *(mockingly)* And all this over a twopenny tin of cocoa!

VIC   *(angry for the first time)* Don't be such a little fool! You know damn well that's got nothing to do with it. That's just another sign that you've let yourself go until you've got no moral sense at all . . .
(COMMANDANT's whistle blows shrilly twice and then again, once.) Blast, that's for me.

NOBBY   *(getting up and lighting the lamp)* Well, thank God that's over. *(She smiles meaningly at VIC.)* The air raid, I mean, of course.

VIC   *(pulling on her coat)* I know what you mean all right. Well, I've done all I can. I wash my hands of you.

(SALOME comes in at the outer door.)

SALOME   I shouldn't. It's much too cold to wash.

(COMMANDANT's whistle blows again.)

VIC Gawd, hark at her! I must beat it.

SALOME Well, that little whistle won't catch me, bending for another ten days. *(She blows a kiss in the direction of the sound.)*

VIC Lucky devil! So long! Have a good time!

SALOME Thanks, Vic. *(As VIC waves farewell from the door)* Good-bye-e-e-e.

(As VIC closes the door, SALOME turns and calls out in a sing-song voice.)

SALOME Anyone here seen Cocky?

(The door to the sleeping quarters opens and JO comes out.)

JO She's on convoy.

SALOME Damn! She wasn't half an hour ago.

JO Perhaps not. Moaner managed to wheedle her into it. She didn't fancy Number Five.

SALOME She might have told me. Oh well, can't be helped, I suppose. Look here, when she comes back, give her a message from me, will you?

JO Aren't you going to wait for her?

SALOME No, that's why I wanted to see her. I've changed my mind. I'm going to pick up the train at Clouey at 10.30. Tell her to look out for me there.

JO All right. Got a date, I suppose.

SALOME I should say so! Like to join me?

JO One of your intimate parties?

SALOME What do *you* think? Dicky calls it a "leave-taking banquet". *(She laughs gaily.)* He's a real sport, is Dicky. You'd adore him.

JO I should loathe the little squirt.

SALOME That sounds as if you won't come.

JO Right first guess.

SALOME *(moving over to NOBBY)* How about you, funny face? Doing anything?

NOBBY No.

SALOME Like an evening with me and the boys?

NOBBY No, thanks. Too risky.

SALOME Don't tell me you funk a little thing like that! Why, I've done it dozens of times and never been copped.

NOBBY It's all right for you – you're practically on leave. I've got to go on convoy at midnight, and if I don't get a lift I can't get back in time.

SALOME Go on, chance your luck. It's worth it.

NOBBY Who are they?

SALOME Dick Pageter and his pal. Nice boys, with lots of money. We'll have a hell of a time.

NOBBY I've a damn good mind to . . . No, I daren't! I'd never get back in time.

SALOME Yes, you would, easily. There are always plenty of lorries on the Clouey road.

NOBBY There wouldn't be, if I wanted a lift. Besides, I should have to come away just when the fun was starting.

JO It's no good your talking to her, Salome. She's reformed.

SALOME What!

NOBBY You keep out of this, Jo.

JO She's reformed. Vic gave her a nice little heart-to-heart talk and she promised to be good and not be led astray, didn't you, mother's precious one?

SALOME *(laughing)* So that's why you wouldn't come!

NOBBY No, it isn't. *(To JO)* You say that again, that's all.

JO Certainly. Mother's . . .

(NOBBY rushes at JO, but SALOME stops her, before she reaches her.)

SALOME Don't be a chump. I've got to get off. Are you coming or aren't you? Make up your mind.

NOBBY Of course I'm coming. Wait while I get my coat.

(She goes into the sleeping quarters.)

JO *(calling after her)* Just another of the girls who fell in the Great War, Mummy.

SALOME You keep out of this. *(She follows NOBBY into the sleeping quarters.)*

JO I wouldn't be in it for a pension.

(She sits down in a chair by the stove and lights a cigarette. SKINNY comes in from the other door, signs her name on the board, and flops down opposite JO.)

SKINNY *(sighing heavily)* Lord, I'm tired.

JO Where've you been?

SKINNY Fetched a couple of nurses from the station. The blasted train was late as usual.

JO The Old Cow's on the warpath to-night. It'll be my turn next. What's the matter with you?

SKINNY I'm simply ravenous. You know I was thinking as I came along just what I could do to a nice steak and kidney pudding with roast potatoes, and apple pie, and a nice chunk of cheddar cheese, and coffee, with cream . . .

JO   Shut up! You make my mouth water.

SKINNY   Don't stop me thinking. It's the only pleasure I've got left.

(SALOME and NOBBY come in again with their coats and hats on. NOBBY goes immediately to the window and, after looking out across the yard, climbs out.)

SALOME   Good-bye-e! We're just off.

SKINNY   *(good-humouredly)* Don't remind me. You might've slipped off quietly and shown a bit of tact.

SALOME   Oh, go on! You don't grudge a girl a few days' leave.

SKINNY   Don't I? That shows how much you know me. I grudge you every minute spent away from this plague spot.

SALOME   Never mind, darling! The war may be over soon, and then we'll all go back together.

JO   Know any more funny jokes?

SALOME   Heaps, dearie, but I can't stop now.

(She starts to get out of the window.)

SKINNY   Hi! Why go by the window? Getting absent-minded, aren't you? You're on leave now! You can use the door.

SALOME   I prefer this way, it reminds me of all the good times I've had.

JO   So long! Keep walking.

SKINNY   And if you can't be good, be careful!

SALOME   *(waving to them as she disappears)* Good-bye-e-e.

SKINNY   That's funny.

JO   What?

SKINNY   Why's Nobby gone with her?

JO   They're having a binge together with the boys.

SKINNY   But how's Salome going to catch the train?

JO   She's joining it later at Clouey. That's where they're going now.

SKINNY   Nobby's got a nerve! She'll never get back before midnight.

JO   Serve her right if she doesn't. I hope the little fool gets caught.

SKINNY   I don't know. I've often thought I'd do the same for a good beefsteak.

JO   Go on. You'd expect a man to give you the whole horse before you even sat on his knee!

SKINNY   Rot! I'd sell my soul for a mess of pottage —

(Her words are cut short by the appearance of LIZZIE who rushes in at the door without warning. She is out of breath and looks scared.)

JO   *(irritably)*: What the hell do you want?

LIZZIE   *(fighting for breath)* Commandant! Quick!

JO   D'you think I keep her in my pocket?

LIZZIE   *(in short gasps)* Where is she? I must find her. Oh, it's terrible! I've been looking all over the place . . .

SKINNY   What's terrible?

LIZZIE   Cocky. They've just found her.

JO   *(catching LIZZIE by the arm)* What d'you mean – found her?

LIZZIE   She's dead. 'It by shrapnel. They've just brought her in. I must find Commandant. Haven't you seen her?

JO   No. You're sure it was Cocky?

LIZZIE   'Course it was, silly!

(She runs out again to look for Commandant. For a few moments JO and SKINNY are too stunned to show any emotion whatever. Suddenly JO leaps to her feet and throws the paper viciously across the room.)

JO   Of all the filthy tricks!

SKINNY   Poor old Cocky!

JO   The cowardly little swine! I'll give Moaner hell for this.

SKINNY   Moaner? What's she got to do with it?

JO   Everything. She got Cocky to take over her convoy because she was in a blue funk.

SKINNY   Why?

JO   She'd been put on Number Five again. You remember what happened last time. *(SKINNY nods.)* Well, she must've thought she was in for another bout. She made Cocky go instead. Blast her eyes! I'll make her pay for that.

SKINNY   But how did you know?

JO   She told me so herself.

SKINNY   What a rotten thing! I wouldn't be in Moaner's shoes for anything in the world.

(As she says these words MOANER appears at the door. She yawns, then stops as she hears her name mentioned.)

MOANER   Sorry to hear that. I don't particularly fancy them myself. *(SKINNY and JO stiffen as they realise her presence. The contemptuous, angry look in their eyes makes her conscious of something unusual in the atmosphere.)* Well, what is it? Has the Old Cow thought up something fresh for me? I know I'm her pet. *(SKINNY turns away, but* JO *continues to glare at her.)* You might at least answer when you're spoken to. What are you staring at me like that for? Anything wrong?

JO *(between her teeth)* Shut up!

MOANER All right. I only —

*(*JO*, suddenly before she can get another word out, slaps her savagely across the face.* MOANER *is taken completely unawares and staggers back against the table. On recovering her balance, she looks at* JO*, holding her face with her hand.)*

MOANER *(curtly)* Thanks. Now perhaps you'll tell me what I've done.

JO *(brutally)* You've killed Cocky! That's what you've done.

MOANER Killed Cocky? What on earth are you talking about?

SKINNY Cocky's dead. She was hit by shrapnel during the raid.

MOANER It's not true! You're not serious.

SKINNY You don't suppose it's something to joke about, do you?

MOANER I'm sorry – I just couldn't realise . . . When did it happen?

SKINNY I told you – during the raid.

JO While she was doing your convoy!

MOANER Oh, God! *(She shudders as she realises her escape and Cocky's fate.)*

JO Doing the convoy you were too white-livered to do yourself. D'you hear, you cowardly little swine?

MOANER *(sinking down into a chair and covering her face with her hands)* Don't . . . Oh, don't, please . . . It's not true . . . It's too horrible! Oh, Cocky, you shouldn't have done it . . . *(She breaks down, sobbing hysterically.)*

JO *(sarcastically)* Pity you didn't think of that before. Pushing your dirty work on to someone else.

MOANER *(despairingly)* You don't understand. . . .

JO We understand well enough.

MOANER I didn't want her to go. . . .

SKINNY *(interrupting sharply)* Then why did you let her take your convoy?

MOANER She came and asked.

JO *(contemptuously)* That's likely!

MOANER It's true, I tell you. We changed over so that she could get away this evening.

JO *(deliberately)* Cocky wasn't on convoy, so why should she want to change?

MOANER She was on at midnight, that's why.

JO *(shouting)* You're lying, and you know it. She was going with Salome on the ten o'clock train.

MOANER *(wildly)* I'm not lying! Ask Nobby, if you don't believe me. She was there all the time.

JO Well, she isn't here now and if she were she'd say the same as I do – that Cocky's dead and you've killed her!

MOANER *(shrieking hysterically)* I tell you I didn't! I never killed her. D'you hear? I never killed Cocky! It wasn't my fault. And don't look at me like that, damn you! I can't bear it – Oh, God – I can't bear it!

(She collapses on the floor, sobbing wildly, and then begins to bang on the bare boards with her clenched fists. As the others stand watching her VIC *comes in.)*

VIC *(at the door)* I say, what's going on? You can hear that row half-way across the yard. *(She suddenly sees* MOANER *on the floor and runs to her at once.)* Moaner! In heaven's name —

MOANER *(hoarsely)* I didn't kill her . . . it's cruel to say it . . . I didn't, I tell you . . .

VIC *(kneeling down and putting her arms round* MOANER *and then looking back at the others)* What the devil have you been doing? *(She starts to raise* MOANER *up.)* There now! It's all right, Moaner . . . Everything's all right! I've got you, old girl.

MOANER I didn't kill her . . .

VIC Of course you didn't . . .

MOANER You believe me, don't you?

VIC Yes . . . yes . . . now hold on . . . *(She begins to propel her towards the door)* You'd better lie down for a bit. Come along, I'll get you something to drink . . .

(On the last words they disappear into the sleeping quarters together. JO *and* SKINNY *sit down morosely.* SKINNY *takes a packet of cigarettes from her pocket, offers them to* JO *and then takes one herself.)*

JO *(as she takes one)* Thanks.

(They both light up and smoke silently. In a moment VIC *comes back into the room and faces them squarely.)*

VIC Now then – what's it all about?

JO *(bluntly)* Cocky's dead.

VIC Cocky! *(She is unable to speak for a moment or two.)* When did you hear?

SKINNY A few moments ago . . . Lizzie told us . . .

VIC   How did it happen?

SKINNY   Shrapnel. During the raid.

VIC   That's what upset Moaner, I suppose?

JO   Yes. She let Cocky take her convoy.

VIC   Why?

JO   Because she funked doing Number Five.

VIC   Looks as though she had good cause to. *(Looking from one to the other musingly)* So that's why you pitched into Moaner. Poor kid!

JO   She deserved it.

VIC   Don't be a fool! It's the luck of the game. Tomorrow it may be you or me . . .

JO   Well to-night it was Moaner's turn – but Cocky took it.

VIC   You can't say that – it's just one of those things. Poor old Cocky! She's got her leave all right – for good, this time! *(A thought strikes her suddenly.)* Does Salome know?

JO   No.

VIC   Well, you might tell her.

JO   I can't. She's cleared off.

VIC   *(surprised)* Where?

SKINNY   To Clouey.

VIC   Clouey?

SKINNY   They went on a sort of farewell binge with a couple of boy friends. Salome's joining the train there.

VIC   Who's "they"?

JO   Nobby went with her.

VIC   *(jumping up)* Nobby! And you let her go?

JO   *(gruffly)* Why not?

VIC   *(angrily)* You dam' fool. She'll get caught. She can't possibly get back in time. You know that as well as I do.

JO   That's her look-out. Serve her right if she does.

(VIC suddenly picks up her coat again and starts putting it on.)

JO   Where are you going?

VIC   Where do you think?

JO   Don't be an idiot, Vic. Let the little fool take care of herself.

VIC   You mind your own business.

(She goes towards the door, but JO is there before her.)

JO   You're crazy! I won't let you do it! *(She bars the way, standing with her back to the door.)*

VIC   You let Nobby go, didn't you?

JO   Yes, but . . .

VIC   Well, now you'll let me!

(She threw JO's arm roughly aside, opens the door and runs out. JO looks after her for a moment, then shrugs her shoulders helplessly.)

Curtain

Scene 2

The same, an hour later. As the curtain rises the COMMANDANT *is in the middle of interrogating* MOANER, *who is sitting in a chair looking very ill. Standing near* MOANER *is* JO, *while* SKINNY *is at the other side of the room. With the* COMMANDANT *is* LIZZIE, *all eyes and ears.*

COMMANDANT   *(sharply)* Westbrooke, I demand an answer!

MOANER   *(dully)* I don't know.

COMMANDANT   If you imagine I shall be put off with such evasions, you are quite mistaken. I am determined to get to the bottom of this unpleasant business. If my instructions had been carried out as they should have been, the death of Cox would never have occurred.

MOANER   No, it would have been me, instead.

COMMANDANT   That is *not* the point Westbrooke, and I shall be glad if you will not misconstrue my words. Once again, I demand an explanation.

MOANER   I can't remember.

COMMANDANT   You *must* remember.

MOANER   I was going out and then Cocky came in. . . .

COMMANDANT   *(impatiently)* Yes, yes, you've said that before. What then?

MOANER   I thought she was going on leave, but she wasn't . . .

COMMANDANT   I know that already. I wish to hear, in as few words as possible, why Cox took your place on the convoy. I understand you were allotted Number Five, a very difficult and dangerous route. That is so, is it not?

MOANER   Yes, Commandant.

COMMANDANT   Last time you were detailed for Number Five, your ambulance was found discarded in a ditch, and you were discovered an hour later running along the road in a violent state of panic, which unfortunately resulted in a nervous collapse. I was willing on that occasion to be lenient with you, as the convoys had been continuous and heavy during the day, but if I thought that cowardice was at the bottom of this regrettable incident, I should have no hesitation in —

JO *(interrupting quickly)* Excuse me, Commandant.

COMMANDANT Well, what is it?

JO I was present when Cox came in and took over the convoy.

COMMANDANT In that case, perhaps you can give me a sensible report of the whole affair.

JO Yes, Commandant.

COMMANDANT What actually happened?

JO Westbrooke was taken ill this afternoon.

COMMANDANT Indeed! Why wasn't I informed?

JO She told us not to say anything about it as she wanted to carry on without making a fuss.

COMMANDANT What was the matter with you, Westbrooke?

MOANER *(feebly)* I – er – I –

JO She was violently sick several times, Commandant. The dinner upset her.

COMMANDANT *(snaps)* Rubbish!

SKINNY *(feelingly)* That's exactly what it was!

COMMANDANT Silence, Skinner! And don't be insolent. *(She turns back to* MOANER.*)* I'm afraid I cannot regard sickness as an adequate excuse for allowing another person to take over your convoy duty, Westbrooke.

JO *(persistently)* She fainted as well.

COMMANDANT When?

JO When Cocky – I mean Cox – came in. That's why Cox offered to take over her convoy.

LIZZIE Coo! She never! I saw Westbrooke with me own eyes come out of that door, cross the yard and get into 'er own ambulance.

COMMANDANT Are you quite certain, Turley?

LIZZIE Cross me 'eart.

COMMANDANT That is very interesting. At what time was this, Turley?

LIZZIE Seven o'clock, Commandant.

COMMANDANT And how did Westbrooke appear to you?

LIZZIE About the same as usual, as far as I could tell.

COMMANDANT I see. *(She turns round to* JO.*)* How do you account for *that*, Overton?

JO *(taking a deep breath)* What Turley says is quite true. Westbrooke *did* go out to the ambulance. She was starting up when she was sick again, so she came back here for a

hot drink. I was making some Bovril. It was then she fainted and Cox offered to go in her place.

LIZZIE Well, I never see 'er come back.

SKINNY *(sotto voce)* Caught you napping, for once!

COMMANDANT I'll trouble you not to interrupt, Skinner. Is what Overton has told me true?

SKINNY Oh, yes, quite true, Commandant.

COMMANDANT *(quickly)* Were you present at the time?

SKINNY No.

COMMANDANT *(maliciously)* Then how do you know it's true?

SKINNY Well – er – you see, when Turley came in and told us Cox had been killed, Overton explained to me how she'd taken over the convoy because of poor Westbrooke's illness. And really, I wasn't surprised, Commandant. The dinner made me feel quite bad too – and I can eat anything as a rule.

COMMANDANT *(to* LIZZIE) Was Skinner with Overton when you came in here to look for me?

LIZZIE *(reluctantly)* Yes, Commandant.

COMMANDANT *(to* JO) Where were the others at the time Westbrooke fainted?

JO Lomax was in the bedroom getting ready to leave.

COMMANDANT And Clarke?

JO She was with her writing a letter for Lomax to take home.

COMMANDANT Where was Newman?

JO On duty, I think.

COMMANDANT *(consulting her notebook)* That seems to be correct. Where are they now?

JO Lomax has gone for her train.

COMMANDANT And the others?

JO *(desperately)* They're – asleep.

COMMANDANT In that case I think I'd better see if they know anything further. Your story is far from satisfactory, Overton, I'm afraid.

JO Sorry, I've done my best.

COMMANDANT And stand to attention when you're spoken to. *(*JO *pulls herself up quickly.)* This slackness is intolerable. Call Newman and Clarke, please.

JO But . . . *(She hesitates.)*

COMMANDANT At once, please. I'm waiting.

JO But Commandant, they've only just gone to sleep, and they've got to be up for midnight convoy. Couldn't you see them then? They've had hardly any sleep this week. And as they weren't here and don't know anything about what happened, it would be a little unreasonable to call them, wouldn't it?

COMMANDANT I trust I am never unreasonable. I will speak to them before the midnight convoy. You will see they come to my room, Turley.

LIZZIE Yes, Commandant.

COMMANDANT That's all for the present . . . Westbrooke, you'd better see the doctor to-morrow and get something to settle your stomach – if it is your stomach!

(She turns to go. As she does so, the door bursts open and NOBBY staggers in supported by VIC. NOBBY, happily drunk, is singing. She tries to throw off VIC's arm.)

NOBBY I can walk myself. Don't be shilly. (She hiccoughs.) Oh! Now, see what you've done to me. (She shakes off VIC's arm and starts to sing.) Any time'sh kisshing time . . . (She staggers into the room coming face to face with the COMMANDANT.)

COMMANDANT (icily) What does this mean?

NOBBY (saluting her playfully) If it ishn't the Old Cow herself! Hooray! Lesh have a party, shall us?

(COMMANDANT, livid with rage, strides to the door and without another word goes out. As the door slams behind her, the curtain falls.)

Act III

Scene 1

It is half-past seven on the following morning and the mess-room table is laid for breakfast. Thick slices of bread and margarine are piled on plates, while the cups and saucers are at the head of the table.

As the curtain rises the COMMANDANT's whistle is heard outside. A few moments later, JO, NOBBY, and SKINNY enter, followed by VIC and MOANER. The latter is still weak and hangs on to VIC's arm as they go to the bedroom together.

SKINNY It doesn't look so good to me.

NOBBY What doesn't?

SKINNY The Old Cow's face.

NOBBY It never has looked very good to me.

JO The shortest roll-call we've had for weeks. She didn't even notice I hadn't washed.

SKINNY Well, that's hard to tell at the best of times.

JO I wonder you've the heart to joke on an empty stomach.

NOBBY Gawd! I've got a splitting head. (She sinks on to a chair.)

SKINNY That ought to be a lesson to you not to mix your drinks.

NOBBY I'd give anything for another hour in bed.

SKINNY You're a fine one to talk about bed.

JO Getting off cheap just because you were tight. We had to turn out twice after midnight.

NOBBY When did you finish?

JO Three a.m.

SKINNY And Commandant's going about looking like a walking graveyard.

NOBBY (in exasperation) Why doesn't she say something and have done with it?

JO I shouldn't be impatient if I were you.

SKINNY I should say not! Let sleeping dogs – er – cows, lie.

NOBBY I wish to God I hadn't been such a bloody fool.

SKINNY It wouldn't've been so bad if you hadn't called her by her proper name.

JO Couldn't you have thought of something a little less farmyard?

NOBBY I must've been absolutely mad!

SKINNY No, just slightly sozzled.

JO The worst of it is she won't believe my story about Moaner, now. We're all for it and a double whack this time.

NOBBY What story?

JO Well, I had to dish up some excuse to stop her getting it in the neck for pushing the convoy on to poor Cocky.

NOBBY What do you mean?

JO Oh, you missed a bit of fun. Moaner got in a panic because she drew Number Five last night, and persuaded Cocky to go instead. That's how Cocky got killed – it ought to have been Moaner.

NOBBY When was this?

JO Seven o'clock.

NOBBY But Moaner didn't ask to change.

JO How do you know?

NOBBY I was there. Cocky came and asked her if she'd change over.

JO What?

SKINNY Why should Cocky have wanted to do Number Five? It's a vile road.

NOBBY Commandant had just told her she

was to go on midnight convoy, which means that she couldn't get off last night with Salome. If she changed over and did the one at seven, it just gave her time to get back and catch the train. Otherwise she had to stick around till morning.

SKINNY   That's different, of course. We all thought Moaner had got wind up. Jo and I pitched into her a bit when we heard about Cocky.

NOBBY   But didn't she tell you?

JO   Yes, she did, but I could've sworn she was lying – I gave her hell! She wouldn't have passed out like that if I hadn't been so damned rough.

SKINNY   Still, you saved her bacon with the Commandant.

JO   I don't know so much.

NOBBY   *(remorsefully)* I seem to have made a mess of it all round. If I'd been here, there wouldn't have been any misunderstanding.

JO   Glad you realise that. You might think a bit sooner next time.

SKINNY   When the deuce is the tea coming? I want my breakfast.

NOBBY   I don't know how you can even look at the stinking stuff.

SKINNY   Well I'm famished. I didn't have an orgy last night.

NOBBY   No need to rub it in.

SKINNY   *(taking a piece of bread and margarine)* I bet this marge is rancid.

JO   It was yesterday. It'll be a bit worse to-day.

SKINNY   *(tasting it and making a wry face)* It is! One day I'm going to force cook to eat the poisonous stuff she dishes up for us.

JO   She'd die of ptomaine.

SKINNY   I know. That's why I'd like to do it so much.

(VIC comes in from the bedroom.)

JO   How is she?

VIC   Better. But she ought to go sick.

JO   Why doesn't she?

VIC   Says she doesn't want anyone to think she's shirking.

JO   Oh!

SKINNY   Damn silly, making her attend roll-call in that state.

JO   I was wrong about her and Cocky.

VIC   Of course you were.

JO   Did she tell you?

VIC   Yes. You must have been crazy to go for her like that. Bad enough for her to hear Cocky was finished without you and

Skinny bullying her for something she hadn't done.

SKINNY   I know. I'm hellishly sorry.

VIC   Why did you do it?

JO   Bit of a shock hearing about Cocky. She was a good sort.

(There is silence between them for a moment. It is interrupted by the appearance of LIZZIE in the doorway. She looks at them all a little maliciously.)

VIC   Well – what is it?

LIZZIE   Commandant'll be 'ere in two minutes.

SKINNY   Did she say what for?

LIZZIE   No, but you'll get what for all right.

SKINNY   That's enough from you, Creeping Lizzie.

VIC   Who does she want?

LIZZIE   Westbrooke's got to be present and all of you what's 'ere now. There won't be no breakfast neither, till it's over.

SKINNY   Till what's over?

LIZZIE   Find out.

(She smiles triumphantly and slams the door. The girls look at each other glumly.)

SKINNY   Little cat! I could wring her neck.

VIC   I'd better tell Moaner.

JO   No, I will.

VIC   All right, but go gently with her.

(JO goes into the sleeping quarters.)

NOBBY   God! I wish it was all over.

VIC   Remember. Let me do the talking, and everything will be okay.

NOBBY   *(bitterly)* I ought never to have gone.

VIC   It's no use saying that now. We'll have to make the best of it.

SKINNY   If only you hadn't called her that farmyard name.

NOBBY   Oh, shut up Skinny.

SKINNY   I won't shut up. It's because of you I've got to wait for my breakfast.

(MOANER comes in supported by JO, who takes her to a chair.)

VIC   *(solicitously)* How's the head?

MOANER   Oh, it's all right, thanks. I'd give anything for a cup of tea though.

SKINNY   We shan't get one till the inquisition's over – and then there'll be no time to drink it, I'll bet.

MOANER   I wish she'd leave us alone for five minutes. What does she want me for again? I can't tell her anything.

JO   All you have to do is remember you were sick yesterday afternoon and you fainted at seven o'clock when Cocky took over your convoy. Is that clear?

MOANER   Yes, I suppose so.

(Footsteps are heard approaching outside.)

VIC   Sh! Take cover.

(The door opens and COMMANDANT *marches in with set lips and stern countenance. All the girls straighten to attention with the exception of* MOANER *who tries to stand but has to cling to the chair for support. The* COMMANDANT *surveys them with a steely glance.*

COMMANDANT   You may sit down, Westbrooke, if you are unable to stand. *(MOANER sinks into her seat.)* I trust you are in a more coherent state of mind than you were yesterday.

MOANER   Yes, Commandant.

COMMANDANT   You will report to the M.O. at ten this morning.

MOANER   Thank you.

COMMANDANT   There will be no breakfast until I have concluded the inquiry into last night's disgraceful incident. Our daily routine must not be upset, and time lost in dealing with the matter will consequently have to be made up in other ways. As you are aware, those of you who behave in such a way as to bring dishonour to our uniform or cause this service to be brought into disrepute, must expect only the extreme penalty – instant dismissal from the ranks. Is that understood?

ALL   Yes, Commandant.

COMMANDANT   That being quite clear, I shall be glad if you will furnish me with a full explanation of your conduct, Clarke. Why did you leave the camp last night without permission?

NOBBY   I don't know, Commandant.

COMMANDANT   You don't know?

NOBBY   No.

COMMANDANT   I order you to explain, Clarke. Refusal to obey orders is direct insubordination. You know what that entails?

NOBBY   Yes, Commandment.

COMMANDANT   Well? *(NOBBY is silent.)* I give you one more chance to answer before I pass on to Newman.

NOBBY   I have nothing to say.

COMMANDANT   I see. Well, Newman,

perhaps you can explain why you went out with Clarke, when you know it is strictly against the regulations.

VIC   I asked her to come with me because I wanted company.

NOBBY   But . . .

COMMANDANT   Silence, Clarke. I gave you your chance to speak before. If you didn't take it, you have only yourself to blame. *(To* VIC.) Where did you go?

VIC   Clouey.

COMMANDANT   You know that Clouey is out of bounds.

VIC   Yes.

COMMANDANT   Then why did you go there?

VIC   Because I wanted a drink.

COMMANDANT   Indeed! You are supplied with all the drink that is necessary here. There is no need to go outside for it.

VIC   *(with a smile)* I wanted something a little stronger, you see.

COMMANDANT   You are aware that intoxicants are forbidden and that it is a punishable offence to bring them into camp?

VIC   I know. That's why I went out.

COMMANDANT   Am I to understand that you persuaded Clarke to go with you on this expedition?

VIC   Yes. I'm sorry I made her drunk. She can't take as much as I can.

COMMANDANT   Is this true, Clarke?

NOBBY   Well – I – er –

VIC   *(quickly interrupting)* It was all my fault, Commandant. She would never have gone if it hadn't been for me.

COMMANDANT   Silence! I was addressing Clarke. Has Newman spoken the whole truth?

NOBBY   *(floundering)* No. . . . *(*VIC *kicks her ankle.)* I mean yes . . . That is . . .

COMMANDANT   Which do you mean?

NOBBY   Well, you see, not quite the whole truth, Commandant. I did get drunk, but she didn't make me. It wasn't her fault at all.

COMMANDANT   So you're both lying? And you're not the only ones, apparently. Overton, why did you say Clarke and Newman were asleep last night when they were not?

JO   I thought they were, Commandant.

COMMANDANT   What do you mean "thought"? Did you go into the bedroom and see them asleep?

JO   No.

COMMANDANT   Then why did you assume they were there?

JO   Because we usually sleep when we're not on duty. We get little enough with convoys every other hour all night.

COMMANDANT   That will do, Overton. Skinner, you supported Overton in her statement to me last night?

SKINNY   Yes, Commandant.

COMMANDANT   When you knew she was lying?

SKINNY   I didn't know she was lying. I thought it was the gospel truth.

COMMANDANT   There is no need to be blasphemous, Skinner. If you must mention the Bible, please do so reverently. Can you tell me anything further?

SKINNY   No, Commandant.

COMMANDANT   Westbrooke, were you present when Newman persuaded Clarke to go with her to Clouey?

MOANER   No, Commandant.

COMMANDANT   What were you doing at the time?

MOANER   I – I was asleep.

COMMANDANT   How very convenient. You weren't being sick, by any chance?

MOANER   No, Commandant.

COMMANDANT   Very well, it seems that I cannot rely on a single one of you to tell the truth, or even to recognise it when it is spoken. There is a conspiracy here to withhold certain facts from me. Of course, I cannot force you to speak, if you are determined to be silent, but I must warn you that I shall be forced to punish severely what is nothing less than open insubordination. Two of you are obviously guilty of more serious offences. You, Clarke, disobeyed orders by leaving here without permission, indulged in strong drink in a place out of bounds, and returned to camp in a state of violent intoxication. Further, you insulted your commanding officer in the vilest of terms, which is, as you are aware, a most serious breach of the rules. Newman, I charge you with the same offences with the exception of the last named, but since you are the elder of the two and have been in the service for a far longer period than Clarke, I consider you the one to whom most blame attaches. There is not the slightest excuse for your conduct. You not only treated the regulations with contempt, but you deliberately and consciously

influenced another to do likewise, which I regard as unforgivable. *(She pauses for a moment, and then adds slowly)* Newman and Clarke, you are both dismissed from the service in disgrace! Certain disciplinary rules must be observed . . .

(The last sentence is drowned by the sound of shouting and running feet outside. The door bursts open, LIZZIE almost falls into the room, panting and red with excitement. COMMANDANT turns on her furiously.)

LIZZIE   Commandant! Commandant! Oh, there you are!

COMMANDANT   How dare you, Turley. Rushing in like this without knocking when you know I —

LIZZIE   But Commandant, I've brought the news.

COMMANDANT   You've brought what?

LIZZIE   The news. I knew you'd want to 'ear the news!

COMMANDANT   For heaven's sake girl, what are you talking about?

LIZZIE   The war! It's over! We've won the bloomin' war!

COMMANDANT   Where did you hear this crazy rumour?

LIZZIE   'Tain't a rumour, Commandant. It's Gawd's truth. The war's over and we're going to march to Berlin and 'ang the Kaiser on a lam' post.

COMMANDANT   Who told you this nonsense?

LIZZIE   Sergeant said it'd just come through from headquarters. They signed the Armistice this morning at five o'clock! They're going to stop firing at eleven.

COMMANDANT   *(dazed)* This morning?

LIZZIE   Yes.

NOBBY   You mean the war's really over!

LIZZIE   Not 'arf, it ain't. We beat the blighters.

JO   *(quietly)* We've won the war!

VIC   *(loudly)* And I'm dismissed! That's funny! *(The others turn to look at her. She begins to laugh softly and then points a finger at the COMMANDANT, who is standing like a statue in the centre of the room.)* You can't dismiss me – I resign!

(She continues to laugh and soon the others are infected. They burst into wild hurrahs. In a moment they are rushing madly to and fro and throwing the bread and margarine into the air. Amid shouts and peals of hysterical laughter, the curtain falls.)

Scene 2

A month later. SKINNY *is sitting at the piano playing in a leisurely fashion.* LIZZIE *is standing by the door, her head cocked on one side listening.*

LIZZIE   Pretty, ain't it?

SKINNY   *(casually)* What?

LIZZIE   That thing you're playing.

SKINNY   Yes, it's rather nice.

LIZZIE   What is it?

SKINNY   Just a song.

LIZZIE   Runs through your head like. Tell us who wrote it so's I can remember, when I get back to Camberwell.

SKINNY   It's by Bach.

LIZZIE   'Oo's 'e when he's at home?

SKINNY   He's dead. He was a German.

LIZZIE   *(horrified)* German! 'Ere, you don't mean ter tell me you're playing a German tune?

SKINNY   Why not? The War's over, isn't it? *(She stops and looks round at* LIZZIE.)

LIZZIE   I know, but – well, it don't seem right some'ow. A dirty Boche!

SKINNY   You thought it was a pretty tune just now, didn't you?

LIZZIE   Well, I don't any longer, see! I ain't a pro-German, if you are!

SKINNY   Perhaps you'd like this better. *(She begins to play "Land of Hope and Glory" very loudly.)*

LIZZIE   Oh, I know that. We used to learn it in school. My sister Elsie can play that.

SKINNY   *(shouting)* Then for God's sake go back to your sister Elsie and stay there.

*(*LIZZIE *sniffs and goes.* SKINNY *crashes out a fearful discord and turns away from the piano, as* JO *appears at the other door.)*

JO   Is that meant to be the Last Trump?

SKINNY   *(carelessly)* If you like.

JO   Well, that's just how it sounded. What's the matter? Got the hump?

SKINNY   I suppose I have.

JO   Don't tell me you're heartbroken because we're going home?

SKINNY   I'm not as happy as I thought I'd be. I thought I should be deliriously excited at the prospect of being in England again, but somehow it just doesn't work out like that.

JO   Things never do.

SKINNY   What's wrong with me?

JO   God knows. Reaction or something. Don't flatter yourself you're the only one.

I've got a touch of the same complaint myself.

*(*VIC *and* MOANER *come in from the outer door, laughing. They sign their names on the board and then proceed to the stove to warm their hands.)*

JO   What's the joke my hearties?

MOANER   Joke?

JO   The one you were crying about as you came in.

VIC   Oh yes, it was rather funny. We were just saying what a lamb Commandant in these days.

JO   *(meaningly)* Lamb?

SKINNY   I shall always regard her as distinctly bovine.

JO   I bet Nobby always will!

(They all laugh at this sally.)

VIC   What d'you think, Jo? She actually asked me if I'd *mind* cleaning the lavatory!

JO   *(thunderstruck)* No!

VIC   Honour bright! I nearly said "Delighted, I'm sure", but I thought it was going a bit too far so I refrained.

SKINNY   What *did* you say?

MOANER   *(in mincing tones)* Not at all, Commandant. Is there anything else I can do for you?

JO   You're asking for trouble.

VIC   Oh, I don't think so. She's really getting to be almost human.

SKINNY   It's the thought of home, I expect.

MOANER   *(incredulously)* Has she a home?

VIC   Of course.

MOANER   Funny! It doesn't seem possible. I'd always imagined her living in a barracks or something.

SKINNY   She's married, I believe.

JO   My God!

MOANER   Really?

SKINNY   So sergeant told me the other day.

MOANER   Wonders'll never cease. You'll be telling me next that she's got half a dozen children and lives at "The Cedars", South Wimbledon.

SKINNY   Oh, I don't think she's run to – er – children yet.

JO   Then she'll have to get a move on if she ever wants to hear the patter of little feet on the nursery floor.

MOANER   Don't go putting ideas into her head, for heaven's sake. I pity the child she had anything to do with.

VIC   Oh, you never know. She's probably

quite harmless when she's not allowed to exercise her authority over other females. It's queer, when some down-trodden little woman gets the chance to boss her own sex, more often than not, it goes to her head and she develops into a hard-faced tyrant with a tongue like a scorpion.

MOANER   Scorpion is right – but why should we be the ones to get stung?

VIC   Oh, we shall all get over it. Have you all packed?

SKINNY   I have.

JO   So've I – except for my boots.

VIC   Your boots?

JO   They're so damned heavy. I think I'll bury 'em. Saves trouble.

MOANER   Now why didn't I think of that?

(The bedroom door opens suddenly and a khaki W.A.A.C. uniform suspended on the point of a stick, is pushed into the room. On it is pinned a label with the words "This uniform going cheap! Any offers?" The girls stare at it for a moment, and then dissolve into laughter.)

SKINNY   What the . . . ?

MOANER   *(reading the label)* This uniform going cheap – any offers?

JO   *(bawls out)* Twopence ha'penny.

SALOME   *(from behind the door)* Any advance on twopence ha'penny?

(She lurches forward into the room as the result of a push from the rear by NOBBY. SALOME is in a white blouse and navy blue bloomers only. NOBBY is still in uniform.)

SKINNY   Rather! Twopence!

SALOME   Oi! Any advance on twopence? Genuine antique, ladies! Alive with memories.

NOBBY   It's alive all right.

SALOME   No advance? Going, going gone! Twopence has it! *(She holds out the uniform to SKINNY.)*

SKINNY   *(drawing away gingerly)* I don't want the lousy thing.

SALOME   Well, what shall I do with it?

JO   Give it to the poor.

SALOME   I wouldn't insult 'em.

VIC   What are you going home in – that rig-out? *(She points to the bloomers.)*

SALOME   No, darling. I bought the duckiest little costume when I was on leave. You'll be all green with envy when you see it.

NOBBY   Well, I think you're a swine. We've all to go home in our rotten uniforms,

because we haven't anything else, so why shouldn't you?

JO   We're not good enough for her that's why.

SKINNY   *(singing)* For – she's going to marry her Tim, tra-la!

SALOME   Chuck it, you B.F.s. I was only going to wear the costume because Tim's meeting me at Waterloo, but if it's going to make you feel like poor relations, I'll get back into this filthy rag.

JO   You won't get any peace till you do, my girl! So you may as well get on with it.

SALOME   Oh, all right. But you're a lot of jealous cats, that's what you are!

(As she goes towards the bedroom, the outer door opens and the COMMANDANT enters, holding a batch of papers in her hand. She looks rather weary and just the slightest bit subdued. SALOME turns, startled at her entrance, while the others rise to their feet. COMMANDANT glances at the notice board and then turns to the girls.)

COMMANDANT   You are all present, I see. First of all — *(She suddenly sees SALOME edging behind JO, holding her uniform up in front of her.)* Good gracious, Lomax! What are you doing?

SALOME   I'm – I was just going to change, Commandant.

COMMANDANT   May I remind you that this is a mess-room, and, while you are about to go home, you are not yet there.

SALOME   Yes, Commandant.

COMMANDANT   While you are here, I shall be glad if you will cease wandering about like a chorus girl. *(SALOME turns to the door.)* I did not say you could go, Lomax. *(SALOME turns back again.)* You had better stay while I give the final instructions. The train leaves at 2.35 p.m. You will occupy the front portion only. I trust you will all conduct yourselves in a manner befitting the service to which you belong.

ALL   Yes, Commandant.

COMMANDANT   You will parade at 1.30 for final roll-call and receive your demobilisation papers. That is all for the moment. I . . . *(She hesitates)* I hope you all have a pleasant journey, and that when you are back in civil life again you may be able to feel that your work here has helped to – ah – broaden your outlook on life and teach you the value of discipline and service.

ALL   Thank you, Commandant.

(COMMANDANT *exists. The girls sit down with the exception of* SALOME.)

VIC   So that's that.

MOANER   I shall refuse to believe it until I'm sitting in the train.

NOBBY   Me too.

SALOME   Well, girls, I may not be home yet, but I'm using this as a boudoir, if it's all the same to you.

(She proceeds to get into her uniform.)

JO   Since when did you have a boudoir, Lady Fitzlomax?

SALOME   (haughtily) Really, Miss Overton, I can't answer such an intimate question.

SKINNY   I say, d'you think the train will have a restaurant car?

JO   My dear Skinny, of course – we're all going to Blighty in a first-class Pullman. Didn't you know?

SKINNY   Oh, shut up! I'm serious. I could do with a decent dinner, I can tell you!

SEVERAL   And so say all of us!

SKINNY   What about having one when we get to London?

NOBBY   You bet we will.

SKINNY   No, I mean all of us – together.

NOBBY   A farewell do?

SKINNY   Yes. How about it? Those in favour, hands up! (All their hands go up at once.) I take it, the motion is carried unanimously, ladies.

SALOME   Where shall it be?

NOBBY   Somewhere in the Strand, of course.

SALOME   Simpson's?

SKINNY   Marvellous! My mouth's beginning to water already. Just think of it. Hors d'oeuvre, soup, chicken, with fried potatoes and brussel sprouts and a bottle of bubbly.

MOANER   Pity Cocky won't be with us.

VIC   Yes, I was thinking that too.

JO   (shortly) Well, you needn't have said it. We don't have to be reminded every five minutes, surely.

MOANER   I'm sorry.

VIC   Perhaps she might be glad to know we're thinking of her, you never know. After all, when we've separated, we shall be just as much lost to each other as Cocky is to us now.

MOANER   Somehow, she never seems lost to me.

VIC   I wonder if we shall remember each other like that.

SKINNY   Why not?

VIC   I don't know. Most people have short memories. In a few years everything will get a little blurred. First we shall forget names, then faces, and then, perhaps, why we ever came out here at all.

SKINNY   I wonder why we did?

NOBBY   What on earth do you mean?

SKINNY   Well, I'm not sure that I know. Do you?

NOBBY   As far as I can remember, I thought it would be simply marvellous to be in France in the thick of it, doing my bit for my country and – and all that rot!

JO   (violently) If that was rot, what are we going to do from now on? At least life has had a purpose out here, even though it has been hell! But all the kick has gone out of it now the war's over.

MOANER   What are we going to do?

SALOME   Well, I'm going to be married for one.

VIC   (with rather a twisted smile) We may not all be as lucky as you, Salome. It's not a very bright prospect is it? Most of the men of our generation maimed in mind or body – the rest dead. A lot of us won't be able to marry, and if we don't, I can't see us settling down to fancy needlework or knitting after this, can you?

JO   No fear! They sent us out to do men's work and we've done it. When we get back, I'm hanged if I'll be fobbed off with a nursery maid's job.

VIC   It looks to me as though we're going to find it a bit difficult to settle to the quiet life when we get back.

SKINNY   (musing) I thought of going on with my music.

JO   Good for you.

SKINNY   (irritably) It's no damn' good at all! Whenever I start to play, I have to give up half-way through.

VIC   Why?

SKINNY   The futility of it all gets me by the throat. I feel as though I could choke at the pretentiousness of everything. You know, in the way of music and poetry and that kind of thing. It just doesn't seem real any more – not as it used to. Once, I could lose myself utterly in music. Now, it hasn't the power to hold me for five minutes.

MOANER   (bitterly) What price art, eh?

JO   All we know is the art of war – and there's precious little art in that, as far as I can see. It's a bloody reality.

VIC   But Jo, art's a reality just as much as war is.

JO   How do you make that out?

VIC   You can't mix the two, that's all. We've seen nothing but mud and blood for the last twelve months. In comparison, music and poetry seem affected and silly – unrelated to life. But only to the life we've led here, not to life in its fullest sense. We're a bit lopsided at the moment, and I don't wonder after what we've been through. But grass will grow again over No Man's Land – and we shall get back to normal too.

MOANER   Nothing will ever be the same again.

VIC   I hope not.

NOBBY   You *hope* not?

VIC   Don't you realise how awful it would be if things weren't different after this? People used to take war for granted, but they won't any longer. They said it was a glorious adventure. But we can tell them a thing or two about it, can't we? Mothers were proud to give their sons – and their daughters! Shall we be proud to give ours?

MOANER   If we have any.

VIC   What I'm getting at is this. When we discovered that all their pretty talk was nonsense, something else gave us the courage to carry on.

NOBBY   That's true. What was it, d'you suppose?

VIC   The knowledge that we were sacrificing all we wanted out of life to win this war – not because the winning of it mattered tuppence, but because it was a war that was going to end wars.

JO   And we've done it!

VIC   Yes, and that was worth a little sacrifice, surely? We've given up our chances of marriage and children – but we've made the future safe for Salome's children – and her grandchildren and great-grandchildren.

SALOME   Hi! Give us a chance! I'm not even married yet.

VIC   Don't you see, there can never be another war after this. We've proved how futile and hopeless and pointless it is. It can never happen again. I feel as though I could look forward ten – twenty years – to 1938 – and hear people saying "No, that generation gave up everything it held dear in life so that there should never be another war as long as the world lasts. They did that for us and we've got to stand by them. They didn't let us down and we mustn't let them down . . . "

MOANER   But if they do . . . ?

VIC   If they do, then we've been through it all for nothing. But they won't, will they?

MOANER   *(musingly)* I wonder.

Curtain

7 Dorothy Hewett 1923–

The Man from Mukinupin
Australia

Introduction

Born in Western Australia in 1923, Dorothy
Hewett ranks alongside Katharine Susannah
Prichard (1883–1969) and Christina Stead
(1902–) as one of the most significant
Australian writers of the twentieth century.
Her writing shares with theirs a concern for
the experience of women, trenchant analysis
of class and economic issues, and
commitment to exposing presuppositions
about race, ethnicity and national identity. It
is interesting to compare her career with that
of another great twentieth-century woman
writer, her contemporary Doris Lessing
(1919–) who grew up in Rhodesia (now
Zimbabwe). Hewett's father, like Lessing's,
was a First World War veteran who pioneered
as a farmer, and her mother suffered the
consequent isolation which Lessing portrays
in *The Grass Is Singing* (1950). This
deprivation and the sexual repression due to
her mother's Protestant upbringing probably
help account for the emotional and physical
abuse to which Hewett was subjected during
her childhood. Like Lessing, Hewett had little
formal education as a child and roamed
freely, especially in her imagination. She too
married and joined the Communist Party,
and, like Lessing, abandoned her first
marriage and child for a second, which she
also left, before commencing her career as a
creative writer.

However, whereas Prichard, Stead and
Lessing are primarily novelists, despite their
sorties into other forms such as the short
story and drama, Hewett is essentially a poet
and playwright. She has written a novel,
Bobbin' Up (1959), short stories, and an
autobiography, *Wild Card* (1990), which
display her lyrical gift for language, but her
revelatory insight finds its most apt
expression through a rich use of physical
metaphor which demands to be given life on
the stage. Furthermore, whereas Lessing first
left her parents' farm for Salisbury, and then
left Africa for London, the metropolitan
centre which her parents had originally
emigrated from, Hewett, a third-generation
Australian, left home for Perth and then
Western Australia for Sydney, New South
Wales. This was the foremost industrial city
in Australia. She still lives there with her
third partner. Lessing writes as an observant
outsider; Hewett writing helps define what it
is to be Australian. That is nowhere as true as
in her most popular play, *The Man from
Mukinupin*.

By 1990, Hewett's autobiography could be
surprisingly frank about apsects of her life,
such as sexual experience, which might be
regarded as *de rigueur* for a male poet but
were scandalous for a woman. It reveals
painful personal events such as a suicide
attempt, the death of her first child, an
abortion, and abuse from her second partner
who was a paranoid schizophrenic. Her
earlier efforts to be equally honest in drama,
dealing explicitly with such taboo subjects as
menstruation and menopause, had resulted in
two of her plays, *The Chapel Perilous* and *The
Tatty Hollow Story*, being banned from
publication or performance in Western
Australia. So there was consternation when
the new English theatre director of Perth
Playhouse, Stephen Barrie, commissioned
Hewett to write a play for the 150th
anniversary of the founding of Western
Australia in 1979. Even the Premier protested.
However, the resultant *The Man from
Mukinupin* is one of her most successful plays,
widely performed particularly by amateur
groups. As she has said, out of the despair and
insecurity of a series of critical disasters, she
wrote a play about reconciliation which
people took to their hearts.

Not that the former rebel against bourgeois
norms forsook her political consciousness

when she left the Communist Party in 1968. Ignoring official narratives of National History about the birth of Australia at ANZAC Cove, she relied on oral culture and her own family's tales to provide living folk-memory of Western Australia's past in the years before she was born. References in the play to JCW's musical theatre, Max Montesole's travelling Shakespeare, Wirth's Circus, even to the steam-train whistling "Yankee-Doodle-Dandy" at the end of the First World War, are all corroborated in her autobiography, where her mother sits singing "There's a Long, Long Trail Awinding". Among the folk-memories are the Great War horrors of Gallipoli and the Somme which had altered her father for all time, and the genocide of the Aboriginal Australians, whose descendants Hewett had visited in Port Hedland in 1946. Without directly representing these episodes of mass slaughter on the stage, Hewett recalls them as founding events by revealing their traumatic effect on two survivors. In this way she achieves some empathy between the races. That may seem a devious approach, but it circumvented censorship, and the account in her autobiography of the abuse she herself had suffered from a traumatised veteran of the Second World War is evidence of the price she had paid to gain such understanding.

Hewett had written both poetry and plays from a young age but the absence of a native theatre tradition or practising theatre group in Western Australia was a drawback to her early development. After university, where her first efforts were staged, there was no one to encourage her or mount her plays until she moved to Sydney. However, she had read widely at the University of Perth (before being sent down for failing her first-year exams) and *The Man from Mukinupin* is evidence of her ability to draw on European traditions and develop them for Australian purposes. As a poetic dramatist, she looked to other dramatists who were also poets. It is not surprising to find the influence of Shakespeare; less to be expected, perhaps, are the traces of Dylan Thomas. Mukinupin shares with Thomas's Llaregyb a population of provincial shopkeepers struggling with a genteel English façade that masks the real passions and pasts of the characters. Hewett has taken one step further Thomas's contrast between daytime respectability and the night-time dream world of desire. Following

Shakespeare's use of doubles in *A Midsummer Night's Dream*, Hewett reveals the repressed unconscious of society. Yet it is not the magic world of English forest-fairies which teases at her characters, but the more sinister, elemental world of pre-colonial and early-colonial Australia. The structure of *The Man from Mukinupin* is loosely based around two linked narratives, the "love-stories" of twin working-class brothers, Harry and Jack, who court two half-sisters, Lily and Polly. The plot is resolved by the day-time wedding of conventional Jack and Polly, and the darker liaison of the criminal, shell-shocked war-hero, Harry, with the half-aboriginal, Lily, who then light out for the wilderness. This apparent romance with its musical-comedy surface disguises an older theatrical form, a saturnalian carnival (Bakhtin 1968).

Despite its strict plotting and named characters, the other play in this anthology which Hewett's most resembles in Stein's *Accents from Alsace*. They both construct a portrait of a community through a collage of quotations, mixing high and low registers in a heteroglossia, a multiplicity of voices which draw on a mixed inheritance (Bakhtin 1981). With its broader scope, Hewett's play is even more polyphonic than Stein's, juxtaposing scraps of Tennyson and Shakespeare with Australian poetry such as Mary Gilmore's "The Aboriginals" and First World War ballads, and placing the grand rhetoric that talks of "daring, enduring and dying", a "bitter heritage" and "the toga of nationhood" alongside Australian slang that speaks about "bummers" "getting snickered" and a "boong-basher's daughter". The ways of life expressed through these voices are also placed cheek-by-jowl, "the jug of cream on a doily", the corset, toupée and "Royal Doulton chamber-pot" of genteel aspirations set alongside the vulgar "jerry" and "clobber", the bull-roarers and didgeridoos, the "shit", "piss" and "bugger" of a less domesticated order. On the one hand, the play is a light-hearted celebration of naïvely superficial common-folk; on the other, a reminder of the darker base of violence and sexuality, associated with the untamed landscape, on which fragile, urban civilisation is constructed.

Through her patchwork of slang and song, poetry and curses, dance and ceremonies, Hewett has displayed how people share in the cultural unconscious by which a society is sustained. *The Man From Mukinupin* celebrates the creation of an imagined community, fertilised by the repetition of pre-Christian rituals of both Aboriginal and European heritage for its pioneering growth into the future. As the play itself dynamically re-enacts rituals, both ancient and recent, the audience and actors participate in the festival of new life, a life that joyfully accommodates the staid as well as the eccentric.

Further reading

Primary

Facey, A. B. (1981) *A Fortunate Life*, Fremantle: Fremantle Arts Centre; Harmondsworth: Penguin.

Hewett, Dorothy (1959) *Bobbin' Up*, Melbourne: Australasian; rep. (1985) London: Virago.

—— (1980) *The Man from Mukinupin: A Musical play in 2 Acts*, Sydney: Currency.

—— (1989) *A Tremendous World in Her Head: Selected Poems*, ed. Kirsten Holst Petersen, Coventry: Dangaroo.

—— (1990) *Wild Card: an Autobiography 1923–58*, Victoria: McPhee/London: Virago.

—— (1992) *Collected Plays Volume 1: This Old Man Came Rolling Home, The Chapel Perilous, etc.*, Sydney: Currency.

Seymour, Alan [1962] (1963) *The One Day of the Year* in H. G. Kippax (ed.) *Three Australian Plays*, Harmondsworth: Penguin.

Thomas, Dylan (1954) *Under Milkwood: A Play for Voices*, London: Dent.

Secondary

Bakhtin, Mikhail M. (1968) *Rabelais and His World*, trans. H. Iswolsky, Cambridge, MA: MIT Press.

—— (1981) *The Dialogic Imagination: Four Essays*, trans. C. Emerson and M. Holquist, Austin: University of Texas Press.

Bell, Diane (1983) *Women of the Dreaming*, Melbourne: Unwin.

Bennett, Bruce (ed.) (1995) *Dorothy Hewett: Selected Critical Essays*, Fremantle: Fremantle Arts Centre.

Damousi, Joy and Marilyn Lake (eds) (1995) *Gender and War: Australians at War in the Twentieth Century*, Cambridge: Cambridge University Press.

Daniels, Kay and Mary Murnane (eds) (1980) *Uphill All the Way: a Documentary History of Women in Australia*, Queensland: University of Queensland Press.

Gilbert, Kevin (ed.) (1988) *Inside Black Australia: an Anthology of Aboriginal Poetry*, Harmondsworth: Penguin.

Summers, Anne (1975) *Damned Whores and God's Police: the Colonization of Women in Australia*, Harmondsworth: Penguin (especially ch. 12).

Thomson, Alistair (1994) *Anzac Memories: Living with the Legend*, Oxford: Oxford University Press.

Williams, Margaret (1992) *Dorothy Hewett: The Feminine as Subversion*, Paddington: Currency.

The Man from Mukinupin _____

[A Musical Play in Two Acts]
First performed by the National Theatre Company
at the Playhouse, Perth on 31 August 1979
Published Sydney, 1980

Dorothy Hewett

_____

Characters

JACK TUESDAY, The grocer's boy who
becomes a J.C Williamson's chorus boy,
doubled with

HARRY TUESDAY, his twin brother, the
shearer who becomes a shell-shocked war
hero.

POLLY PERKINS, the town beauty, Jack's
sweetheart and the storekeeper's daughter,
doubled with

LILY PERKINS, known as TOUCH OF THE
TAR, Harry's sweetheart and the half-caste
half-sister of Polly.

MISS CLARRY HUMMER, the ex-wardrobe
mistress of J. C. Williamson's, now the
town dressmaker, doubled with,

THE WIDOW TUESDAY, Jack and Harry's
mother: a Dickensian lady.

MISS CLEMMY HUMMER, ex-tightrope walker
from Wirth's Circus, now mistress of
ceremonies for the night people.

EDIE PERKINS, Polly's deaf mother, a reciter
of ballads.

EEK PERKINS, Mukinupin storekeeper and
Polly's father, doubled with

ZEEK PERKINS, his twin brother, a water
diviner and star gazer.

MERCY MONTEBELLO, an ageing
Shakespearean actress, who marries Cecil
Brunner.

CECIL BRUNNER, travelling salesman in
manchester goods and lingerie, doubled
with

MAX MONTEBELLO, Italian actor/manager,
and

THE FLASHER, town flasher and madman.

Setting

The action takes place in Mukinupin, a
typical West Australian wheatbelt town east
of the rabbit proof fence. The time is 1912 to
1920.

Two unravelling wicker chairs are placed
around a small table down right for the
MISSES HUMMER, presenters of the play.
Downstage left is the Perkins' General Store,
with a counter and stools. Closer to centre
stage is a cardboard pillared portico: the
Mukinupin Town Hall. In Act II this is
inscribed with the legend: "Lest We Forget",
and a cardboard war memorial of a soldier
with a kelpie dog at his feet is placed upstage
left of the Town Hall.

Act I

*In darkness the weird night music begins on the
sound track, continuing until the mood of night
and eeriness has been well set. The music is
interspersed with a line of dialogue, an
occasional giggle, scream, shout of laughter or a
coo-ee.*

ZEEK'S VOICE   (*chanting*) Water . . . Water . . .
Water . . .

WIDOW TUESDAY'S VOICE   (*chanting*) Moth
and rust . . . Rust and moth . . .

TOUCH OF THE TAR'S VOICE   (*calling*)
Coo-ee . . . Coo-ee . . . (*a high giggle*).

HARRY TUESDAY'S VOICE   (*calling
imperiously*) Lily! Lily Perkins!

TOUCH OF THE TAR'S VOICE   (*mocking,
fading out*) Harr-ee! Harr-ee! Harr-ee!

EDIE PERKINS' VOICE   (*moaning*) Wash your
hands . . . put on your nightgown . . . don't
look so pale.[1]

(*The background music rises to crescendo as,
against the back scrim palely lit, and back to
audience, is spread-eagled the shadow of the
FLASHER in raincoat and felt hat, flashing.*)

143

FLASHER Look Polly! Look Polly! Look Polly! *(Wild laughter, a scream, blackout.)*
ZEEK'S VOICE *(continuing and growing in volume)* Water . . . Water . . . Water . . .

(ZEEK'S VOICE is broken by the sound of CLEMMY HUMMER knocking onstage with her crutch. Pause, silence. The church bells begin ringing and in dim blue light we see CLEMMY standing, back to audience, leaning on her crutch, downstage right, like a mistress of ceremonies. Enter the dancers, ZEEK, HARRY, TOUCH OF THE TAR, and WIDOW TUESDAY, all absolutely unrecognisable in their roles as rustic clog dancers. They are each carrying pitchforks and are dressed in gum boots, and wheat sheaves, so that they look like moving haystacks. They dance and sing the "Five Man's" Morris in a circle, with CLEMMY joining in as a kind of hobbling doppelganger.)

THE FIVE MAN'S MORRIS

ALL We'll dance the Five Man's Morris
We'll cart the sheaves away
We'll dance the Five Man's Morris
On Polly's wedding day.

We'll stook it and we'll fork it
We'll cease our labours soon
When the haystacks rise like magic
And we've stacked them to the moon.

(Chorus)

Bringin' in the sheaves, bringin' in the sheaves
We'll bless all Mukinupin bringin' in the sheaves.

The bells will toll and gold will roll
Around us in a ring
We'll bless all Mukinupin
When we bring the harvest in.

We'll dance the Five Man's Morris
We'll hear the teams roll by
When the evening star has vanished
And the Cross hangs in the sky.

(Chorus)

Bringin' in the sheaves, bringin' in the sheaves
We'll bless all Mukinupin bringin' in the sheaves,

(Exit the dancers as CLEMMY HUMMER turns downstage.)

CLEMMY Goodnight Zeek, Goodnight Flasher, Goodnight Harry Tuesday, Goodnight Lily Perkins, Goodnight Widow Tuesday . . .

(Her voice dies away with weariness, she yawns, the faint light of morning steals over the stage, a rooster crows, a magpie carols, as she hobbles to one of the two unravelling wicker chairs set beside a small table downstage right. She seats herself painfully, with the aid of her crutch, and relaxes, closing her eyes. As the stage lightens we can see backstage up right a cardboard pillared portico with "MUKINUPIN TOWN HALL 1912" in gold lettering. Downstage left is the Perkins' General Store with clothesline far left. Enter CLARRY HUMMER carrying a silver teatray set with coffeepot, sugar bowl, two coffee cups, a jug of cream on a doily. Both the MISSES HUMMER are smartly, brightly, and theatrically dressed from a bygone age: MISS CLEMMY a trifle askew, and on the edge of eccentricity.)

CLARRY *(brightly)* Six a.m., Clem.

(CLEMMY wakes with a start, yawns, goes into their routine.)

CLEMMY First light.

(CLARRY has set down the tray and herself, and is beginning to pour the coffee.)

CLARRY The alarum clocks are ringing.
CLEMMY Across the salt lakes.
CLARRY East of the rabbit proof fence.

(They giggle. CLARRY hands CLEMMY her coffee. They sit sipping.)

CLEMMY Feels like another scorcher.
CLARRY Dust in summer.
CLEMMY Mud in winter.
CLARRY AND CLEMMY That's Mucka.

(They laugh delightedly at their little routine. The town hall clock strikes six. CLARRY checks it against her pocket watch fastened to her waist.)

CLARRY Town Hall clock's on time.

(Enter EEK PERKINS, dressed in a conservative business suit and hat, checking his pocket watch. He takes up position in front of the scrim, shakes his watch and holds it to his ear.)

CLARRY Eek Perkins is checking his watch.
CLEMMY *(giggling)* Like the white rabbit.
CLARRY Time's stopped.

CLEMMY   But he doesn't know it.

CLARRY   Doesn't know much, really.

CLEMMY   Profit and Loss.

CLARRY   Just a Mukinupin boy.

CLEMMY   Knows how to get on.

CLARRY   Get on what?

CLEMMY   *(in a stage whisper)* Gin jockey, they call him. *(CLARRY pretends to be shocked, but giggles.)*

CLARRY AND CLEMMY   No rain about, Mr P.?

EEK   *(mournfully)* Not a cloud in the sky, Miss Clarry, Miss Clem. *(They all shake their heads.)*

ALL   So bad for the crops.

EDIE   *(off, reciting coming closer)*
I sprang to the stirrup and Joris and he;
I galloped, Dirck galloped, we galloped all three . . . [2]

(Enter EDIE PERKINS in smart beaded black: black bonnet trimmed with jet and carrying a huge ear trumpet. She joins EEK at the scrim still reciting.)

. . . "Good speed!" cried the watch,
As the gate-bolts undrew . . .

EEK   *(loudly)* Mrs Perkins!

EDIE   " . . . 'Speed!' echoed the wall to us galloping through . . . "

EEK   Edie Perkins!

EDIE   *(unaware)*
. . . Behind shut the postern, the lights sank to rest,
And into the midnight we galloped abreast.

CLARRY   Edie Perkins, always was a good hand at a recitation.

CLEMMY   But amateur, hopelessly amateur.

CLARRY   And deaf as a post. Another cup, dear?

CLEMMY   Tone deaf. Please, dear.

EDIE   Eek Perkins, we'll never get there on time.

EEK   Get where, Mrs Perkins?

EDIE   *(loudly)* What's that? *(She raises her ear trumpet)*

EEK   *(yelling)* Get where?

EDIE   Back to Mukinupin. Where's Polly? *(Agitatedly)* Where's my Polly?

POLLY   *(off)* I'm here, Mother,

(Enter POLLY PERKINS, hair tied behind in a big bow dressed in calf-length simple white muslin, white straw boater and smart, button-up boots. She takes up position in front of the scrim.)

EDIE   Ay?

(POLLY kisses her cheek.)

POLLY   Here, Mother!

EEK   Are you, coming with us, Polly?

POLLY   Where, Pa?

EEK   Back to Mukinupin before opening time.

POLLY   Why, Pa?

EEK   Polly, Polly Perkins, you're always asking questions.

POLLY   It's the only way to get any answers . . . isn't it?

(Enter JACK TUESDAY, whistling "Polly Put the Kettle On". He is dressed in black trousers, white shirtsleeves and a grocer's boy's white apron.)

JACK   Ask me a question, Pol?

POLLY   Do you love me, Jack?

JACK   More than all the tea in china.

(Enter CECIL BRUNNER in shabby black with bowler hat, a sample case and a pink rosebud in his buttonhole.)

CECIL   Have an acid drop, Miss Polly?

POLLY   Oh, thanks ever so, Mr Brunner.

(CECIL removes an acid drop from his waistcoat pocket, gives it to POLLY, who dusts it, hesitates, pops it in her mouth. JACK grabs POLLY by the hand and twirls her into the set.)

JACK   Run faster, Polly, faster.

POLLY   Why? Why?

JACK   So Cecil Brunner can't ever catch you. *(They laugh together, and whisper secrets. CECIL is stiff in front of the scrim.)*

CECIL   I come to Mukinupin twice a year, travelling in manchester goods and . . . ladies' unmentionables. *(CECIL crosses to the shop counter and raises his hat to the two MISSES HUMMER.)* Lovely weather, Miss Clarry, Miss Clem.

CLARRY AND CLEMMY   Summer'll never end.

EDIE AND EEK   No good for the crops.

(They all nod their heads. EEK picks up a roll of bunting, gestures to JACK to bring the ladder and goes out front of the shop. He holds the ladder while JACK climbs up with the bunting and fixes it above the shop-front. He hands JACK hammer and nails. EDIE crosses behind counter and examines CECIL's goods.)

EDIE   When the time comes, Mr Brunner

will make our Pol a good husband. *(She smiles benignly on* CECIL.*)*

POLLY *(giggling)* With acid drops in his pocket.

EEK Good, hard working, sensible stamp of a chap.

POLLY *(pouting)* Wears a corset and a toupée.

EDIE Wears a Brunner rose in his buttonhole. *(She leans forward to sniff at it.)*

EEK Well dressed, good family, not like young Jack.

EDIE Who, Father?

EEK Young Jack Tuesday. *(*EDIE *moves out towards the front of the shop.* JACK *climbs down the ladder, and the three of them admire the sign.* JACK *stuffs the hammer in his pocket.) (Reading proudly)* "Perkins' General Store, 1912".

EDIE What was that, Mr Perkins? Speak up, Mr Perkins. *(*JACK *carries the ladder backstage.)*

EEK *(roaring)* Not like young Jack *(quietly)* or his jailbird twin brother, Harry.

EDIE Not like your barmy twin brother, Zeek.

EEK *(angrily)* Not much to choose between them.

EDIE *Eeek* and *Zeek?*

EEK *(furiously)* Jack and Harry Tuesday . . . like as two peas.

EDIE *Eek and Zeek Perkins* . . . identical twins!

POLLY *(defiantly)* I love Jack Tuesday.

EEK You'll love Cecil Brunner.

JACK You love pink roses. I'll get you some.

*(*JACK *begins to sweep the shop with the straw broom.* POLLY *unwinds her skipping rope, hands the two ends to* EEK *and* EDIE, *who turn rope for her.* CECIL *watches, smiling.)*

POLLY *(chanting)*
Roses are pink, violets are blue,
I've got a boyfriend and so have you.
Tell your mother to hold her tongue,
Tell your father to do the same,
'Cause he's the one who changed her name.
Count the sheep going into the pen,
Count them over and over again.

POLLY *(skipping pepper)* Fifty, sixty, seventy, eighty, ninety, one hundred.

(The rope turns faster and faster, till, breathless, POLLY *gives up.* EEK *goes behind*

his counter and makes up his ledger. EDIE *hangs the mat on the clothesline with* CECIL's *help, and begins to beat it with the broom.* POLLY *takes her rope and skips slowly round the stage.* CLARRY *begins packing up the coffee things.* CLEMMY *takes a novel out from under the pillow.)*

CLARRY There's little Polly Perkins skipping down the street.

CLEMMY Like the Queen of the May.

CLARRY Growing up like a wildflower.

CLEMMY There's Jack Tuesday sweeping out the Perkins' General Store.

CLARRY He's sweet on Polly.

CLEMMY That'll put the cat amongst the pigeons.

POLLY *(pausing)* If I threw a bottle with a love letter in it into the middle of the saltbush plain would anyone answer?

CLARRY Course not – dead and buried.

CLEMMY Under the sea.

EDIE *(calling)* Get a move on, Polly, or I'll tan your BTM.

CLARRY What's that you're reading, dear?

CLEMMY *(wickedly whispering) Passion in the Dust* by Marie Corelli.

CLARRY Oh! Clem! *(*CLARRY *crosses to exit with tray, smiling.)* Edie Perkins is beating out her Persian carpet.

CLEMMY Never get the dust out of *that*, not in a hundred years.

(Exit CLARRY. CECIL *and* EDIE *relay the mat,* CECIL *returns to* EEK, *and they talk shop.* POLLY *sidles up to* JACK *who pretends to ignore her.* EDIE *exits out back.)*

JACK Whadda you hangin' around for, Polly Perkins? I'll give you a chinese burn.

POLLY Mind your lip, Jack Tuesday. You're as bad as your brother Harry.

JACK My brother's all right.

POLLY Your brother's bad.

JACK Who says so?

POLLY Everybody knows about bad black Harry, in Fremantle jail. Everyone that matters.

JACK Who matters?

*(*EDIE *re-enters, carrying a bowl of pink roses which she places on the end of the shop counter.)*

EDIE *(calling)* Polly! Polly Perkins, you keep away from the rough end of town or the Flasher'll get you.

(EDIE *joins* EEK *and* CECIL BRUNNER, *backs to audience as* CECIL *displays his wares.*)

POLLY   *(to* JACK) I saw you kissing Touch of the Tar down the rough end of town.

JACK   That was Harry. She's Harry's girl.

POLLY   It was you, Jack Tuesday. I always know you by the dimple in your cheek.

JACK   *(touched)* Do you, Pol? Anyway, she's gone walkabout with the sandalwood cutters. (JACK *has been carefully sweeping towards the bowl of roses. He grabs the bunch, puts it behind his back, ditches the broom and whistles back across stage, passing* CLARRY *as she re-enters with her sewing basket.* POLLY *pretends not to notice.*) *(cheerfully)* Morning Miss Clarry, Miss Clem.

CLARRY AND CLEMMY   Morning, Jack.

JACK   Not a cloud in the sky.

CLARRY AND CLEMMY   But so bad for the crops. (*They all grin conspiratorially.* JACK *brings the roses out in front of his chest.*)

JACK   *(awkwardly)* Here, Pol, I picked these for you.

POLLY   *(sweetly)* Oh! You never? Oh! You shouldn't 've. Oh! Jack, they're so pretty.

JACK   Not as pretty as you are.

POLLY   Pretty as Touch of Tar?

JACK   Prettier.

POLLY   *(primly)* Pretty is as pretty does. She puts apples down the front of her dress to make two bulges.

JACK   *(embarrassed)* I know. (POLLY *turns sideways.*)

POLLY   If I stand sideways can you *see* anything?

JACK   See what?

POLLY   A difference?

JACK   Oh! . . . Since when?

POLLY   Since last time you *looked*, silly!

(JACK *swings her round.*)

JACK   Not much. (POLLY *pouts,* JACK *laughs and tries to kiss her clumsily.*) Polly! (POLLY *twists away.*)

EDIE   *(Calling)* POLLY! Put the kettle on!

POLLY   It's time to go in. The midges are biting.

EDIE   And we'll all have tea!

(POLLY *dances off.* JACK *comes centre for his song, accompanied by* CECIL BRUNNER, EEK *and* EDIE *and the two* MISSES HUMMER. *During the song* POLLY *returns with tea, teacups, milk jug and silver teapot and serves tea.*)

POLLY PUT THE KETTLE ON

JACK: *(Sings)*
On Monday mornings in the street
there is a girl I love to meet,
she captures every heart.
The blinds go up, the curtains part,
and nothing could be finer,
and I love her more than all the tea in China.

(*All sing and dance as* POLLY *re-enters.*)

ALL   For it's Polly Perkins, pretty Polly Perkins,
All the boys give her the eye.
Pretty Polly Perkins is the girl for me,
So Polly put the kettle on and we'll all have tea.

Hey, Polly!

(JACK, CECIL *and* EEK *give long wolf whistles.*)

CECIL
In Mukinupin Polly is the Mukinupin belle,
There's not a gal to touch her, I know because I fell
For pretty Polly Perkins when first she caught my eye
And I lingered on the corner just to see her passing by.

ALL   And we lingered on the corner just to see her passing by.

EEK   O she passes by in Mucka with such a lovely air;
Her dress is made of muslin, there's a ribbon in her hair,
And every man in Mucka is leaping to his feet
When little Polly Perkins drops her ribbon in the street.

(POLLY *drops her ribbon,* JACK *and* CECIL BRUNNER *scramble for it but* JACK *wins, triumphantly.*)

ALL   Hey, Polly!
For it's Polly, Polly Perkins, pretty Polly Perkins.
All the boys in the street are giving her the eye,
Little Polly Perkins is the girl for me,
So Polly put the kettle on and we'll all have tea.

Hey, Polly!

(JACK, CECIL *and* EEK *give wolf whistles.*

POLLY *passes round the cups. There is laughter, chatting.)*

POLLY Tea, Miss Clarry; tea, Miss Clem. One lump or two?

CLARRY AND CLEMMY Thank you, dearest Polly, don't mind if we do.

(Laughter. EDIE PERKINS comes centre to recite, to accompaniment on the piano.)

EDIE Airy fairy Lilian,
Flitting, fairy Lilian,
When I ask her if she love me
Claps her tiny hands above me,
Laughing all she can;
She'll not tell me if she love me . . . [3]

ALL Put her in a billycan.

EDIE *(oblivious)* Cruel little Lilian . . .

(CECIL BRUNNER comes forward and bows.)

CECIL I'm afraid the time has come to say farewell. My good grey mare and sulky are waiting, and I am a knight of the road. *(He crosses to POLLY and kisses her hand.)* Goodbye, Miss Polly, goodbye till next time.

EDIE Say goodbye to Mr Brunner, Polly.

POLLY Goodbye, Mr Brunner.

CECIL Cecil. *(He waits but POLLY only smiles vaguely.)* Dare I hope, Miss Polly? Dare I carry with me on my journey the memory of one dark rose with the dew-drops in her hair? *(POLLY hangs her head, JACK clenches his fist.)*

EEK Good stamp of a chap, that Brunner. He'll make a go of it. *(CECIL shakes him by the hand, then pauses before JACK, who begins to whistle and look elsewhere.)* Take Mr Brunner's bag, Jack. Hop to it, lad.

CECIL Goodbye, sweet ladies. *(They all wave, JACK picks up the bag, looking sulky.)*

CLARRY AND CLEMMY God speed, Mr Brunner.

(CECIL BRUNNER exits, followed by JACK, EDIE stands waving as CECIL disappears. POLLY puts her tongue out at his retreating back. EDIE turns and catches her at it.)

EDIE Polly Perkins! It's time you put your hair up, my lady, *and* lengthened your skirts. *(EEK pulls a chair out from behind the counter and sits down to read the paper, his back to the women. POLLY props a mirror on the counter and begins to do up her hair, trying different styles. EDIE drags out some bolts of material – silks and satins – from*

behind the counter and staggers downstage with them.) We'll get Miss Clarry and Miss Clemmy to make you up something stylish. What do you think of this, Miss Clarry? *(EDIE holds a bolt of satin up against POLLY.)*

CLARRY Too old for Polly, Mrs Perkins. Too sophisticated. Don't you think so, Clemmy?

POLLY But I'd *love* something sophisticated.

CLEMMY She needs – Stand up, dear – she needs a beaded pink georgette.

POLLY Ooh, Lovely! *(POLLY pulls off her dress, helped by EDIE, and stands in her slip.)*

CLARRY Clemmy always had perfect taste, always.

CLEMMY But you were the dressmaker, dear. I'll always remember how you dressed the divine Sarah.

CLARRY *La dame aux camélias* in white, slipper satin.

CLEMMY You were a goldmine for JCW's. I only hung by my teeth from the Big Top in dyed pink, see-through muslin.

CLARRY You were a marvel, dear. If only you'd used a net.

CLEMMY I ascended in a balloon above Melbourne, singing tra-la-la-boom-de-ay. *(She begins to sing and attempts a dance.)*

CLARRY Fun and music are what the people want, dear.

CLEMMY After I fell I had a cat, rat and canary show.

CLARRY In the theatre everything is possible. Stand up here, Polly.

(EDIE brings the pink georgette and a packet of pins. POLLY climbs up on the table and slips the pink georgette over her head. EDIE stands by with the pins. CLARRY kneels at POLLY's hem, pins in her mouth, as CLEMMY tries an odd wavery little dance around them, leaning on her crutch. The cries of the two women punctuate CLEMMY's speeches.)

CLARRY AND EDIE *(in turn)* Hold still Polly! Pull your bottom in! She needs a little pad *on her lower spine!* But sway backs are *so* fashionable! Don't wriggle, Polly! Polly! *(POLLY gives an occasional "Ouch!" as a pin goes in.)*

CLEMMY Ta-ra-ra-boom-de-ay, ta-ra-ra-boom-de-ay . . . remember Annette Kellerman, Clarry, swimming at the Aquarium? And the wax works in Bourke Street, Baby Bliss the fat lady and the midgets, General and Mrs Mite? You've got a dip in the hem there, dear.

POLLY Oh! Tell us about it, Miss Clemmy.

CLARRY Keep still, dear.

CLEMMY Ta-ra-ra-boom-de-ay, ta-ra-ra-boom-de-ay. Well! we had to cancel Ben Hur because of the bubonic plague but Lillian Russell looked beautiful up to the last till her voice went off, and she had to pay me to sing her finales for her.

POLLY *(enchanted)* Lillian Russell!

CLEMMY And Nellie Stewart was principal boy in *Cinderella*. All the gallery girls called "Nellie, Nellie!" and threw her floral tributes.

POLLY *(ecstatic)* Nellie Stewart!

CLEMMY *(stopping dead)* But then His Majesty's burnt down on a Palm Sunday and I fell from the high wire and ended up . . . in Mukinupin.

POLLY Oh! Miss Clemmy, Miss Clemmy, how could you bear it?

CLEMMY Dead and buried under a sea of scrub.

EDIE Don't wriggle, Polly.

CLARRY Almost finished. There! *(She rises stiffly.)* Doesn't she look a picture?

EDIE Marvellous, Miss Clarry. Marvellous! Such dash, such style, such a waste in Mukinupin.

POLLY *(getting down)* How do I look, Miss Clemmy? *(CLEMMY clasps POLLY to her.)*

CLEMMY Dearest Polly, you look like . . . like Gladys Moncrieff in *Peg O' My Heart*.

POLLY Oh! Miss Clemmy, do I, do I? *(POLLY whirls around the stage. EDIE puts up her ear trumpet.)*

EDIE Who? Who?

POLLY *(whirling EDIE with her)* Gladys Moncrieff, Mummy.

EDIE She does too, she does too. *(EDIE rushes across to EEK and rattles his paper.)* Father, Father, look at our Polly! She's the spitting image of Gladys Moncrieff.

EEK Looks like Polly Perkins to me. *(POLLY dances over to him, hugs and kisses him, laughing.)*

POLLY Dearest Pa, I'm so happy I could . . . bite your ear off. *(POLLY dances about singing "ta-ra-ra-boom-de-ay". EEK looks pleased, rustles his paper.)*

EDIE Listen to her, hitting a high C like an opera star. Why, even I can hear her.

EEK The line's gone through to Jiliminning.

EDIE What's that Father? Speak up.

EEK *Jiliminning . . . Line's through!*

EDIE *(proclaiming)* "The mighty bush with iron rails is tethered to the world";[4] and our daughter is singing like . . . Jenny Lind.

EEK Make a good wife for some steady feller. Says here some Archduke's been assassinated at . . . some outlandish place.

EDIE Where?

EEK Sar-a-jevo.

EDIE Never heard of it.

CLARRY Thank God we live in Mukinupin.

CLEMMY Nothing ever happens here.

POLLY Summer's ending. I've put my hair up and lengthened my skirts. Everything changes.

(EDIE exits with tea things. The sisters sit. POLLY comes centre for song.)

SUMMER BIRD

POLLY

I saw the summer bird
blue as the sky,
that was her song you heard
down by the creek she went
I saw her flying so high,
Summer bird – fly, summer bird – fly.

The summer bird is blue,
blue as the creek water,
I'll give her song to you
if you tell me who taught her

All the notes in the scale
and some I've never heard;
through winter's frost and hail
come back, my summer bird.
Summer bird – fly, summer bird – fly.

I'll see the summer bird,
blue as the day;
that was her song you heard
before she flew away
into the wattle tree
Summer bird – fly, summer bird – fly.
Summer bird – fly.

(JACK re-enters holding two tickets triumphantly.)

JACK Pol, Pol, I've got us two front row tickets for Max and Mercy Montebello for *The Strangling of Desdemona* in The Mukinupin Town Hall.

POLLY Oh, Jack! You're a marvel!

(POLLY embraces the delighted JACK. General excitement as they all crowd round, except for EEK who continues ostentatiously reading his paper, rustling the sheets.)

ALL *The Montebellos!*

JACK In the flesh. And two complimentaries

for Miss Clarry and Miss Clemmy Hummer in honour of their long association with the profession.

CLARRY   How thoughtful!

(JACK and POLLY rush about setting up the seats outside the Town Hall.)

CLEMMY   They played the Hippodrome in the old days.

CLARRY   I dressed her for Rosalind in those skintight, satin breeches. Her figure could take it. She was so lissome. Remember, Clem?

CLEMMY   *(grimly)* The incomparable Mercy. Who could ever forget *her*!

(EEK stands and reads aloud:)

EEK   August the third, 1914. Should the worst happen after everything has been done that honour will permit, Australians will stand beside our own to defend her to our last man and our last shilling.

(No one takes any notice of him. There is a roll of drums. Enter MAX MONTEBELLO, very Italian, with a sweeping moustache, wide-brimmed black hat, and a cloak. He stands at the Town Hall entrance and strikes an attitude. There is a breathless hush.)

MAX   Ladies an' gentlemens. *(Another drum roll, and a sweeping bow. A pause while EDIE bundles up EEK, JACK throws off his apron and takes POLLY's arm, the MISSES HUMMER move upstage, arm in arm.)* Actor-Manager Max Montebello presents . . . fresha from ze triumps in Kununoppin and Koolyanoboff, and under distingué patronage . . . *MADAME MERCY MONTEBELLO. (Enter MERCY, a faded beauty in a white nightgown, curtseying grandly.)* Ze world's greatest act-resse in ze Pathetique and Triumphant 'eroines of Shakespeare, wiz illustrative act-ing of ze varrying emotions of ze great Masters incomparable 'eroines. *(The audience clap enthusiastically. MAX bows. MERCY curtseys. MAX holds up his hand in a commanding gesture.)* Despite ze vicious rumour, despite ze tragic times, despite Madame's perigrinations aroun' ze bent surface of dis 'oary ol' planette, I would like to ensure our aud-ience that 'er majestic voice shows absolutely no sign of de wear or de tear. *(He gestures at MERCY and she attempts to hit a high note.)*

JACK   You can do better than that, Pol. *(MAX glares but MERCY curtseys and smiles winningly again, touching JACK'S heart. He leaps to his feet, ashamed.)* *(Gallantly)* Three cheers for Madame Mercy. *(Mukinupin claps but POLLY pulls JACK down in his seat, shushing him. MERCY exits, blowing kisses to the delighted JACK.)*

MAX   Zank you, Zank you, Mukinupin. And now I would like to draw ze attention of ze audience to ze refined presence of Miss Clarice and Miss Clementine; Miss Clarice, once J. C. Williamson's most distingué costumière, Miss Clementine, ze great-est female wire-walker in ze Sousern 'Emisphere. *(Much applause as the MISSES HUMMER rise and bow.)*

JACK   *(standing)* Hooray, hooray for Miss Clary and Miss Clemmy.

MAX   And as ze curtain raiser for ze great tragedy of Mr Shakespeare, our local artiste . . . *(He fumbles for the name. JACK jumps up and whispers in his ear.)* Ah! yes . . . it is . . . MADAME EDEE who vill favour us wis one of 'er mosta delightful recitations from ze maudlin bard, ze Poet Laureate, Alfred Lord Tenny-son.

(MAX bows and withdraws. Excited cries from audience of, "Surprise! Surprise!" as EDIE, shoved on stage by EEK, rises all smiles and moves centre.)

EDIE   *(very nervously)* "The May Queen!"
(Pause for applause but there is none.)
(Firmly) "The May Queen" by Alfred Lord Tennyson. *(Scattered applause.) (In a rush:)*
    If you're walking call me early, call me early, Mother dear,
    For I would see the sun rise upon the glad New Year,
    It is the last New Year that I shall ever see,
    Then you may lay me low in the mould and think no more of me

(Sniffles, loud sobs, and EEK blows his nose with vigour. EDIE warms to it:)

    Goodnight, goodnight, when I have said goodnight for evermore,
    And you see me carried out from the threshold of the door;
    Don't let . . . don't . . . don't let . . .

(She casts about wildly for the word.)

POLLY   *(in a stage whisper)* Effie!

EDIE   Ay? *(She puts up her ear trumpet.)*

POLLY   *(louder)* Effie!

EDIE *Who?*
ALL *EFFIE, EFFIE, EFFIE!*
EEK *(bellowing)* For God's sake woman, *EFFIE!*
EDIE *(scornfully)* But I will see the sun rise upon the glad New Year
ALL So if you're waking, call me, call me early, Mother Dear

(Applause as EDIE returns to her seat and MERCY enters in her nightgown, singing.)

MERCY

The poor soul sat sighing by a
  sycamore tree.
Sing all a green willow
Her hand on her bosom and her head
  on her knee.
Sing willow, willow, willow;
The fresh streams ran by her, and
  murmur'd her moans;
Sing willow, willow, willow;
Her salt tears fell from her, and
  soften'd the stones;
Sing willow, willow, willow:
Sing all a green willow must be my
  garland,
Let nobody blame him, his scorn I
  approve, –

Hark, who is't that knocks?

I call'd my love false love; but what said
  he then?
Sing willow, willow, willow:
If I court moe women, you'll couch
  with moe men.

Who's there? Othello?

MAX *(entering blackface)* Ay, Desdemona.
MERCY Will you come to bed, my lord?
MAX 'Ave you pray'd tonight, Desdemona?
MERCY Ay, my lord.
MAX If you bethink yourself of any crime
  Unreconcil'd as yet to 'eaven and grace,
  Solicit for it straight.
MERCY Alas! my lord, what may you mean by that?
MAX Well, do it, and be brief; I will walk by:
  I woulda not kill zy unprepared spirit,
  No, heaven forfend, I woulda not kill zy soul.
MERCY Talk you of killing?
MAX Ay, I do.
MERCY Then heaven have *Mercy* on me!
MAX Amen! wis all my heart.
MERCY If you say so, I hope you will not kill me.

MAX Hum!
MERCY And yet I fear you; for you are fatal then
  When you eyes roll so.
  Why I should fear I know not,
  Since guiltiness I know not; but yet I feel I fear.
MAX Zink on zy sins.
MERCY They are loves I bear to you.
MAX Ay, and for zat zou diest.

(JACK hisses loudly, but is restrained by POLLY.)

MERCY That death's unnatural that kills for loving.
  Alas! why gnaw you so your nether-lip?
  Some bloody passion shakes your very frame;
  These are portents: but yet, I hope, I hope
  They do not point on me.
MAX Peace and be still!
MERCY I will so: What's the matter?
MAX Zat hankerchief which I so lov'd and give zee
  Zou gav'st to Cassio.
MERCY No, by my life and soul! Send for the man and ask him.
MAX Sweet soul, taka heed, taka heed of perjury;
  Zou'rt on zy death-bed.

(JACK leaps to his feet, anguished.)

JACK No, no! *(POLLY pulls him down. Everybody shushes him.)*
MERCY Ay, but not yet to die.
MAX Yes, presently;
  Zerefore confess zee freely of zy sin;
  For to deny each article viz oass
  Cannot remove nor choke ze strong conception
  Zat I do groan vithal. Zou art to die.
MERCY Then Lord have mercy on me!
MAX I say, amen.
MERCY And have you mercy too! I never did
  Offend you in my life; never lov'd Cassio
  But with such general warranty of heaven
  As I might love; I never gave him token.
MAX He hath confess'd.
MERCY What, my Lord?
MAX That he hath us'd thee.
MERCY How? Unlawfully?

MAX   Ay.

JACK   *It's a lie! (He wrestles with* POLLY *to climb over his seat.)*

MERCY   He will not say so.

MAX   No; his mouth is stopp'd:

MERCY   What is he dead? Alas! he is betray'd and I undone.

MAX   Out, strumpet! Weep'st zou for him to my face?

JACK   *Villain! Villain!*

MERCY   O! banish me, my lord, but kill me not!

(JACK weeps loudly.)

MAX   *(put out)* Down, strumpet!

MERCY   *(delighted)* Kill me tomorrow; let me live tonight!

(JACK thumps the seat.)

JACK   Yes! Yes! Yes!

MAX   *(nervously)* Nay, if you strive –

MERCY   But half an hour!

JACK   *(groaning)* Just half an hour.

MAX   *(glaring)* Being done, zere is no pause.

JACK   Bastard!

MERCY   But while I say one prayer!

MAX   It is too late.

(He smothers her. JACK *leaps for the stage.)*

JACK   BLOODY BASTARD! *(He grabs* CLEMMY's *crutch and charges* MAX *with it. They grapple and roll on stage.)*

MERCY   O! falsely, falsely murder'd. A guiltless death I die.

JACK   MURDER, BLOODY MURDER! *(*JACK *fetches* MAX *a terrible blow with the crutch.)*

MAX   Jesus, Mary and Joseph.

JACK   *(standing over him)* She loved you, cruel Othello. Take that and that and this.

*(*MAX *crawls to* MERCY *and crouches beside her.)*

MAX   Oh, bloody period! I kiss'd zee ere I
          kill'd zee;
          No way but zis,
          Killing myself to die upon a kiss.
          (In a stage whisper to JACK) O Spartan
          dog!

*(*MAX *dies, with great fervour.* JACK *stands with crutch upraised. But, unable to control himself, throws himself over the bodies, weeping. Mukinupin give a standing ovation.)*

JACK   O Spartan dog!

*(*MAX *rises, takes* MERCY *by the hand.*

MERCY *pulls* JACK *to his feet and rushes him forwards in bow after bow. Gradually* JACK, *realising he is a star too, takes full advantage of the situation, even taking a solo bow. He kisses* MERCY's *hand, and shakes* MAX's *hand.* MAX *quells the audience with a gesture.)*

MAX   Zank you. Zank you, Mukinupin. I must say that nevaire before 'ave we 'ad such an extraordinary reception. Zis young man . . . *(*MAX *brings* JACK *forward.)* . . . should 'ave a most remarkable career. I predict great zings for . . . *(He bends to whisper, then holds* JACK's *hand high)* . . . for Meestar Jack Toosday. *(Applause)* And now, p'praps as a fitting close to zis most wonderful night MR TOOSDAY may like to entertain you wis zomesing of his own choosing. *(He consults* JACK.) I GIVE YOU . . . MUKINUPIN'S OWN MR ZACK TOOSDAY in "An 'AM, AN EGG AND AN ONION".

*(*JACK *comes forward, abashed, as* MAX *and* MERCY *run offstage hand in hand, and join the audience. But he soon gets back his self-confidence, and begins his song with suitable tap dance accompaniment.)*

AN 'AM, AN EGG AND AN ONION[5]

JACK   I'd 'ave it for breakfast each mornin'
          If I could I would 'ave it for tea,
          An 'am, an egg and an onion
          Is the fav'rite banquet for me.

          I took a job in the city
          but when I lined up for me pay,
          The boss said "an egg and an onion
          is all that you're gettin' terday".
          So I said, "WHERE'S THE 'AM?"

ALL   So 'e said, "WHERE'S THE 'AM?"

JACK   I went out on the town wiv me
          sweet'eart
          the cafe that we went to was naice,
          for an 'am and an egg and an onion
          but there wasn't an egg in the place.

          So I said, "WHERE'S THE EGG?"

ALL   So 'e said, "WHERE'S THE EGG?"

JACK   I got married last Saturdee arvo',
          the missus was cookin' me tea,
          there was 'am and an egg but no
          onion,
          she says "Give up onions for me."

          So I said, "WHERE'S THE ONION?"

ALL So 'e said, "WHERE'S THE ONION?"

JACK I packed all me clobber and 'opped it,
I caught the first train outa town,
for an 'am and an egg and an onion,
I went to a pub and sat down.

No 'am?

ALL NO 'AM!

JACK No egg!

ALL NO EGG?

JACK No onion!

ALL NO ONION?

JACK So I went outback on a station,
the cook 'ad been there for years,
cookin 'am, cookin' eggs, cookin'
  onions
till it all come out of our ears.

'Ave an 'am, 'ave an egg, 'ave an onion,
'e'd say wiv 'is soupy grin,
the bloody crook, it was all 'e could
  cook,
so I up and clobbered 'im.

(Mukinupin, plus the MONTEBELLOS, *dance down the aisle and join* JACK *onstage for the finale.)*

ALL 'Ave an 'am, 'ave an egg, 'ave an onion,
and just for a change if you can,
'ave an egg, and an 'am and an onion,
or an onion, an egg and an 'am.

(The MISSES HUMMER *dance off,* EEK *and* EDIE *return to the shop,* EEK *behind the counter.* POLLY, JACK, MERCY *and* MAX *are left centre on the red carpet.* JACK *leaves* POLLY *alone as* MERCY *beckons him over. She puts her arm round* JACK.)*

MERCY Jack Tuesday, if every you need a job you'll always find one waiting with Max and Mercy Montebello. Isn't that right, Max?

MAX Thassaright, Mercy.

MERCY You're a natural, Jack. You're meant for the bright lights. What are *you* doing in . . . Mukinupin?

JACK *(overcome)* I'm a grocer's boy, ma'am, in Perkins' General Store,

MERCY A grocer's boy! *(Turning to* POLLY) And this is . . . ?

JACK *(eagerly)* Polly Perkins, ma'am. She's the . . . store-keeper's daughter.

MERCY Oh! I . . . see! And very sweet, very

pretty too. H'dy' do, Polly? *(*POLLY *curtseys grimly.)*

POLLY Very well, thank you, ma'am.

MERCY Well, Polly, your Jack's got a great future in the halls. He's wasted here in Mukinupin. Surely even *you* must see that?

POLLY *(defensively)* He could work his way up to be manager.

MERCY Manager! Manager! *(She turns to* MAX *and they smile and shrug together.)* Oh, well of course, if that's what he wants. Is that what *you* want Jack, dear?

JACK Well . . . as a matter of fact . . . *(Looking wildly around)* I couldn't leave Polly. *(*MAX *raises his eyes to heaven.)*

MAX He couldn't leava Polly.

JACK That's right.

MAX AND MERCY He couldn't leava Polly.

MERCY If you ever change your mind, Jack Tuesday, remember Mercy Monte . . . is waiting. *(*JACK *kisses her outstretched hand and* MAX *and* MERCY *exit.)*

POLLY *(furious)* Mercy Monte is *waiting*! Why, she's old enough to be your mother.

JACK *(grinning)* She didn't act like my mother. I think she's sweet on me, Pol. *(*JACK *preens himself,* POLLY *is disgusted.)*

POLLY Speaking of mothers, I can see the Widow Tuesday bowling down the main street in a horse and buggy done up with string. It's your Ma, Jack.

JACK *(groaning)* Oh, Gawd!

POLLY And I bet both my button-up boots she's come about the mortgage once again.

*(*JACK *takes up his broom, puts on his apron and begins sweeping vigorously. Enter the* WIDOW TUESDAY *dressed in widow's weeds, with a heavy black veil. She sweeps up to* EEK *behind his counter and falls on her knees, in a Dickensian travesty.)*

WIDOW TUESDAY Foreclose, Ezekial Perkins! Foreclose, and put me out of my misery.

EDIE *(harshly)* Get up, Mrs Tuesday.

EEK *(testily)* Please get up, Mrs Tuesday.

WIDOW TUESDAY I am the Widow Tuesday, Mrs Tuesday no longer, Mr Tuesday 'as gone to 'is reward. *(*EDIE *puts up her ear trumpet.)*

EDIE What's that, Mrs Tuesday?

WIDOW TUESDAY *(screaming)* Mr Tuesday is no more.

EDIE *(grimly)* Drank himself to death, I'll be bound. Well, we can't be held responsible.

WIDOW TUESDAY   I throw myself on your mercy, Eek Perkins. I grovel at the usurer's feet.

JACK   Aw, give it a rest, Ma.

EEK   I'm not a hard man.

WIDOW TUESDAY   'Earts 'ard as flint *and* stonier.

EDIE   *(complacently)* We all suffer.

EEK   What about your sons . . . Widow Tuesday?

WIDOW TUESDAY   Young 'Arry and young Jack? Should the sins of the fathers be visited upon the children, Eek Perkins?

POLLY   Of course not, Pa.

EDIE   Hold your tongue, miss.

WIDOW TUESDAY   *(moving to chair)* My 'Arry's detained.

EEK   At His Majesty's pleasure?

EDIE   Who?

EEK   *(shouting)* Harry Tuesday . . . got two years.

WIDOW TUESDAY   'Arry is as 'Arry does, but my Jack's 'is mother's boy.

JACK   Aw Ma, put a sock in it.

EEK   Jack's not a bad boy, but he doens't keep his place. He has . . . aspirations.

WIDOW TUESDAY   Towards whom?

EEK   Towards our daughter; towards Polly, Widow Tuesday.

WIDOW TUESDAY   *(heavy sarcasm)* I'd never 'ave believed it. Is it true, Jack?

JACK   Is what true, Ma?

WIDOW TUESDAY   That you and Polly Perkins . . . ?

JACK   Are in love? Why, yes it is true. *(Grinning)* There, it's the first time I've come right out and said it.

EEK   It can't be allowed.

EDIE   Said what?

JACK   *(singing)* I'm in love with Polly Perkins, I'm in love with Polly Perkins. *(JACK waltzes with the broom, then throws it away, and takes POLLY in his arms. They waltz together.)*

JACK   *(singing)*
> I'm in love with Polly Perkins and she's in love with me
> Pretty Polly Perkins is my fatality,
> She's like a rose in summer, her pink cheeks all abloom
> Lovely Polly Perkins illuminates the room.

(JACK falls on one knee as POLLY circles him.)

> I cannot live without her, she makes the landscape glow
> Pretty Polly Perkins . . .

EEK, WIDOW TUESDAY AND EDIE   No! No! No!

JACK   No?

POLLY   No?

EEK   Never, Jack Tuesday.

EDIE   She's just put her hair up.

WIDOW TUESDAY   She's too young, Jack. *(JACK turns to POLLY.)*

JACK   Polly?

POLLY   Not yet, Jack. I'm too young. I've . . . just put my hair up. *(Moving towards him)* Oh Jack. *(JACK takes her face in his hands.)*

JACK   Lovely Pol, if you don't marry me I'll enlist in the W.A. Light Horse and go to Palestine. *(POLLY clasps her hands.)*

POLLY   And be a hero. Oh, Jack!

EDIE   *(reciting)*
> Then up spake brave Horatius,
> The captain of the gate,
> To every man upon this earth
> Death cometh soon or late,
> And how can man die better
> Than facing fearful odds,
> For the ashes of his fathers,
> And the temple of his gods?[6]

WIDOW TUESDAY   Don't you go puttin' the mocker on my Jack. *(She takes out a large white handkerchief, weeps copiously. EEK pats her shoulder.)*

EEK   There, there. . . .

EDIE   Tears, idle tears.

WIDOW TUESDAY   Idle, are they? Well, let me tell you, Mrs Perkins, or whatever you calls y'self, if you'd a had my sorrows you'd never stop bawlin'. I was a civilised 'uman bein' before Mr Tuesday brought me to this God forsakin' 'ole.

EEK   Character and success go hand in hand.

WIDOW TUESDAY   *(darkly)* Mr Tuesday was never much of a mixer and there's some I would never 'ave mixed with, in the old days.

EDIE   What's that?

EEK   *(shouting)* There's some she'd never have mixed with!

EDIE   Who?

WIDOW TUESDAY   There's some as is no better than they should be.

EEK   *(brightly)* Price of wheat going up, price of wool firming.

WIDOW TUESDAY   Some 'as got skeletons in their cupboards . . . and they're not white ones.

EEK (*desperately*) Go home and you'll find there's been a thunderstorm.

WIDOW TUESDAY (*gloomily*) Rust and moth, moth and rust. Mr Tuesday was a good provider, swallered a packet of Aspros every mornin', and shot 'isself through the 'ead goin' rabbitin'. There was no blot on 'is escutcheon.

EDIE No what?

EEK (*bellowing*) No blood, I mean, NO BLOT ON HIS ESCUTCHEON!

EDIE Whose escutcheon?

WIDOW TUESDAY If the cap fits, wear it. I've 'ad me say.

EEK (*desperately*) I'll take out a second mortgage, Widow Tuesday. Always ready to help a battler.

WIDOW TUESDAY You've got your head screwed on right, Mr Perkins, and God will reward yous.

EDIE What she say?

EEK GOD WILL REWARD US!

WIDOW TUESDAY God 'elps them as 'elps themselves. Comin' Jack? (*JACK moves across from* POLLY *to take his mother's arm.*)

POLLY Spring's coming. I can hear the buggy wheels turning into the street for the tennis court dance.

JACK Save the last one for me . . . the lights-out dance.

(*POLLY smiles.* JACK *exits with* WIDOW TUESDAY. POLLY *tries a few dance steps.*)

POLLY (*singing*)
I'm in love with Jackie Tuesday
And he's in love with me.
Handsome Jackie Tuesday
Is my fatality.

I cannot love without him,
He makes the landscape glow,
I don't want to lose him,
And I don't want him to go.

(*Enter* CECIL BRUNNER *with sample case.*)

EDIE Why, it's Mr Brunner. You remember Mr Brunner, Polly?

POLLY Of course, Mother.

CECIL Why, Miss Polly you're quite the gracious lady. How time does fly.

POLLY Thank you, Mr Brunner.

CECIL Why don't you call me Cecil?

EDIE Yes, why don't you call him Cecil?

CECIL Please don't stand on ceremony.

POLLY I don't want to be too familiar.

CECIL But I want you to be too familiar.

POLLY I'm a nice girl, Mr Brunner.

CECIL Cecil.

POLLY Cecil.

CECIL Dare I hope – Polly?

POLLY Hope for what?

CECIL That you'll have another acid drop.

POLLY Don't mind if I do.

(*While* CECIL *and* POLLY *begin their song,* EDIE *is going through his samples, holding up petticoats and nightgowns.*)

HAVE ANOTHER ACID DROP

CECIL
Have another acid drop –
POLLY
Don't mind if I do.
CECIL
Take another acid drop,
promise to be true.

I'm a knight upon the road,
flogging lingerie,
I sell the stuff of romance
in a corset and toupée.

(POLLY *and* EDIE *are exclaiming over a trousseau-type negligee.* POLLY *pulls her dress off and with* EDIE's *help tries it on.*)

As I move about the country,
the saltlakes and the scrub,
there's a mirage that haunts me
in every outback pub.

When I fold up my corset,
and take off my toupée,
there's little Polly Perkins
in my lingerie.
POLLY
I'm little Polly Perkins
in a white negligee.
CECIL
I give a rosebud to her,
and beg her to be true,
I offer her an acid drop –
POLLY
Don't mind if I do.
CECIL
But when I wake at daybreak,
I know the bird has flown,
Little Polly Perkins
will never be my own.

So take a case of samples,
take a rose bouquet,
take a heart and wear it
on your white negligee.

Take another acid drop,
tell me you'll be true,
have another acid drop.
POLLY
Don't mind if I do.

(POLLY *whirls about the room in her new negligee while* CECIL *talks to* EDIE, *showing off his wares upstage.* JACK *has re-entered during the song and stands downstage left, glowering at* POLLY.)

JACK   Take it off.
POLLY   Why?
JACK   It's . . . indecent, that's why.
POLLY   Why?
JACK   Because it . . . shows.
POLLY   Shows what?
JACK   Everything!
POLLY   Don't you like it?
JACK   No.
POLLY   Liar!
JACK   *He* gave it to you.
POLLY   Mr Brunner.
JACK   *(mocking)* Cecil!
POLLY   He likes me.
JACK   D'ya want to be an old man's darlin'?
POLLY   I'm not an old man's – anything.
JACK   Then take it off.
POLLY   No. I'm not a young man's – anything, either.
JACK   I thought you was.
POLLY   Then you thought wrong. Mother says –
JACK   *(mocking)* Mother says!
POLLY   You're too . . . familiar.
JACK   You didn't used to think so.
POLLY   When?
JACK   Behind the floursacks in the storeroom after closin' time.
POLLY   You're not a gentleman.
JACK   Mother says!
POLLY   I shouldn't waste myself.
JACK   *(angrily)* Don't, then.
POLLY   I don't intend to. *(She tosses her head.)*
JACK   You'll soon be rid of me.
POLLY   What's that mean?
JACK   Miss Polly with her hair up.
POLLY   *(hurt)* Don't you like *it*, either?
JACK   It's nothin' to me.
POLLY   That's all right, then. *(She turns away.)*
JACK   I got other fish, bigger fish . . .
POLLY   What, then?
JACK   Joined up.
POLLY   Joined up! *(She turns back.)*

JACK   Goin' to the war . . . *(a laugh)* to be a hero.
POLLY   What for?
JACK   To fight the Hun. Better than a grocer's boy. Or a – nightie traveller.
POLLY   You're not going. *(She crosses and confronts him.)*
JACK   Goodbye, Polly. *(He takes off his apron and begins to move away.)*
POLLY   Come back.
JACK   Can't come back. The war'll be over in a month or two.
CECIL   England needs you, Jack.
EEK   The only good German is a dead German.
EDIE   Keep clean and fight fairly.

(Re-enter the two MISSES HUMMER *with a large Australian flag. They stand downstage well in view and wave it. As* JACK *puts on his Army uniform, slouch hat and leather leggings and hoists his kitbag on his shoulder,* EEK, EDIE, CECIL *and* POLLY *dance and sing him off to the war. The two* MISSES HUMMER *join in the singing.*)

YOUR COUNTRY NEEDS YOU IN THE
TRENCHES

ALL   *(except* JACK)
Your country needs you in the
   trenches,
Follow your masters into war,
And if you cop it we'll remember you
At the Mukinupin Store.

Economic domination
That's what we're fighting for,
Join up and save the Empire,
We've got to win the war.

You'll murder them at Wipers.
And at Bathsheba Wells,
Only one more stunt, boys,
And then you'll get a spell.

Face the test of nationhood,
Keep Australia free,
England needs you, Jack, to fight
For me, and me, and me.

Your country needs you in the
   trenches,
Follow your masters into war,
And if you cop it we'll remember you
At the Mukinupin store.

And if you cop it we'll remember you
At the Mukinupin store.

EDIE AND POLLY
> Your mothers and your sisters,
> Your sweethearts and your wives,
> Won't hand you a white feather,
> If you'll only look alive.

EEK AND CECIL
> Look alive, for Crissake look alive,
> The brasshats are all toffs,
> But we've gotta beat the Boch,

ALL   For England Home and Beauty look alive.

> Your country needs you in the trenches,
> Follow your masters into war
> And if you cop it we'll remember you at the Mukinupin Store.

EEK   Fight for the West, laddie.

JACK   The West, why it's the freest, richest, happiest land on earth. I'll fight for it.

(As JACK exits waving, POLLY sobs, EDIE with her arm around POLLY recites:)

EDIE   Hail beauteous land, hail bonzer Western Australia,
> Compared to ye all others are a failure.[7]

(They all cheer. POLLY tears herself away and runs after JACK.)

POLLY   Come back, Jack . . . Oh! please . . . come back.

(Her voice breaks and she exits, running. EEK and CECIL exit through the shop, but EDIE lingers, looking after POLLY, shading her eyes against the setting sun.)

EDIE   *(reciting)*
> The red sun sinks in the springtime heat
> And waves of shadow go over the wheat.[8]

(A pause, then EDIE calls, as if to a child:)

Polly, Polly Perkins, keep away from the rough end of town, speak when you're spoken to, and then only to the Bank Manager's daughter.

(She exits through the shop, and the MISSES HUMMER are left, staring dreamily into the evening, CLARRY with the Australian flag draped across her knees. Very faintly the weird night music begins on the sound track. CLEMMY stands leaving on her stick looking into the distance.)

CLARRY   *(softly)* Red sky at morning, shepherd's warning.

CLEMMY   *(whispering)* Red sky at night, shepherd's delight. *(Pause)* I think I can smell rain.

CLARRY   You're always imagining things, Clem. *(The night sounds begin as the stage darkens . . . A last crow calls, a dingo howls, an insect begins tapping; there is a wolf whistle, a coo-ee, then a wild scream. CLARRY starts up.)* What's that?

CLEMMY   Don't be a fool, Clarry. It's only the Flasher down in the creekbed.

CLARRY   *(relieved)* And the girls giggling under the pepper trees, holding hands.

CLEMMY   *(darkly)* The blacks like wild ducks crying under the guns.

(There is a change of tone now which CLARRY has been fighting off.)

CLARRY   *(faintly)* The sky was full of crows . . . wasn't it?

CLEMMY   And arsenic in the waterholes.

(There is a quavering voice a long way off.)

ZEEK   *(off)* Water . . . Water . . . Water . . .

CLARRY   *(alarmed again)* Who's that?

CLEMMY   You know who it is.

CLARRY   *(relieved)* Zeek Perkins . . . of course, it's only old Zeek.

CLEMMY   It's the dowser . . . looking for stars and water.

CLARRY   *(sympathetically)* He hasn't been right since he did that perish in the desert, and they brought him in with the skin shrivelled off him like bacon rind. They said he followed a mirage for days, crawling naked under the sun. That was an awful thing, Clem.

(Enter ZEEK dressed in ragged clothes, barefoot, with a cabbage-tree hat and a long white beard. He carries a hurrican lantern, a waterbag and a diviner's rod. On his back is strapped a primitive telescope. He looks a mysterious, yet benign, figure.)

ZEEK   Water, water, everywhere but not a drop to drink.

CLARRY   Goodnight, Zeek Perkins. *(ZEEK moves in a circle around the stage pointing his diviner's rod at the earth.)*

ZEEK   Bad water . . . too much salt in it.

CLARRY   *(standing)* It's late and I'm going to bed, and so would you, Clem, if you had the sense you were born with.

CLEMMY   I'm not sleepy.

CLARRY *(moving off)* No more of it.

CLEMMY *(innocently)* No more of what?

CLARRY Take care, Clemmy, please take care.

(CLEMMY smiles mysteriously. POLLY's voice is heard in the distance.)

POLLY *(offstage, calling)* Jack . . . Jack . . . Come back, Jack . . .

(CLEMMY exits. The mysterious night music begins again. There is a loud wolf whistle and POLLY runs on, calling . . .)

POLLY Jack! Jack!

(ZEEK is setting up his telescope. POLLY runs to him.)

POLLY Oh! Uncle Zeek, you haven't seen Jack Tuesday tonight, have you?

ZEEK The river of the water of life is bright as crystal. If anyone thirst, let her come to me.

POLLY I *have* come to you. *(She shakes his arm.)* Uncle Zeek, where's Jack Tuesday? *(ZEEK guides her to the telescope.)*

ZEEK *(confiding)* Look in there, Polly, there's deserts and stars and the five days of creation.

POLLY *(half-crying)* I don't want your deserts and stars. I want Jack. *(ZEEK grips her arm so fiercely that she cries out.)*

ZEEK Then drink, Polly . . . drink fire, blood, sand and water.

(ZEEK forces her head back and tips the waterbag towards her mouth. POLLY chokes on the water, and struggles away.)

POLLY You're just a crazy old man.

ZEEK *(still pouring the water out)* You can run it through an hour-glass.

POLLY An old humbug, who knows nothing. *Nothing*, do you hear? *(But ZEEK has lost interest in her. He has his eye to the telescope. POLLY turns away, raging and sees CLEMMY watching her. She runs to CLEMMY.)* Oh, Miss Clemmy, how glad I am to see you! I'm looking for Jack Tuesday, and I can't get any sense out of anybody.

CLEMMY *(silkily)* Why, dearest Polly, what's the matter?

POLLY *(in tears)* My Jack's gone, Miss Clemmy. He's gone to the war without saying goodbye or anything.

CLEMMY *(innocently)* But why?

POLLY Because he thinks I don't love him any more. But he's wrong. He's terribly wrong. Of course I love him.

CLEMMY Do you, Polly?

POLLY Yes, yes I do. I'm sure I do.

CLEMMY You're too young to know anything about love.

POLLY Of course I'm not. How can you say that? I'm exactly the right age to fall in love. I just want him . . . to wait a little. *(CLEMMY grabs POLLY's arm cruelly.)*

CLEMMY Silly Polly Perkins. What's love? Is this . . . Love? *(CLEMMY knocks hard onstage with her crutch. The night sounds and the weird music augment each other. The FLASHER leaps onstage in a long, ragged overcoat, felt hat pulled down low over his eyes. POLLY is pushed towards him by CLEMMY.)* The Mukinupin Flasher!

FLASHER *(whispering)* Look Polly! Look Polly! Look Polly! *(He gives a great leap, opens his coat wide and shuts it again, giggling. POLLY screams.)* Look, Polly. Did you ever see such a whopper? *(He flashes again.)*

POLLY *(crying)* Uncle Zeek, Uncle Zeek, can't you see what's happening?

ZEEK *(to telescope)* There is a chaos of waters, but the waters of chaos are the waters of life.

(The FLASHER circles POLLY.)

FLASHER *(chanting)*
    My mother said I never should
    Play with the Flasher in the wood.
    If I did, she would say
    Naughty girl to disobey.
    . . . Look Polly! Look Polly! Look!

(POLLY sinks to her knees, moaning.)

POLLY Miss Clemmy, Miss Clemmy! *(CLEMMY puts her hand heavily on POLLY's shoulder.)*

CLEMMY Polly Perkins, you've strayed down the wrong end of town after dark, so now you're going to get more than you bargained for. *(The FLASHER droops in the corner, like a crow, waiting. ZEEK stands stiffly, mesmerized beside his telescope. CLEMMY knocks imperiously with her crutch.)* ENTER THE BLACK WIDOW OF MUKINUPIN.

(The WIDOW enters, gaunt and heavily veiled, like Death.)

WIDOW TUESDAY *(chanting)* Moth and rust . . . Rust and moth . . .

POLLY   Oh! Widow Tuesday, please save me, please.

WIDOW TUESDAY   Don't ask *me* to pity *you*, Polly Perkins.

POLLY   For Jack's sake.

WIDOW TUESDAY   Mr Tuesday was dragged ten miles in the stirrup with a bullet through 'is skull. *(She gives an awful scream of demoniac laughter, and a great leap in the air.)* And we all got the barcoo rot.

(She doubles up with more laughter but CLEMMY knocks again for silence and the bullroarers, the didgeridoos and the tapping sticks begin. They rise in intensity as the music grows louder and the WIDOW TUESDAY, with a wild scream, begins to chase the FLASHER [flashing as he runs], ZEEK and POLLY round and round in a mad game of tag. The music stops abruptly, the FLASHER is left standing centre. He takes a matchbox out of his pocket, shakes it and puts it to his ear.)

FLASHER   Down in the creekbed I have found the secret of perpetual motion. I fasten the earphones to my head. I listen to the wireless waves. Marconi the Great one, Speak to me! *(He rattles the matchbox and whispers)* Marconi, Marconi, must I kill? *(He pauses with a sly look, then with a wild yell he throws off his raincoat and in a flapping white nightshirt chases POLLY, the WIDOW and ZEEK round and round in a counter circle.)* Marconi, Marconi, must I kill? *(The FLASHER stops abruptly, puts the matchbox to his ear and shakes it.)* Marconi, Marconi . . . *(He begins to whimper, then loudly)* Marconi, Marconi *(a whisper)* must I kill? *(They all stand poised for flight. Smiling)* Marconi says I must not frighten the ladies. Marconi says . . . *(The music changes, becoming more sinister, the bull-roarer insistent.)*

ALL   *(chanting in a circle)*
We have come over the mire and moss,
To dance a round with the hobby hoss,
Sing heigh down down with a derry
   down-ay,
Come in, come in, thou hobby hoss.[9]

CLEMMY   BRING IN THE HOBBY.

THE WIDOW   *(screaming)* BRING IN OLD BALL!

(She slaps her thighs, jigging on the spot. With a leap and a skirl of sound the HOBBY enters. The HOBBY [HARRY TUESDAY] wears a
simulated horse's skull on a broomstick, with glass bottles for eyesockets, and a lolling red tongue. He wears a long cloak, so that he appears to be prancing or galloping, and is about eight feet high.)*

ALL   *(screaming)* THE HOBBY! THE HOBBY!

(The HOBBY pretends to bite the women, nudging up their skirts, paying particular attention to POLLY. All except CLEMMY flee from the HOBBY. He pursues the terrified POLLY, who, half-fainting, is swept into his arms. As they chant the Hobby Song the HOBBY exits running, carrying POLLY, pursued by the FLASHER.)

FLASHER   Marconi, Marconi, must I kill? *(They exit. ZEEK moves back to his telescope, chanting.)*

ZEEK   Fire and brimstone, fables and fancies.

(With a roll of drums, CLEMMY comes centre. The WIDOW TUESDAY throws down a coil of rope.)

WIDOW TUESDAY   Clemmy Hummer, the greatest female high-wire walker in the world!

(The WIDOW TUESDAY claps madly. To the drums rising in a crescendo CLEMMY walks gingerly across the wire, wavers, but goes on. A foot slips, she falls with a terrible scream and crumples on the stage. The WIDOW runs forward, helps her up, returns her crutch and assists her to the wicker chair.)

CLEMMY   I used to balance on a rope amongst the stars.

ZEEK   Sun, moon and stars, all sweet things.

(HARRY TUESDAY re-enters as himself, dressed in tight-fitting moleskin trousers and a black Jackie Howe singlet. He has a rifle and ammunition slung across his body, carries a bottle of beer in one hand, and the Hobby's head in the other. He is JACK TUESDAY's identical twin in looks but there the resemblance ends. HARRY is wild, drunken, and full of bitterness.)

HARRY   Grog shops closed, no more fun and games. *(HARRY sits on the edge of the stage.)*

CLEMMY   You didn't frighten her too much, did you Harry?

HARRY   No . . . just give 'er a bit of a thrill, that's all. She'll think she had a nightmare.

WIDOW TUESDAY   When did you get back, son?

HARRY   Stole a horse and rode inter town ternight.

WIDOW TUESDAY   Dad's dead. Shot himself through the head.

HARRY   The old timers always reckoned anybody was mad took up land east of the rabbit proof.

CLEMMY   Tell us about Fremantle, Harry. Tell us a story.

HARRY TUESDAY'S SONG[10]

HARRY

The bloody stones they break your
    bones,
inside Fremantle yard;
and it's a curse there's nothin' worse
than doin' two years hard.

I killed a sheep 'twoud make you weep
for need of a coupla pence,
I kept the law and hung the fleece
out on the squatter's fence.

The squatter is a stingy man
for stealin' of his ewes,
inside the yard you'll do it hard,
kowtowin' to the screws.

The Judge will throw you in the can,
he will not grant no bail,
and you can rot till you're forgot
inside Fremantle jail.

When I came out then I had nought,
not a pocketful of pence,
so now I kill and eat me fill,
hang nothin' on the fence.

Me boots are full of mud and blood,
me coat is stiff with pain,
I'll never shear the bloody sheep
out on the One Tree Plain.

But one dark night I'll start a fight,
I'll wake the silent town,
I'll give the law a little fright,
I'll shoot the bastards down.

I won't forget and they'll regret
they give me two years' hard,
to break me bones acrackin' stones
inside Fremantle yard.

(The WIDOW TUESDAY beats her thigh with enthusiasm.)

WIDOW TUESDAY   Good on you son, you're not a crawler like young Jack.

HARRY   Where's Touch of the Tar?

WIDOW TUESDAY   Reckon she went bush.

HARRY   You seen 'er, Miss Clemmy?

CLEMMY   No, Harry. After you were jailed she left home.

HARRY   Pissed off with a bloody sandalwood cutter, I bet. She always 'ad a weakness for sandalwood. Liked the blue flames. Her and me usta sit and . . . make up pictures . . . in the fire . . . y'know?

ZEEK   Avoid the tail of the Scorpion, but the Wolf will burn forever.

HARRY   (half-laughing) That old bastard hits the nail on the head too often. Gooday, matey, what you see in there?

ZEEK   The Cross is a timepiece, Harry, a guide to travelling men. By May it is upright, by August it slopes to the sou'-west, as the earth rolls. Come, take a look in here, my son, and you will see.

(HARRY crosses and takes the telescope.)

HARRY   (squinting up) Think I could foller Touch of the Tar with this thing?

ZEEK   The clouds of Magellan are often lost in the dreaming.

(HARRY hands the telescope back to him with a laugh.)

HARRY   It's a big world up there, old timer. And a hard one down here.

WIDOW TUESDAY   Come on home, Harry. It'll be just like old times, you and me, with the boiled wheat and the 'roo in the camp oven.

HARRY   Jesus, Ma! What a homecomin'.

WIDOW TUESDAY   You don't need that girl. She's black.

HARRY   Half black. Comes from good white stock. (Laughing) They reckon she was fathered by Eek Perkins. She's a boong-basher's daughter.

WIDOW TUESDAY   I got another mortgage out of the ol' bugger by hintin' I knew more than I ought to.

HARRY   Ah, everybody knows, but nobody's sayin'. Bush towns are like that.

ZEEK   (to his telescope) The crows are fatted with the murrion flock.

HARRY   Yeah. They reckon ol' Eek spent a lotta time down in the creekbed with them gins, before he took up murderin' 'em, an' become a lay preacher. (He doubles up with mirth.) Y'know, me and him 've got a lot in common. Oh, I know what they call me – a kombo and a gin jockey, but I don't give a stuff. I never went after 'em with guns –

not yet, anyway – and Touch of the Tar, she's just right for a jailbird.

CLEMMY   She's a good girl, Harry.

HARRY   Maybe . . .

CLEMMY   And she likes you.

HARRY   She don't like me, she loves me, and that means she hates me more than half the time. Well . . . maybe she's gone for good, and I won't weep over 'er. *(He moves restlessly away as if listening for someone.)* But where is the black bitch? *(Pause)* How's ol' Jack? Still counter jumpin'?

WIDOW TUESDAY   Gone for a soldier. Left me on me own with the farm and a second mortgage.

HARRY   Did he now? Never thought he had the guts. But a king and country man, a' course. Well, that's Jack all over. He always fell for the bullshit.

WIDOW TUESDAY   Come home, Harry love, now that you've seen the world . . .

HARRY   From Fremantle jail.

WIDOW TUESDAY   You can take up the shearin' again. You're the only gun shearer east of the rabbit proof.

HARRY   Come 'ome, back ter Stinkwort Holler, not me, Ma. Jack's a joined up. I'll do the same. He's got the right idea for once. Get away from the tattletales, see the world, put a bullet in a few bastards. *(The* WIDOW *begins to weep noisily.)* So long, Miss Clemmy. *(He kisses her awkwardly.)* You won't see Harry Tuesday till he comes home a hero. *(He grins and takes the* WIDOW's *arm.)* Goodbye, Zeek.

ZEEK   We'll miss you, Harry lad.

HARRY   Say goodbye to Touch of the Tar for me. Tell 'er to be true. *(*HARRY *doubles up at his own joke.)* C'mon, Ma. Dry your crocodile tears, and help me pack me clobber. *(Exit* HARRY *and the weeping* WIDOW.*)*

ZEEK   *(into telescope)* Hercules is well down towards the north with Lyra the harp and Cygnus the Swan.

(Enter TOUCH OF THE TAR, *a dark beauty in a ragged dress, torn across one breast, with bare, dirty feet.)*

TOUCH OF TAR   You seen 'Arry Toosday ternight, Miss Clemmy?

CLEMMY   He's just left with his Ma.

TOUCH OF TAR   *(bitterly)* Two years and don't give a damn about me.

CLEMMY   He asked after you.

TOUCH OF TAR   Arsed after me did 'e, the

bastard? 'E knows where ter find me. Our ol' place . . . in the creekbed.

CLEMMY   He's gone for a soldier. *(*TOUCH OF TAR *whistles.)*

TOUCH OF TAR   Sweet J-e-s-us! What come over 'Arry? 'E only fights when 'e's shickered. *(Mournfully)* Never even said goodbye or up your bum.

CLEMMY   He left a message.

TOUCH OF TAR   *(eagerly)* What?

CLEMMY   "Say goodbye to Touch of the Tar for me." He thought you'd followed the sandalwood cutters.

TOUCH OF TAR   *(bitterly)* Did 'e? Thought I'd gone orf like any ol' black woman. Don' 'e know who I am? I'm Lily Perkins. They reckons me Daddy slept with every coloured woman in the camp. *(Pause)* Trouble with me is, Miss Clemmy, it's give me ideas. I 'xpect too much for a coloured girl, don' I? *(During this dialogue* JACK *has entered and slumps on the Town Hall steps. He is very drunk.* JACK *hiccups.)* *(Sharply)* Wassat?

CLEMMY   *(softly)* Somebody just came in.

TOUCH OF TAR   *(delighted)* 'Arry. *(She runs across, stops, hesitates, shyly.)* That you, 'Arry? *(No answer. She moves closer, shaking his arm.)* 'Arry!

JACK   It's not Harry, it's Jack.

TOUCH OF TAR   *(disappointed)* I thought you was 'Arry.

JACK   People sometimes do, but not for long. *(Pause.)* Sorry!

TOUCH OF TAR   You look lonely.

JACK   I am . . . and drunk.

TOUCH OF TAR   You like me leedle bit, Jack?

JACK   *(uncomfortably)* Dunno . . . maybe.

TOUCH OF TAR   You like ter come wiv me . . . down the creekbed somewhere? 'Ave a go?

JACK   Why?

TOUCH OF TAR   *(bitterly)* 'Cause they reckon I'm hot bitch: y'know, take on anythin'.

JACK   Don't sell y'self short.

TOUCH OF TAR   Why not? I'm nothin'!

JACK   *(gently)* Touch of the Tar . . .

TOUCH OF TAR   Don't call me that. I'm Lily . . . tha's me name . . . Lily. Pretty, ain't it?

JACK   *(humbly)* I didn't know.

TOUCH OF TAR   No, nobody does, much, an' if they ever did they forgotten. Mind you, it's not me ol' people's name. Tha's another one altogether.

JACK   Old people?

DOROTHY HEWETT

TOUCH OF TAR   Ol' people, me Mumma's people, but they all gone. Nothin' left now, few gnamma 'oles, stone tools, scarred trees, ol' junk thas all, nothin'. Sometimes I 'ear em on the wind.

JACK   *(uneasy)* Hear what?

TOUCH OF TAR   'ear 'em, cryin' an' screamin', y'know. They reckon they was done in, down the creekbed, fulla bones. Me bastard Daddy was in on that. Ever seen 'em?

JACK   No.

TOUCH OF TAR   Come wiv me. I'll show you.

JACK   I don't wanta. *(Pause)* I'm waitin' for a lift.

TOUCH OF TAR   Scared, are you?

JACK   No, I'm goin' to the war. I got pissed, that's all.

TOUCH OF TAR   Then . . . come.

(Slowly, as if mesmerized, JACK is pulled across the stage by TOUCH OF TAR.)

TOUCH OF TAR   You'll like it, Jackie, you see. You call me, go on, you say, "Lily".

JACK   Lily.

TOUCH OF TAR   You drunk now, but later . . . you won't mind. You say it agen . . . "Lily".

JACK   Lily.

TOUCH OF TAR   See. Nice, aint it? Come on, Jack, I'll take care of you. It's nice . . . in the creekbed. Warm an' dark an' soft, she-oak trees: real nice for us. You'll see.

(They exit.)

ZEEK   Observe the transit of Venus across the face of the sun.

(CLEMMY sits dozing in her wicker chair. A voice is heard off, approaching and reciting mournfully.)

EDIE   Where fled the quarry, leaping
      By hill and creek and plain,
      They lie together, sleeping,
      The hunter and the slain.[11]

(Enter EDIE in long white calico nightgown, sleepwalking and wringing her hands. She circles the stage. CLARRY wakes, startled.)

EDIE   Wash your hands, put on your nightgown, don't look so pale.

ZEEK   Where hast thou been, sister. Killing swine?

EDIE   Never again from the night, the night that has taken

Shall ever the tribes return to tell us their tale,
They lie in a sleep, whence none shall ever awaken . . .
(She washes her hands as she walks.)
Here's the smell of the blood still.

ZEEK   And all will vanish, stars, gas, dust, planets, moons.

EDIE   Driven to drown in the swamps – but the wind their dirge; the hunted of the dogs: *(in her ordinary voice)* and now you're a blackdog and I'm damned, damned.

ZEEK   The large dog Sirius and the little dog, Canis Minor, mark how they move.

CLEMMY   *(firmly)* Go to bed now, Edie Perkins.

EDIE   To bed, to bed; Come, come, come, come, give me your hand, Eek Perkins. What's done can't be undone. Their blood is black on our hands that nothing can purge.

(EDIE exits, still asleep. Enter CLARRY in dressing gown and hair curlers with nightlight in her hand.)

CLARRY   *(fearfully)* Are you there, Clemmy? What was that?

CLEMMY   Only Edie Perkins sleepwalking again. I told her to go to bed.

CLARRY   I thought she'd got over it.

CLEMMY   Not as bad as she used to be. It was on every couple of weeks once.

CLARRY   Poor thing! *(Sitting)* To carry that guilty conscience all the days of your life.

CLEMMY   She drove him to it.

CLARRY   Out of wicked jealousy. "Get rid of the black heathens", she screamed at him, and he did.

CLEMMY   All of them were in it, the whole town, egged on by the wives. And now there's only Touch of the Tar – I mean Lily Perkins – to remind him.

CLARRY   It got out of hand.

ZEEK   *(babbling)* The creek ran with blood. "Come on", Eek shouted, "grab your gun", but I took my telescope and went the other way. Some of 'em run out over the salt lake, crying like plovers. They never came back. It was bedlam, and when I looked in my telescope the dog star was raging to the west.

CLEMMY   I've always hated the place.

CLARRY   Mukinupin?

CLEMMY   Exiled here like shags on rocks.

CLARRY   I know you've missed it, Clemmy,

but who wouldn't? Up there in the Big Top with the crowd holding their breaths.

CLEMMY   I could see the five Wirth sisters playing at statues on their powdered horses, looking up, everybody looking up . . . and then . . . suddenly . . . *(She covers her face with her hands.)*

ZEEK   Moons rise, stars fall. . . .

CLARRY   Don't brood on it, dear. It's such a long time ago.

CLEMMY   I'm like a bird with a broken wing.

(On the sound track the night sounds begin.)

CLARRY   *(sleepily)* Who's that giggling in the creekbed?

CLEMMY   Touch of the Tar.

CLARRY   *(murmuring)* I can hear a madman screaming.

CLEMMY   It's only the Flasher, tuning into Marconi. *(They giggle. Pause.)*

CLARRY   I think I can hear a willy wagtail. Listen Clem, *(murmuring)* sweet pretty creature . . . sweet pretty creature. *(Her voice dies away.)*

CLEMMY   I couldn't dance much, y'know Clarry, I couldn't really hit a high C, and my legs were terrible, but by God . . . I could walk that high wire. *(Pause)* Goodnight, Clarry. Sweet dreams.

(The MISSES HUMMER *sleep.)*

ZEEK   And certain stars shot madly from their spheres flying between the cold moon and the earth. *(The night sounds fill the stage. Enter* HARRY TUESDAY, *ready for the road, with rifle, bandolier and swag, wearing a Digger's hat. He sits and rolls a smoke, dropping his swag at his feet.)* How goes the night, boy?

NEW HOLLAND SONG[12]

HARRY

New Holland is a barren place,
in it there grows no grain,
nor any habitation
wherein for to remain.

She is my gold, my darling,
she gives me drought and rain,
when I plough and sow her
upon the saltbush plain,

She is my bitter heritage,
she is my darling one,
she drowns me in the winter
and she bakes me in the sun.

I'll plant her and I'll rape her,
I will not run her down,
upon her gold and torment
I'll build my shanty town,

Cut her plains with sheep pads,
mine the black beach sand,
push the iron ranges down
and salt the Great South Land.

And then she will repay me,
for she will give no grain,
nor any habitation
wherein for to remain.

*(*HARRY *picks up his swag and moves off, singing. During the song* ZEEK *has been packing up his telescope.)*

ZEEK   The moon shines with a good grace. Well shone, Moon. *(*ZEEK *takes his divining rod, moves along stage front, places a stone in the place of greatest pull, and measures foot to foot along the stage. He pauses and turns centre.)* *(Triumphantly)* Dig here. You'll get water at sixty feet. *(The shadowy figure of* ZEEK *is left, centre, holding his divining rod like a prophet.)*

Act II

The stage is empty and set exactly the same as in Act I. The time is 1918. A steam train can be heard approaching in the distance, a train whistle blows "Yankee Doodle Dandy" insistently several times like a signal. Enter the townspeople in various stages of early morning undress: The HUMMER SISTERS *yawning in dressing gowns,* EDIE PERKINS *in hair curlers,* EEK *still in shirtsleeves, with lather on his face and a cut-throat razor in his hand.* CECIL BRUNNER *has forgotten his toupée. They stand about bewildered and exclaiming to each other.*

ALL   What is it? Did you hear the train? Playing a tune. Yankee Doodle Dandy!

*(*EEK *comes centre, holds up his hand.)*

EEK   Hark!

(They all stand silently listening. The train whistle repeats the refrain. Enter POLLY PERKINS *running on, wild with excitement, dressed in a white blouse, black skirt and button-up boots, waving a telegram.)*

POLLY   The war's over. It just came through on the wire.

(The town crowd around POLLY, *calling out . . .)*

VARIOUS   When? What happened? Tell us, Polly. What's she saying?

*(*POLLY *unfolds the telegram importantly, and comes centre.)*

POLLY   *(reading)* London, November the eleventh, 1918, ten fifty-five a.m., most urgent. Armistice signed at five o'clock this morning.

EEK   *(reverently)* Ah! The wonders of modern science.

CLEMMY   *(wryly)* Even in Mukinupin.

POLLY   *(softly)* Jack will be coming home.

*(*EDIE *runs up and down with her ear trumpet.)*

EDIE   What she say, what she say? Speak up, Pol, do.

EEK   *(roaring)* War's over!

ALL   War's over! War's over! War's over!

(They move in a ritual circle, shaking hands, smiling, exclaiming. CECIL, *embarrassed, suddenly remembers his toupée, adjusts it hurriedly, and kisses the ladies' hands. When he reaches* POLLY *she ignores him, remaining apart in a dream of* JACK *as the train plays "Yankee Doodle Dandy" and the church bells ring out. They all sing a wartime medley beginning with "Yankee Doodle" and moving into one or two of the following: "Keep the Home Fires Burning", "Tipperary", "Take Me Back to Dear Old Blighty", or "Pack Up Your Troubles". During the songs* EEK *and* CECIL *exit and bring back a huge boomerang of flowers, the* HUMMER SISTERS *exit, return dressed in their best, carrying a floral star five feet across.* EDIE *takes the curlers out of her hair;* POLLY *primps in a hand mirror;* EEK *wipes the lather off his face, and as the train hisses and whistles and they move into the solemn tones of the Recessional,* EDIE *and* POLLY *produce a bunting sign with* "WELCOME HOME MUKINUPIN'S HERO".

Enter JACK TUESDAY, *in Digger's uniform, carrying his kitbag and looking bewildered. They all crowd round, singing their lungs out, while* JACK *stands centre, surrounded by floral tributes.* CECIL *and* EEK *carry* JACK *shoulder high along the street, with the others following. They place* JACK *on the table top, pile the flowers around him, still singing.* EEK *holds up his hand for silence and reads his speech from the Town Hall steps.)*

EEK   Fellow citizens, I feel I stand here today in the reflected glory of the Australian soldier. *(Loud cheers from everybody except the embarrassed* JACK.) After five years of the most dreaded war the world has ever known; the fearful horrors of trench warfare, a Europe drenched in gore; we stand here to welcome home our returning hero . . . *(*EEK *brandishes his cut-throat razor.)* It is true that not the faintest breath of these horrors ravaged our fair young shores, but we gave our sons to face the test of manhood, and, in the grey light of early dawn, leap out upon unknown shores to dare, endure and die. *(Cries and sobs from the crowd.* JACK *hangs his head.)* Yes, Australia was there, and Mukinupin was there, to crush Germany and re-divide the world. At one stride our young Commonwealth put on the toga of nationhood, vindicated the rights of man, and maintained the moral order of the universe. Let us pray.

(Still fiercely brandishing his razor EEK *falls on his knees and begins the Lord's Prayer.* JACK *hesitates but follows, they all join in, except* EDIE, *who, sublimely unknowing, begins to recite.)*

EDIE   The bugles of the Motherland
    Rang ceaselessly across the sea,
    To call him and his lean brown band
    To shape Imperial destiny;
    He went by youth's grave purpose willed,
    The goal unknown, the cost outweighed,
    The promise of his blood fulfilled –[13]

EEK   *(furious)* Will you hold your tongue, Mother.

EDIE   *(crossly)* The bravest thing God ever made.

(They all break into "Mademoiselle from Armentières". JACK *grins and they all, except* EEK, *rise and circle* JACK, *hand in hand, singing.)*

ALL   Speech, speech.

JACK   *(embarrassed)* I'm glad to be back – and still alive. *(Hoorays, coo-ees.)*

POLLY   *(with pride)* My JACK's a hero.

JACK   No Pol, I'm not. You've got it all wrong. That's Harry. *(Dead silence.)*

ALL   *(amazed)* Harry!

JACK   That's right. Harry got the VC at Hill

60 – for extraordinary gallantry – under fire. There was nobody left in 'is bloody platoon.

ALL No!

JACK *(cheerfully)* Harry always was a wild bugger. So you see, you got the wrong snoozer. Can I get down now? *(EEK rises from his knees.)*

EEK This is most embarrassing, Jack Tuesday.

JACK Yeah, I know, it is a bit of a bummer. Mind you, I'm still not as embarrassin' as Harry.

EEK Where is . . . Harry?

JACK Jumped ship at Albany, deserted and went bush. But I wouldn't bother about gettin' out the red carpet for Harry. He's shell-shocked, off his chump, takes fits and dribbles. Barmy Harry, they call 'im.

(POLLY runs forward and clasps JACK in her arms.)

POLLY Well, I don't care anyway. I'm just glad you're back, safe and sound.

CLARRY AND CLEMMY Hear, hear!

JACK *(grinning)* Me too. Jeez, Pol, you look good enough to eat. *(JACK hugs POLLY.)*

POLLY I missed you, Jack. You only wrote twice.

JACK Ah! Well, you know I was never much of a hand with the pen.

EDIE What's he say?

EEK *(bawling)* He's not a hero . . . or much of a hand with the pen!

EDIE I might have known it. *(Disgusted, she rolls up the bunting.)*

EEK Well, Jack, we won't hold this against you. Even if you're not a hero.

CECIL No, indeed.

EEK You did your bit and now we're prepared to do ours. *(But JACK has been canoodling with POLLY, much to CECIL's chagrin, and doesn't take much notice. EEK clears his throat.)* Jack Tuesday, I'm prepared to offer you your old job back again in Perkins' General Store. I'll always support a trier. *(EDIE holds out the broom for JACK to take.)*

JACK I'll die laughin'.

CECIL You could do worse, Jack. Mukinupin's quite the little metropolis.

EEK Work hard, produce plenty and pay your debts, that's Mukinupin.

CLARRY We're just one big happy family in Mucka.

POLLY Father shaves in a silver mug and Mother *(giggling)* uses a Royal Doulton chamber pot with forget-me-nots round the rim.

EEK Some of you doubted, but I never doubted.

POLLY And oh, Jack, guess what! I've got a vieux rose bedroom, with a big clock going tick-tock-tick on the landing.

JACK I don't want to be a grocer's boy in Perkins' General Store.

POLLY Oh, Jack.

EEK I can understand that.

CECIL Oh, perfectly understandable.

EEK I'll make another offer. What about . . . the land?

JACK Ma's dead of gallopin' consumption, so you can keep the lousy farm. It's only stinkwort and poison bush anyway.

POLLY Oh, Jack, you'll never get on.

JACK Get on! Be a farm labourer, workin' sun-up till dark six days a week, live in a tin shed with a stretcher in it for a quid a week and me keep. Come off it, Pol. No. I'm goin' shearin'.

EEK AND CECIL With the red-raggers and no-hopers.

(EEK exits, disgusted, with CECIL. EDIE and the HUMMER SISTERS gather up the floral tributes and exit.)

POLLY Oh, Jack, I've waited so long for you to come home. Ever since that last night when we quarrelled. You never even spent your last night in Mukinupin with me.

JACK *(uneasy)* I know, Pol.

POLLY Where did you spend it, then?

JACK I got shickered.

POLLY *(disgusted)* Somebody said you were with Touch of the Tar.

JACK Did they?

POLLY Well, were you?

(As JACK and POLLY confront each other, EEK and CECIL re-enter with ladder and bunting, and put up a large sign in front of the Mukinupin Town Hall. It reads, "LEST WE FORGET". The MISSES HUMMER enter, staggering under a cardboard statue of a soldier with a kelpie dog at his feet. EDIE follows with a bunch of flowers. They set it all in place and when they have all finished their respective jobs they exit.)

JACK   Ask no questions and you'll hear no lies. (POLLY *turns her back on him.*)

POLLY   Go shearing then – see if I care.

JACK   I'm only back two minutes, and you're at me again.

POLLY   I hate you, Jack Tuesday.

JACK   No you don't, Pol. (JACK *comes behind her and clasps her waist, kissing her ear.*)

POLLY   I thought it would be so lovely, just you and me, like it used to be, behind the dust on the counters.

JACK   Nothin's changed, Pol.

POLLY   Everything's changed, but you've changed most of all.

JACK   I've grown up, that's all. I've seen the world, Pol. I've got to live me own life, and you've got to let me.

POLLY   And what about *my* life? How can I marry . . . a shearer?

JACK   (*teasing*) No vieux rose bedroom, no silver shavin' mug or forget-me-not jerry.

POLLY   I think I'll marry Cecil Brunner. *He's* got a position.

JACK   You'll never marry *him.*

POLLY   You better watch out, Jack Tuesday, because, if you treat me badly, I just might, y'know.

JACK   Don't threaten me, Polly. (*He catches her waist.*) I don't treat you badly, do I? Do I?

POLLY   It's too long ago. I don't remember. (JACK *pulls her towards him. She struggles but, when he kisses her, responds.* POLLY *breaks away.*) Ah Jack! You make it so hard for me.

JACK   I won't be shearin' forever. It's only a stopgap. I'll make it – one a' these days.

POLLY   Make it, how?

JACK   I dunno. I just know – I will, and then we can be married and you can go on bein' the lady.

POLLY   I don't believe you.

JACK   I tell you it's true. I'll be a . . . a . . . (*A long pause*)

POLLY   You'll be a what?

JACK   I'll be an . . . actor, that's what I'll be. I'll be an actor, Pol.

POLLY   (*scornfully*) An actor?

JACK   That's right. Remember the Montebellos?

POLLY   That old woman who made sheep's eyes at you?

JACK   Remember how impressed they were?

POLLY   I remember how she buttered you up, that's all. *He* wasn't impressed.

JACK   He was jealous. He could see . . . another performer in the offing.

POLLY   You're impossible. (*She turns away.*) It's all dreams, Jack, just pipe dreams.

JACK   You don't believe in me, that's your trouble. You just don't believe in me at all.

(POLLY *exits and* JACK *comes centre for his song.*)

FLASH JACK OF MUKINUPIN[14]

I trudged beyond Jitarning Soak,
I passed the Kunjin plain,
I left behind the rabbit proof,
wet wool and drizzlin' rain,

In mud and blood in Flanders' fields
the whizzbangs were all poppin',
Flash Jack survived with his nine lives,
Come back to Mukinupin.

(*Chorus:*)

Tumble in their beds, boys,
Skirts above their heads, boys,
I can do a respectable tally meself,
I take a lot of stoppin',
And they know me round the
    backblocks
as Flash Jack from Mukinupin.

And it's all around the country,
in me moleskins and me hat,
I'm the latest kind of flasher
out on the One-Tree Flat.

At Kunna and at Mucka
I will kiss the girls and then
I'll call in at the shanty
and say fill 'em up again.

(*Repeat chorus:*)

And all the girls in Mucka
will take a shine to me,
I'll love 'em and I'll leave 'em
underneath the pepper tree,

Before me time is all cut out,
and I've called it a day,
I'll have every girl in Mucka
in the family way.

(*Repeat chorus:*)

(JACK *dances towards the war memorial, takes out a cigarette, lights it and seats himself at the foot of the memorial. Enter* MERCY MONTEBELLO, *carrying a hatbox and suitcase and dressed in the height of fashion. She has just come off the train. With languid* grace MERCY *removes her gloves and hat, and gazes round her with undisguised loathing. She goes to the mirror to fix her hair then runs her finger over the furniture.)*

MERCY Mukinupin, Mukinupin. Hasn't changed a jot in five long years; dust still as thick, silence still as deep, flyspots still as various. Ah! Max, Max. *(She sits, holding her head in her hands in a Victorian pose.)* Your Mercy has fallen upon evil days. *(She pulls herself together, takes up writing paper and pen.)* But nil desperandum, as the Greek philosopher says; Mercy Montebello can still make a silk purse out of a sow's ear. *(She gazes out front for inspiration, sucking her pen.)* Dearest Jack . . . no, that won't do. Dear Jack – too formal. My dear Jack . . . that's better . . . My dear Jack, I arrived by train this morning and thought I might in remembrance of older and happier times . . . just . . . drop you this line . . .

(MERCY rises, essays a few graceful dance steps, as she speaks the following dialogue to music.)

>   Do you remember the old times?
>   I remember too well,
>   I've been waiting all morning
>   in a suite at the Royal Hotel.

>   I've come to Mucka by train, Jack,
>   Desdemona is free.
>   Max collapsed into the footlights
>   whilst he was strangling me.

>   Don't hope to see a beauty,
>   I'm just a faded rose,
>   But I'd like to take your hand, Jack,
>   before I take my repose.

(MERCY sits for the last lines of her letter.)

>   I haven't any designs, dear,
>   Cross my heart, hope to die,
>   But I'll wear a hat with a feather,
>   And you wear a spotted tie.

>   I recall when we met, Jack,
>   the wheat was a burnished yellow,
>   we were innocent, young, then;
>   love, Mercy Montebello.

(MERCY places the letter in an envelope and firmly licks the flap.)

MERCY That should bring him running.

(Enter CECIL BRUNNER in bowler hat, carrying a huge bunch of long-stemmed pink roses. He bows over MERCY's hand. MERCY rises.)

CECIL *(stuttering)* Welcome, Madame Montebello. What an honour . . . our little town . . . etc., etc.

MERCY So charming of you, Mr . . . Mr . . . ?

CECIL Brunner, but please call me Cecil.

MERCY I wouldn't presume.

CECIL The presumption is all on my part, Madame.

MERCY *(aside)* It is rather, but how can I make use of his presumption . . . ? *(To CECIL)* Mr Brunner. . . . Cecil . . . your roses are exquisite. *(She takes them.)*

CECIL They do not come within coo-ee of your unearthly beauty, Madame.

MERCY Within coo-ee. What an odd expression. Is that local dialect?

CECIL I fear so, Madame. I am, after all, only a humble colonial.

MERCY A humble man may dare where others fail. What is your calling, pray?

CECIL I travel, Madame.

MERCY Travel, travel where? Are you a strolling player, one of *our* fraternity?

CECIL A knight of the road, certainly, but I travel in ladies lingerie.

MERCY *(shocked)* An underwear salesman!

CECIL You could . . . describe me as such.

MERCY If you have come to make a sale, I assure you . . . the cupboard is bare.

CECIL *(with dignity)* I come only as a sincere admirer, Madame.

MERCY Do you happen to know a Mr Jack Tuesday? Is he still in the district?

CECIL I have that doubtful privilege. Jack Tuesday has just returned from the war.

MERCY Covered in glory, no doubt.

CECIL *(bitterly)* Masquerading as some sort of hero.

MERCY I am seeking Mr Tuesday, because I think he may be able to repair my fading fortunes.

CECIL Jack?

MERCY He is handsome, well set up, has a pleasant singing voice, can dance nimbly, and has something of a presence. In short, with my assistance he could make a career for himself on the boards.

CECIL Jack . . . an actor?

MERCY Trust in me, my experience Mr . . . er . . . Cecil. It is not inconsiderable.

CECIL *(thoughtfully)* You would take him away from here?

MERCY   *Certainement.* You could hardly make a career in the Mukinupin Town Hall. *(She shudders and takes up her letter.)* I have written him a letter asking him to meet me here. *(Pause)* He had, I think . . . some species of . . . fiancée?

CECIL   Polly, but they're not really engaged. Only she . . .

MERCY   Fancies him, well, what female wouldn't? That's my point. He'd make such a divine principal boy.

CECIL   *(gloomily)* Would he?

MERCY   You have some aspirations in Polly's direction yourself?

CECIL   I did have, but begin to despair. *(MERCY claps him on the shoulder.)*

MERCY   Take heart, sir. Deliver my message and your troubles are probably over.

CECIL   Do you really think so? *(He takes the letter.)* Oh, Madame, if it were only true.

MERCY   Come, who could resist Mercy Montebello? *(MERCY sashays around the room.)*

CECIL   Who indeed! *(He bows low over her head again.)*

MERCY   Fly, Mr Cecil. You are, indeed, the messenger of fortune. *(He moves off. MERCY puts up her hand.)* Mr Cecil. *(He pauses.)* Could you, would you, lend me my fare out of town?

CECIL   Certainly, Madame. *(He fumbles in his pocket and hands her the money with a bow.)*

MERCY   God will reward you, for it's pretty certain Mercy Montebello cannot. *(She kisses his cheek. He presses his hand to his blushing cheek and stumbles out, in a daze.)* God speed, Mr Cecil.

(MERCY moves across to the glass and begins making up. CECIL crosses to JACK, elaborately casual.)

CECIL   Evenin', Jack.

JACK   Evenin'.

CECIL   Bit on the gloomy side? *(No answer)* I've a message for you. Every cloud has a silver lining.

JACK   From Polly?

CECIL   From Mercy Montebello. *(JACK leaps up.)*

JACK   Mercy . . . in town? *(He grabs the letter and begins to read.)*

CECIL   At the Royal . . . somewhat down on her luck.

JACK   She wants to see me, and I'm to wear . . . a spotted bow tie. *(He looks worried.)* I haven't got one.

CECIL   Feel free.

(He unties hiw own spotted tie and hands it to JACK, who knots it untidily around his neck.)

JACK   How do I look?

CECIL   *(dryly)* Magnificent!

(JACK starts to move across the stage. He stops.)

JACK   Is she still . . . as . . . beautiful?

CECIL   As a gazelle – if a little long in the tooth. *(JACK grins.)*

JACK   Thanks, Cec. I'll do as much for you some day. *(CECIL exits. MERCY stands, looking nervous. JACK stands, looking nervous.)* Mercy . . . it's me. Jack. I got your letter. *(MERCY dabs at her eyes with a handkerchief.)*

MERCY   *(tearfully)* Oh, Jack!

JACK   *(clumsily)* Don't cry, Merc. I'll look after you. *(MERCY lays her head on his shoulder.)*

MERCY   Dear Jack. Still as handsome as ever, and as kind.

JACK   *(gallantly)* And you're still as beautiful.

MERCY   You recognised me?

JACK   Who could ever forget . . . Mercy Montebello.

MERCY   The world apparently. Ah! Jack, Jack, the public are so fickle. Since Max . . . passed away. *(She sobs a little.)*

JACK   Don't talk about it . . . please.

MERCY   I've had no-one to turn to A woman alone is *(gesturing)* . . .

JACK   Turn to me.

MERCY   What gallantry . . . my dear.

JACK   Any bloke would envy me, Merc.

MERCY   Let me fix your tie . . . *(She does so, very provocatively. Their eyes meet.)* There, that's better. *(MERCY sways away, sits and takes a flask of gin out of her purse.)* Have a spot, Jack.

JACK   Don't mind if I do.

(She fills two glasses and hands one to JACK.)

MERCY   To us. *(They drink.)* And now – down to business.

JACK   Business? *(MERCY tinkles with laughter.)*

MERCY   Don't get the wrong idea, Jack. This is – strictly a business proposition. *(She makes outrageous eyes at him.)* I thought you understood that.

JACK   Oh!

MERCY   Come, Jack. I'm old enough to be
   your Ma.
JACK   *(gloomily)* I 'spect you are.
MERCY   But that doesn't stop us having a
   great deal to give each other.
JACK   *(cheering up)* You reckon?
MERCY   I reckon; so listen carefully to what I
   have to say. *(JACK nods and leans forward
   in his chair.)* I'm looking for a new partner.
   I can't work alone. I need a foil, with
   masculine bravado to offset my . . .
   womanly tenderness. Anyway, I'm
   thinking of leaving the classics and moving
   into something more picturesque and
   tuneful, with *exotique* settings and catchy
   songs . . . something with a genuine
   appeal to the romantic longings of our
   audiences. You follow me? *(JACK nods
   violently.)* And that, dear Jack, is where you
   come in.
JACK   *(stupidly)* Where do I come in?
MERCY   *(gaily)* I'm asking you to be my
   partner in this enterprise.
JACK   Why me?
MERCY   Look at you. *(She pulls him to his
   feet and twirls him round.)* You have such
   grace, such charm, such . . . *élan*. Every
   woman in the audience will fall in love
   with you. In short, dear Jack, you have the
   sex appeal.
JACK   Have I? *(MERCY laughs at him.)*

MERCY AND JACK'S DUET

MERCY
   Oh! Would you like to sing
   a short duet with me?
   I wouldn't ask for more than this.
JACK
   I'll be laconic,
MERCY
   Strictly platonic,
JACK AND MERCY
   Let's seal it with a kiss.
MERCY
   Oh! Jack, we're going places,
   in silks and laces,
   we'll know how far to go,
   we'll give them a show, a dream,
   they've never seen a show like ours
      before.
JACK AND MERCY
   We'll stop in all the best hotels,
   when we step out they'll ring the bells.
MERCY
   You'll order cocktails,
   I'll dress up to kill,

JACK AND MERCY
   And up in lights we'll have
   our double bill.
MERCY
   We'll be seen in all the chic
   and stylish places,
JACK
   You'll take my arm,
   we'll have such charm,
MERCY
   Élan.
JACK AND MERCY
   We'll have our faces in the magazines.
JACK AND MERCY
   So would you like to sing
   a short duet with me?
   I wouldn't ask for more than this,
JACK
   I'll be laconic,
MERCY
   Strictly platonic,
JACK AND MERCY
   Let's seal it with a kiss,
   with a kiss.

(They kiss, but MERCY breaks away.)

MERCY   The only problem is – will you take
   my offer seriously?
JACK   Oh, I will, I will.
MERCY   What plans have you for your
   future?
JACK   No plans. Oh well, I was thinkin' of
   goin' shearin'. But of course I'd drop all
   that like a hot potater.
MERCY   But what about your little friend . . .
   little Miss Whatsisname . . . Polly?
JACK   Polly'll be delighted. She wants me to
   get on.
MERCY   She may not want to lose you.
JACK   That's true. *(Pause)* I don't suppose,
   Miss Mercy, we could find a place for
   Pol?
MERCY   I wonder. *(She drums on the table
   with her fingers.)* I don't really see why not.
   She's a pretty little thing . . . front of house,
   perhaps.
JACK   Oh Merc, you're such a brick. If we
   could only take Pol I'd be the happiest man
   on earth.
MERCY   Then it's decided. I won't even
   unpack. We'll leave on the train this
   evening. Have you got your fare?
JACK   Too right. I've got me deferred pay.
MERCY   Capital! Now where can we find
   your Polly?
JACK   She'll be in a vieux rose bedroom with

a clock ticking on the landing, dreaming of being a lady.

MERCY   In Mukinupin! Poor thing. Well then, Jack my dear, let us go and change your Polly's life.

(JACK *picks up* MERCY's *bags while she puts on her hat and fixes it before the mirror. They move off together and* JACK *raps loudly on the counter.*)

JACK   Pol, are you there?

(*Enter* POLLY *dressed to the nines.*)

POLLY   (*sweetly*) Yes, Jack.

JACK   (*awkwardly*) Polly, you remember Miss – Madame Montebello.

POLLY   Oh, I do. You're looking very well, Madame.

MERCY   Thank you, Polly.

JACK   Madame has a . . . proposition to make.

POLLY   Please do sit down. (*They do so, very stiffly.*) A proposition?

JACK   Yes, a business proposition.

POLLY   Indeed?

JACK   And it includes you. Oh Pol, please say yes, it means the whole world . . . to both of us.

POLLY   What is . . . this business proposition?

MERCY   In short, Miss Polly, my husband is dead and I am looking for a partner. (POLLY *gives a horrified gasp.*) (*Patiently*) A business partner. I need a principal man.

POLLY   But Jack's a grocer's boy.

JACK   (*grimly*) Not any more I'm not.

MERCY   We all have to be discovered – somewhere.

POLLY   In Mukinupin?

MERCY   Even in Mukinupin. You must not stand in his way, my dear. Your Jack has talent – and charm. He's wasted in these . . . desert places.

POLLY   (*wailing*) So you're taking him away. (JACK *takes her hand.*)

JACK   No, Polly, listen Madame Montebello – Mercy – wants you too.

POLLY   For what? A bit of window dressing?

JACK   (*bitterly*) Spoken like a true Perkins. Polly, the drapers' daughter!

MERCY   You could be very useful to us, Polly. Front of house, public relations, who knows? You could play it by ear.

POLLY   It doesn't appeal to me, Madame.

JACK   But why not, why not?

POLLY   Just because . . .

(JACK *leaps up, grabs her shoulders and shakes her.*)

JACK   Because *what*? Don't play games with me, Polly Perkins. (POLLY *starts to cry.*)

POLLY   Because I won't be used: that's why, Jack Tuesday. (*To* MERCY) Oh, you think you can pull the wool over my eyes, you and your fine feathers. I can see right through *you*. It's Jack you're after, always has been. You and your business arrangements!

MERCY   I beg your pardon?

JACK   How dare you speak to Madame Montebello in that tone of voice. Apologise!

POLLY   I won't, I won't.

JACK   Apologise!

POLLY   I'm a nice girl.

JACK   Not nice enough.

POLLY   You'd be in clover, Jack, wouldn't you, with the two of us? You could switch around.

(JACK *slaps her face. She runs crying offstage. A long pause as* JACK *shakily lights a cigarette.*)

MERCY   (*quietly*) Well, Jack, it won't work, will it?

JACK   (*miserably*) I could come with you anyway.

MERCY   But I don't think you will.

JACK   Oh, Merc, I don't know what to do.

MERCY   If you make up your mind, I'll be at the station waiting for the train out of Mukinupin. *Au revoir*, Jack. (JACK *moves across to her.*)

JACK   Thank you for asking me.

MERCY   The offer's open – always, Jack. (*She lifts up her face for a kiss. They kiss gently, then passionately.*) You kiss – so passionately.

JACK   (*breathless*) So do you. (MERCY *moves across and picks up her bags.*) Let me carry your bags.

MERCY   I can manage. I'm an independent woman.

(*She exits.* JACK *sits at the table. He takes two bottles of beer out of his knapsack and puts them down belligerently. Enter* CECIL BRUNNER. JACK *loosens his tie and tears it off.*)

JACK   You can take your bloody tie.

CECIL   What's up, Jack?

JACK   (*mimicking him*) What's up, Jack? I'll tell you what's up – all hell and damnation, that's what's up. (CECIL *sits opposite him.*)

CECIL   It can't be as bad as that.

JACK   Can't it? (*He looks at* CECIL *suspiciously.*) Now I come to think of it, how was it that you delivered that note from Mercy Montebello?

CECIL   I was just passing by.

JACK   (*drinking heavily*) Oh, yeah.

CECIL   And Madame Montebello asked me to deliver her letter. (*Pauses defensively.*) I've always admired her. She's a very fine figure of a woman.

JACK   (*savagely*) Like you've admired Polly. (*He leans across the table.*) Listen, Brunner, if I thought that you deliberately set me up . . .

CECIL   I don't know what you're suggesting.

JACK   I bet. You've always wanted Polly, since she was a little bit of a kid. Well, haven't you?

CECIL   (*stiffly*) I love Miss Polly – yes, it's true.

JACK   And you thought if you got me out of the way you'd have a better chance? All's fair in love and war.

CECIL   I want to marry her.

JACK   Well, maybe now you'll get your wish. How does that affect you?

CECIL   I'll always be here if she needs me.

JACK   After all, you're more her type . . . (*with scorn*) a travelling salesman.

CECIL   (*with dignity*) There are worse things.

JACK   You reckon?

CECIL   I'd give her . . . security.

JACK   That's what she wants, alright. Okay Cec, you're on your own, by Christ, and I hope you make it. (*He rises, swaying noticeably.*) The Perkinses'll be pleased, and Pol'll be a lady. It's what she's always wanted, and no hard feelin's.

(JACK *claps* CECIL *on the shoulders and lurches over to the war memorial where he sits drinking. Enter* EDIE *behind the counter.* CECIL *crosses to her and begins unpacking his sample case.*)

CECIL   I've got some lovely stuff for the summer trade, Mrs Perkins.

EDIE   You always have such good taste, Mr Brunner. (CECIL *begins displaying his wares.*)

CECIL   This trousseau set's a real stunner.

EDIE   (*coyly*) I'd like to see our Polly modelling that.

(*During the following scene* CECIL *exits.*)

JACK   (*singing*)

Polly lies over the ocean,
Polly lies over the sea,
Polly lies over the ocean,
O bring back my Polly to me.
Bring back, bring back,
O bring back my Polly to me.

(*Enter* TOUCH OF THE TAR *in her ragged dress, barefoot. She sidles up to* JACK.)

TOUCH OF TAR   It's Jack Toosday, isn't it?

JACK   (*sulkily*) Y'know it is. (*She sits beside him.*)

TOUCH OF TAR   Could never mistake yous. You an' 'Arry.

JACK   Everybody does.

TOUCH OF TAR   You're diff'rent. (*Giggling*) I oughta know. (*She leans her head against* JACK's *knee.*)

TOUCH OF TAR   I like you, Jackie.

JACK   Good luck, Lily.

TOUCH OF TAR   Don' you talk to me like that. Why you talk about luck ter me?

JACK   Because you need it. You an' me both. Here, take a swig. (TOUCH OF THE TAR *drinks heavily. They share the bottle.*)

TOUCH OF TAR   Me bastard farver come from Mucka.

JACK   I know.

TOUCH OF TAR   I'm not a prostitute . . . no way. I just hates men.

JACK   You don't hate me.

TOUCH OF TAR   Why not?

JACK   Because I never hurt you.

TOUCH OF TAR   Why do I like you?

JACK   Because we're both . . . outcasts.

TOUCH OF TAR   Why doncha get off with me agen?

JACK   It wouldn't be any good in the mornin'.

TOUCH OF TAR   I'm not good enough for you. Thass it.

JACK   For either of us.

TOUCH OF TAR   Then give us two bob, will y'?

JACK   Don't talk to me like that.

TOUCH OF TAR   Ah, I don't give a fuck, anyway. I'm tired of it, hangin' about on the edge of town, treated like shit.

JACK   You an' me both, Lil.

TOUCH OF TAR   Lets go then, Jackie.

JACK   You're Harry's girl.

TOUCH OF TAR   I'm nobody's. Come on, take a real good look at me, in the daylight. I'm nobody's, but I'm pretty, ain't I?

JACK   Yeah, you are.

Figure 8 Queensland Theatre Co. production of Dorothy Hewett's *The Man From Mukinupin*, November 1989 (directed by Aubrey Mellor), showing Alan David Lee as "Jack Tuesday", twin-brother to the shell-shocked VC, "Harry Tuesday", sitting next to Rebecca Riggs as "Lily Perkins (Touch of the Tar)" who is half-sister to "Polly Perkins", in front of the war memorial in Act II. Later, a drunken Harry is to sit in the same place, reinforcing the contrast between the artificial construction of the Australian Digger as war hero, and the mundane reality of actual war veterans. [Photo: Fiora Sacco.]

TOUCH OF TAR   Then let's piss off, Jackie, you an' me. You could do a lot worse.

JACK   You really want to go?

TOUCH OF TAR   Too right. What's keepin' us here?

JACK   You couldn't go like that. (TOUCH OF THE TAR *stiffens.*)

TOUCH OF TAR   What's wrong with me?

JACK   You look like a tramp.

TOUCH OF TAR   Ah shit, you're jus' like all the rest – white men. (*She takes another swig.* JACK *stands up, swaying slightly, and pulls her to her feet.*)

JACK   No, if you go with me, you'll go like a lady. You're pretty an' you're nice and you'll go like a lady. D'ya hear?

TOUCH OF TAR   (*sulkily*) Go where?

JACK   Everywhere; the whole wide world, maybe. You an' me and Madame Montebello.

TOUCH OF TAR   She wouldn't want me. She's a stuck up bitch, I bet.

JACK   No she's not. She's an actress. Maybe you could be one, too.

TOUCH OF TAR   Me? (*She laughs incredulously.*)

JACK   Get some decent clobber on you and you'd be a knock-out, Lil. Come on. (JACK *begins dragging* LILY *in the direction of Perkins' store, but she hangs back.*)

TOUCH OF TAR   Where we goin'?

JACK   To buy you a new dress and a pair of shoes and a hat and –

TOUCH OF TAR   I'm not goin' in there.

JACK   You're comin' with me.

TOUCH OF TAR   That bitch won't serve me.

(JACK *drags* TOUCH OF THE TAR *across the stage to* EDIE PERKINS.)

JACK   We need a dress, and shoes, and a hat, everythin' to fit.

EDIE   What's that?

JACK   You heard. (*He roars into her ear trumpet.*) Dress. Hat. Shoes.

EDIE   We don't serve blacks in here. (JACK *pounds on the counter.*)

JACK   You're servin' me. Get it. Me! Now . . . Dress, hat shoes and the best – none of your rubbish. I want somethin' like – somethin' like Polly'd wear.

EDIE   (*faintly*) Polly would wear.

JACK   Get it.

(As EDIE *brings out a white muslin dress with sash, a big picture hat and black pumps with bows* TOUCH OF THE TAR *exclaims*

with delight. She peels off her dress, tries on the new clothes and dances about the room.)

TOUCH OF TAR   Jesus, Jack! Look at this. Oh! Ain't it just lovely?

JACK   And I want a parasol.

(*Enter the two* MISSES HUMMER; CLARRY *with her sewing basket and* CLEMMY *leaning on her stick. They sit in their armchairs.* CLARRY *takes out her sewing,* CLEMMY *fans herself with her sandalwood fan.* JACK *pays* EDIE.)

CLEMMY   It's a scorcher.

CLARRY   A hundred and fourteen in the shade.

CLEMMY   Drought and rabbits.

CLARRY   Rabbits and drought.

CLEMMY   Looks like the end of the world, dear.

CLARRY   Salt's rising.

CLEMMY   Soak's gone bitter.

CLARRY   Honeysuckle's dying.

CLEMMY   Even the birds are dropping out of the sky.

CLARRY   And the tanks are empty. We'll have to start carting soon.

CLEMMY AND CLARRY   No good for the crops.

(*Exit* JACK *and* TOUCH OF THE TAR. EDIE *starts to sob. Enter* EEK PERKINS *with his paper. He sits in the armchair, ignoring* EDIE.)

CLARRY   There's that myall girl, Touch of the Tar, sashaying down to the siding, dressed up to kill.

CLEMMY   Lily Perkins!

CLARRY   Leaving town.

CLEMMY   With Jack Tuesday.

CLARRY   Poor Polly.

CLEMMY   Polly's lying down in the best bedroom with eau de cologne on her hankie.

CLARRY   Listening to Galli Curci on the phonograph.

CLEMMY   (*giggling*) Singing "My Tiny Hand is Frozen".

CLARRY   She's always been the little lady.

CLEMMY   And a bit too big for her boots.

EDIE   I was a refined and cultured woman, Mr Perkins, before you brought me to this sink of Sodom.

EEK   Town's like an oven.

EDIE   Dressing up a black gin to look like our Polly.

EEK   Ninety-seven enlisted men and twenty-four died. Not a bad record for Mucka.

(The light begins to fade as HARRY TUESDAY *enters in ragged moleskins, a black singlet, a slouch hat, bare feet and drinking a bottle of beer. He is already very drunk. He sits at the foot of the war memorial.)*

CLARRY   *(whispering)* There's Harry Tuesday.

HARRY   I was awarded a VC an' two bars for givin' a corp, a kick in the arse. *(He chuckles wildly.)*

CLEMMY   Harry's back home.

CLARRY   It's a wonder he's saved his neck this long. (HARRY *begins to sing drunkenly.)*

HARRY   *(singing)*
>   I wanta go home, I wanta go home,
>   I don't wanta go to the trenches no
>   more,
>   where hand-grenades an' whizzbangs
>   they roar.[15]

(Speaking) I'm shickered, an' may the best man win.

EDIE   I never speak, I cannot speak of these matters, without I . . . choke with emotion.

EEK   The Albany doctor'll be blowing up soon.

HARRY   *(singing)*
>   So send me over the sea
>   where the Heinies can't get at me,
>   O my, I'm too young ter die
>   I wanta go home.

EDIE   Lowest creatures on God's earth. They're all only animals . . . animals . . .

HARRY   And there was nobody left in the whole bloody platoon. *(He collapses, laughing again.)*

EDIE   Well, I hope she's gone for good, that's all. I hope she's gone for good. *(Firmly)* Because I tell you, Eek Perkins, I've never been so humiliated – serving your bastard. (EEK *drops his paper and stares at her. There is a long pause. He picks it up again.)*

EEK   Wheat's up seven and fourpence ha'penny a bushel. *(Long pause.* EDIE *stares hiccuping into the night;* EEK *reads his paper.)* The only way you can teach a nigger is with a big stick. (CLARRY *sews,* CLEMMY *fans herself, as* HARRY *continues to sing into the darkness.)*

HARRY
>   Where whizzbangs are flyin' and brave
>   men are dyin'
>   for bastards like you, dinky-di,
>   dinky-bloody-die,

>   dinky-die, dinky-di, dinky-di.
>   dinky-bloody-di . . .

*(*HARRY *moves off, singing and taking a swig from his bottle, as the lights come up on* POLLY *entering with bolts of material.* POLLY, CLARRY *and* CLEMMY *make a semi-circle sewing bee;* EEK *changes his paper for the earphones of a crystal set.* POLLY *begins sewing.)*

POLLY   It's lonely in Mucka, isn't it, Miss Clem?

CLEMMY   It always was Polly.

POLLY   Funny, I never noticed it before.

POLLY'S SAD SONG

POLLY
>   Oh! the plovers all call
>   and the autumn leaves fall
>   on the town in the turn of the year,
>   as I sew a fine seam I sit and I dream
>   for what has become of my dear?

EDIE, CLARRY AND CLEMMY
>   Oh! What has become of her dear, oh
>   dear,
>   Oh, what has become of her dear?

>   Will he ever come back
>   down the wallaby track
>   with a song on his lips just for me?
>   Or should I forget in the wild and the
>   wet:
>   is my love just a fond memory?

EDIE, CLARRY AND CLEMMY
>   Is her love just a fond memory, ee-ee,
>   her love just a fond memory?

CLEMMY
>   How well she remembers
>   that burning December
>   when he left on the train like a toff,
>   as the train whistle blew, she suddenly
>   knew
>   Jack Tuesday was having it off.

EDIE, CLARRY AND CLEMMY
>   Oh! Yes, he was having it off, off, off,
>   Oh, yes he was having it off.

*(*POLLY *weeps.)*

CLARRY
>   It was always her fate
>   to be fatally late,
>   and she knew he would never be true,
>   but alack and a day she let him slip
>   away,
>   with a virginal flutter or two.

EDIE, CLARRY AND CLEMMY
>She'd a virginal flutter or two, oo–oo,
>a virginal flutter or two.

(POLLY *sobs louder.*)

CLARRY AND CLEMMY
>And hour by hour
>her heart's turning sour,
>while she sits here and sews a fine seam,
>she'll never get laid, she'll be just an old maid

EDIE
>With a hope chest that's full up with dreams.

ALL
>Her/my hope chest is full up of dreams, it seems,
>her/my hope chest is full up of dreams

(CECIL BRUNNER *has entered during the song, and now comes forward into the circle.*)

CECIL   Good evening, ladies.

ALL   Good evening, Mr Brunner – I mean, Cecil.

CECIL   Quite a snap in the air this evening. Have an acid drop. (*They all smile, incline their heads and take one.*)

CECIL   I hope I'm not intruding.

ALL   Oh! No, no, no!

CECIL   But I do have something of the utmost importance to say.

POLLY   I'm sure it must be very interesting.

CECIL   To Miss Polly.

EDIE   What's he saying?

CLARRY   (*shouting*) It's private.

EDIE   To who?

CLEMMY   Polly.

EDIE   Oh! (*They all look at each other. EDIE rises.*) Miss Clemmy! Miss Clarry! (*They both rise, smile archly.*)

CLARRY AND CLEMMY   Good evening, Mr Brunner.

CECIL   (*embarrassed*) I don't mean to be precipitous.

CLARRY, CLEMMY AND EDIE   Of course not, Mr Brunner.

(EDIE *farewells the* MISSES HUMMER *backstage, then crosses to* EEK *and shakes him.* POLLY *moves across to an old style phonograph.*)

POLLY   I'll just put a record on. It's the latest hit. They're dancing to it everywhere: Sydney, London, New York.

EEK   Secede, that's what we need – secession. I've said so for years. Wipe Canberra off the face of the earth, and go it alone. (EDIE *keeps on shaking him.* EEK *takes off his headphones.*) Eh?

EDIE   Early night, Mr Perkins, dear.

EEK   But it's only just gone seven.

EDIE   Early to bed, early to rise, makes a man healthy, wealthy and wise.

(EDIE *makes faces at* EEK; *grumbling, he exits with her.* POLLY *has begun dancing round the room to the strains of "You Made Me Love You", humming the tune.*)

POLLY   Dance, Mr Brunner?

CECIL   These modern dances! I don't think . . . I know how.

POLLY   Of course you do. Look – it's easy. (*She demonstrates a few steps.*) Anyone can pick it up . . . in two ticks. (CECIL *moves into* POLLY's *arms.*) Isn't it scrumptious?

CECIL   Oh! Miss Polly, if only we could go on dancing like this forever.

POLLY   You're pretty good really – for a beginner.

CECIL   (*archly*) You could give me dancing lessons.

POLLY   Would you like that?

CECIL   It would be . . . scrumptious.

POLLY   That's right. (*Laughing*) You're a card. I like a sense of humour. (*She begins to sing the words of the song.*)
>You made me love you,
>I didn't want to do it,
>I didn't want to do it,
>You made me love you . . .

CECIL   How appropriate!

POLLY   And all the time you knew it.
>. . . You made me happy,
>Sometime, you make me glad;
>But there were times, dear,
>When you made me feel so sad.

CECIL   Miss Polly . . . could we stop dancing now?

POLLY   Oh no, don't you love it?

CECIL   I can't talk and dance at the same time. It needs too much concentration. (POLLY *whirls across and turns off the gramophone.*)

POLLY   Well, and you were saying?

CECIL   Polly. You must know how I've been hoping –

POLLY   (*lightly*) While there's life there's hope – so they say.

CECIL   Hoping that . . . one of these days . . . you'd do me the honour of being my bride.

(POLLY *turns away. Enter* HARRY
TUESDAY, *right, much the worse for wear.
He sits under the monument with a bottle of
beer.*) Oh, I know you were in love with
Jack Tuesday, but he went away, under
suspicious circumstances.

POLLY   He went away to be an actor.

CECIL   With two women in tow . . . *(moving
towards her)* My dear Polly, how could you
ever take him back after that?

POLLY   No, of course I couldn't.

CECIL   No decent woman could.

POLLY   Of course not. *(Pause.* CECIL *moves
closer.)*

CECIL   Marriage is a big step.

POLLY   There's not many eligible men in
Mukinupin. No, let's face it, there aren't
any eligible men in Mukinupin. I could
hardly marry Harry Tuesday. *(She giggles.)*

CECIL   You probably don't think I'm eligible,
either. But I love you, Polly, I always have,
and I would make you a faithful husband.

POLLY   I know that . . . Cecil.

CECIL   And we could travel all round the
country. It's an interesting life.

POLLY   Almost anything's better than
Mukinupin.

CECIL   Then will you . . . marry me?

POLLY   I don't see why not.

CECIL   Does that mean yes?

POLLY   I suppose so. *(*CECIL *takes* POLLY *in
his arms. She is very unresponsive.)*

CECIL   Oh! Polly, my dearest, you have
made me the happiest man east of the
rabbit proof. Of course, I'll have to ask your
father formally for your hand.

POLLY   Well then, let's get it over with.
*(*POLLY *goes upstage and calls off)* Mother,
Daddy, Mr Brunner – I mean Cecil – has
got something to tell you! *(Enter* EDIE *and*
EEK *looking self-conscious.)* They must have
been listening outside the door. *(Amused,
she exits, tweaking* EEK's *ear. He looks
pleased.)*

EDIE   What was that, dear?

CECIL   Mr Perkins, may I have your
permission to ask your daughter's hand in
marriage?

EEK   Yes. But I don't like your chances.

CECIL   *(dignified)* She has already said, yes.

EEK   Well! Did you hear that, Mother? I'll get
out the cigars.

EDIE   Hear what?

EEK   Our Pol getting married to Cecil here.
*(*EDIE *bursts into tears and clasps* CECIL *to
her.)*

EDIE   Oh! Mr Brunner – Cecil – you've made
me the happiest of women.

EEK   Our Pol, grown and wed! It's hard for a
man to lose his only daughter.

EDIE   But we're not losing a daughter – we're
gaining a son. *(Self-conscious laughter.)* Give
Cecil a glass of strawberry cordial, Father.

EEK   Got nothing stronger. I'm a wowser –
and proud of it. *(They all drink their cordial.)*
A toast – to Cecil and Polly.

EDIE   To Cecil and Polly. Have you decided
on a long or a short engagement? I think a
spring wedding's always appropriate, don't
you? And it'd give her time to get her
trousseau together. I'll just run across and
tell Miss Hummer. She'll have to start in
sewing right away. *(*EDIE *stands dreaming
in the doorway.)* I can see her now in white
georgette embossed with lily of the valley,
an ivory train caught by a coronet of
pearls. We were married in the spring,
weren't we, Eek? I was a city girl. I'd never
seen the real country. At first we lived in
that tin humpy at the back of the store, and
I hung up all the family portraits, tinted to
kill. They stared down at us, night and day;
and sometimes I heard the dingoes howling
from the salt lakes and the blacks . . .
(shuddering) The willy-willies blew the dust
and the sheets of corrugated iron along the
main street. Sometimes I thought, "I'll die
of the loneliness" – but, of course, I didn't.
They were such long, hot summers; but I
must have got used to them.

*(*EDIE *exits dreamily.* HARRY *sings
drunkenly, unaccompanied.)*

HARRY

> New Holland is a barren place,
> in it there grows no grain,
> nor any habitation
> wherein for to remain.
>
> I'll plant her and I'll rape her,
> I will not run her down,
> upon her gold and torment,
> I'll build me shanty town.

CECIL   I think I ought to tell you, Mr
Perkins –

EEK   Call me Eek.

CECIL   That I do hope to keep Polly in the
manner to which she's become
accustomed.

EEK   Thank God we got rid of that young
loafer, Jack Tuesday. Not the other one,
though. He's still out there howling under

the war memorial. National disgrace! We didn't put *that* up to be desecrated. Oh, I know they tell me he's a hero, but I can't stomach it. Feller like him, disgrace to the town, danger to the women folk. *(They smoke their cigars and drink their cordial.)*

EEK   It's queer though, Cec. As one white man to another, have you ever noticed? Women *like* a bastard, stirs something in them – maternal instinct. But I'm glad our Polly came to her senses. She was sweet on Jack Tuesday, no doubt about it, proves what I just said. They all love a swine. Come on, Cec lad, and we'll join the ladies. *(EEK rises and moves front to stare up at the sky.)* Rain about. Just in time for the seeding.

CEC   Good for the crops.

EEK   Superphosphate will save us all.

(They exit back, chummily, as the sky darkens and the light changes towards an early rainy evening.)

HARRY
   She is my bitter heritage,
   she is my darling one,
   she drowns me in the winter
   and she breaks me in the sun

(TOUCH OF THE TAR enters dressed in the bedraggled finery of her former appearance, barefoot and dirty, trailing her broken parasol. She moves uncertainly centre.)

TOUCH OF TAR   That you, 'Arry?

HARRY   *(very drunk)* No. Who's zat, eh, who's zat?

TOUCH OF TAR   It's me – Lily.

HARRY   Lily . . . Lily who?

TOUCH OF TAR   It's Lily Perkins.

HARRY   Oo! We've got tickets on ourselves, haven't we? Lily Perkins, eh? *(Laughing wildly, he rises and staggers over to her.)* Why, it's ol' Touch of the Tar 'erself. But what's all this, eh! What's all this – flash clobber? *(He tears at her dress and it comes away in his hands.)*

TOUCH OF TAR   Me name's Lily Perkins. *(HARRY begins to push her across the stage.)* Don' you touch me.

HARRY   Why?

TOUCH OF TAR   'Cause you're an animal, thass why. You're a wild animal. Whadda you want, anyway? What you ever want from me? Same ting all the time, same ting.

HARRY   Your blood, that's what.

(More lightning flashes and the thunder begins to roll.)

TOUCH OF TAR   *(taunting him)* They reckon you're mad now, not right in the 'ead? *(HARRY circles her dangerously.)*

HARRY   Thass right.

TOUCH OF TAR   But you always was, I reckon, always was barmy, can't blame it on no war. Mad 'Arry Toosday.

HARRY   Stupid bitch! I'd like ter king hit you with this bottle.

TOUCH OF TAR   Why doncha then, you dingo? *(She skilfully dodges as he brings the bottle down on stage, smashing it off for a weapon.)*

HARRY   What are y', eh? You're a harlot, that's what y' are. You never been faithful to me. Tell me, go on. How many times. *(He springs at her, knocks her down and raises the bottle over her head, kneeling over her.)* Who'd you go with, eh? Who'd y' go with?

TOUCH OF TAR   Your bloody brother, that's who. I went with Jack. *(She laughs wildly.)*

HARRY   I'll kill the dirty crawler. *(He raises the bottle but changes his mind.)* Ah, you're shit, you stink, you're not worth markin'. What can you expect from a gin, anyway? A man 'd have to be mad. *(He gets up and staggers away to the memorial.)*

TOUCH OF TAR   Me name's Lily, Lily Perkins.

HARRY   Nick orf.

TOUCH OF TAR   I reckon I don't like you 'Arry . . . but I love you, by Jesus. *(No answer.)* Why didn't y' kill? I wanta die anyway. I come home ter die. *(Pause)* But I ain't got no home. *(There is a tapping of sticks, very softly. The bullroarer begins like an echo of itself, far away.* TOUCH OF THE TAR *listens, humming to herself, tapping on the stage with her broken parasol.)* Rain's comin' up. I heard the black cockatoos fly over. Then we'll sleep in peace, we'll break the drought. *(TOUCH OF THE TAR sits cross-legged centre stage to the beating of sticks, the bullroarer and the rolling thunder.)* You don't love me, 'Arry, an' I c'n do wivout you. I usta think I couldn't, that I'd die or somethink, but when the coppers come for you I never died, an' when you went to their bleedin' ol' war I never died neither, and 'ere I am still hangin' about on the edge of town . . .

(She laughs wryly and begins to circle in a

weird little dance, humming to herself, unfolding her broken parasol that hangs over her head like a parody. Her dance begins slowly, but gradually becomes wilder and wilder as the storm increases.)

TOUCH OF THE TAR'S SONG[16]

Lily Perkins is me name, the creek bed
  is me station,
It's no disgrace, 'cause me black face is
  the colour of the nation.
O boomerai an' mind her eye an' dance
  roun' in the bindi,
I got a boy in Mukerup an' one in
  Muckinbimbi.
Me Daddy is as white as flour, me Mam
  was black as coal,
an' then they comes, the Caflik nuns,
  an' taught me 'bout me soul.
I wish'd they'd left me in the creek
  where me ol' people dies,
the liddle child they found who cried,
  among the bindieyes.
I 'ad a liddle dream that I might catch a
  fallin' star,
but they took me down ter whitey town
  an' called me Touch o' Tar,
but when the wild duck cries at night it
  seems I gotta rise
with beatin' wings an' voice that sings
  out of the bindieyes.

(The rain begins. She holds out her arms to it like a fertility rite, and puts up her ragged parasol. HARRY hunches into a battered Army greatcoat.) It's rainin', 'Arry. The rain's come. (To the sound of rain and thunder she dances on.)

Lily Perkins is me name, the creekbed
  is me station,
I am the spirit of the place, the colour
  of the nation,
Oh! boomerai an' mind yer eye an' don'
  kick up a shindy,
we'll all waltz in and out agen an' dance
  the wild corroboree.

(During the song ZEEK enters, dressed as before, with lantern, telescope, etc.)

ZEEK   'Night, Lily. Creek's risin'.
TOUCH OF TAR   'Night, ol' Zeek. You make rain wiv that thing?
ZEEK   Only God makes the rain.
TOUCH OF TAR   But nothin' for poor Lily, eh? (She gives a sad little giggle as she moves off.) But never mind, 'Arry, we'll all die laughin', eh? (TOUCH OF THE TAR exits.)
ZEEK   Feelin' bad, Harry?
HARRY   Pretty crook! The booze has got me, an' the gas . . . poison gas y'know. (Pause.) There's a kind of bottomless horror, when the gruesome wind is blowin, and the ice is crackin' in the paddocks.
ZEEK   They reckon you won the Victoria Cross.
HARRY   Thass right.
ZEEK   What y' do with it?
HARRY   Give it ter Touch of the Tar for a fuck. (He explodes into laughter.) Nah, she wouldn't even take it, ignorant boong, I pawned it an' got shickered in Albany. I ain't never been back. (ZEEK is peering through the telescope.)
ZEEK   There's somethin', out in that creekbed – and, by crikey, it's Touch of the Tar.
HARRY   Ah, she can swim like a blackfish. She couldn't drown if she wanted to.
ZEEK   She's got a rock tied round 'er middle. She'll drown alright.
HARRY   Silly bitch, we all gotta die. Why don't she just wait 'er turn. I'll die – like a dog in the scrub.
ZEEK   She's goin' down alright.
HARRY   It's bloody freezin' in there. I'm not goin' ter catch me death ter save 'er black hide.
ZEEK   And she ain't comin' up agen.
HARRY   Ah! Bugger 'er. (But he is galvanized into action and races off.)
ZEEK   Water of life. Water of chaos. Water of destruction. The child in the womb is lapped with water, the pastures of the wilderness drip, the hills gird themselves with joy, the meadows clothe themselves with flocks, the valleys deck themselves with grain. We will irrigate the desert with the spring of living water, freshen the waters of the dead salt lake and make the well at the world's end swarm with fish . . . (HARRY staggers on carrying the dripping TOUCH OF THE TAR in his arms. Thunder and lightning.)
HARRY   Give us a hand here, Zeek. (ZEEK hobbles across and together they bring TOUCH OF THE TAR round.) She's comin' round.
ZEEK   Hey, Touch of the Tar!
HARRY   Don't call 'er that. She don't like it no more. She likes Lily. Pretty name, ain't it? Suits 'er too.

(TOUCH OF THE TAR opens her eyes and smiles.)

TOUCH OF TAR   You still mad at me 'Arry? *(Feebly she tries to sit up.)* It didn't work wiv Jack. Thass why I come back, okay?

HARRY   Okay!

TOUCH OF TAR   'E said 'e was an outcast, but he weren't 'nough of an outcast for me.

(HARRY pours some of the grog down her neck and she chokes and splutters.)

HARRY   There, get that inter y'. Better stuff than water.

(HARRY cradles TOUCH OF THE TAR tenderly in his arms as ZEEK goes back to his telescope.)

TOUCH OF TAR   'Arry, I got so tired.

HARRY   Of what?

TOUCH OF TAR   Of bein' the town slut, the town joke, the black velvet. You name it, I'm tired of it.

HARRY   We'll make it all right, Lil.

TOUCH OF TAR   *(happily)* You called me Lil.

HARRY   It's your name, ain't it?

TOUCH OF TAR   Do you love me, 'Arry?

HARRY   Die without y'. But I'm walkin' on ice with you, Lily. I always am. *(She shivers.)*

TOUCH OF TAR   Jeez, but I'm cold.

HARRY   Don't whinge. I can't stand a whinger. *(HARRY crosses to ZEEK's pack, takes a blanket and wraps her up carefully.)*

TOUCH OF TAR   When you was away . . . in them trenches . . . I usta think. 'E's out there . . . in the dark . . . callin' to me . . . like me ol' people . . . wonderin' why I don't never come to 'im. *(Thunder, lightning.)*

HARRY   They was all dead, every man Jack of 'em, lying out there in the moonlight, starin' up at the sky. I said, "Mate, how about givin' us a hand here?" then, "Hey! You bludgers, there's work ter be done", and then I knew, I was all on me pat malone.

TOUCH OF TAR   Will we get married, 'Arry?

HARRY   They called it, no man's land.

TOUCH OF TAR   I believe in God, do you?

HARRY   Didn't use to, but I wanta be square now, Lily, an' do the straight by you. We'll leave this rotten town. We'll go across them salt lakes with the quail risin' up under our feet . . . Hey, Zeek, know anythin' about this marryin' business?

ZEEK   *(alarmed)* Marryin'? Me? No, I never been a marryin' man.

HARRY   Me neither, but now I'd like . . . a bit of a ceremony. *(ZEEK scratches his head.)*

ZEEK   Eek's the lay preacher, but I was never much of a one for churches. Y'see I'm a *religious* man. *(He pauses, thinks.)* Hang on a minute. *(ZEEK rummages in his pack and pulls out a pocket Shakespeare.)* Just the ticket.

HARRY   What's that?

ZEEK   Will Shakespeare: merry, tragical, tedious and brief. *(He looks up towards the sky.)* Rain's easin', cloud's passin'. And now the moon like to a silver bow, new bent in heaven, shall behold the night of our solemnities. Go . . . bring the rabble. *(Enter silently the FLASHER, who takes ZEEK's hurricane lantern, lights it, and holds it up behind him. ZEEK rummages in his pack for a pair of battered glasses and places them solemnly on his nose. HARRY and TOUCH OF THE TAR kneel before ZEEK. There is the sound of a tapping stick and the weird night music begins, interrupted by the tapping sounds and the faint bullroarer.)* Highest Queen of State, Great Clemmy comes. I know her by her gait.

(Enter CLEMMY, ZEEK takes her arm.)

CLEMMY   Why has thou, Zeek, summoned me hither to this short grass'd green?

ZEEK   How does my bounteous sister? Go with me
   To bless this twain, that they may prosperous be,
   And honour'd in their issue.

CLEMMY   This is a most majestic vision, and Harmonious charmingly.

HARRY   For Christ's sake get on with it.

CLEMMY   Hush, and be mute,
   Or else our spell is marr'd.

ZEEK   Look down ye gods and on this couple drop
   A blessed crown, quiet days, fair issue and long life.
   Give me your hands, and by the merry rite of spring
   I charge you lovers you are eternally knit.

(ZEEK moves off to gaze in his telescope as HARRY and TOUCH OF THE TAR rise and embrace. The FLASHER and CLEMMY form an arch of gum leaves. HARRY and TOUCH OF THE TAR move ceremoniously under the

arch as CLEMMY and the FLASHER sing.
TOUCH OF THE TAR and HARRY move off
into the distance like a mirage over the
saltlakes. ZEEK has lost interest in the
proceedings and is back amongst the stars.)

THE MARRIAGE SONG

CLEMMY
Honour, riches, marriage-blessing,
FLASHER
Long continuance and increasing,
ALL
Hourly joys be still upon you
As we sing our blessings on you.
Earth's increase and harvests plenty,
barns and cradles never empty;
vines with clustr'ing branches growing,
wheat with goodly burden bowing.
Spring come to you from the farthest,
In the very end of harvest!
Scarcity and want shall shun you.
All our blessings now are on you.
Honour, riches, marriage-blessing.

(ZEEK jumps up and down in excitement.)

ZEEK (yelling) By the jumping bleeding
bloody Jesus I've found another planet.

(CLEMMY, centre, gazes wistfully after
HARRY and TOUCH OF THE TAR. She beats
with her crutch on the stage.)

ZEEK The stars are above, wherever we are.
We walk the earth and gaze into eternity,
we ride with Andromeda, see the holes in
heaven . . .
FLASHER And find the secret of perpetual
motion. (Exit the FLASHER murmuring to his
matchbox.) Marconi the Great one, speak to
me.

(ZEEK jumps up and down with excitement.)

ZEEK (yelling) By the jumping bloody Jesus,
I've found another planet!

(Exit ZEEK carrying the telescope. CLEMMY
moves to her wicker chair and sits, hands
folded. Lights up in the Perkins' parlour.
CLEMMY rises and comes forward to greet
POLLY, who enters in her wedding gown
carrying a portrait of JACK, followed by
CLARRY, fixing her train and EDIE fussing
after her with the bridal bouquet. POLLY
comes centre, looking melancholy and
exasperated, tugging at her veil and displacing
it as the two women fix it and CLEMMY tugs
her dress here and there.)

POLLY'S SAD WEDDING SONG

POLLY
They dress me up in my wedding
gown,
but the love of my life is out of town,
he's been out of town for many a day;
through autumn and winter and spring
he's away,
but the plover's song is still achingly
sweet,
like a wave of shadow over the wheat.

(Still holding the photograph, POLLY climbs
on the table with help from the women to
have her hem adjusted in a similar scene to
that in Act I.)

O Mother, dear Mother, I'm queen of
the May,
you woke me up early on my wedding
day,
but never again will I fall asleep,
to the song of the plover so achingly
sweet,
so put on my veil and give me my ring,
and teach me the song it is proper to
sing.

(To photo:)
I've something borrowed and
something blue,
but I haven't a thing that belongs to
you;
happy is the bride that the sun shines
on,
happy the crops that the rain rains on,
but I'd like to run on my leaden feet
like a wave of shadow over the wheat.

They dress me up in my wedding
gown,
but the love of my life is out of town,
he's been out of town for many a day;
through autumn and winter and spring
he's away,
but the plover's song is still achingly
sweet,
like a wave of shadow over the wheat.

(EDIE takes Jack's photograph from POLLY
and tosses it away. POLLY is helped down
from the table and stands waiting. Enter EEK
dressed in clerical collar and good black suit.
He gives POLLY his arm and they move off in
the direction of the Mukinupin Town Hall
with EDIE weeping and the two MISSES
HUMMER following. CECIL BRUNNER enters
through the Town Hall archway and stands

waiting, dressed in a morning suit. POLLY *is crying quietly.)*

ALL *(except* POLLY*)*
Don't be late for your wedding, dear
   Polly we pray,
Polly we pray, Polly we pray,
If your bridegroom is jilted he'll cry
   lack-a-day,
Cry lack-a-day cry lack-a-day,
Don't be late for your wedding, dear
   Pol.

(As they reach the Mukinupin Town Hall, POLLY *turns front to dry her eyes.* EEK, *very concerned, draws her aside.)*

EEK   My darling child, are you sure you're happy?

POLLY   Of course I'm happy, Daddy. Can't you see – they're tears of joy.

EEK   It's not too late to turn back.

POLLY   Too late, Daddy.

EEK   Better late than never. Oh Pol, a loveless marriage is a sin against the spirit.

POLLY   Isn't it possible to make the best of it?

EEK   *(sadly)* It is *possible.*

POLLY   I'll do it, then. All girls cry on their wedding day.

(She turns back, moves to CECIL's *side, smiling bravely.* EEK *leaves her side and, taking his prayer book from his pocket, mounts the steps in front of the Town Hall.)*

EEK   Beloved brethren of Mukinupin, we are gathered together here in the sight of God and in the face of this congregation to join together this man and this woman in holy matrimony instituted of God in the time of man's innocency. *(*JACK TUESDAY *and* MERCY MONTEBELLO *have entered far right, carrying their ports, and both dressed in the height of fashion. Nobody notices them.)* It is not by any to be enterprised and taken in hand lightly, unadvisedly or wantonly, but reverently, discreetly, advisedly, soberly and in the fear of God. Therefore if any man can shew any just cause why ye may not be lawfully joined, let him now speak . . .

JACK   *(coming forward)* Yes, I can. *(They all swing round.* POLLY *stares as if she had seen a ghost.)*

EEK   *(faintly)* . . . or else hereafter hold his peace.

JACK   I can't hold my peace.

EEK, EDIE, CLARRY AND CLEMMY   Why?

JACK   Because she doesn't love him.

EEK   Is that right, Polly?

POLLY   *(faintly)* Quite right, Father.

EEK   Then, why didn't you say so? It's too bad of you, Pol.

EDIE   *(angrily)* What's she say, what's she say?

CLARRY   *(shouting)* She won't marry Cecil!

EDIE   Oh, my God, my God, my smelling salts! *(She goes to faint and is supported to a chair by the* MISSES HUMMER. EEK *goes to minister to her.* POLLY *turns to* CECIL.)

POLLY   Mr Brunner – Cecil – I owe you an apology.

CECIL   It is a sad disappointment – Miss Polly.

POLLY   It's more than that. I've been cruel and dishonest and I should be punished for it, as I've no doubt I will be, Oh, Jack! *(*JACK *moves forward and takes* POLLY's *hands.)*

JACK   Marry me, Polly, that'll be punishment enough.

POLLY   But what about – Madame Montebello? *(*MERCY *laughs lightly.)*

MERCY   Why, my dear – I'm old enough to be his Ma.

POLLY   Yes, I know, but you're . . . so . . . beautiful.

MERCY   Thank you, I'm sure, but that doesn't alter the case.

POLLY   But I thought . . .

MERCY   A fertile imagination, Miss Polly, is no substitute for good sense.

CECIL   Hear, hear. *(*MERCY *smiles at* CECIL *and bows.)*

POLLY   And Touch of the Tar . . . ?

JACK   She ran away, back to Mukinupin, within a week.

MERCY   I'm afraid she just . . . didn't fit in. Oh, come, come, my dear, why don't you just take your Jack, and stop the cross examinations.

JACK   Merc, you've hit the nail on the head as usual. But what about . . . ?

MERCY   What about me? Why Jack – a comely woman can always fall on her feet, given the right set of circumstances.

CECIL   And they are, Madame?

MERCY   An eligible bachelor, and an eye for the main chance. *(*MERCY *makes roguish eyes at* CECIL *who is quite overcome.)*

CECIL   Oh, Madame Montebello, if you could only take a broken heart . . .

MERCY   And make it whole? Why certainly,

my dear, we could have a double wedding. *(She moves into his arms.)*

CECIL   I could hardly hope for such happiness. Miss Polly . . . ?

POLLY   I'm so happy for you, Cecil. So relieved for us all.

JACK   Me too. Put it there, Cec. (JACK *shakes* CECIL *violently by the hand.)*

MERCY   So now, if we could perhaps re-arrange ourselves. (POLLY *runs across to* EEK.)

POLLY   Oh Daddy, Daddy, I want to marry Jack, and Mercy wants to marry Cecil, so it's all turned out for the best after all.

CLARRY AND CLEMMY   Oh! Polly, how marvellous!

EDIE   What's she say, what's she saying now?

CLARRY AND CLEMMY   It's a double wedding, Mrs Perkins.

EDIE   Bigamy! Oh my God . . . the smelling salts, the smelling salts?

EEK   Are you sure you've got it right this time, Polly?

POLLY   Oh! Daddy yes, yes, absolutely scrumptiously sure.

EEK   What are your prospects, young man?

JACK   *(proudly)* I've got a contract with the Firm for three years at three quid a week in the second back row of the chorus and, we're off to tour Maori land in *The Maid of the Mountains* with Our Glad.

ALL   *(except* MERCY) Oh! Wonderful! What luck! Marvellous news, Jack! etc.

JACK   And there'll be a place for Pol, too, she's got great legs and we know she can hit a high C. Oh, Pol, Pol, we can go anywhere from here. Ziegfield is paying Evelyn Laye five thousand a week.

POLLY   Oh Jack, you're such a marvel.

JACK   *(grinning)* Just a Mukinupin boy and proud of it.

MERCY   Jack will go far, I promise you. *(Hastily)* And Polly too, of course.

JACK   It's all settled then.

(JACK and POLLY move off, arm in arm, MERCY and CECIL follow, EEK and EDIE, reconciled, follow and then the MISSES HUMMER, for the Wedding Dance.)

THE WEDDING DANCE

JACK

> Everything is turning up roses,
> Everything is turning out fine,

Man proposes and God disposes
To turn the water into wine.

There's a definite silver lining,
Blue skies don't turn to grey,
The sun will always come out shining
On a Mukinupin wedding day.

CECIL

> Mercy Montebello, will you marry me?

MERCY

> Why, Mr Brunner, *certainement* – ly.

JACK

> Polly Perkins, will you be my wife,
> To live together for the rest of my life?

POLLY

> To live together in a dream of love,

JACK AND POLLY

> To kiss and cuddle like a turtle dove.

EDIE

> Eek Perkins, will you give your daughter
> To be his ever loving bride?

EEK AND EDIE

> Through the storms of life and sunshine
> Walking gladly side by side,

ALL   *(chanting)*

> In sickness and health, for richer for poorer, for better or worse,
> To love and to cherish till death do us/them part.

EEK

> Those whom God has joined together let no man put asunder.

ALL   Everything is turning up roses,
> Everything is turning out fine,
> Man proposes and God disposes
> To turn the water into wine.

There's a definite silver lining,
Blue skies don't turn to grey,
The sun will always come out shining
On a Mukinupin wedding day.

(POLLY and JACK have danced over to the suitcases; the train whistle is heard off. As EDIE and EEK, CECIL and MERCY, and the two MISSES HUMMER wave, weep and throw kisses, JACK and POLLY exit, carrying the luggage as the song dies away . . .)

POLLY AND JACK

> On a Mukinupin wedding day . . .
> on a Mukinupin wedding day . . .
> on a Mukinupin wedding day . . .

EEK   *(to EDIE)* Dry your eyes, Mother. It's time to open up Perkins' General Store.

EDIE   Where's my Polly now?

EEK   Gone to make her fortune. She's a chip off the old block.

(EEK goes behind the counter and rings up his cash register. EDIE takes a feather duster and begins dusting the shop, and anything else within sight. The light begins to fail.)

EDIE   *(sniffing)*
Life is real! Life is earnest!
And the grave is not the goal;
"Dust thou art to dust returnest",
Was not spoken of the soul.
Lives of great men all remind us
We can make our lives sublime,
And, departing, leave behind us
Footprints on the sands of time.[17]

(CLARRY takes up the shop broom and begins purposefully to sweep the stage. CLEMMY hobbles to her wicker chair and fans herself with her sandalwood fan. CECIL strolls across, arm in arm with MERCY.)

EEK   I suppose you'll be off on the road again soon, Brunner?

MERCY   Certainly not. Cecil and I are opening up the best fish and chip shop in Mukinupin.

CECIL   Have another acid drop, my precious.

MERCY   Certainement, my love.

(MERCY and CECIL promenade, arm in arm, backstage to the scrim and stand as if posed forever in a photograph album. EEK rings up his last change in the till, and follows them to the scrim.)

EEK   Coming, Mother?

EDIE   I won't be long, Mr Perkins. *(EDIE hobbles out front, shading her eyes.)*

EDIE   *(reciting again)*
Art is long, and Time is fleeting,
And our hearts, though stout and brave,
Still like muffled drums, are beating
Funeral marches to the grave.

(She moves backstage, and she and EEK pose for their eternal photographs against the scrim.)

CLARRY   *(briskly)* Time to go, Clemmy. I've locked all the doors, swept the stage and blessed the place. *(CLEMMY rises painfully to her feet.)* Take my arm, dear, and we'll . . . whirl off into the dark. *(The weird night music begins on the sound track very faintly, as they move off.)* What about Polly and Jack?

CLEMMY   Oh, they'll never come back. They're playing *Chu Chin Chow* with Oscar Ashe and the camels.

CLARRY   And Harry and Touch of the Tar have gone bush over the saltlakes. Do you think they've found Paradise?

CLEMMY   Paradise is mighty hard to find.

CLARRY   Like Zeek Perkins fishing in the dust all the days of his life.

CLEMMY   He never found fresh water in Mukinupin.

(The night music grows in volume as CLARRY and CLEMMY take their immortal places before the scrim. Silence. A pause, then the FLASHER gives one of his unearthly screams from the creekbed.)

MERCY   And now the Mukinupin Glee Club of the Ladies' Auxiliary of the RSL presents . . . *(A drum roll as MERCY turns and gives it all she's got . . .)* THE MUKINUPIN CAROUSEL *(MERCY bows and they all sweep into the final song and dance routine. The dance should be circular and reconciliatory in mood.)*

ALL   Take a whirl on a carousel,
into the dark on a carousel,
deserts and stars have served us well,
so let's all ride on a carousel.

MERCY AND CECIL
Skeletons, acid drops, tea in china,
dry the dishes, what could be finer,
counting the sheep going into the pen,
counting them over and over again.

EEK AND EDIE
Fire and blood and sand and water,
the church bells toll for the
    storekeeper's daughter,
birth and magic and moth and rust,
close the curtain because we must.

CLARRY AND CLEM
Love-in-the-mist and salvation jane,
down in the creekbed praying for rain,
ring a roses and round we go,
close the curtain and end the show.

ALL   Take a whirl on a carousel,
into the dark on a carousel,
desert and stars have served us well,
so let's all ride on a carousel.

(The music plays faster and faster as they whirl into a total blackout, and darkness falls on Mukinupin.)

The End

Notes

1 *The Man from Mukinupin* makes many references to popular and classical works familiar to the reader, particularly Shakespeare. Besides detecting Lady Macbeth behind Edie's sleepwalking scene, the reader will recognise Montebellos' "The Strangling of Desdemona" as a travesty of *Othello* and the marriage ceremony of Miranda and Ferdinand from *The Tempest* in the "wedding" of Lily and Harry. Quotations from *A Midsummer Night's Dream* are also to be found, particularly in Zeek's speeches. Below are the sources of other quotations and pastiches which may be less easily identifiable.

2 Robert Browning, "How They Brought the Good News from Ghent to Aix".

3 Alfred Lord Tennyson, "Lilian".

4 Henry Lawson, "The Roaring Days".

5 Traditional song.

6 Thomas Babington Macaulay, "Horatius", in *Lays of Ancient Rome.*

7 A traditional West Australian anthem. The author is unknown.

8 After Tennyson.

9 An old English fertility chant, quoted in Richard Cavendish (ed.), *Man, Myth and Magic,* New York, 1970.

10 Harry Tuesday's song owes something to the traditional folk song, "Jim Jones".

11 Mary Gilmore, "The Aboriginals".

12 For the first verse and the thought behind "The New Holland Song" the author is indebted to Randolph Stow's character, Byrnie, in his novel *Tourmaline* (London, 1963). The last lines of *Tourmaline* read:
   Beware my testament!
   (Ah, my New Holland; my gold, my darling.)
   I say we have a bitter heritage.
   That is not to run it down.

13 Will Ogilvie, "The Australian".

14 A parody of the traditional folk song, "Flash Jack from Gundagai".

15 A traditional Diggers' song from the Great War.

16 Touch of the Tar's song owes something to the traditional folk song, "Old Black Alice".

17 Henry Wadsworth Longfellow, "A Psalm of Life".

8 Wendy Lill 1950–

The Fighting Days
Canada

Introduction

Wendy Lill grew up in Ontario, Canada, but has since lived in Manitoba and New Brunswick. Part of a new generation of women who influenced Canadian theatre from the 1970s, she has worked in documentary and film as well as drama. Her first play was *On the Line*, but she made her name with *The Fighting Days*. This was premiered in 1983 at the Prairie Theatre Exchange, in Winnipeg, Manitoba, the city where the play's action takes place in 1910–17. The narrative draws loosely on the novel, *Aleta Day* by Francis Marion Beynon (1884–1951), which Lill uses to dramatise certain features of the Canadian women's suffrage movement in relation to the 1914–18 War.

Aleta Day was published in London in 1919, by the pacifist, C. W. Daniel (who was also responsible for publishing two other anti-war novels, Theodora Wilson Wilson's *The Last Weapon* (1916) and Rose Allatini's *Despised and Rejected* (1918), both of which were banned). Semi-autobiographical, Beynon's novel tells of her own political development. It relates her childhood experiences of a bullying, incompetent Methodist father and her move from rural Manitoba to the city, to her growing awareness of patriarchal ideology. That awareness led to her conversion to feminism and the women's suffrage movement, and her pacifist stand during the movement's crisis over Canadian conscription during the First World War. Lill's play compresses these events, dropping the temperance argument of *Aleta Day* and somewhat melodramatic aspects of its plot, in order to concentrate on Beynon's real-life dilemmas over the war. However, she adapts Beynon's creation of a fictional romance in her book. This enables Lill to display women's emotional enslavement to patriarchal values, while highlighting the connections between wider feminist politics and personal decisions with regard to marriage, sexual choice and intellectual emancipation. *The Fighting Days* also incorporates letters which Beynon actually received and published replies to whilst working as a journalist. This extends the voices in the play, to express the concerns of ordinary women of the period and to demonstrate their growing war-fever.

Having trained as a primary teacher, Francis Beynon moved to Winnipeg in 1908 to join her elder sister, Lillian, who was working on the Manitoba *Free Press*. There she met the influential feminist, Nellie McClung (1873–1951), author of a best-selling novel of 1908, *Sowing Seeds in Danny*, and tireless campaigner for both temperance and women's suffrage. Lillian married Vernon Thomas, another journalist, in 1911. In 1912 Lillian became the first president of the Manitoba Political Equality League and that year Francis took over as women's editor for a popular newspaper, *The Grain Growers' Guide*. She used the opportunity to address the so-called "prairie wives" on feminist issues, frequently citing Olive Schreiner, and to argue her pacifist views. In January 1915, McClung, the two Beynon sisters and other members of the League took part in an uproarious stage production at the Walker Theatre in Winnipeg. Entitled *Votes For Men*, this was a role-reversal burlesque, in which McClung played the role which parodied the conservative, anti-suffrage Premier of Manitoba, Sir Rodmond Roblin. Following a campaign that revealed gross corruption in the existing provincial legislature, the liberals were voted in to replace Roblin. In January 1916, they extended the provincial and national franchise to women in Manitoba, together with the right to stand for election, the first province where this was achieved.

Figure 9 Members of the Political Equality League with its petition of nearly 40,000 signatures for the enfranchisement of women, presented to the Manitoba Legislature on 23 December 1915. In the front row, with Dr Mary Crawford, is Mrs Amelia Burritt, aged 94, who secured 4,250 names. Lillian Beynon Thomas is in the back row with Mrs F.J. Dixon. [Provincial Archives of Manitoba, N9905]

However, in June 1917, the Canadian Prime Minister, Sir Robert Borden, introduced a "Compulsory Enlistment Bill" in Parliament, to be followed by an election in December. This so-called "Khaki Election" was in effect a vote of confidence in military conscription and Borden altered the national franchise to achieve his aims. Whilst extending the vote to all women over 21 who had sons, husbands or brothers in uniform or who were themselves serving overseas, he disenfranchised all "aliens": immigrants from Eastern Europe (i.e. Germany or Austria-Hungary) who had arrived less than 15 years previously. This racist move, which effectively disenfranchised immigrant women, accentuated the Anglo-French split over conscription and divided the Canadian women's suffrage movement. It also

provoked a public rupture between the Beynon sisters and McClung who, proud her son had enlisted, fully supported the Prime Minister. Vernon Thomas was fired because of his anti-war stance, and moved to the USA with Lillian. Opposing conscription and racial discrimination, Francis was forced to resign her post in 1917 and also fled to New York. The novel was her written response to those events, expressing her "grief and anger over the militarism that swept through Canadian society and politics" (Hicks's intro. in Beynon 1988: xiv). She never lived in Canada again.

Thus, in recovering Canadian women's history by means of Francis Beynon, Lill chose certain key issues. These issues, concerning the divisive effect of the Great War on the women's suffrage campaign and the conflicts women experienced between patriotism and feminism, are shared by the history of women in other countries such as Britain, the USA and France. Women in Australia and New Zealand already had the vote by 1914, but they too suffered from the racism, ethnic prejudice and xenophobia encouraged by pro-war propaganda. Allied governments' so-called "intelligence units" used wartime censorship laws to impede the international women's peace movement. It was courageous of Lill to publicise these issues, which had arisen again in the 1960s and 1970s over the Vietnam War. Her play can be seen as a thoughtful rejoinder to an earlier feminist play by Diane Grant and Company: *What Glorious Times They Had: Nellie McClung, a Satire*, first performed in Toronto in 1974. Also based on the friendship between McClung and the Beynon sisters, Grant's play centred on the burlesque, *Votes for Men*, and stopped with Manitoba women gaining the vote in 1916. It thus evaded the war and the subsequent rift between the play's main characters. Lill's play, by passing from the outbreak of war in 1914 at the end of Act I, to Christmas 1916 at the beginning of Act II, slides over the provincial issues to focus on national and international politics.

However, both plays should also be set against two plays by Madeleine Greffard: *L'incroyable histoire de la lutte que quelques-unes ont menée pour obtenir le droit de vote pour toutes* (1980) [The incredible story of the fight which some women put up in order to get the vote for all women] and *Pour toi je changerai le monde* (1981) [For you I shall change the world]. These plays, performed in Quebec in the early 1980s, recount the struggles of early Quebec feminists. They would remind us that neither Grant nor Lill (let alone Beynon or McClung) alluded to the question of French-speaking feminists in Canada at the time of the Great War, despite the fact that in the 1970s the War Measures Act again resulted in the loss of liberties for many Quebec citizens. Not only French-Canadian feminists were drawn into the near civil war that erupted on both occasions. Whereas Canadian women won the right to vote federally in 1918 and most provinces had granted suffrage to women by 1925, in Quebec women did not gain the vote until 1940. Lill's play itself exemplifies its own

central problem: the difficulty of achieving political sisterhood in the face of nationalism.

Further reading

Primary

Beynon, Francis Marion (1919) *Aleta Day*, London: C. W. Daniel; reprinted (1988) with an introduction by Anne Hicks, London: Virago.

Chown, Alice A (1921) *The Stairway*, Boston: Cornhill; reprinted (1988) with an introduction by Diana Chown, Toronto: University of Toronto Press.

Craig, Grace Morris (1981) *But This Is Our War*, Toronto: University of Toronto Press.

Grant, Diane & Co (1976) *What Glorious Times They Had – Nellie McClung, a Satire*, Toronto: Simon & Pierre.

Lill, Wendy (1985) *The Fighting Days*, Vancouver: Talon.

McClung, Nellie (1915) *In Times Like These*, New York: Appleton; reprinted (1972) with an introduction by Veronica Strong-Boag, Toronto: Toronto University Press. (War essays)

—— (1945) *The Stream Runs Fast*, Toronto: n.p. (Autobiography)

Secondary

Cleverdon, Catherine Lyle (1950) *Woman Suffrage Movement in Canada*, Toronto: University of Toronto Press.

Gwyn, Sandra (1992) *Tapestry of War – a Private View of Canadians in the Great War*, London: HarperCollins.

Morton, Desmond and J. L. Granatstein (1989) *Marching to Armageddon: Canadians and the Great War 1914–1919*, Toronto: Lester & Orpen Dennys.

Read, Daphne (ed.) (1978) *The Great War and Canadian Society*, Toronto: New Hogtown Press.

Roberts, Barbara (1985) *"Why Do Women Do Nothing to End the War?": Canadian Feminist-Pacifists and the Great War*, Ottawa: n.p.

Socknat, Thomas (1987) *Witness against War: Pacifism in Canada, 1900–45*, Toronto: University of Toronto Press.

The Fighting Days

[A Play in Two Acts]
First performed at the Prairie Theatre Exchange, Winnipeg on 16 March 1983
Published Vancouver, 1985

Wendy Lill

Characters

FRANCIS BEYNON

LILY, her sister

NELLIE McCLUNG

GEORGE McNAIR, editor of *The Rural Review*

Act I

[Place and time]

Winnipeg 1910–14

Scene 1

Dark stage. Funeral music fading into the sound of a train. Lights up. FRANCIS, *18, and her sister* LILY, *25, are on the train.* FRANCIS *is looking out the window, lost in thought.* LILY *is crocheting.*

LILY   Do you think Father's up there right now watching us?

FRANCIS   I never really believed in that part. Did you?

LILY   No, I guess not. Some things just sort of stick with you. He said he'd be joining Grandpa in heaven the day after he died, so there'd be no point in trying to put anything over on him. *(She smiles.)* I remember you saying that if he was going to heaven, you didn't want to go there. That you'd rather go to hell.

FRANCIS   But I never really stood up to him. Had I been braver, Lily, I would have defied him.

LILY   You were braver than the rest of us. It was you Father went after. You seemed to bring out the worst in him.

FRANCIS   Why do you think that was?

LILY   Mother says it was your questions that made him angry. He thought they sprang from an "undisciplined spirit" . . . whatever that means.

FRANCIS   You know when he used to ask "are you right with God?" What did you say?

LILY   I said "yes" every time and then he stopped bothering me.

FRANCIS   But how does one know whether they're RIGHT with God?

LILY   I don't know, Fanny.

FRANCIS   Do you believe deep in your heart that Methodists are the only ones with immortal souls?

LILY   Not any more. Not since I moved to the city.

FRANCIS   What happened then?

LILY   I guess I started to think . . . bigger. I met people who believed in all sorts of things. Some of my friends are Presbyterians. Vernon, the young man I'm seeing at the newspaper, is an agnostic.

FRANCIS   An agnostic? I've never even heard of that church. What does he believe?

LILY   Well . . . he believes . . . well, he's not sure there really is a God . . . he's just not sure.

FRANCIS   *(concerned)* Oh.

LILY   But he's very nice, Fanny. He went to school in England. He reads a lot, just like you.

FRANCIS   If you like him, Lily, I'm sure I will. *(Silence)* Lily, what about the Catholics?

LILY   What about them?

FRANCIS   Are they all right too?

LILY   Yes, they're all right too.

FRANCIS   That's good. I always thought it was sad that Mrs Sawatsky was going straight to hell after raising all those kids. Lily, what do you remember most about him?

LILY   "Serve the Lord with fear, with trembling kiss his feet, lest he be angry and you perish . . . for his wrath is quickly kindled." There was always so much wrath.

FRANCIS   I'll always remember looking to see if his workboots were by the kitchen door. That meant he was in the house and I'd get that frightened feeling in my stomach. Lily, did you think he was ever going to die? I didn't. The horse died on its feet on the hottest day of the summer. Gippy and Rex crept off by themselves and died. I was scared that Mother would die in the yard with a load of wet laundry in her arms and that look on her face and I'd be left alone with him. I shouldn't have said that.

LILY   You can't help the way you feel. *(Squeezing her sister's hand)* Let's not talk about it any more. *(Pause)*

FRANCIS   Lily, does this mean I'm free now?

LILY   Free?

FRANCIS   Free. Free to sing in the house, push peas around on my plate, screw up my face, play cards, read books . . .

LILY   *(laughing)* All of those things! And Mother will be sixty miles away with Uncle George and not worrying over your soul any longer.

FRANCIS   Thank heavens!

LILY   I'm going to take care of you now. We'll get a nice bright room in the West End with elm trees out front. We'll go to picture shows and tea rooms and libraries . . .

FRANCIS   Libraries!

LILY   And you can meet my newspaper friends and join my suffrage club.

FRANCIS   Your what?

LILY   My suffrage club. Oh, you'll learn about that soon enough.

FRANCIS   *(looking doubtful)* Do you think I'll fit in?

LILY   Of course you will. You're going to love the city!

FRANCIS   Do you think so?

LILY   *(hugging her)* I do. And furthermore, the city will love you! Oh Fanny, you're a brick!

Scene 2

Women's Press Club. Sound of people climbing stairs, voices, NELLIE *and* LILY *enter, mid-conversation;* FRANCIS *follows behind.*

NELLIE   *(reciting)* "I do not want to pull through life like a thread that has no knot. I want to leave something behind when I go. Some small legacy of truth, some *word* that will shine in a dark place . . . " What word? What word? I want that word to be . . .

(They become aware there is no heat in the room.)

LILY   Warmth!

NELLIE   *(going to radiator and banging it)* Didn't Isobel pay our rent this month?

LILY   Maybe they think they can get rid of us by freezing us to death.

(LILY and NELLIE continue working on speech. FRANCIS walks around the room, fingering things.)

LILY   I would start the other way, Nellie.

NELLIE   With the alarm clock? You don't think McNair will call me a drippy tap in need of a washer?

LILY   Well, it would not be as bad as when he said you rattled along like an old tin can.

NELLIE   Or the time I squeaked along like a set of rusty bagpipes.

LILY   *(laughing)* But nothing will top the time he called Isobel as useless as a button on a hat. *(They all laugh.)*

NELLIE   The perils of public speaking!

LILY   You won't believe this fellow, Fanny.

FRANCIS   Who is he?

NELLIE   He's a wart on the nose of progress. He's a loose nut in a machine trying to go forward!

LILY   He's the editor of *The Rural Review*. We won't be much longer, Fanny. Anyway, I'd leave the alarm clock in. It's an idea that strikes people right between the eyes.

NELLIE   You're right. I'll leave it in. *(To FRANCIS)* Your sister gives me my best ideas, yet never gets any of the credit!

LILY   Nor any of the abuse. Suits me fine.

NELLIE   Whenever I see you, Francis, I seem to be working on some silly speech. There's more to life than that. I haven't even had a chance to get to know you. *(Indicating sofa)* I want you to sit down here and tell me all about yourself.

FRANCIS   There's nothing to tell.

LILY   Don't be shy, Fanny. *(To NELLIE)* She devours every book she can get her hands on. She knows more about newspapers than I do after four years at *The Free Press*. *(To FRANCIS)* You've got lots to tell!

FRANCIS   Well, I grew up on a farm . . .

NELLIE   So did I! We've already got something in common! When I was a girl, I loved to read books too, but I was always the first one yanked out of school to herd the cows. I would tear around from one field to another, chasing cows and hating every one of them!

FRANCIS   I felt exactly the same way!

NELLIE   Did you?

FRANCIS   But they had to be moved or they'd eat through all the grass.

NELLIE   Oh, I know they had to be moved, but I couldn't understand why I had to chase them all the time. It was always Nellie that had to do it. Never my brothers.

FRANCIS   But they had to go to school so they could handle the affairs of the farm.

LILY   But she wanted to go to school too! She wanted to learn to read.

NELLIE   I wanted to learn how to read more than I wanted to sing in heaven!

FRANCIS   But what was the point if you were just going to get married?

NELLIE   But if I was going to be a mother and a wife, wasn't I the most important of all? Didn't I have to be a light . . . a beacon?

LILY   With a husband and all those children in her care?

NELLIE   Just imagine, Fanny . . . imagine how wonderful it would have been if your mother had read Tennyson before you fell asleep at night . . .

> Willows whiten, aspens quiver,
> little breezes, dusk and shiver,
> through the wave that runs forever
> by the island in the river
> flowing down to Camelot.
>
> Four grey walls and four grey towers
> overlook a space of flowers
> and the silent isle imbowers
> the Lady of Shallot

FRANCIS   (entranced) That's beautiful! I always wanted to write . . . Just like you and Lily! I thought if I could write things down, they'd be clear to everyone . . . all the things I felt inside. I would be clear to everyone and I wouldn't feel so alone.

NELLIE   Did you ever try?

FRANCIS   Yes, but I didn't really have anything to say.

NELLIE   Don't ever say that, Francis! Not ever. Any woman with a mind, a pair of eyes and a heart, already has more than it takes to write for any newspaper in this country!

LILY   (laughing) Oh, Nellie!

NELLIE   That's a good line! I should use it somewhere.

FRANCIS   You make it sound so easy.

NELLIE   It's not easy, but it's worth the effort. Isn't it, Lill?

LILY   That depends on whether you ask me before or after my editor has torn apart my story.

NELLIE   Details. But the point is we women have finally got a chance to write for one another now. Do you agree?

LILY   I agree.

NELLIE   Good! (Turning to FRANCIS) Francis, we're not chasing cows any more. We've got no one to blame but ourselves for not doing what we want. Do you understand? (FRANCIS nods.) Which leads us back to the problem at hand, the speech for tomorrow night. You're coming, aren't you?

FRANCIS   Oh, yes, I'll be there!

NELLIE   Good!

Scene 3

The auditorium. FRANCIS *and* LILY *enter and sit down. A gentleman in his late thirties sits down beside them and takes out a notebook.* NELLIE *takes the podium. Applause begins.* FRANCIS *is riveted.*

NELLIE   My name is Nellie McClung and I'm a disturber. Disturbers are never popular. Nobody likes an alarm clock in action, no matter how grateful they are later for its services! But I've decided that I'm going to keep on being a disturber. I'm not going to pull through life like a thread that has no knot. I want to leave something behind when I go; some small legacy of truth, some word that will shine in a dark place. And I want that word to be . . . DEMOCRACY! Democracy for Women. Because I'm a firm believer in Women, in their ability to see things and feel things and improve things. I believe that it is Women who set the standards for the world and it is up to us, the Women of Canada, to set the standards . . . HIGH! (Applause) Maybe I'm sort of a dreamer, maybe I'm sort of naive . . . but I look at my little girls and boys and I think I want a different world for them than the one I was born into. I look at them and my heart cries out when I see them slowly turn towards the roles the world has carved for them: my girls, a life of cooking and sewing and servicing the needs of men; and the boys, scrapping and competing In the playground, then right up into the corridors of government, or even worse, the battlefields. I want them to have a choice about their lives. We mothers are going to fight for the rights of our little girls to think and dream and speak out. We're going to refuse to bear and rear sons to be shot at on faraway battlefields. Women need the vote to bring about a better, more equitable, peaceful society, and we're going to get it!

(Standing ovation. LILY and FRANCIS applaud happily. The gentleman looks on without enthusiasm. NELLIE comes over.)

LILY   You were superb!

FRANCIS   Oh, yes!

NELLIE   Was I loud enough?

MCNAIR   *(aside)* Excruciatingly.

(NELLIE notices him; stiffens.)

NELLIE   Why, Mr. McNair. I thought I saw a bit of tartan in the crowd. I hope you found my speech enlightening.

MCNAIR   It's always interesting to hear a woman speak in public. It's sort of like seeing a pony walking on its hind legs. Clever, even if not natural.

NELLIE   Well, I hope this time you'll manage to spell my name correctly. There are two c's. It is McClung, not McLung.

(MCNAIR gets out his notebook and corrects the spelling.)

MCNAIR   What a pity. I thought that was a rather good play on words.

LILY   *(steering NELLIE away)* Let's go and find Isobel to see what she thought. Help yourself to some lemonade, Fanny. I won't be long.

(NELLIE and LILY exit. FRANCIS goes over to a refreshment table. MCNAIR follows.)

MCNAIR   At least I can be assured of a little refreshment at these events. Saves the evening from being a complete waste.

FRANCIS   I thought her speech was wonderful.

MCNAIR   She rattles along like an old tin can. And she repeats herself. She said the same thing at the Walker Theatre last week.

FRANCIS   It sounded spontaneous to me.

MCNAIR   That's a knack she's got.

FRANCIS   Well, why did you come a second time if you thought so little of it the first?

MCNAIR   I'm a reporter. I never give up hope.

FRANCIS   A reporter?

MCNAIR   The name's McNair. George McNair.

FRANCIS   The editor of *The Rural Review*.

MCNAIR   *(flattered)* That's correct. Does your husband take *The Review*?

FRANCIS   I'm not married. But if I was, I'm sure he would, since it's the best farm paper this side of Kingston.

MCNAIR   What's in Kingston?

FRANCIS   *The Advocate*, of course.

MCNAIR   *The Advocate*? It's a rag!

FRANCIS   I disagree.

MCNAIR   It's a liberal propaganda sheet . . . and it's weak on markets.

FRANCIS   You're weak on crop summaries.

MCNAIR   You don't say? May I be so bold as to ask your name?

FRANCIS   Francis Beynon. Francis Marion Beynon.

MCNAIR   Ah, I see. You're the one who writes for *The Free Press*.

FRANCIS   No, that's my sister Lillian. She was the one with Mrs McClung. They're very close friends.

MCNAIR   Well, she's not a bad little writer.

FRANCIS   Oh, Lily's very good. But don't you think her paper's soft . . . soft on facts, soft on the truth, soft on banks, soft on the railways . . .

MCNAIR   . . . but hard on farmers.

FRANCIS   And even harder on suffragists.

MCNAIR   Oh, you're one of those, are you?

FRANCIS   Yes, I guess I am.

MCNAIR   Well, I'd better go and write this up.

FRANCIS   I'm curious, Mr McNair. Why didn't you send your women's editor tonight?

MCNAIR   Couldn't. She went and . . . passed away.

FRANCIS   Oh, I'm sorry to hear that.

MCNAIR   Well, she was over seventy. She wouldn't have taken to this type of event much either. Anyway, she's history and I'm stuck without a living soul to attend these interminable meetings!

FRANCIS   Perhaps you might think of hiring someone with more modern ideas.

MCNAIR   Easier said than done, little Miss.

FRANCIS   Perhaps you might think of hiring me.

MCNAIR   You? Hiring you? I don't even know you.

FRANCIS   Sir, I come from a farm and I am a woman. I know all about bedbugs and woodticks, runny eyes in chicks, cracked tits on milkers, cakes without eggs . . . and how to avoid the minister's visit.

MCNAIR   I'm sure you do.

FRANCIS   My grammar's good. Lily taught me how to type. And I wouldn't wallow in sentimentality like that last one. No offence meant.

MCNAIR   Miss Beynon, you're making a speech. It's unwomanly.

FRANCIS   It's not unwomanly, Mr. McNair. It's 1912. And I'm simply trying to interest you in my qualifications.

MCNAIR   (interested) Well, perhaps you should try to interest me in the cold light of day. Shall we say nine o'clock tomorrow morning? Mind you're not late!

FRANCIS   No!

(MCNAIR walks towards the door, then turns.)

MCNAIR   And don't forget to bring your lunch.

(He exits.)

FRANCIS   (to herself) I think I've got myself a job!

Scene 4

FRANCIS approaches the desk, sits down, and begins to write her first editorial. She is tentative.

FRANCIS

To the Women of The Rural Review:

It is my great pleasure to begin my new task as editor of the homemaker's page. I have lived on a western farm myself and when I was a girl, rode the calves home from the pasture and chased the wild geese off the wheat fields back of the granary. In my mind's eye, I can still see my mother, standing alone against the faraway fields of wheat, sun hat in hand, her skirts blowing away with the wind, looking for a rare visitor to come down the road. I now know that she was only one of the thousands of lonely women of the prairies . . . far from neighbours, far from towns, far from doctors.

Within this page, I hope you will all be able to get closer to one another. I hope you will begin to see this as YOUR page, where you can write and think and dream and rage . . . and in every way, help one another.

The page is now YOURS.

Francis Marion Beynon

(Throughout the play, women of the prairies will respond to FRANCIS' editorials through letters.)

WOMAN

Dear Miss Beynon:

This is my first letter to your homemaker's page – though I've had talks galore with you up here . . . (Pointing to head) I live on the prairie with not many neighbours but I'm really not at all lonely. I had a serious operation last May and then a few weeks after, our little house and everything in it burned down. But in the midst of it all, God has blessed us with another little baby. (Weak smile) Our eighth. So life is never dull. Could you please send me your little booklet "How to Tell the Truth to Children?" It is comforting to know that children can be told . . . the truth, and still retain the cleanness of thought and purity we wish for them. I've enclosed 5 cents for postage. My husband says what a rigmarole letter . . . though I can't write in a hurry . . . so please forgive.

Your sincerest reader, Sunbeam

Dear Miss Beynon:

I got something to say to your reader – Titewad's Wife. I have had three husbands and I think you got to have three husbands before you gets your fair av'rige. My first was terrible thin. My second was terrible fat. Men run that way. Always one thing or the other. Either terrible drinkers or don't drink at all. Either terrible tempers or no tempers at all. Some as cheap as pig dirt, others with an open hand. Don't see how us women folks stands 'em. Men's upsesses and downsesses has wore me out. My third husband was just plain av'rige. He just wasn't one thing or another. He was just so ordinary I couldn't stand him any longer and I divorced him. So to you lady I say, it's only after you have three husbands you know what you really want, and that's no husband at all.

Always Yours, Chucklehead

Scene 5

The Women's Press Club. FRANCIS *is answering letters from her readers.* LILY *and* NELLIE *are helping.* NELLIE *is pregnant.*

FRANCIS *(holding up letter)* How do you remove warts from animals and humans?

LILY Apply the water you pour off beans after they're boiled soft.

FRANCIS *(reading)* I am five months pregnant and I have a terrible time lacing my corset good and tight. Any suggestions?

LILY That's your department, Nell.

NELLIE Tell her to throw her corset in the closet. That's what I've done. *(Patting her stomach)* Otherwise, our children will grow up with a terror of small rooms.

FRANCIS Is there any way to lengthen the life of my stockings?

LILY Tell her to rub paraffin on their soles.

FRANCIS What is the best colour of paint to go with oatmeal wallpaper?

NELLIE Either bone or brown.

FRANCIS Do I have any advice on how to keep baby chicks in the pink?

NELLIE For heaven's sakes, Francis, you don't have to answer everything. Give that one to the Hen Department at the paper!

FRANCIS *(laughing)* There is no Hen Department. I don't know how I'd answer all of these without you.

NELLIE Well, we wouldn't want you to lose your job.

LILY Don't worry, Fanny, you'll be able to answer this kind of stuff in your sleep in no time.

NELLIE I have better things to do. Let's stop now and practise.

FRANCIS There's just one more. "Would someone be so kind as to tell me how I can clean feathers. I have an owl and would be very pleased if I could find out how to clean it?"

NELLIE An owl? Is it a dead owl?

LILY What would anyone want with a dead owl?

FRANCIS "I have an owl" is all she, wrote.

LILY Maybe she wants to clean it out, then cook it.

NELLIE Cook an owl? How disgusting.

LILY No, I think it must be a stuffed owl if she's interested in its feathers. It's probably been sitting on her mantelpiece for years and the feathers are dirty.

NELLIE Cornstarch, then. How would you cook an owl anyway?

LILY Probably just like a duck.

NELLIE But there wouldn't be much to it, would there?

FRANCIS Maybe she has a pet owl . . . like some people have pet crows.

NELLIE Animals don't need anyone to clean them. They clean themselves. I wish people would be more precise.

LILY It must be dead, then. Tell her to rub the feathers in cornstarch and, if by chance, she wants to eat it, tell her to clean it out like a duck and cook it with lots of spices.

NELLIE Great! Let's get on with the practice.

(NELLIE cranks up the Gramophone. FRANCIS puts away her papers. NELLIE hands out scarves, begins to demonstrate the dance.)

LILY Don't strain yourself, Nell. You might shake it loose.

NELLIE Would that be so terrible?

FRANCIS and LILY Nellie!

NELLIE Well, I've had four already. How many does a modern woman need? My Jack is already 15. How about you and Vernon?

LILY I would like three but Vernon thinks it would interrupt his concentration.

NELLIE I think Vernon concentrates far too much! *(They laugh)* And you, Francis?

FRANCIS No one will even want to marry me.

NELLIE Don't be silly! Come here and I'll show you how to do this. *(FRANCIS gets up, moves about awkwardly at NELLIE's tutelage.)* This is an interpretive dance. You just let your body move in whatever way you feel. It's very naughty. I saw it at the Palladium last time we were in London. They go mad for dancing over there. If the British suffragists can do it, so can we. Imagine you're a swan.

FRANCIS I feel like a prairie chicken!

NELLIE Close your eyes. It helps you forget about yourself. Stick out your hips, Fanny. Farther.

FRANCIS If McNair could see me now. He thinks it's queer for a woman to speak in public!

LILY What's he going to think when he sees us doing an interpretive dance at the Press Club Christmas party? *(They laugh).*

NELLIE Maybe he'd go back to Glasgow where he belongs, working for some reactionary tabloid. He's like a Scotch thistle bristling for a fight. And you know, he drinks.

LILY   Don't be too hard on McNair. Fanny doesn't mind him. She told me that under all that bluster is a good heart.

NELLIE   Well his mind skids when it comes to suffrage! And he drinks.

LILY   (laughing) You've already said that! I think your mind skids when it comes to McNair.

FRANCIS   He's not that bad, Nellie.

NELLIE   What's good about him?

FRANCIS   Well . . . he wears plaid earmuffs to work on cold mornings. And sometimes during the day, I can hear him in his office humming to himself . . . "Bonnie Dundee".

NELLIE   Francis, you've taken a shine to him. He's almost old enough to be your father!

FRANCIS   No, I haven't.

NELLIE   Then why are you blushing?

FRANCIS   Because I feel preposterous doing this dance.

LILY   (coming to her rescue) You're doing fine. Here, let me fix your scarf.

NELLIE   I think she's going to miss you when you marry Vernon. Who will do up her buttons and make her hair nice?

LILY   She can look after herself.

NELLIE   Well, now that we've got warts and matching wallpaper out of the way, we'll have to get her working on the larger issues. Tomorrow you can come along to my Women for Peace Committee. We've started a world disarmament campaign, and then, after that, we'll drop in on the Christian Temperance meeting. We can always use new recruits, Francis. It's always the same old girls on everything.

FRANCIS   I'd love to come.

NELLIE   Good. All right now, let's all three try it together . . . from the top.

(Music crossover into next scene.)

Scene 6

The newspaper office. FRANCIS is practising her dance step. The door opens; she hears MCNAIR approaching. She slides back behind her desk. MCNAIR enters.

MCNAIR   Let's see what you've got on your page this week. (He pulls the page out of the typewriter and begins to read aloud.) "We have too long been contented with the kind of motherhood that can turn its back on mere children toiling incredible hours in factories making bullets and ammunition and uniforms for some faraway war and yet calmly say, 'Thank God it's not my children.' What we need now is a new spirit of national motherhood." And someone who can write shorter sentences. National motherhood. National motherhood? You make it sound like the railway, Miss Beynon.

FRANCIS   (deflated) I quite liked that expression.

MCNAIR   Is it yours?

FRANCIS   Well . . .

MCNAIR   It sounds like something off of Mrs McClung's bat. You seem to have an opinion about everything lately. National motherhood, intemperate husbands, the German war machine, the profession of parenthood, the Boy Scout movement, and suffrage ad nauseum. But I find myself wondering . . . what happened to your columns on mothers and babies, ginger snaps and peonies? What about the little crocheted sweaters for the wee ones. Hmmmm? What about those things? They're important, too.

FRANCIS   Do you think they are more important than freedom from cruel husbands and fathers, from hypocritical ministers, from war-mongering politicians?

MCNAIR   Oh, don't bludgeon me with adjectives. Just say what you mean.

FRANCIS   I'm sorry.

MCNAIR   Unfortunately, the things you mention will always be with us. Scotch broth and shortbread and a garden full of bluebells make them a bit more tolerable. My mother knew that. She would never have bothered herself with voting and chasing men out of bars.

FRANCIS   But was she happy?

MCNAIR   Happy? I don't know. She seemed content. She smiled a lot.

FRANCIS   You mean she just put up with it.

MCNAIR   Perhaps. But the point is, she had enough to do in the home. You'd be wise to keep that in mind.

FRANCIS   If you think that women belong in the home, why did you hire me?

MCNAIR   I had no choice. What self-respecting man would want to write about "women's things"? Unfortunately, you don't seem interested in writing about them either.

FRANCIS   Mr McNair, are you not finding my work satisfactory?

MCNAIR   Did I say that?

FRANCIS   You imply that.

MCNAIR   I do not. I think that the suffrage question is . . . interesting, but you take it much too far. Mrs McClung need only pen one of her silly little verses and it somehow finds its way into your editorials.

FRANCIS   Mrs McClung is at the forefront of the suffrage cause.

MCNAIR   She is a dilettante and a debutante. And a hypocrite. She's an upper class snob who wouldn't have given my poor mother the time of day.

FRANCIS   That's not true. Nellie McClung is fighting for the vote for women.

MCNAIR   For women who don't need the vote. For women who've got something better than the vote! Influence! And furthermore, the proper lineage!

FRANCIS   No!

MCNAIR   No? Then tell me why your suffrage club list is full of names like Steward, Titheradge, Ward, Galbraith, Gordon, and not . . . Lewycky, Schapansky and Swartz?

FRANCIS   Well, maybe their husbands won't let them come.

MCNAIR   They're not there because your suffrage club doesn't want them there. Neither do they want them living next to them on Chestnut Street nor their children sitting beside theirs at school.

FRANCIS   Mr McNair, I believe in democracy for *all* women. I do!

MCNAIR   Then you're in the minority. Isobel Graham has gone on record saying she's afraid the entire western hemisphere is sinking under the weight of the immigrants.

FRANCIS   Isobel has . . . a blind spot.

MCNAIR   And Laura McLaughlin, another one of your leading lights, is heading up the fight to eliminate any foreign language in the schoolyard.

FRANCIS   That's because Laura thinks it's important that newcomers learn English.

MCNAIR   That's because she hates the very idea of them.

FRANCIS   I admit there are some members who don't feel comfortable with all the strangers in our midst, but that will change. It takes time to alter attitudes. It takes time to remove the walls of class and privilege and ethnic differences that . . .

MCNAIR   Oh, don't start that again! The fact is the suffragists are an exclusive club. And you'd do well to stay away from them.

FRANCIS   I find it curious how you suddenly spring to the defence of foreign women. Because in the year that I've known you, you have never shown interest in *any* women having the vote, whether their name was Gordon or Schapansky! I'm beginning to think that you just enjoy muddying the waters!

MCNAIR   *(winking)* I enjoy arguing with you. You argue like a man!

FRANCIS   Well, I am not.

MCNAIR   And I'm glad you're not.

FRANCIS   *(flustered)* I believe in the vote for women, all women, and I am going to keep fighting for it.

MCNAIR   Now don't get so flustered. It's not that important, is it?

FRANCIS   Mr McNair, let me try to explain something to you. When I was a child, on the farm, I was constantly asking questions. Does God ever change his mind? Why was he angry all the time? Why couldn't I talk to the Polish children on the next farm? Why didn't my father help them out like the other neighbours? But nobody wanted to answer my questions. There seemed to be a secret fraternity at work that I didn't understand. My father and the Methodist minister and later my teachers thrashed and sermonized and ridiculed me until my spirit shrank and I began to doubt my very worth.

MCNAIR   It doesn't seem to have been a lasting affliction. You seem to have quite an unswerving confidence.

FRANCIS   Well, I don't. I still cower at the voice of authority. Even now, I tense up as you, my editor, come into the room. Do you understand what I'm talking about?

MCNAIR   Yes, I think so, but I'm not sure what it has to do with suffrage.

FRANCIS   Oh, but it's all connected! When I came to the city, I met women fighting for the freedom to think and worship and question for themselves. Women who challenge authority . . . who look it right in the eye and say, prove you're worthy of respect! I felt like I'd been let out of prison. I felt like a great gleam of sunlight had broken through the fog. And I didn't feel alone any more!

MCNAIR   You're a funny one. You remind me of those little birds I found trapped in the house when I was a child. My mother would make me catch them and let them go free outside. And whenever I caught them, I could feel their little hearts beating in my hand, and I wanted to tell them not to be afraid, that I wasn't going to hurt them. You're like one of these little birds. Miss Beynon, I understand you live alone since your sister married. Perhaps you might be needing someone to look in on you once In a while.

FRANCIS   I would like that very much.

MCNAIR   Good, then. 1 will do that. It's time you associated with someone who still holds womanhood sacred.

FRANCIS   No! I don't need anyone to hold womanhood sacred. I hold womanhood sacred myself. I do!

MCNAIR   Well, you hold it at quite a distance. It might help your cause if you applied some rouge to your cheeks occasionally. Good day, Miss Beynon, I'll let you get back to national motherhood.

(MCNAIR *exits*. FRANCIS *sits down a her desk and begins typing angrily.*)

FRANCIS
    Men say that women have enough to do in their homes without worrying about going to the polling station. I have been doing some thinking about this. Prairie women have been trapped too long inside the home, lonely and dependent from the day they wed till the day they die. And yet, aren't we as necessary to prairie society as the sun and the rain are to the fields? Don't we deserve to be seen as whole people, with the same rights and responsibilities as the men we work beside? That's why I want the vote, because a vote is like being given a voice when before we were silent. It s like being set free after years of captivity. In the end, isn't what we're really talking about – freedom? I think so. But I've talked long enough. Please write and tell us what freedom means to you.
                                        F.M.B.

WOMAN
    Dear Miss Beynon
    Some go to the Bible for proof that woman should not have the freedom to vote. I can see nothing there to convince me that women have no interest outside her house. The very fact that God placed Eve outside in his big garden and not inside the four walls of a kitchen ought to prove she was intended to be a companion to her husband and to see and understand whatever interests him.
    I have to thank you and your sister Lily and Nellie McClung for all the wonderful work you're doing in elevating women to their rightful place as queen of the home.
                        Sincerely, Western Sister
P.S. Could any of the readers tell me how to take rust out of a white dress?

Dear Miss Beynon:
    Freedom for me would be a public restroom in town. A place where a woman could go after a long trip in from the country. Please work on that.
                                        Sunflower

Dear Miss Beynon
    I agree with you that freedom would come with getting the vote. If women had it sooner, there wouldn't be so many laws on the books which are a disgrace to civilization . . . not to mention humanity.

Dear Miss Beynon
    I am 31 years old, the mother of 7 children, the eldest 11 years, the youngest 8 months. I would like to have any information I can get about birth control. That would be freedom for me.

Dear Miss Beynon
    With all this talk of women's freedom, maybe there's something you're forgetting. And that's the foreigners. Haven't we got enough trouble with them over there, without letting them think they can run our country too? Can we bear dilution by the ignorance, low idealism and religious perversity of the average foreigner? I say no! We must keep them back. Give us good sound British stock women, already civilized, already subject to both earth and heaven for conduct.
                                        Wolfwillow

FRANCIS   I have to take exception to a recent view from Wolfwillow about immigrants within our country. It seems tragic to me the number of people, who without being able to give a single reason, instinctively hate or fear or distrust every person who does not belong to the same race or religion as themselves. What is the harm of people being different? Is anyone who is original in their thinking really so frightening? *(LILY is reading remainder of editorial at the beginning of the next scene.)* If our country of Canada is going to achieve its potential as a great nation, we must begin to recognize the contributions of people from all lands who decide to make it their HOME.

For my part, I would say that the real foreigners are not those who have been raised in different countries, but those whose standards and ideals of life are so immoveable as to not allow for communication with others.

Scene 7

The Women's Press Club. LILY *is reading* FRANCIS' *editorial in the newspaper.* NELLIE *is seated.*

LILY   It's beautiful, Fanny.

FRANCIS   You mean that?

LILY   Yes I do! I knew you'd put your heart and mind to work and come out with something that rang absolutely true! *(Hugging her)* She's quite a girl, isn't she, Nell?

NELLIE   At least she doesn't come to us for advice on hens any more.

LILY   Is that all you've got to say?

FRANCIS   Do you like it, Nell?

NELLIE   I'm surprised that McNair let you run such an idealistic little piece.

FRANCIS   He said he thought it was sort of . . . hopeful.

LILY   Well it is hopeful, and I'm proud of you! Nell, aren't you?

NELLIE   She's a quick learner.

FRANCIS   Nellie, do you like it?

NELLIE   Like it? I think the sentiments are admirable, but I wonder if it takes everything into account.

FRANCIS   What do you mean?

NELLIE   Such as what's going on in Europe right now. Some of the countries where these foreigners hail from are rattling their sabres at Britain even as we speak. People are frightened. God only knows what might happen over there. That's all, Fanny.

LILY   Well, I think we should go have an ice cream to celebrate her efforts.

NELLIE   You two go along. I've got some work to finish first.

(LILY and FRANCIS leave. FRANCIS is crestfallen.)

Scene 8

FRANCIS' *suite.* FRANCIS *is straightening things and looking in the mirror. She is nervous. The doorbell rings; it's* McNAIR.

FRANCIS   Good afternoon, Mr McNair.

McNAIR   Good afternoon, Miss Beynon. I hope I'm not disturbing you.

FRANCIS   No, not at all. Won't you come in.

McNAIR   I guess you're wondering why I dropped a note about visiting today.

FRANCIS   I thought perhaps you were going to be in the neighbourhood.

(McNAIR takes a letter from his pocket and hands it to her.)

McNAIR   Not exactly. Here's a letter I received from a group of your readers from Minnedosa. It seems they take exception to your column on the foreign question. *(FRANCIS reads, looks upset.)*

FRANCIS   I thought it was the most heartfelt thing I'd written.

McNAIR   It was mercifully short of adjectives.

FRANCIS   It sounds as if they hate me.

McNAIR   Not you, Miss Beynon, just what you're saying.

FRANCIS   Maybe I was a bit outspoken. Even Nellie seemed cool when she read it.

McNAIR   Did you believe in what you wrote?

FRANCIS   Yes

McNAIR   Well then?

FRANCIS   *(reading on)* They're asking for my resignation. That's why you've come, isn't it?

McNAIR   I wouldn't be much of an editor if I could be intimidated by bigots such as these. I follow a hardy little gleam myself called freedom of the press. You're doing a good job, Miss Beynon. I'm not saying I agree with everything you write. Believe me, I don't. I'm not a big reformer, as you know. But as long as you write with fairness and reason, and punctuation . . . I'll back you. I came to tell you that.

FRANCIS   *(indicating the letter)* But what about this?

McNAIR   Forget about the letter. Your column obviously struck a chord in some of your readers, and they didn't like the sound of it. But that's not your problem.

FRANCIS   Except that I have this tight feeling in my stomach that I haven't felt since I was a child.

MCNAIR   If you want to be liked by everyone, you're in the wrong line of work.

FRANCIS   Perhaps I am.

MCNAIR   Don't say that. You'll grow a thicker skin in time. Look at me.

FRANCIS   Is that what that is?

MCNAIR   I think you're a fighter, and when the occasion arises, you'll come out strong.

FRANCIS   Thank you. I hope you're right. Could you stay for a while and have some tea?

MCNAIR   That would be lovely, Miss Beynon.

FRANCIS   Please call me Francis.

MCNAIR   All right, Francis, please call me McNair. (FRANCIS *exits to kitchen.*) How does one occupy one's time when not fighting for women's rights?

FRANCIS   I've been known to go to concerts in the park and even some plays. Lily and I have been to every tea room in the city. Sometimes her husband Vernon takes us out to the country in his roadster.

MCNAIR   Perhaps some afternoon you might enjoy a trip up to Winnipeg Beach. I hear it's a popular spot with the fashionable crowd. Though being seen with me would perhaps not be quite so fashionable.

FRANCIS   (*re-entering with tea tray*) I would be delighted to be seen with you.

MCNAIR   Perhaps some time the two of us could go to church . . . or did the fierce God of the Methodists scare you off altogether?

FRANCIS   No, I've made my own truce with God. In fact, I met God one afternoon in a corner of the pasture.

MCNAIR   Did you?

FRANCIS   I'd gone out before a thunderstorm to find the cows. I remember looking all around and seeing nothing but a few shacks between me and the faraway edges of the world. Then over the east, a snake of fire wiggled down the sky, followed by a crash of thunder. Then a breeze stirred my hair and I felt I was riding on the wings of a bird. I knew God passed by in that breeze because for a moment, I wasn't afraid of anything – not my father, or the minister, or doing compositions, or Lily's warts . . . or anything at all.

MCNAIR   I don't know whether you're a heathen or not, but you breathe a clean wholesome look upon life. My mother would have liked you, Francis. Perhaps getting that letter wasn't so unpleasant after all. It's given us a chance to . . .

(MCNAIR *notices an orange sash on a chair, with the words VOTES FOR WOMEN. He goes over and picks it up.*)

MCNAIR   What trumpery is this?

FRANCIS   That's my sash for the suffrage parade.

MCNAIR   Your sash?

FRANCIS   Yes. We're all wearing them . . . for effect.

MCNAIR   Surely, Francis, you're not going to make a spectacle of yourself like that?

FRANCIS   Well, that all depends on what one calls a spectacle.

MCNAIR   I call an army of matrons marching down Main Street in orange sashes a spectacle. My God, you'll have the whole city staring gape-mouthed at you. Laughing and hooting and hollering. It's outrageous.

FRANCIS   Now wait a minute!

MCNAIR   A whole generation of women being turned upside down, turned into shrill opinionated harpies, when they should be at home, having lots of good strong children!

FRANCIS   Like a bunch of good breeding hogs!

MCNAIR   There' s nothing wrong with good breeding. And there's not enough of it happening any more. Instead, we're being swamped by a bunch of immigrants who don't even know "God Save the King". None of you ladies seem to care that we'll be at war in a month, and there'll be real armies marching down Main Street.

FRANCIS   Of course we care, but we can't just drop women's suffrage because a bunch of countries can't settle their differences.

MCNAIR   You're a babe in the woods.

FRANCIS   And you're a . . . you're unspeakable! You're everything that people say about you.

MCNAIR   Well if what you mean is that I don't delude myself and that I'm not a dreamer, I suppose you're right.

FRANCIS   Well, I am a dreamer! And I believe there are changes coming. Wonderful changes . . . that will allow everyone to live in freedom. Those days are coming but we have to fight for them.

MCNAIR   There is something very wrong

with you. I would not permit my wife, if I had one, to carry on the way you do.

FRANCIS   Well I would certainly not permit my husband, if I had one, to substitute his conscience for mine! Good day, McNair!

(With a melodramatic sweep of her hand, she indicates the door. MCNAIR *leaves.* FRANCIS *picks up the sash, turns it over in her hands, looks miserable.)*

Scene 9

At the suffrage parade. FRANCIS *is standing in the crowd, listening to* NELLIE *speak. The atmosphere is jolly, excited.*

NELLIE   *(with megaphone)* All right, sisters, you've got your instructions for the parade. Afterwards, we're invited to Government House for tea and sandwiches with the Premier and the Mayor of Winnipeg. You look beautiful out there. We've come a long way, sisters. The day has finally arrived when we've beaten back the bigotry which says that men are better than women. This day strikes a blow for social equality!

(The suffrage march begins. It is a victorious moment. FRANCIS *is in the midst of it, elated.)*

FRANCIS   Oh I am thankful to be living in these fighting days, when there are so many things waiting to be done, that we have no time to sit and feel sorry for ourselves, when Humanity is seething and boiling and stirring with a thousand conflicting interests, which in the end will work themselves out to the final good of the race. And we women have just begun to dabble with our fingertips in this great eddying stream of life!

(Suddenly the suffrage music turns into military music. Parade sounds become the sound of heavy boots. The expression on FRANCIS' *face changes from victory to confusion and fear. A drill sergeant calls out "Company, halt!")*

Act II

[Time and Place]

Winnipeg, 1916–17.

Scene 1

FRANCIS *is in her apartment. It is Christmas time. She is writing her Christmas editorial, 1916.*

FRANCIS   The Christmas edition of *The Review* will have to go out this year without a Christmas editorial on the women's page. Vainly I have tried to call up the old jubilant spirit of Christmas . . . without success. To observe this great celebration, while Christian Europe is busy contradicting its teaching "Peace on Earth, Good Will to Men", seems almost a sacrilege. The pen writes haltingly and unconvincingly upon the subject . . . and finally stumbles and stops altogether.

(Light up on LILY, *seated on the sofa, rolling bandages.* FRANCIS *is pacing.)*

LILY   We took bones last night. It's astonishing how many ways there are of being injured. We learned that anything ending in "itis" is an inflammation. First aid is a rude sort of thing. You just grab an old gent's cane or umbrella for splints and a lady's clothing for bandages. Carrie Markham says she just knows she'll be wearing her best and Frenchest lingerie when she'll have to tear it into bandages for some poor private.

Then we did drowning . . . with a REAL man to demonstrate. In one method, you have to hold the tongue of the drownee out with a handkerchief. The tongue is a rather slippery member. Sometimes one has to put a needle through it to keep it outside the mouth. That's in case there is a lot of blood in the throat. . . .

FRANCIS   Lily, what are you talking about?

LILY   My first aid class.

FRANCIS   The war is three thousand miles away. Why are you taking first aid?

LILY   It's good to be prepared.

FRANCIS   Prepared for what?

LILY   Prepared in case we have to do our bit.

FRANCIS   Are you off to France to save men . . . drowning on the battlefield?

LILY   Of course not.

FRANCIS   Is the conflict going to spread to Canada?

LILY   That's not the point.

FRANCIS   Then what is the point of these endless first aid classes? To me, it all seems . . . daft.

LILY   Everything seems daft to you lately. Even what I'm doing!

FRANCIS   That's 'cause you're doing the strangest things. (LILY *gets up to leave.*) Where are you going?

LILY   I shouldn't have come. I hoped maybe we could talk about . . . just talk . . . but you're being . . . oh, I don't know how to describe it!

FRANCIS   I'm sorry, Lily. Please don't go. I need to talk, too.

LILY   All right then. You start.

FRANCIS   Lily, do you remember when Ned Stone's father came back from the Boer War? He said he'd seen British soldiers rounding up women and children and putting them in compounds. He said he saw them dying like flies. I walked home across the field, trying to imagine people dying like flies . . . you and Mother and Mrs Gregory and the Hawkin girls . . . Lily, that's what's happening over there! Last month, one hundred thousand men died in one day!

LILY   I know. I read the paper.

FRANCIS   Lily, what do you really think of the war?

LILY   I don't want to think about it.

FRANCIS   Why not?

LILY   It gives me a headache.

FRANCIS   (*exasperated*) Well, that's a small price to pay compared to some!

LILY   There you go again!

FRANCIS   I'm sorry. It's just that I look at those boys on the parade ground. They're almost too young to shave yet, but there they are, marching around, waving their bayonets, making funny noises, jumping to attention. It all seems so . . . pointless.

LILY   How can you say that? They're fighting for democracy, so that you and I can live in freedom. Isn't that what they're fighting for?

FRANCIS   So they say. I heard Vernon talk last night at the Labour Temple. I thought you'd be there.

LILY   I couldn't miss my class.

FRANCIS   Couldn't pass up splints and tourniquets to hear your husband speak out against the war?

LILY   I know what he said. He gave me a private rendition last night when he came home. The British peers own part of the armaments plants in Germany. The first guns captured from the Germans were made in England. The only people who will win the war will be the munitions makers. Conscription is a violent attack on the rights of the individual. . . .

FRANCIS   Well?

LILY   Well . . . it makes sense . . . and I believe him. But I just don't know how to put it all together . . . what Vernon's saying, what others are saying. I . . . it would be a lot easier if he wasn't giving public lectures.

FRANCIS   Lily! Vernon has a right to speak in public.

LILY   Except that half the paper won't talk to him now and the copy editor checks my stories twice before they go to press. He assumes I think like Vernon.

FRANCIS   Well, don't you?

LILY   Well, yes, but . . .

FRANCIS   Then you've got to stand up for him, Lily! You've always fought for people's right to express themselves. The issue here is freedom!

LILY   But I thought it was freedom that we're fighting for over there? Well, whatever it is, there are millions of young men going out and fighting for it. How can they all be wrong?

FRANCIS   But how can you ever be free by killing people or being afraid that someone's going to kill you?

LILY   I can see why Father hated your questions.

FRANCIS   Now's not the time to be quiet, Lily. My God, even McNair's not hoodwinked by all this flagwaving hysteria! He's getting his teeth into war graft and profiteering.

LILY   Well that's fine for him. He's too old to have to worry about it.

FRANCIS   What do you mean?

LILY   Conscription is coming, Fanny.

FRANCIS   Lily, is that what you're worried about? Vernon wouldn't go, would he?

LILY   No. He's a pacifist.

FRANCIS   Well, that's good, isn't it?

LILY   I suppose.

FRANCIS   You don't sound happy!

LILY   I am. I am. It's just that if he won't go, does that make him . . . a coward?

FRANCIS   Do you think he's a coward?

LILY   No. But I think . . . if Vernon won't go, what about Nellie's Jack? He enlisted the day he turned eighteen.

FRANCIS   Oh, I hate this!

LILY   So do I! *(She bursts into tears)* Isn't it strange, Fanny. One day we're collecting signatures for the vote, and the next, we're signing people up for the patriotic fund. I can't even remember any more who signed what. Last July at Nellie's cottage, Vernon was playing ball with Jack on the beach, and all of us were lolling in the hammocks . . . I don't know what to think any more, Fanny. I'm trying not to think. That's why I'm taking these silly classes from women in red, white and blue dresses. I have to DO something!

FRANCIS   *(going over to comfort* LILY*)* I know, Lily. *(The doorbell rings.)* That must be McNair. He's early. I'll be right back.

*(*MCNAIR *enters, sees* LILY*)*

MCNAIR   Lily! *(Noticing she is crying)* I hope I'm not interrupting something. I could go away and come back later.

LILY   No, please don't leave on my account. I'm all right now.

MCNAIR   I just thought I'd peruse the papers in pleasant company before we went to the party. *(He sits down on the sofa and opens the papers.)* Just pretend I'm not here. *(Awkward pause.)* Here, this will cheer you up! *(Reading)* "The Boer War has brought us the khaki brown and the mopish scout hats, and just as we were feeling at home in these sombre shades, war was declared in the Balkans, and that brought us, blessedly, I might add, those pretty peasant waists and rich, bright-hued embroideries of the southern climes. Let's hope we never to go war with the Eskimos." Fantastic mind behind that report.

FRANCIS   Why would that cheer us up?

MCNAIR   Well, at least neither of you is responsible for it. *(*FRANCIS *laughs.)* Listen to this. *(reading)* "The patriotism of those war manufacturers who are skinning kin and country with their faulty gear and second-rate boots is the kind that should be recognized by a coat of tar and feathers. But instead, they'll probably get a title!" My God, that man can write!

FRANCIS   Who wrote it?

MCNAIR   I did!

*(*LILY *and* FRANCIS *both laugh.* LILY *collects her things.)*

LILY   Oh, you're a ray of sunshine on a cloudy day, McNair. I'm going home to get ready now.

MCNAIR   *(standing)* We'll see you later then.

*(*FRANCIS *goes to the door with her. They hug.)*

FRANCIS   We'll see you soon.

*(*FRANCIS *comes back into the room and starts pacing.* MCNAIR *watches.)*

MCNAIR   You've got a bee in your bonnet.

FRANCIS   Would you ever think of fighting in the war?

MCNAIR   It's a bit late in the day for me to enlist.

FRANCIS   But if you weren't too old, would you even consider it?

MCNAIR   I suppose I would.

FRANCIS   Why?

MCNAIR   Why? Because it's getting bloody hard to stay out of it! If you're of age and not in uniform, women look at you as if you're not quite complete. And the men simply hate you.

FRANCIS   But why is that? What business is it of theirs? It's your life!

MCNAIR   Am I coming in on the tail end of an argument?

FRANCIS   Yes, you are. I'm sorry. *(She sits down beside him.)*

MCNAIR   If I was younger, I would go to war, Francis. I have a responsibility to fight for the freedom of my country.

FRANCIS   What does that really mean?

MCNAIR   Well, it means to protect our homes, our loved ones . . . our women. Men are supposed to sacrifice their lives for women. Haven't you noticed? Since the war started, I haven't heard a peep from your Women for Peace Committee. Why do you think that is?

FRANCIS   They're knitting socks and rolling bandages.

MCNAIR   But why do you think that is?

FRANCIS   I don't know. I don't know.

MCNAIR   Because when it comes right down to it, women need protection, and they know it. At least most of them do. And that's why they swoon into the arms of the first waiting soldier.

FRANCIS   Why do you say things like that to me?

MCNAIR   I can't resist. Your cheeks colour up in such a pretty way.

FRANCIS   Well, I'm tired of knitting socks. It's time to DO something!

MCNAIR   All right. Put on your coat and we'll go to the party.

FRANCIS   I'm serious.

MCNAIR   You've taken some pot shots at the Patriotic Fund. You're always haranguing us about the treatment of foreigners. *(FRANCIS dismisses this.)* My editorials started the ball rolling towards the investigation on rotten boots. I think we're doing our bit by keeping the war honest.

FRANCIS   McNair, I remember my first column about the war. *(Recollecting)* "We women will keep our purpose clear – true democracy – and with our purpose, transport our men, our country, through the troubled waters of war!" I saw womanhood as some great unsinkable ship which would buoy up everyone!

MCNAIR   That's an admirable image.

FRANCIS   Except that it was wrong! We thought we were sailing the vessel of freedom, but there seems to be a thousand others out there with the same claim. How can freedom take so many forms? I don't know what to think any more. Lily's on the verge of tears all the time and Nellie's a flagwaving patriot. We've got the vote now, but we're too anxious or terrified to figure out what to do with it. The letters I get are filled with war and loss and fear . . .

MCNAIR   And while you're at it, you're the worst of all! You're constantly brooding over every war report as if you'll learn something new by counting up the stacks of dead.

FRANCIS   You're right. I am the worst of all. I feel so utterly useless!

(MCNAIR puts his arm around her, leads her to the sofa.)

MCNAIR   Come here and sit with me. You can't do anything more than you're already doing. War is always hard on high-strung women.

FRANCIS   That's a fine remark.

MCNAIR   It was meant by way of comfort. I know it's hard on you.

FRANCIS   And not on you. In your heart, you believe this war is right, don't you?

MCNAIR   Of course it's not right. War is never right. But God almighty, woman, it's Christmas Eve. Can't you just be content to watch the candles flicker and the snowflakes fall? Do you have to notice every tragic face, every heinous act? Why can't you just notice . . . me!

FRANCIS   I'm sorry, McNair. I do notice you. All the time. I do!

MCNAIR   Well then, why don't you try to imagine a little house with a garden full of bluebells, and a trellis and a little baby in your arms . . . a little pal. That's what I do. Makes me feel better.

FRANCIS   You're such a romantic.

MCNAIR   And what's wrong with that?

FRANCIS   Nothing, except why do you always picture me in a garden with a baby? Do you think I'd be happy just doing that? If I stopped thinking altogether?

MCNAIR   Well, give it a try. Just put your wee mind to it . . . little pink and white gurgling bundles . . . tiny fingers . . .

FRANCIS   *(laughing)* Oh, how unfair that men can't give birth! You'd be such a perfect mother.

MCNAIR   Oh, the world is too unfair.

(They kiss.)

Scene 2

The Press Club Christmas party.

LILY   And now for a bit of light entertainment from the carefree sisters of the typewriter and the interrogation mark. Nellie McClung, with our assistance, will give her musical rendition of her much loved poem . . . LET'S PRETEND.

NELLIE   *(accompanied by LILY and FRANCIS:)*

> Let's pretend the skies are blue,
> Let's pretend the world is new,
> And the birds of hope are singing all the day.
> (CHORUS) All the day!
> Short of gladness, learn to fake it,
> Long on sadness, go and shake it!
> Life is what you make it, anyway.
> Let's pretend the skies are blue,
> Let's pretend the world is new,
> There is wisdom without end . . . in the game of
> Let's Pretend!

(MCNAIR applauds. The three women join him.)

LILY   That was splendid, Nellie!

FRANCIS   Oh yes! *(To MCNAIR)* Wasn't it?

MCNAIR   A frothy little delight, I must say.

NELLIE   A rare compliment!

MCNAIR   As rare as your rhymes!

FRANCIS   Shall I pour the lemonade?

NELLIE   Thank you, dear.

LILY   There will be no bickering tonight . . . and no talk of the war. Is that clear? This is a Christmas party.

MCNAIR   I'll drink to that.

NELLIE   You would.

MCNAIR   And where is your better half tonight, Nell?

NELLIE   At a patriot drive.

MCNAIR   And yours, Lill?

LILY   (reticent) At an anti-conscription rally.

MCNAIR   Well, thank God some of us are doing something irresponsible tonight . . . (Awkward silence) I heard a funny story the other day. In the spring, they're going to build a roof garden on the legislative building. To supply fresh cut flowers for the politicians.

FRANCIS   The cabinet ministers can go up and take some air on their roof farm!

LILY   It will be quite inspiring to see Premier Norris in overalls doing his agricultural duty.

(They laugh. Another awkward silence.)

FRANCIS   There's a new play at the Walker I want to see.

LILY   What's it called?

FRANCIS   It's called The Guns of . . . oh, we'll talk about it another time.

(Another awkward silence.)

LILY   I hear Sadie Vaugh is expecting!

FRANCIS   That didn't take long.

NELLIE   I think that's called war-risk insurance.

MCNAIR   More lemonade, Nell?

NELLIE   Please.

MCNAIR   I don't hear much about suffrage now that you've got the vote. I guess you can't blame every social ill in Manitoba any longer on your political disability.

NELLIE   Well, we still haven't got the federal vote. But it's coming.

MCNAIR   Yes, so I hear. But when it does, you'll find the privilege as empty as last year's bird's nest.

NELLIE   We'll see.

MCNAIR   You'll end up choosing between two scoundrels, one not much better than the other. I've often felt, when I vote, that I'm not exercising much more political influence than the horses that haul me to the polling station.

NELLIE   Nor probably much more intelligence.

MCNAIR   You're being rude, Nell.

NELLIE   And you're being patronizing.

FRANCIS   You're both being . . .

LILY   (to FRANCIS) Themselves.

MCNAIR   I'm simply telling your friend not to feel badly that she hasn't turned the world around.

NELLIE   We closed the bars.

MCNAIR   Aye, that you did. Deprived many a young lad one last good belt before going off to the slaughter.

NELLIE   (angrily) Don't talk like that about our boys!

LILY   Please don't fight, you two.

MCNAIR   It would have done them no harm . . . the odd nip. You should try it yourself sometime!

FRANCIS   The music is starting up. Why don't we dance.

NELLIE   You're disgusting!

MCNAIR   And you are a hypocrite!

NELLIE   I am not!

MCNAIR   Aren't you? Then tell us why you told the Prime Minister to exclude foreign women from the upcoming federal election. So much for women's suffrage!

FRANCIS   That's not true!

MCNAIR   I read it in the Free Press.

LILY   Nell, you didn't tell me.

NELLIE   There wasn't time. He was only in town for a couple of hours.

LILY   But you could have called . . . .

NELLIE   Well, I didn't. And it's done. McNair likes to sensationalize. I simply suggested that the foreign women be excluded as a temporary war measure. A war measure. It's not a new idea. Let's not ruin our evening.

LILY   McNair, will you dance with me? I need some time to clear my head.

(MCNAIR and LILY exit. FRANCIS and NELLIE are left in stunned silence.)

FRANCIS   There was a speech you made once about leaving a word behind to shine in a dark place. It was years ago. Do you remember?

NELLIE   There've been so many, they kind of float together.

FRANCIS   It was at the William Avenue Library. It was a summer night. Lily and I walked there from our suite on Arlington. I smelled lilacs; the man next door was out watering his lawn . . . his wife was sitting

203

on the verandah, watching, rocking . . . .
You said that night . . . I want to leave
some word behind to shine in a dark place
. . . and I want that word to be democracy.

NELLIE You have a good memory.

FRANCIS I was so moved by that statement,
I would have jumped off a cliff that night, if
you'd asked me.

NELLIE You've been a hard worker.

FRANCIS I don't understand anything any
more, Nellie. Help me!

NELLIE Oh, Francis, there was a reason for
this. I suggested excluding the foreign
women only until the war is over.

FRANCIS But what does the war have to do
with it?

NELLIE Francis, there are districts where
almost every single English-speaking man
has enlisted. The moral tone of the
electorate has drastically changed.

FRANCIS Moral tone?

NELLIE The only way to protect our . . .
traditions . . . is to limit the vote to Empire
women.

FRANCIS But don't the foreign women have
the same "traditions"? Justice, love,
equality? How can you turn your backs on
them . . . if you truly believe in women?

NELLIE (with difficulty) It's not that simple.
The foreign community . . . does not view
conscription favourably.

FRANCIS Oh, I see! How efficient you are! If
one doesn't view conscription favourably,
then lop off their vote or their heads,
whichever is easiest!

NELLIE You make me tired, Francis. You
were a raw green girl from the country
when I first met you, too scared to open
your mouth without your sister's
prompting. It was Lily and I who brought
you out, who. filled you with every ideal
you have today. And you dare to stand
there and question me on what's right and
wrong!

FRANCIS But this is wrong! What you're
doing is a total contradiction!

NELLIE Oh, don't tell me about
contradictions. You have no right. You
have nothing to lose in this war. You know
nothing of the pain and nausea I feel when
I read the casualty lists. You moon around
over that drunken tory who'd rather have a
woman strapped to the sink than marching
in a suffrage parade. You have no right! It
is I who is paying every minute this war
continues. We have to end it, don't you

understand! We have to win this wretched
horrid war!

(FRANCIS *is stunned into silence;* NELLIE *is
shaking. The music stops.* MCNAIR *and* LILY
return.)

FRANCIS What about Women for Peace,
Nell?

NELLIE Stop it.

FRANCIS Was that just another phrase that
flowed off your tongue?

LILY Fanny, don't talk like this! Please!

FRANCIS Did you ever really believe we
could stop war or change anything at all?

NELLIE Of course I did! I do!

LILY Stop this!

MCNAIR Francis, calm down!

FRANCIS Why are you all trying to shut me
up!

MCNAIR There's nothing anyone can do
about the war now! Germany declared war
on Britain. We couldn't have stayed out of
it. We have a responsibility to the mother
country.

FRANCIS Don't we have a responsibility to
our children . . . to build a peaceful world?
Isn't that what we've always believed, Nell?

NELLIE: I believe that freedom still has to
be paid for. It's like a farm that has to be
kept up. Another instalment of the debt
has fallen due. That's what I believe.
There's a private in the Princess Pats who
carries my picture in his cap, Francis.
There are times when the doubter is
intolerable!

(FRANCIS *looks from one to the other, then
walks out.*)

Scene 3

FRANCIS *is at her desk at the paper, writing an
editorial.*

FRANCIS

When a coincidence of engagements
brought Sir Robert Borden and Mrs Nellie
L. McClung to Winnipeg together recently,
McClung made use of the opportunity to
ask the Prime Minister to grant the federal
franchise to all British and Canadian born
women, excluding the foreign women.

In this, Mrs McClung was speaking for
herself alone, and not for the organized
women of the suffrage provinces. I hope
that the majority of the women who fought
and won the suffrage fight, on the ground

that democracy is right, still believe in democracy.

Personally, if I had a religious faith or a political conviction which wouldn't stand the test of a great crisis, and which had to be discarded whenever an emergency arose, I would rise up and take it out and bury it in a nice deep grave and pray that it might have no resurrection day!

For my part, I believe in democracy just as invincibly today as I did in the yesterday of my own political minority, and if a serious attempt is made to exclude these new women citizens from the franchise, my tongue and pen will do their little best by way of protest.

F.M.B.

(FRANCIS opens her mail.)

WOMAN
Dear Miss Beynon
You say that Mrs McClung was speaking for herself alone, but I say her instincts as a patriot told her the right thing. My husband Jake and our three sons are in the war now and they're all of voting age. Yet their voices won't be heard. The foreign women have their husbands safe and sound by their sides and we all envy them. They may think differently and they may not, but how can we be sure? I think perhaps we should not take the chance.

Sincerely . . . Lonely at Home

Dear Miss Beynon
I think that Lonely at Home should have five votes, not just one! One for herself and four for the manhood she has sent off to war! And I say, more power to Mrs McClung's elbow! You say you believe in democracy. Well democracy means government by the people. In this crisis I say British people! Shall our men go and fight the Hun across the sea while their country is being turned over to a foreign power? A thousand times NO!

Fiercely . . . Wolfwillow

(FRANCIS puts down the letters, gets up and puts on her coat.)

Scene 4

The train station. Sounds of the train sighing and hissing. FRANCIS *is helping* LILY *with her suitcases. They are both agitated, upset.*

LILY Vernon took the two big suitcases when he left last week. I've got my hat boxes. I guess that's everything. *(Looking lost)* That's all, I guess.

FRANCIS *(handing her a book)* I've brought you a book. Carl Sandburg.

LILY Thank you.

FRANCIS Have you eaten? They probably won't serve lunch till one.

LILY I've just had breakfast. I couldn't eat another thing.

FRANCIS I made you some cookies to have with tea.

LILY Thank you.

FRANCIS Did you write Mother and give her your new address in New York?

LILY No. Could you do that, Fanny?

FRANCIS Oh, Lily!

LILY Fanny, please!

FRANCIS What should I tell her?

LILY Tell her Vernon's been offered a good job in New York and couldn't pass it up. Do you think she'd believe that? Tell her I'm going to be the new editor of *The New York Times*. Oh, I don't know what to tell her!

FRANCIS Why not tell her the truth? That Vernon walked onto the floor of the Legislature to shake hands with the only politician with enough courage to make an anti-conscription speech.

LILY Don't tell her that.

FRANCIS And for that he was fired! So you decided to go to a country where democracy still means something.

LILY Oh, I should have done it myself.

(NELLIE arrives and looks from one to the other.)

NELLIE Hello, Francis. *(To LILY)* Lily, I wanted to say goodbye.

LILY Oh, I'm glad you came. *(They hug.)*

NELLIE Here's a book for the train.

LILY Kipling! Fanny brought me Sandburg. *(She looks from one to the other.)*

NELLIE Have you had anything to eat? It takes forever for them to serve lunch. Here's some biscuits.

LILY Fanny brought me some cookies! The two of you will have me rolling off the train in New York. *(Looking from one to the other)* Well, here we are. The carefree sisters of the typewriter and interrogation mark. Any parting shots? *(She grabs both of their hands.)*

FRANCIS I still don't know the difference

between baking soda and baking powder. I'm going to send the hard questions on to you in New York.

NELLIE   I'll never forgive Vernon for taking you away.

LILY   Vernon had no choice, Nell. No one will hire him here now. At least in New York, he can write about what he believes.

NELLIE   You mean he can make a mockery of what our boys are fighting for!

FRANCIS   That's not what he's doing!

LILY   Please, please, let's not talk about Vernon. Let's talk about ourselves. Can we? I feel so helpless right now. It used to be we'd talk about love and sisterhood . . . now we only talk about death and destruction. Will you take care of Fanny while I'm gone, Nell?

NELLIE   Of course I will.

FRANCIS   I'll be fine on my own.

NELLIE   You're very hard on people, Francis. When the war is over, we'll get the suffrage issue straightened out and there'll be a vote for everyone. Believe me, just like we've always dreamed. When the war is over.

CONDUCTOR   (offstage) All aboard!

FRANCIS   Have you got everything, Lily?

NELLIE   I have to go. I've got two meetings before lunch. It never ends. Write big long letters. Goodbye, Lily.

(LILY and NELLIE hug. NELLIE exits.)

LILY   She was apologizing to you and you wouldn't accept it. I understand how Nellie feels. She supports the war because her son is fighting in it. She has no choice. But that's no reason to turn your back on her, your best friend, your teacher, just because she didn't meet your high standards. How arrogant you are!

FRANCIS   But she gave up her dream.

LILY   No she didn't! She just lost sight of it for a while. It happens to all of us, and it will happen to you. You'll marry McNair and have children, and you won't be so eager to pick up a banner or lead a parade. You'll shift your zeal and compassion to those you love . . . and the dream won't seem so crystal clear any more!

FRANCIS   If that's the price of love, I'm not sure I can pay it. I want to be free, Lily. I don't know what more to say than that.

LILY   Fanny, you're never really free. You can frame a declaration of independence every day, but you won't be free. We're

bound by our affections more than any legal contracts, or governments or causes. We're all trapped by something. The heart doesn't choose wisely, it just chooses.

(Sound of the train whistle. Both sisters fight back tears.)

FRANCIS   Oh, don't leave. I don't know what I'll do without you.

LILY   I've got to. It's time.

FRANCIS   I love you, Lily.

LILY   Fanny, you're a brick. (They hug. LILY leaves.)

Scene 5

FRANCIS enters her office. MCNAIR is there. She takes off her hat and coat.

FRANCIS   I've got four typewriters now – mine, Lily's and two of Vernon's – and none of them work very well. Have you ever been to New York, McNair?

MCNAIR   I landed there when I first came over. I read a different paper every day for two weeks, and never found the same opinion twice. Don't worry, Francis. They'll find work.

FRANCIS   I guess so. McNair, do you think I'm . . . hard on people?

MCNAIR   Very! You're like a terrier worrying a bone.

FRANCIS   Why do you think that is?

MCNAIR   Because you've got a vision of the world that's clearer than most.

FRANCIS   Then why do I feel so frightened all the time . . . frightened that I'm wrong, or that I'm right, that I'm not doing enough, or that I'm doing too much . . . that I'll end up alone. When I was given a mind that questioned everything, why wasn't I given a spirit that feared nothing? I used to think that everything was possible, but I just don't know any more.

MCNAIR   You're just tired, Francis, and you miss Lily. Why don't you open your mail? That will put the fight back into you.

(FRANCIS opens her letters.)

WOMAN
Dear Miss Beynon:
    I say hurray for Borden and conscription. Let's round up those slackers who are hanging around the city poolrooms and get them into uniform. The time has come to send more than socks and tobacco to our

heroes in the fighting line. What we need is Men Men and more Men!

Western Sister

FRANCIS
Dear Western Sister:

It is easy for us to be brave with other people's lives, but I don't believe in their hearts that the people of Canada want compulsory enlistment. Let's have a referendum to ask Canadians whether they want conscription!

WOMAN
Dear Miss Beynon

Referendum? Referendum now? For three years our boys have fought for us and our cause. Referendum now, while our enemy prepares destruction for our battered heroes? Surely not referendum but reinforcement! And quickly to our waiting sons!

Dear Miss Beynon

What we are fighting here is a holy war against the very Prince of Darkness, and therefore every man owes it to God to support conscription. And if there is any man out there who says his conscience won't allow him to slay his fellow man, then he's laying down too strict a rule for his conscience.

FRANCIS   That is not God's plan! I believe that God is democracy, the only true democracy. He filled the world with human beings, no two of whom are alike and I'm sure he meant them to be left free to develop their differences and to report on life as they see it. War has never been in God's plan – the Lord of Peace – only that of man.

WOMAN
Dear Miss Know-It-All:

"There shall be wars and rumours of war, but the end is not yet." Do not go taking the name of the Lord in vain and putting your half-cooked ideas on him. You used to be alright when you talked about votes for women, but you're a disgrace to the female race the way you go on about peace. Anyone who talks like that is a traitor and probably has foreign friends.

(FRANCIS *takes over the reading of the letter from the woman who has written it. She reads it aloud as* MCNAIR *comes into the room.*)

FRANCIS   "My husband told me to say that he's proud of his country and proud to fight for it, and if you don't keep your mouth shut, you might find someone will shut it for you."

MCNAIR   (*taking the letter from* FRANCIS) This is a threat! Who wrote this?

FRANCIS   Would you sign a letter like this?

MCNAIR   This has got to stop. You've gone too far!

FRANCIS   I've gone too far?

MCNAIR   When it gets to the point that people are sending you hate mail, like this, yes! People who write letters like this are unbalanced. You might get hurt, Francis.

FRANCIS   It was you who told me that if I believe in something, I should have the courage to write about it.

MCNAIR   But this is different. The war is making people crazy. A man was nearly beaten to death at an anti-conscription rally last night. These are dangerous times. Where are you going?

(FRANCIS *has risen. She puts on her hat and coat.*)

FRANCIS   To a meeting.

MCNAIR   What meeting?

FRANCIS   A women's meeting, McNair, at the library. Nellie McClung is giving a talk. I'd like to hear what she has to say.

MCNAIR   I'll walk you there.

FRANCIS   Thank you.

(*They exit together.*)

Scene 6

A women's meeting. NELLIE *is addressing the audience.*

NELLIE   The Wartime Elections Act has just given us Dominion women the vote, and I think we should use it to vote for conscription. Yesterday, I received a letter from my son in France asking when we're going to send more troops. He says they're holding on as best they can, but they're getting weaker. Are we backing our boys or not? A thousand voices chatter reasons for delay, but across the seas comes one voice loud and clear. Who calls Canada? Our boys are calling us! Tonight is the beginning of the federal election campaign and the issue is conscription. Now is our chance to work for the candidates who are going to help our boys. We have no time to lose. The more women we can get out the better . . .

FRANCIS   Mrs McClung, I have a question?

NELLIE   We don't have much time.

FRANCIS   I won't be long. How can our boys be fighting for freedom if we are not giving them the freedom to decide whether or not they'll give their lives?

NELLIE   That's not an easy question to answer. I've struggled with it in my heart. But sometimes, individual freedom has to be sacrificed for collective freedom. Peace can only be achieved when we band together and let the enemy know that we will not budge.

FRANCIS   I have another question.

NELLIE   We have a lot of work to do.

FRANCIS   How can peace be achieved, how can we get any nearer to peace, when a lot more people are being sacrificed?

NELLIE   I think you're trying to be disruptive, Miss Beynon. Your views on the war are well known. I don't know whether there's any point in taking up more time.

FRANCIS   Please, I'd just like to make one suggestion. *(She goes up to the front.)* Why don't we tell the politicians that we women, the mothers, wives and sisters of Canada, want to bring this war to a peaceful conclusion right now, before any more blood is shed!

NELLIE   If there aren't any more questions, we should get down to forming committees. We have six candidates to start working for . . .

FRANCIS   Can I talk for a minute please . . . just a minute! The real issue of this war is not conscription or the war over there. The real issue is being fought right here in halls like these. The real issue is whether militarism shall grow and prosper or whether it shall decline and fall. We, as women, in our first chance to use our franchise, are being asked to vote for war! To vote for sending more sons and husbands away to fight and be killed. Let's use our vote to say NO to war! And let's not exclude our sisters because they speak another language –

WOMAN IN AUDIENCE   Shut up. Just shut up! You don't know what you're talking about! You've got nothing to lose! Get out of here! GET OUT!

NELLIE   Please, can we have order. Miss

Beynon, I believe you have your answer. Now, let's get back to business.

(FRANCIS leaves, anguished.)

Scene 7

The newspaper office. MCNAIR is seated.
FRANCIS *storms into the office.*

FRANCIS   I just received a call from the censorship board. Those scoundrels told me not to write anything about the conscription bill which might "arouse" opposition!

MCNAIR   Sit down, Francis.

FRANCIS   Since when have British citizens relinquished the right to discuss unmade legislation?

MCNAIR   Sit down, Francis.

FRANCIS   Is this Canada or is this Prussia? Has everyone gone war mad?

MCNAIR   *(shouting)* Sit down, Francis! *(FRANCIS finally sits.)* I want to talk to you. I've been getting calls all week from readers. About you. One woman said she'd seen you handing out anti-war pamphlets at Portage and Main on two occasions, and that you were haranguing passers-by.

FRANCIS   *(jumping up)* I was not haranguing them. I was trying to engage them in conversation.

MCNAIR   The publisher called me a while ago. He's running for parliament on the conscription issue. He wants me to . . . he wants your resignation. I told him I would talk to you.

FRANCIS   *(in disbelief)* He wants me to resign from my job?

MCNAIR   Yes.

FRANCIS   No! I won't! He can't get away with something like that! We can get my readers to back me!

MCNAIR   Francis, your readers haven't been very supportive lately. *(He slams the letters down on the desk.)* Haven't you noticed?

FRANCIS   What about you?

MCNAIR   Don't you ever get tired of rowing upstream?

FRANCIS   McNair, what about you? The paper has a role to play in presenting all sides of the war issue. We've got to get people thinking! Really thinking! Really questioning!

MCNAIR   The issue has already been discussed to death. Borden has granted the Empire women the vote and they're going to use it to ram conscription down our throats!

FRANCIS   No! No!

MCNAIR   Yes! And there's nothing you can do about it. Or should do about it!

FRANCIS   So you simply suspend freedom of the press . . . freedom to express opinions?

MCNAIR   Nobody gives a damn about your opinions, or my opinions either! We've just got to win the war and then you can hold any damned opinion you like. Just swallow hard and hold on.

FRANCIS   Do you want me to resign?

MCNAIR   Yes. No. I don't have any choice. *(FRANCIS turns to leave.)* Francis, wait. Look at me. *(FRANCIS turns.)* You've got lines on your face now that don't go away when you stop smiling. I can see a hint of grey in your hair along the temples. You're not a young girl any more. Francis, I love you. I want to marry you. I want to take care of you. I want you to stop worrying about what you can't change. Let me take care of you now. Don't say anything. Let me talk. I've saved enough money to buy a house. Leave the paper. You won't have to put up with any more abusive letters, you won't have to turn yourself inside out with issues. I know how it tortures you. Just let it all go!

FRANCIS   McNair, I love my work.

MCNAIR   I know you do, Francis, but I'm asking you to marry me! You can forget about everything else.

(FRANCIS shivers, moves away.)

FRANCIS   It's cold in here suddenly. *(Slowly, with difficulty)* You said to me once that I was like a bird struggling to get free though it loved the warmth of your hand. I love you, McNair. I love your warmth. But I. . . . *(her voice breaks)* can't . . . do what you want. It would be too much like a closed hand. And I'd always be straining to get free. Do you understand?

(MCNAIR searches her face, almost speaks, then thinks better of it. Instead, he comes over to FRANCIS, puts his arms around her, holds her for a moment, then leaves. FRANCIS is left standing alone. A wave of emotion flows over her as she realizes the extent of her aloneness now. A wail comes from deep inside her. She drops her head, remains silent for a long while, then slowly walks over to her desk and begins to collect up her belongings. As she begins to formulate her last editorial, we see her resolve and vision and brightness returning to her.)

FRANCIS   Every once in a while, one comes to a parting of the ways. I have come to that today. It is with deep feelings of regret that I am severing my connection with *The Rural Review*. I had hoped through this page, that we women of the prairies could help advance the cause of women, and I believe that in some small ways, we have done that. It would have been a much bigger thing if we could have claimed to have erased tyranny and war and intolerance. I now think that that is a work to be measured in generations. But someday, when we who are here now are dead and gone, and the little acorns that were planted on our graves have grown into flourishing trees and fallen into decay, it will come to be recognized that there is no crime in being different, in doing one's own thinking. It may even be that in that dim and shadowy future, the world will have sense enough to value peace, and we will be able to live free of the fear of war. This, in the end, is the only thing that really matters. By the time this reaches print, I will have left for the Mecca of all writers on this continent, the city of New York. There, I will continue to work towards that future. One can only follow "The Gleam" as one sees it, and hope that it does not prove to be a will-o-the-wisp.

And that is all.

Curtain

9 Christina Reid 1942–

My Name, Shall I Tell You My Name
Northern Ireland

Introduction

Christina Reid was born in Belfast in 1942. Her father was a docker and her mother worked part time as a waitress. As Reid told the American journalist, Elizabeth Shannon, she had "an Ulster Protestant Unionist background" but she did not support the Unionists at all, finding their actions "indefensible". She became left-wing although, "detesting anything religious", she never marched in the peace demonstrations. She has struggled to rid herself of labels (Shannon 1989: 212–16). Reid wrote from childhood, yet like other women she stood outside the great renaissance of Northern Irish cultural activity in the 1960s and 1970s, which was led by male poets such as Seamus Heaney at Queen's University, Belfast. Nor was she involved in the formation of Field Day by Brian Friel and Stephen Rea in Derry in 1980. This was partly because she only went to Queen's University as a mature student in 1982/3 and did not make those connections. Her cultural networks were other. As she says, "I'm working-class, and working-class women spend all our time with other women and children" (Shannon 1989: 212). This makes her typical of Irish women writers: "the telling of tales by other women forms the well of their creativity" (ibid.: 213). In Reid's case she believes her writing comes from what she heard sitting around a kitchen-table, from her mother and grandmother, who were great storytellers. Her earliest experience of theatre was the women of her family dressing up to enact stories "that were a mixture of fact, fantasy and folklore" (Jeffs' introduction in Reid 1993: v).

Her writing career took off when she was in her mid-30s, after her mother died. Reid dramatised one of her own stories for a drama competition and won a prize. Other awards soon followed: in 1980 she won the Ulster Television Drama Award for her play, *Did You Hear the One About the Irishman . . . ?*; in 1983 the Thames TV Playwright Scheme Award for *Tea in a China Cup*; and in 1986 both the Giles Cooper Award for her radio-play, *The Last of a Dyin' Race* and the George Devine Award for her theatre play, *The Belle of the Belfast City*. Dissatisfaction with her life fuelled her drama, but making that public led to the breakup of her marriage. Writing enabled her to become self-supporting and in 1987 she divorced and moved to London with her three teenage daughters. Since then she has written episodes for several radio and television series, including *Citizens* and *Streetwise*, and been writer-in-residence at the Young Vic, London (1988–9). Her plays have been performed not only in Dublin, Belfast, Manchester and London, but also in the USA, where the Royal Shakespeare Company toured in 1985 with *Did You Hear the One About the Irishman . . . ?* Her best-known plays are probably *Joyriders* (1986) and its sequel, *Clowns* (1996), which she is amalgamating into one screenplay.

Elizabeth Shannon found Northern Ireland

> like a secret society for men. They belong to all-male clubs, invent childlike, mysterious handshakes, march to loud drumbeats, make deals, stir up hatreds, and try – some of them – to find solutions to the problems that they and men of previous generations have created.
>
> (Shannon 1989: 4)

From all this activity they have excluded women. To Shannon it seemed that, as a result, women's voices had "gradually faded, died away in Northern Ireland" (ibid.: 4). This accords with Reid's own perceptions about Northern Ireland:

> The public faces of the Protestant and Catholic paramilitaries are all men. All the

people who talk about religion and the Church are all men. The politicians are all men. Women are never the leaders, the faces, the voices. Ian Paisley and the Pope are basically in total agreement over what a woman's role in the home should be.

(Reid 1997: xv)

Yet Reid's plays are evidence of the ways in which Irish women have in fact made their voices heard, from Anne Devlin to Eavan Boland, from Mary Robinson to Nell McCafferty. As Reid says, concentration on male violence on stage and screen "leaves too many songs unsung" (Banks 1994: 555). Reid sings these other songs.

One of Reid's main themes, prominent in both *Tea in a China Cup* and *My Name, Shall I Tell You My Name*, is women's responses to the ways in which masculine identity is constituted by violence and national identity by war. The Dublin Easter Rising against the British in 1916 is recalled in Eire as the birth of the Irish Republic. This has produced a cultural amnesia in the South about the fact that 100,000–150,000 Irish volunteers served in the British Army 1914–18, and that 35,000–40,500 of them "gave their lives in the Great War, 1914–18" (to quote the neglected Irish National War Memorial at the edge of Dublin). In the North, on the other hand, not only is the Great War remembered annually at local November Armistice ceremonies, but since 5,500 Ulstermen died on 1 July 1916, the Battle of the Somme is commemorated during the July Orange parades that also mark the Siege of Derry, the Battle of the Boyne and the Protestant ascendancy. It was the Battle of the Somme that the Catholic Republican playwright, Frank McGuinness, made central to his examination of how Unionist identity is celebrated, in his 1985 play, *Observe the Sons of Ulster Marching towards the Somme* (McGuinness 1996: x). Recreating on stage the bloody red hand of Ulster and the bloody beating of the lambeg drum, and reciting the names of those who died, McGuinness showed that myths of martial heroism are as important to the Northern Unionist mentality as Yeats made them to the Nationalists in his dramatic portrayals of Cuchulain.

Reid has followed the alternative Irish dramatic tradition to Yeats's pre-industrial legends: the mock-heroism of that other Protestant, working-class dramatist, Sean

Figure 10 "In Glorious Memory": banner carried by the Larne Loyalists Orange Lodge, Co. Antrim, in the Orange Day parades, showing the Ulster Division of the British Army, going "over the top" at the Battle of the Somme, 1 July 1916, based on the painting by J. Prinsepp Beadle referred to in Reid's play.

O'Casey. Her plays share with O'Casey's the rich community-life and desperation of the urban poor, and she similarly alleviates the bleakness of her narratives with jokes, dance and song. But her writing is woman-centred. *Tea in a China Cup*, which makes imperial history manifest on stage in a growing collection of framed army photographs, of young Belfast men in the uniforms of the British Army from the First and Second World Wars and the post-war conflicts, finally rejects that legacy as "not worth anything anyway". Beth, the protagonist, realises that "my head is full of other people's memories" and that these don't help her to know who or what she herself is: "On the hill there stands a lady, who she is I do not know". This echoes the refrain from Dolly's song in *The Belle of the Belfast City*: "Please won't you tell me who she is." Andrea poses that same question of female identity in *My Name, Shall I Tell You My Name*, Reid's radio play set simultaneously in Derry and Holloway Prison, London in 1986. (First broadcast on

211

BBC Radio 4 from Belfast in March 1988, the
play was adapted for the stage and performed
by Yew Theatre Co., first at the Dublin
Theatre Festival, 1989, and then at the Young
Vic, London, 1990.)

In *My Name, Shall I Tell You My Name*,
Andrea is encouraged by her grandfather, a
veteran of the Somme, to learn and repeat the
names of his dead comrades. This duty, to
name and praise dead warriors, was the role
of the bard. Yeats was fulfilling that role in his
poem "Easter 1916"; McGuinness's character,
the elder Pyper, fulfils the same role in
Observe the Sons of Ulster. This practice
reinforced the belief that the land was
redeemed by sacrifice in combat. Andrea's
response is part of her rejection of the Orange
rituals, such as the commemoration of the
Siege of Derry, the tradition that the Army
"makes a man of you" and the other
prejudices that encourage violence, racism
and exploitation in place of generous
fellow-feeling: "The men go off to war and the
weemin' and the children stay behind and
keep the home fires burnin' till the men get
back." The cruel segregation that results from
such bigotry is signified in Reid's play by the
closing of her grandfather's tin-box and the
slamming of the iron prison-door. Andrea is
speaking from Holloway as a result of going to
the Women's Peace Camp at Greenham
Common. In the dense allusiveness of Reid's
writing, Andrea is thus associated via the
suffragette hunger-strikers with the IRA
hunger-strikers in the Maze prison in 1981,
and her grandfather's belligerent
intransigence with Margaret Thatcher's.
Andrea is starving for her grandfather's love,
but her plea for a no-man's land where they
could declare a truce is also a political plea for
common recognition. It is the same plea that
underlies *The Belle of the Belfast City*. Andrea
subverts her grandfather's litany by reciting
the names as she lights peace candles at
Greenham, and adding new names. But her
plea is not simply for tolerance; it is for her
grandfather to be able to say, as she does: "I
love you, even though I have grown to hate
everything you believe in."

Further reading

Primary

Devlin, Anne (1986) *Ourselves Alone*, London:
Faber.

McGuinness, Frank (1996) *Observe the Sons of
Ulster Marching Towards the Somme* in
Plays: 1, London: Faber.
O'Casey, Sean [1928] (1985) *The Silver Tassie*
in *Seven Plays by Sean O'Casey*, ed. R.
Ayling, London: Macmillan.
Reid, Christina (1986) *The Last of a Dyin' Race*
in *Best Radio Plays of 1986*, London:
Methuen.
—— (1993) *Joyriders and Did You Hear the One
About the Irishman?*, introduced by
Caroline Jeffs, London: Heinemann.
—— (1997) *Plays: 1*, introduced by Maria M.
Delgado, London: Methuen.
Reid, J. Graham (1982) *The Hidden
Curriculum* in *The Plays of Graham Reid*,
Dublin: CoOp Books.
Yeats, W. B. [1939] (1966) *The Death of
Cuchulain* in *Selected Plays* ed. A. N.
Jeffares, London: Macmillan.

Secondary

Banks, Carol (1994) "Christina Reid" in K. A.
Berney (ed.) *Contemporary British
Dramatists*, London: St James Press, pp.
607–9.
Boyce, George (1993) *The Sure Confusing
Drum: Ireland and the First World War*,
Swansea: University College.
Jeffery, Keith (1993) "The Great War in
Modern Irish Memory" in T. G. Fraser and
K. Jeffery (eds) *Men, Women and War*,
Dublin: Lilliput, pp. 136–57.
Liddington, Jill (1989) *The Long Road to
Greenham: Feminism and Anti-Militarism in
Britain since 1820*, London: Virago.
McMullen, Anna (1993) "Irish Women
Playwrights since 1958" in T. R. Griffiths
and M. Llewellyn-Jones (eds) *British and
Irish Women Dramatists since 1958: a
Critical Handbook*, Milton Keynes: Open
University, pp. 110–23.
Miller, David (ed.) (1998) *Rethinking Northern
Ireland: Creative Ideology and Colonialism*,
London: Longman.
Murray, Christopher (1997) *Twentieth-century
Irish Drama: Mirror up to Nation*,
Manchester: Manchester University Press.
Orr, Philip (1987) *The Road to the Somme: Men
of the Ulster Division Tell Their Story*,
Belfast: Blackstaff.
Shannon, Elizabeth (1989) *I Am of Ireland:
Women of the North Speak Out*, Boston:
Littlebrown.

My Name, Shall I Tell You My Name

[Radio Play for Three Voices]
First broadcast on 14 March 1988 by BBC
Northern Ireland, producer Kathryn Porter

Christina Reid

Characters

ANDY, aged 71–93 (Born 1893)

ANDREA, aged 24 (Born 1962), Andy's
  granddaughter

ANDREA, as a child

Derry 1964, Andy's house
ANDREA *aged 2/3*
ANDY *aged 71/72*

ANDY My name, shall I tell you my . . .
ANDREA Name . . .
ANDY It's hard, but I'll . . . .
ANDREA Try . . . .
ANDY Sometimes I forget it, that's when
  I'm . . .
ANDREA Shy . . .
ANDY But I have another, I never forget.
  So . . .
ANDREA Easy . . .
ANDY So . . .
ANDREA Pretty . . .
ANDY And that's . . .
ANDREA Granda's Pet.
ANDY You're just perfect. You're my joy.
  The light of my life. Do ye know that?
  Come on now. Walk. Walk to me. Don't be
  afraid. You can do it. It's only three little
  steps. And your old granda would never let
  ye fall.

Derry and London, 1986
ANDREA *aged 24 in London*
(She is drawing as she talks.)

ANDREA It's my earliest memory,
  stumbling into his arms, sitting on his
  knee, mimicking the last word of each line
  of that poem. The love in his voice, the
  delight in his face . . . I was wearing a pink
  dress, with white lace . . . here on the
  pocket and the hem . . . and he held out a
  biscuit to entice me to walk to him . . . no,
  not like that . . . between his thumb and
forefinger . . . this should in truth be two
drawings, not one. I didn't learn to walk
and talk on the same day. But that's how I
remember it . . . perhaps because the two
events were joined in his memory . . . I
taught you to talk and I taught you to walk,
he used to say. Your old granda taught you
how to make your way in the world . . .
Now I talk to my drawings, to myself . . .
who does he talk to now, I wonder? Maybe,
like many old men he just talks. To
himself. To the wall. To the memories
locked away in his old tin box. I wonder if
he still keeps my very first drawing there.

ANDY *aged 93 in Derry*
*(He is unlocking the tin box and removing and
unfolding Andrea's first drawing.)*

ANDY She drew me before she drew
  anything else. God knows what she's
  drawin' now . . .
ANDREA Draw it out. Work it out. I won't
  cry. I mustn't cry . . .
ANDY She was always laughin'. Nothin'
  daunted her. Brave an' bright an' beautiful.
  The cleverest child in the street an' the
  best lookin'. Her mother, my Annie, kept
  her spotless. Nice wee starched frocks,
  white socks, shiny patent leather shoes.
  The nearest thing Derry ever seen to
  Shirley Temple, ringlets an' all. A wee
  beauty if ever there was one . . .
ANDREA The eye of the beholder . . . Truth
  is, I was a plain child with hair as straight
  as a rush. Every night, my mother bound
  my hair in cloths to make it curl. And
  every morning I had to sit still and not
  complain while she teased and tortured the
  hair into ringlets. Then she'd tie it all up
  with a satin ribbon, and she'd look at me,
  and she'd sigh, "God child. You must have
  been far down the queue when God was
  handin' out the glamour . . . "
ANDY She was a picture. She must have

been at the head of the queue when God was handin' out the good looks . . . and the best behaviour. A chip off the old block, so she was. Just like her mother before her. She was always a good wee girl too, my Annie. The best of the bunch. The last of my daughters. It was my wife's idea to call her Annie, after me. "It's the nearest we'll get to Andy." she said, "for I'm havin' no more children." Well, she'd had five, so she'd done her bit, even if they were all girls.

ANDREA   I was born on his sixty-ninth birthday. His last grandchild. His only granddaughter. To please him, my mother called me Andrea. They say he didn't sober up for three days afterwards.

ANDY   Sure there's nuthin' to equal a wee girl. And I'm the man would know. Five daughters, all good girls. And be God, if they didn't all produce sons when their time come. Every time another grandson was born, the wife used to laugh an' say to me "That'll learn ye to complain about never havin' had no sons." An' then Andrea come along. Worth all the grandsons put together. See wee lads? They're never at peace. Always runnin' about an' shoutin' an' makin' a nuisance of themselves. No respect. Not like her. She never put a foot wrong . . . when she was a child . . .

ANDREA   I was an insufferable little madam. Not a bit of wonder my brothers and cousins couldn't stand me. They used to taunt me when he wasn't around. "Granda's Pet! Granda's Pet! Give us a chorus of the 'Good Ship Lollipop', Shirley!" He walked in one day and caught them at it. Scattered them with his walking stick.

ANDY   Wee hallions! They'da laughed on the other side of their faces if I had got the houl of them. I told their mothers, you're far too soft on them wee lads. A bloody good hidin's what they need. My mother used to beat the livin' daylights outa me if I as much as said a word outa place. Made a man outa me. That an' the army . . . Man, them were the days with the lads in France. Real men. Heroes. Ulster Protestant Orangemen. We'll never see their like again . . . Joseph Sloan, Billy Matchett, Isaac Carson, Samuel Thompson, Hugh Montgomery . . .

ANDREA   . . . Hugh Montgomery, Frederick Wilson, James Elliott, John Cunningham, Edward Marshall . . . a litany of the Glorious Dead. Pale faces in a sepia photograph in his tin box. Just a handful of the five and a half thousand Ulstermen who died on the first day of the Battle of the Somme. By the time it was all over, the total number of dead, British, French, and German, was one point two million. My grandfather was one of the two survivors from our road. He was 23 years old.

ANDY   A glorious victory. Their finest hour. An inspiration for painters and poets.

ANDREA   It was the first proper painting I ever saw. It hangs in the City Hall in Belfast. We went there on the train from Derry when I was about seven, to visit his eldest daughter. But his real reason for going was that he wanted to stand with me in front of that painting . . . and teach me another poem . . .

ANDY *aged 76 and* ANDREA *aged 7*
(They are walking the marble corridors of the City Hall in Belfast. The footsteps stop.)

ANDY   There it is. There they are. I'll read ye the inscription . . . The Battle of the Somme. Attack by the Ulster Division 1st July 1916. Presented to the Lord Mayor Alderman James Johnston and the Corporation of the City of Belfast as a gift to the citizens from the Ulster Volunteers to commemorate "one of the greatest feats of arms in the annals of the British Army." Now what do ye think that, eh?

ANDREA (CHILD)   Why is that man wearing short trousers?

ANDY   He's the officer.

(Sound of the ADULT ANDREA drawing increases in speed and intensity)

ANDREA (ADULT)   The officer is young, golden, angelic face . . . a Boy Scout leading men in long trousers into battle. Fritz is being taken prisoner . . . top of the painting . . . more to the left . . . and another German soldier lies dying . . . not there . . . bottom left . . . An Ulsterman walks away from the dying man . . . he carries a bayonet . . . blood covered . . . he looks . . . not victorious . . . he looks nothing . . . blank . . . His eyes were wide open, but he looks blind . . .

ANDY   Can ye read the Poem on the brass plate? Have a go. I'll help ye with the big words.

(The CHILD ANDREA reads the poem. ANDY helps her when she falters.)

ANDREA (CHILD)   On fame's eternal
  camping ground.
Their silent tents are spread.
And Glory guards with solemn round
The bivouac of the dead.

ANDY   See that one there with the bayonet?
  Spittin' image of Billy Matchett. Poor Billy
  . . . I was one of the lucky ones, got injured
  minutes after we cleared the trenches, so
  they found me quick. Wasn't too far out, ye
  see. Got the knee operated on the same
  day. Billy got hit further out on the
  battlefield. Three days before they found
  him. They got him back to England, but the
  oul gangerine killed him. A terrible death,
  they say. Better to get killed outright. Billy
  was the best Lambeg drummer Derry had
  ever seen. The Orange Lodge paid for his
  headstone. White marble with a black
  soldier inset. Done him proud. Billy's son,
  wee Billy, took over the beatin' of the
  Lambeg drum when he grew up. Carryin'
  on the name. Carryin' on the tradition,
  which is how it should be. That's what life's
  about, child. Knowin' who ye are, what ye
  come from. Don't you ever forget that.

ANDREA (ADULT)   My name . . . shall I tell
  you my name . . .

ANDY   And now young Billy's dead too. Cut
  off in his prime. Second World War.
  Dunkirk. Still, his son, another Billy has
  stepped into his father's shoes.

ANDREA (ADULT)   God's good and life goes
  on.

ANDY   When we get back to Derry I'll take
  ye to see wee Billy beatin' the Lambeg
  drum.

ANDREA (CHILD)   Will he let me beat it?

ANDY   You couldn't even lift it. Sure the
  drum's bigger than you are.

*(Billy is beating the drum surrounded by an
admiring crowd.)*

ANDY   Go on ye boy ye! Yer granda'll never
  be dead as long as you're alive! Hey, Mrs
  Machett, lift wee Andrea up on my
  shoulders so she can see your Billy better.

ANDREA   Wee Billy Matchett was a huge fat
  perspiring man. The Lambeg drum was
  strapped to his chest. He had been beating
  the drum for a long time and his hands
  were bleeding. The blood trickled over the
  tattoos on his arms . . . Ulster is British . . .
  No Surrender . . . Remember the Somme
  . . . Dunkirk . . . The Relief of Derry. Billy's
  little bird-like wife kept darting forward
  with whiskey for his parched mouth and a
  cold sponge for his burning frenzied face.
  She didn't attempt to sponge away the
  blood. That was sacred. I wasn't frightened.
  I was puzzled. I couldn't understand why
  the great fat man was hurting himself like
  that. It didn't make sense. And why was his
  silly little wife so pleased about it? Maybe
  she didn't like him. Maybe she was hoping
  he'd drop down dead. I was about to ask
  my grandfather what it was all about when
  suddenly he began to sing . . .

ANDY   *(sings)*
  We'll fight for no surrender
  We'll come when duty calls
  With Heart and Hand and Sword and
    Shield
  We'll guard Old Derry's Walls.

ANDREA   And then I understood that this
  was about war.

ANDY   When Billy stopped drummin' he
  lifted Andrea off my shoulders an' held her
  above the cheerin' crowd. I was that proud
  I could hardly speak.

(Sound of the CHILD ANDREA*'s small voice
amid the cheers)*

ANDREA   Granda, there's blood on my frock.

ANDY   Never worry yourself. We're goin'
  home now and your mother can soak it in
  cold water before it dries in. That way it
  won't leave no mark.

ANDREA (ADULT)   Wee Billy Matchett
  dropped dead on 12th July while he was
  beating the big drum before the 12th of
  July parade. They say his funeral was
  nearly as big as the parade itself. The big
  drum was set on the ground alongside the
  open grave and wee Billy's son, 10 year old
  little Billy, solemnly hit the drum three
  times as soil was sprinkled on the coffin.
  My grandfather patted little Billy on the
  head and said "You carry the name and one
  day, when you're older, you'll be man
  enough to carry the drum" . . . God's good,
  and death goes on.

*(Andrea's drawing merges with the sound of
the drumming. This sound fades.) (Sound of
the tin box being opened, and Andy's war
medals being removed)*

ANDREA (CHILD)   Can I put your medals
  on, Granda?

ANDY   No love, Medals is for men.

ANDREA   Why?

ANDY Because that's the way things are. The men go off to war, and the weemin and the children stay behind and keep the home fires burnin' till the men get back.

ANDREA (CHILD) Since my grandmother's death, my mother had been keeping two home fires burning. For eight years she'd been running his house as well as her own, trudging half a mile in all weathers to light his fire, do his shopping, cook his meals, because he'd stubbornly refused to have a home help.

ANDY Strangers in yer house, pokin' around, knowin' yer business. I'll have none of that carry-on. I have five daughters. They know their duty.

ANDREA His daughters were ageing women, and had other duties. Irish husbands, Irish sons. My mother, being the youngest and the fittest and a widow, fell for it all. She dutifully cared for him, and he obstinately ignored all her arguments about his entitlement to a free home help.

ANDY Entitlement! That's the trouble with the world the day. People thinkin' they're entitled from the cradle to the grave. And the ones that do the most complainin' about hard times wouldn't know what a day's work looked like. On the sick or on the dole. They don't want to work. That's their trouble. From the day that I come back from the Great War till the day that I retired from the Linen Mill, I never went sick once. Not even when the oul knee was that sore I could hardly walk let alone work. I never used my war wound as an excuse to lie in my bed and live off the State.

ANDREA (CHILD) My mummy says it's time you let the State do something for you.

ANDY My country give me medals. Honoured me. I won't demean that by lookin' for a handout. Now, tell me who else got medals. Tell me the names.

ANDREA (CHILD) Joseph Sloan, Billy Matchett, Isaac Carson, Samuel Thompson, Hugh Montgomery . . .

ANDREA (ADULT) . . . Hugh Montgomery, Frederick Wilson, James Elliott, John Cunningham, Edward Marshall . . . and Edward Reilly, the only other survivor. He turned down his medal. His face and his name were cut off the end of the photo.

ANDY Turned down his medal. Turned traitor. Canvassed for the Labour Party after the war. Made speeches against the Government and the Monarchy. Betrayed all the brave men who fought and died so that we could be British and free. Turncoats and Communists. Catholic throwbacks the lot of them. What sort of a name's Reilly for a Protestant family? Intermarried way back to raise themselves out of the gutter. But it never leaves them. Popery. Bad Blood. Nationalism. Communism. Same difference.

ANDREA I didn't even know that Edward Reilly existed until I was nearly 16. His grandson Eddie was small and dark and fierce and looked like John Lennon. I was that lovesick, I took to wearing oriental eye make-up, because I had some sort of confused notion that if I looked like Yoko Ono Eddie would automatically fall madly in love with me. Instead, he told me his grandfather's version of the Battle of the Somme. How the Ulster Divisions were sent in first. High on alcohol and Ulster Protestant Pride. How they wore Orange sashes and went into battle singing songs about the Battle of the Boyne and the siege of Derry, as if the Catholic King James had been resurrected and was leading the German Army.

ANDY Makin' mock of brave men, just like his grandfather before him.

ANDREA His grandfather didn't mock them. He mourned them. They were brave men, his friends, and he loved them. And he lay in the mud for three days listening to Billy Matchett screaming and sobbing and moaning. He could hear Billy, and he could see him, but he couldn't help him, because his own legs were broken and he was half buried in an avalanche of mud and blood and bits of the bodies of Joseph Sloan, Isaac Carson, Samuel Thompson, Hugh Montgomery . . .

ANDREA (CHILD) . . . Hugh Montgomery, Frederick Wilson, James Elliott, John Cunningham, Edward Marshall.

ANDREA (ADULT) And Edward Reilly who survived and wept every time he told that story to his grandson.

ANDY Like an oul woman. Nobody never seen me cry.

(A metal door slams and echoes in the distance.)

ANDREA I won't cry. I won't let them see me cry. Give me some of your fierce, proud strength Grandfather. Did you ever cry I wonder, when no one was there to see . . . Perhaps you didn't dare in case you could never stop.

ANDY   I told her. You keep away from that skite Eddie Reilly. He's a Commie, like his granda. No good'll come of it.

ANDREA   I was dying to go to the bad with Eddie Reilly. I increased the oriental eye make-up and powdered my lips white.

ANDY   You want to have seen the state of her. Like a demented Geisha Girl with a heart disease.

ANDREA   I don't think Eddie ever noticed what I looked like. He was only ever interested in talk and books. In getting at the truth. His truth, as opposed to my grandfather's. I wanted to talk of love, not war . . . nor walking sticks . . .

ANDY   Who paid for your walkin' stick, Granda! I knew the minute she asked who'd put her up to it!

ANDREA (CHILD)   My granda's walking stick has a real ivory top. The man who owned the mill bought it for my granda when he retired.

ANDY   Done me proud he did. Presented it to me personally.

ANDREA (ADULT)   Presented it. But didn't pay for it. The mill workers paid for it. They organised a collection and mill owner gave a pound towards it.

ANDY   Sir John was a gentleman. As was his father.

ANDREA   On the day that you retired, young Sir John descended from his carpeted office on high and delivered a short speech about loyal workers who'd served his father and now served him.

ANDY   He shook me by the hand and called me one of the true blue breed, and wished me a long and happy retirement.

ANDREA   You worked your guts out in that mill for over 40 years and he gave a pound towards your retirement present. I doubt he even knew your name before that day.

ANDREA (CHILD)   My name shall I tell you my name . . .

ANDY   Tellin' her yarns. Fillin' her head full of nonsense. Them Reillys were always disturbers.

ANDREA (ADULT)   Questioning things that mustn't be questioned. It was the first time I ever hurt him. "Who paid for your walking stick, Granda?" He flew into a rage and then sulked for days. There was more to the story than I realised. His workmates

wanted to buy him the best stick in the shop, but they were ten shillings short, so my mother made up the difference. "He never knew the ins and outs of it," she said, "He just assumed Sir John bought it, and nobody never told him no different." But of course he knew. If Eddie Reilly's granda knew, then so did mine. My mother said it wasn't a question of knowing. It was a question of loyalty and pride, and I was too young to understand the importance of these things. And how I could hurt him like that in defence of a waster like Eddie Reilly, she'd never know.

ANDY   She soon learned her lesson, trustin' the Reillys.

ANDREA   It was all over the road before I heard it. Eddie Reilly had got the girl from the sweetshop pregnant and they were getting married. I couldn't believe it. Doris Braithwaite was a tall skinny blue-eyed blonde. Not a bit like Yoko Ono. I was so incensed that I gave Eddie back all his books and told him he was a rotten traitor just like his grandfather before him. I thought of destroying my John Lennon records, but couldn't find it in my heart to go that far. Instead I settled for scrubbing off the black eye-liner, gave up Socialism for Art and Drama, and got top grades in my "A" levels . . . and hurt my grandfather for the second time by opting to go to an English university.

ANDY   It wasn't that I wasn't proud of her. I was the one always knew she had it in her. But I don't see why our Queen's University in Belfast wasn't good enough for her.

ANDREA   There is no drama course at Queen's.

ANDY   Drama! What sort of a career's that for a respectable girl! They're all floozies and nancy boys. Stick to the sums and the writin'. Train for a proper job.

ANDREA   I want to design sets for the theatre. I want to be an artist. I am an artist. I get that from you. No-one else in the family can draw.

ANDY   Like my mother said, you'll never make a livin' paintin' pictures . . . I was 13 when I won the scholarship. There was a competition. The mill owners organised it. Ye had to write a composition. Anything to do with the mill. I wrote about my mother. She was widowed young an' after my da died, she earned her keep by ironin' the linen handkerchiefs for the mill. An' every time she had a hundred done, she wrapped them in brown paper, an' I took them down the road to the mill, an' collected the money. Anyway, that's what I wrote about. An' I drew pictures to go along with it. Pictures of her heatin' the irons on the stove, foldin' the handkerchiefs. She was that neat. The handkerchiefs looked like nuthin' when they arrived, an' they were all crisp an' lovely when she'd finished. I loved the smell of them handkerchiefs. Like bread bakin'. Anyway, I won – I suppose because I was the only one drew pictures as well as writin' the composition. There was a bit in the paper about it. An' my mother got into a terrible state about everybody knowin' she ironed handkerchiefs to make ends meet. I always thought she wrapped them in brown paper to keep them clean. But the real reason was that she didn't want people knowin' her business. She was a proud woman . . . The prize was a place in one of them posh schools, or ten pounds. My mother took the money. Well, she needed it . . . an' they give me a job in the mill as well as the ten pounds. I worked there till the war started, an' they took me on again when I got back . . . It's not that I don't want you to have your chance Andrea, I just think that London's no place for a good girl. They're not like us over there. . . .

ANDREA   He paid my plane fare. Wouldn't hear tell of me going by boat. Insisted on coming to the airport with me. Before we left Derry, he gave me a pep talk on the dangers awaiting me on the mainland. Implied there were white slave traders lurking on every corner. What he didn't say was that he was hurt at me considering that anything in England could be better than anything in Ulster. It's one of those paradoxes of the Ulster Protestant mentality – being more British than the British, but believing that anyone leaving the province for mainland if they don't have to, is somehow letting the side down, slighting the family, betraying the cause.

ANDY   I wanted her to be safe an' looked after proper, with regular meals an' hot milk on her cornflakes. The English put cold milk on their cereal of a mornin'. God, your heart wouldn't lie in it. I fixed her up with a room at Freda Sloan's. I knew Freda would see her right.

ANDREA   Walking into Freda's home was like stepping back into his. There they were, framed above the fireplace – my grandfather and her dead husband's dead father Joseph Sloan, and . . .

ANDREA (CHILD)   Isaac Carson, Samuel Thompson, Hugh Montgomery, Frederick Wilson, James Elliott, John Cunningham, Edward Marshall.

ANDREA (ADULT)   Edward Reilly had been cut off the end of the photograph. Freda and Joe Sloan hadn't left Derry. They'd brought it to London with them. Freda was kind and strict and interfering, like a well intentioned warder in an open prison. *(She gasps as the metal door slams and echoes in the distance again.)* You can run away from an open prison . . .

ANDY   Dear Andrea, Freda Sloan is very upset about you leaving, and so am I . . .

ANDREA   Dear Granda, I'm sorry for upsetting you and Freda. She was very good to me and I did thank her, but she lives miles away from the University. It was costing me a fortune in tube fares, and I was always late for lectures. The house I'm in now is very nice. I share it with five other students and we can help each other with the work and share books and expenses, so that saves us all a bit of money. Don't worry about me . . .

ANDY   I know it's natural that they grow up and find their way in the world, but at least if they do it near home they can visit ye regular. England's awful far away. It's not as if ye can put your foot on the bus or the train and come home for the weekend.

ANDREA   Dear Granda, Yes, I'm working hard, and eating properly, and getting plenty of sleep. Thank you for the postal order. Do you mind if I buy a sweatshirt with it instead of a hat and gloves . . .

(Sound of ANDY *unlocking the tin box and removing Andrea's letters and postcards from London.)*

ANDY   Dear Granda, Thanks for your letter and the fiver. I bought a book about war poetry. We're doing an improvised play about war through the eyes of writers. No, I won't be able to get to the cenotaph to see the big Armistice Day parade. I have a lot of essays to write and it will take me all weekend. I'll be thinking of you in the Derry parade . . .

ANDREA   I spent the entire weekend in bed

with my new landlord. My grandfather had warned me about white slave traders, and I found mine in Hanif. Oh my love, what are you doing now, and are you thinking of me? Remember that weekend. Remember. We sat in bed on that Sunday morning, eating chocolate and reading war poetry for the Monday tutorial. The poem was among some stuff you'd photocopied in The British Library.

ANDREA (CHILD)
>On Fame's eternal camping ground
>Their silent tents are spread
>And Glory guards with solemn round
>The bivouac of the dead.

ANDREA (ADULT)   Poems of American Patriotism. It's not about The Somme at all. It's about the American War with Mexico. Written in 1847 by Theodora O'Hara to commemorate the bringing home of the bodies of the Kentucky soldiers who fell at Buena Vista and were buried at Frankfort at the cost of the State. 1847. 1916. I expect it's much the same no matter what war you die in . . .

ANDY   Army trainin' keeps ye fit. Stands ye in good stead for the rest of your days. All my daughters dead and gone, and here's me, 93 years old and' still goin' strong. There's ones in this place only 70 odd, an' they're never out of their beds. You have to keep on your feet or you get old before your time.

ANDREA   I went home for my mother's funeral. Afterwards, he told me that' he'd been offered a place in an Old People's Home nearby. He didn't ask me to stay and look after him, but it was there, unspoken, and I felt guilty for not offering, for wanting to be with Hanif more than I wanted to be with him.

ANDY   I don't mind it here. It's clean an' orderly, an' meals regular as clockwork. I'm not sayin' it's like bein' in your own wee house but sure nothin' ever is. My grandsons is mostly scattered all over the globe. No jobs, no prospects here for them. The two that stayed on in Derry visit the odd time. Christmas. Easter. That sort of thing. I have great-grandchildren in Canada and Australia that I've never seen. All wee lads. No great-granddaughters.

ANDREA   I went back to visit him once. It was the last time I ever saw him. I went specially to tell him . . . to tell him . . . It

was four years ago. 1982. The day after the sinking of the Belgrano.

1982.
(The background murmur of voices in the dayroom of the old people's home.)

ANDY   You picked a grand day to come visitin'. Isn't it great news. Britain rules the waves again. By God, if she'd been Prime Minister when that scum rose out of the Bogside, the Troubles would have been over in a day. She'd have sent the big gunboats into Derry an' wiped them off the face of the earth. I admit I was a bit took back when they elected a woman, but she's a goodun. The equal of any man. No messin' about. Get stuck in there. Show the bastards who's the boss. What I wouldn't give to be a young man again. Fightin' fit and' rarin' to go. Still, Maggie has two of my grandsons, carryin' on the tradition, carryin' on the name. I'll bet your English friends are real proud of ye, havin' a brother and a cousin in the Falklands. Have ye heard from either of them?

ANDREA   I went to see them at Southampton before they sailed. They looked so young.

ANDY   Same age as me when I went to war. It'll make men of them.

ANDREA   Granda . . . could we go to your room and talk . . .

ANDY   A good idea. This oul dayroom gets awful crowded in the afternoons. *(In a whisper)* An' we can have a wee drink to celebrate. One of the ward orderlies slipped me a wee bottle on the q.t.

(Sound of whiskey being poured in Andy's bedroom.)

ANDY   Here, get that down ye. It'll put a bit of colour in your cheeks. You're lookin' peaky. Is there something wrong?

ANDREA   I've come home specially to tell you somethin'.

ANDY   Are you in some sort of bother?

ANDREA   I'm getting married . . . I'm having a baby . . . I need your blessing.

ANDY   You're only a child yourself.

ANDREA   I'm 20. He's 22. I wanted to tell you first, before anybody else in the family. I don't care what my brothers or my cousins think, but I don't want you thinking bad of me . . .

ANDY   Ach child, you never had a bad bone

in your body. Don't upset yourself on my account.

ANDREA   I was so afraid you'd be angry. I thought you might disown me. All the way over on the plane I kept rehearsing what I would say. How I would word it. I didn't intend to blurt it out like that.

ANDY   Is he a good man? Is he fond of you?

ANDREA   Yes.

ANDY   Well then. That's all that matters. An' he must be a decent man, doin' the right thing by ye. Although mind you, he should of come with ye. Not sent you to face the music on your own.

ANDREA   He couldn't come. He's in hospital. He'll be alright soon. He got beaten up, you see a gang of skinheads broke into the house one night when he was there by himself. He was studying and he hadn't pulled the curtains. It was dark outside. They could see him, but he didn't see them until they . . .

ANDY   Why would anybody do the like of that?

ANDREA   They were drunk. They'd been out celebrating the English Fleet sailing for the Falklands.

ANDY   Rabble. Too cowardly to join up and fight like men. Was your man badly hurt?

ANDREA   Yes, yes he was. But he's over the worst. He'll be alright. As soon as he comes home we're getting married.

ANDY   How will you manage for money? I've got a wee bit put by. I was gonna leave it to you, but you can have it now if ye need it.

ANDREA   We'll be okay. His grandfather owns the house we live in. We have a roof over our heads. And one of the other students is moving out soon, so we're going to turn her room into a nursery.

ANDY   You'll still need cash, you'll have a lot to buy. I'll arrange it. It's not much mind, but it's yours. His grandfather owns the house eh? His family must be well to do.

ANDREA   His father's an accountant. His mother lectures at the university.

ANDY: You're movin' up in the world. Don't be forgettin' what ye come from.

ANDREA: Don't be daft.

ANDY: It happens.

ANDREA   Hanif's not a snob.

ANDY: What the hell sort of a name is that!

ANDREA   Oh God, I meant to tell you that part of it slowly too. (She is taking a photo out of her bag.) Look, this is him. It was

taken outside his parents' house. Isn't it lovely. They live in Kensington . . .

ANDY   He's an Argy.

ANDREA   He's British. His father's from Bristol. His mother's from Pakistan.

ANDY   Get out of my sight!

ANDREA   Granda . . .

ANDY   I won't be related to a half-caste! A nig-nog.

ANDREA   Don't, please don't . . .

ANDY   Get rid of it! Get rid of it! I'll have none of that carry-on in my family! We have a name to upkeep. We're respected in this town!

ANDREA   Please. don't do this . . . talk to me . . . listen to me . . . don't . . .

ANDY   Don't you ever come back to Derry! Do you hear me! Get back to England and keep your black bastard there with you. I won't have my name dragged down. Associated with the like of that. Get out of my sight! Get out!

(Sound of the metal door, closer this time.)

ANDREA   I mustn't cry. I mustn't cry. Don't draw his face. No more of his face. Draw Annie. Golden and beautiful like her father. What are you doing today. Being spoiled rotten by your doting grandfather. My grandfather will have been awake since daybreak. It's the seventieth anniversary of the Battle of the Somme today. He'll be up and washed and dressed, and wearing his medals. He'll have made his own bed. It's the only domestic thing he ever did, making his own bed. They taught him that in the army. He'll be sitting waiting for the British Legion car to collect him. Oh God please let him have this day. Don't let him read the papers. That press photographer was from Derry. He went to school with my brother. He recognised me. I know he did.

(Sound of a newspaper being opened by Andy.)

ANDY   Derry girl arrested at Greenham. Conchie! Trollop! Traitor! If you were here in this room, I would kill you with my own two hands!

ANDREA   Sometimes I wish they'd killed Hanif outright and not left me to live with a stranger. I don't really mean that, Annie. I love the man your father was, tender, loving, easy-going, full of fun . . . But I hate what he's become. I was so sure he would recover completely from the attack once you were born . . . and he was a lot better . . . for a while . . . and I thought, "He's got over it. No more dark silences, no more bouts of silent weeping." And then it started all over again. "Pull the curtains . . . is the door locked . . . don't leave Annie in the garden, they watch the house you know." His injuries healed so fast, and there was no brain damage, but he's been in hospital six times in the last four years, and each stay has been longer than the last. I feel guilty every time I take him back in, even though I know he's happier in hospital than he is at home. He feels safer there, you see. How can he feel safe with them and not with me! And how can my grandfather hate me, having loved me all those years! There's no rhyme nor reason to love, is there? I never wanted Hanif to change, and he did. And I always hoped my grandfather would change, and he never will.

(Sound of ANDY *taking his medals out of the tin box.)*

ANDY   I'll go to the Somme Parade the day. Wear my medals with pride. Hold my head high, despite what she has done. And well dare anybody mention her name in the same breath as mine. My loyalty and courage have never been in question. I've always fought for what's right. I wore these medals the day I joined Carson's army, after the Great War. We beat the English Government then, and we'll beat them this time round too. Anglo-Irish Agreement be damned! Lloyd George couldn't defeat us in 1920 and Maggie Thatcher won't defeat us in 1986. Carson may be dead, but his spirit lives on in the Protestants of Ulster.

ANDREA (CHILD)   *(Sings)*
  Lord Edward Carson had a cat
  It sat upon the fender
  And every time it caught a rat
  It shouted no surrender!

ANDREA (ADULT)   Lord Edward Carson, the English lawyer whose rhetoric rallied the Ulster Protestants to fight the Home Rule Bill. The English lawyer who prosecuted Oscar Wilde.

ANDREA (CHILD)   My granda cut his thumb with a pocket knife and signed the Ulster Covenant with his own blood.

ANDREA (ADULT)   Maybe I'll sign these

drawings, "The Ballad of Holloway Gaol" . . . No, that would be giving myself an importance I don't deserve. I'm not like the other women who were arrested. I'm not a campaigner, a fighter, I never have been. I was brought up in a city with soldiers on the streets and armed police, and I never thought about it. I don't remember Derry without barbed wire, checkpoints. The war was always there, a part of everyday life, like getting frisked when you go shopping by security forces in security zones. I didn't go to Greenham to protest about a lethal security zone. Nothing as noble as that. Hanif had gone back into hospital, and his father had taken Annie to the seaside, and I was lonely and depressed. Couldn't face being in the house alone. Hanif's sister said, "I'm going to Greenham for the weekend. Come with me." So I did, Because I had nothing better to do. I hated it. The cold and the rain and the mud. I've always liked my home comforts. I wandered down to that main gate because I was miserable and bored . . . and curious. And there they were, all those women, sitting in the road in front of a bloody great army vehicle. And they were singing. I thought it all looked rather silly, I even felt a bit embarrassed on their behalf . . . and then the riot squad moved in. There was no riot till they created it. I just stood there, on the edge of it all, watching, not knowing what to do. And then this elderly woman sat down on the ground beside me. She was carrying a cake. A silly chocolate cake with three candles. And she lit them, and she said, "One for my nephew crippled in the Falklands Campaign. One for my fiancé killed at Dunkirk. One for my grandfather shellshocked at the Battle of the Somme." And then she got up and she walked to the gate and sat down in the road. She left the cake and the box of candles on the ground beside me. She knew she'd be arrested, and she left the cake behind. Like a light burning in a window. Two Policemen dragged her into the back of a wagon. She was at least 60 years old . . . I lit the rest of the candles. Held them in a bunch in my hand, cupped my other hand round them to stop them going out, and walked up to the two policemen. I held out the candles, and I said, "These are for Joseph Sloan and Billy Matchett and Isaac Carson and

Samuel Thompson and Hugh Montgomery and Frederick Wilson and James Elliott and John Cunningham and Edward Marshall . . . " And when they heard my accent, one of them called me a stupid I.R.A. cunt and threw me into the wagon. The candles were lost in the mud. *(Sound of a door being unlocked nearby)* I had intended to say that three of the candles were for Edward Reilly and Hanif and my grandfather, but there was no time. *(Sound of Andrea's cell door being opened)* Perhaps I'll say it in court.

(As ANDREA *and the warder leave the cell, a military band is heard. Their footsteps merge with the marching feet and crowd noise at the Somme Commemoration Parade in Derry. The band plays "Marching through Georgia" and* ANDY *sings along with the band.)*

ANDY

We are, we are, we are the Billy Boys
We are, we are, we are the Billy Boys

(The band music continues in the distance as ANDREA *speaks.)*

ANDREA   You can't do this again . . . I have a period . . . Don't tell me it's normal procedure. It's harassment. I was strip-searched when I was brought here. I haven't been anywhere else. What could I have hidden . . . My name? You know my name . . . What's your name? . . . and in whose name do you do this . . .

(The band music increases)

ANDY   *(Sings)*

We are, we are, we are the Billy Boys
We are, we are, we are the Billy Boys.

ANDREA (CHILD)   Granda, there's blood on my frock . . .

(The band noise cheering crowd and marching feet increase in volume and die away, and are replaced by the sound of ANDREA *back in her cell, drawing.)*
(The music and marching feet recede and are replaced by the sound of ANDREA *drawing.)*

ANDREA   I didn't cry in court, but I didn't make any heroic speeches either. I just told them my name and refused to promise to be a good little girl and keep the peace. So, I'm a guest of Her Majesty for the next three weeks. It was the chocolate-cake

lady's third offence, so she got three months. The magistrate asked her why a woman of her years kept disturbing the peace, and she said "Because I want my granddaughter to die of old age, that's why." When we were arrested, she advised me to concentrate on someone I loved, to give me strength. I close my eyes and try to picture Annie or Hanif or my mother, but my heart and my hands reach out to him, and I draw his face over and over again . . .

ANDREA (CHILD)   It's for you, Granda. It's for you.

ANDY   What is it?

ANDREA   It's a picture of you.

ANDY   So it is. Aren't you the clever girl.

ANDREA   And I said our poem for the teacher, all by myself.

ANDY   You never did.

ANDREA   I did.

ANDY   You're havin' me on.

ANDREA

My name, shall I tell you my name
It's hard, but I'll try
Sometimes I forget it. That's when I'm shy
But I have another, I never forget
So easy. So pretty.
And that's Granda's Pet.

ANDREA (ADULT)   For four years now, you haven't answered ANY OF MY LETTERS. Do you throw them away unopened, or do you lock them away with the medals and the photos and the memories in the old tin box? I miss you. I need you. I need to make my peace with you. I love you in a way that I've never loved anyone else. I love you, even though I have grown to hate everything you believe in. How can I make you understand it myself? . . . You must have moments of doubt. You must have. You're stubborn and you're proud, but you're not a fool . . . loyalty, patriotism. Them or us . . . you won't ever question what all that has done to you, because you daren't. Once you question even a small part of it, you end up questioning it all. And to do that would be to negate your whole life, everything you've lived and survived by . . . I wonder what you're doing now . . . I wonder if you're ever afraid . . . I wonder if you ever think of me . . .

ANDY   Bright and brave and beautiful. The cleverest child in the street. A good girl

MY NAME, SHALL I TELL YOU MY NAME

ruined by bad company. Not her fault alone. Sure a woman's only as good as the bed she lies in, and even the best of women can be led astray by the wrong man . . . I wonder did she ever get to design a set for a play . . . I suppose she draws different pictures now . . . but she drew me before she drew anything else, an' that's somethin' nobody and nuthin' can change nor take away from me . . .

ANDREA   They say that one Christmas Day during the First World War, a group of British and German soldiers called a halt to the fighting and declared a truce, just for an hour. There must be an hour, a place, where he and I can meet. A Piece of Common Ground. A No-Man's Land. If it's possible for strangers, then it's possible for us. Or maybe it's easier to declare a truce with someone when you don't bear their name . . . or their face . . .

ANDY   I walked in the Somme Parade the day. Wore my medals with pride. Held my head high. Done the heroes proud. The Legion collected me, and brung me back in a big car. Every year. Regular as clockwork. They always look after their own. An' they're gettin' my picture painted. They're gonna hang it up in the Legion Hall. I'm the only one of the regiment left, an' they want to honour me . . . I usta draw pictures myself, but I never kept it up, an' I lost the way of it . . . I won a prize once, but that was a long time ago . . . a long time ago.

Appendix: checklist of (published) plays by women relevant to World War I: 1915–39

(*Note*: Playwrights' dates are given in parentheses; the publication dates for plays are set in square brackets.)

Borden, Mary (1886–1968) [1929] "In the Operating Room" in *The Forbidden Zone*, London: Heinemann.

Box, Muriel (1905–91) [1935] *Angels of War*, in John Bourne (ed.) *Five New Full-Length Plays for All Women Casts*, London: Lovat-Dickson & Thompson.

Burrill, Mary P. (1884–1946) [1919] *Aftermath*, in *Liberator*, April 1919. Reprinted in Kathy A. Perkins (ed.) (1989) *Black Female Playwrights: an Anthology of Plays before 1950*, Bloomington: Indiana University Press, pp. 57–66.

Dane, Clemence (pseudonym of Winifred Ashton 1887–1965) [1922] *A Bill of Divorcement*, London: Heinemann. Performed London, 1921.

Draper, Ruth (1884–1957) *Vive La France! 1916*, *Le Retour de l'Aveugle*, and *In County Kerry*, in Morton Dauwen Zabel (ed.) (1960) *The Art of Ruth Draper: Her Dramas and her Characters*, London: Oxford University Press, pp. 205–17. Performed New York 1916–20.

Dunbar-Nelson, Alice (1975–1935) [1918] *Mine Eyes Have Seen*, in *The Crisis* 15, April 1918, pp. 271–5. Reprinted in James V. Hatch and Ted Shine (eds) (1974) *Black Theater, USA: 45 Plays by Black Americans, 1847–1974*, New York: Free Press, pp. 173–7.

Glaspell, Susan (1876–1948) [1921] *The Inheritors*, Boston: Dodd Mead. Performed Provincetown, 1921; London, 1925.

Gore-Booth, Eva (1870–1926) [1930] *The Buried Life of Deirdre*, London: n.p.

Hamilton, Cicely (1872–1952) [1922] *The Child in Flanders*, London: French. Reprinted in J. W. Marriott (ed.) (1925)

One-Act Plays of Today: Second Series, London: Harrap. Performed London 1919.

Jennings, Gertrude (1877–1955) [1916] *Poached Eggs and Pearls: A Canteen Comedy in 2 Scenes*, London: French.

—— [1917] *Allotments*, London: French.

—— [1917] *Waiting for the Bus*, London: French.

John, Gwen (?) [1925] *A Peakland Wakes*, in *Plays of Innocence*, London: Benn. Broadcast Cardiff, 1924.

—— *Luck of War* [1925] in *Plays of Innocence*, London: Benn. Performed London, 1917.

Kraze, Friede H. (1870–1936) [1915] *Erfüllungen: Ein Stück von Heute für Morgen*, [Fulfilments: A Play of Today for Tomorrow] Stuttgart: Bonz.

Langner, Ilse (?) [1930] *Frau Emma kämpft im Hinterland* [Frau Emma Fights Behind the Lines], Berlin: Fischer.

Lask, Berta (1878–1967) [1924] *Die Befreiung: 16 Bild aus dem Leben der deutschen und russischen Frauen, 1914–20* [Liberation: 16 Tableaux from the Lives of German and Russian women, 1914–20], Berlin: Remmele.

Lazars, Maria ("Esther Grenen" ?) [1933] *Der Nebel von Dybern* [The Fog of Dybern], Berlin: Stettin.

Lee, Vernon (pseudonym of Violet Paget 1856–1935) [1915] *Ballet of the Nations: a Present Day Morality*, London: Chatto.

—— [1920] *Satan, the Waster: a Philosophic War Trilogy*, London: Cape.

Lenéru, Marie (1875–1918) [1922] *La Paix – 4 Actes* [Peace – 4 Acts], Paris: Grasset. Performed Paris, 1921.

Miller, May (1899–?) [1930] *Stragglers in the Dust*, in Kathy A. Perkins (ed.) [1989] *Black Female Playwrights: an Anthology of Plays before 1950*, Bloomington: Indiana University Press, pp. 145–52.

O'Hara, Constance Marie (1907–?) [1935] *The*

Years of the Locusts, Boston: Baker. Performed Philadelphia, 1933; Birmingham, UK, 1938.

Pilcher, Velona (?) [1929] *The Searcher: a War Play*, London: Heinemann. Performed London, 1930.

Smyth, Ethel (1858–1944) [1925] *Entente Cordiale: a Post-War Comedy in One Act* in E. Smyth (1928) *A Final Burning of the Boats, etc*, London: Longman, Green.

Stein, Gertrude (1874–1946) [1922] *Accents In Alsace* and *Please Do Not Suffer*, in *Geography and Plays*, Boston: Four Seas. Reprinted in Cyrena N. Pondrom (ed.) (1993) *Geography and Plays*, Wisconsin: University of Wisconsin Press.

—— [1932] *Am I to Go or I'll Say So*, in *Operas and Plays*, Paris: Plain Edition.

Stopes, Marie Carmichael (1880–1958) [1918] *The Race* in *Two New Plays of Life*, London: Fifield.

Tennyson-Jesse, Fryn (1889–1958) and

Harold Harwood [1918] *Billeted*, London: French. Performed London, 1917.

Vivanti, Annie (Chartres) (1868–1942) [1928] *L'Invasore: dramma in tre atti* [The Invader: play in three acts] Milan: Mondadori. Performed Turin, 1915.

—— [1918] *Le Bocche inutili: dramma in tre atti* [Useless Mouths: Play in Three Acts], Milan: Quintieri.

Wentworth, Marion Craig (1972–?) [1915] *War Brides: A Play in One Act*, New York: Century.

West, Rebecca (pseudonym of Cicely Isabel Fairfield, 1892–1983) [1928] *The Return of the Soldier: A Play in 3 Acts*, adapted by John van Druten from R. West's novel, London: Victor Gollancz.

Winsloe, Christa (1888–1944) [1930] *Gestern und Heute* [Yesterday and Today] adapted by Barbara Burnham as *Children in Uniform*, Boston: Baker. Performed London, 1932.